ESSENTIAL PAPERS ON PSYCHOSIS

Peter Buckley, M.D.
Editor

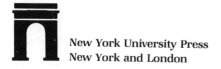

New York University Press
New York and London

Library of Congress Cataloging-in-Publication Data

Essential papers on psychosis.

  (Essential papers in psychoanalysis)
  Includes bibliographies and index.
  1. Psychoses.   2. Psychotherapy.   I. Buckley,
Peter, 1943–   . II. Series.
RC512.E88   1987   616.89   87-5804
ISBN 0-8147-1096-4
ISBN 0-8147-1097-2 (pbk.)

Clothbound editions of New York University Press
books are Smyth-sewn and printed on permanent
and durable acid-free paper.

p 10 9 8 7 6 5 4 3 2

I

E   *Essential Papers on*

E   *Essential Papers*

E   *Essential Papers on Narcissism*

E   *Essential Papers on Depression*

For Eric

Contents

Acknowledgments

We wish to gratefully acknowledge the *International Journal of Psycho-Analysis* for permission to reprint the following: N. J. London, "An Essay on Psychoanalytic Theory: Two Theories of Schizophrenia. Part 1: Review and Critical Assessment of the Development of the Two Theories. Part 2: Discussion and Restatement of the Specific Theory of Schizophrenia," Vol. 54, pp. 169–93, 1973; T. Freeman, "Narcissism and Defensive Processes in Schizophrenic States," Vol. 34, pp. 415–25, 1962; E. Jacobson, "On Psychotic Identifications," Vol. 35, pp. 102–8, 1954; H. Rosenfeld, "On the Treatment of Psychotic States by Psychoanalysis: An Historical Approach," Vol. 50, pp. 615–31, 1969; H. F. Searles, "Transference Psychosis in the Psychotherapy of Chronic Schizophrenia," Vol. 44, pp. 249–281, 1963; N. Cameron, "Introjection, Reprojection, and Hallucinations in the Interaction between Schizophrenic Patient and Therapist," Vol. 42, pp. 86–96, 1961.

We wish to gratefully acknowledge the *Psychoanalytic Quarterly* for permission to reprint the following: V. Tausk, "On the Origin of the 'Influencing Machine' in Schizophrenia," Vol. 2, pp. 519–56, 1933; R. C. Bak, "Masochism in Paranoia," Vol. 15, pp. 285–301, 1946.

We wish to gratefully acknowledge the *British Journal of Medical Psychology* for permission to reprint the following: H. F. Searles, "Sources of Anxiety in Paranoid Schizophrenia," Vol. 34, pp. 129–41, 1961; H. F. Searles, "Phases of Patient-Therapist Interaction in the Psychotherapy of Chronic Schizophrenia," Vol. 34, pp. 169–93, 1961.

Introduction

In his autobiographical account of his psychosis, Daniel Schreber (1, pp. 83–5) wrote the following:

In consequence of my every increasing nervousness and the resulting increasing power of attraction, an ever growing number of departed souls felt attracted to me—primarily those who may have retained some special interest in me because of personal contacts with me during their life—and then dissolved on my head or in my body. This process frequently ended with the souls concerned finally leading a short existence on my head in the form of "little men"—tiny figures in human form, perhaps only a few millimetres in height—before finally vanishing. . . . I suppose that these souls, when they first approached me, still possessed a fairly large number of nerves and in virtue of them still retained a fairly strong awareness of their identity. Each time they approached me they lost part of their nerves in favour of my body through the power of attraction; finally they consisted only of one single nerve, which for some mysterious reason not further explicable, assumed the form of a "little man" in the above sense. This was the final form of existence of these souls before they vanished completely. . . .

Connected with these phenomena, very early on there predominated in recurrent nightly visions the notion of an approaching end of the world, as a consequence of the indissoluble connection between God and myself. Bad news came in from all sides that even this or that star or this or that group of stars had to be "given up"; at one time it was said that even Venus had been "flooded," at another that the whole solar system would now have to be "disconnected", that the Cassiopeia (the whole group of stars) had had to be drawn together into a single sun, that perhaps only the Pleiades could still be saved, etc., etc. While I had these visions at night, in daytime I thought I could notice the sun following my movements; when I moved to and fro in the single-windowed room I inhabited at the time, I saw the sunlight now on the right, now on the left wall (as seen from the door) depending on my movements. . . .

From the sum total of my recollections, the impression gained hold of me that the period in question, which, according to human calculation, stretched over only three to four months, had covered an immensely long period; it was as if single nights had the duration of centuries, so that within that time the most profound alterations in the whole of mankind, in the earth itself and the whole solar system could very well have taken place.

This vivid self-report contains descriptions of phenomena often encountered during what Bowers (2, p. 19) has aptly termed "the psychotic state of consciousness"—hallucinatory experiences ("the little men"), the sense of impending cataclysm ("the end of the world"), self-referential delusions ("the sun following my movements"), distortions of the sense of time ("as if single nights had the duration of centuries'') and megalomania (''the indissoluble connection between God and myself'') and it is the purpose of this book to bring together important psychoanalytic papers which shed light on the psychological nature of such psychotic states and address aspects of their psychotherapy.

The abandonment of reality exemplified by Schreber's account typifies psychosis. For Freud (3, p. 183) this was the cardinal differentiating factor between neurosis and psychosis:

In a neurosis the ego, in its dependence on reality, suppresses a piece of the id (of instinctual life), whereas in a psychosis, this same ego, in the service of the id, withdraws from a piece of reality. Thus for a neurosis the decisive factor would be the predominance of the influence of reality, whereas for a psychosis it would be the predominance of the id. In a psychosis, a loss of reality would be necessarily present, whereas in a neurosis, it would seem, this loss would be avoided. (3, p. 185)

Freud acknowledged that every neurosis disturbed the individual's relation to reality in some way, but ''in neurosis a piece of reality is avoided by a sort of flight whereas in psychosis it is remodelled.''

Accompanying the loss of a capacity to maintain links to reality may be disorganizations of cognition, language, and affect. The harrowing effect of this on the afflicted individual as the personality begins to unravel cannot be underestimated. As John Perceval (4, p. 3) described it,

The Almighty allowed my mind to become a ruin under sickness . . . in addition to the power of discerning evil in others, I fancied that I had the power to discern evil in myself, and to know by the sensation of my palate, throat and hearing, whether I was speaking in accordance with the will of God, or against his will, and consequently against the laws of nature.

Many psychoanalysts hold the view that in psychosis the unconscious becomes conscious. Fenichel (5, p. 422) stated that ''because the primary process and the archaic ways of thinking have come to the fore again, schizophrenics are not estranged by these mechanisms any more.'' In his original topographic model of the mind, Freud viewed the unconscious as functioning according to the primary process. Instinctual energy in the unconscious is free or mobile and able to be displaced from one mental content to another. In the primary process system there is no sense of time, wishes function according to the pleasure principle seeking immediate satisfaction through discharge of excitation, and the rules of logic and reason no longer prevail. This is in opposition to the functioning of the systems Preconscious and Conscious wherein secondary process and the rules of reason, logic and the fact of external reality predominate. In contrast, in the system Unconscious, magical thinking dictated by the pleasure principle holds sway. Primary process thought makes its appearance in dreams, in the mental life of small children, and in the thinking of psychotic individuals. Fenichel (5, p. 422) postulated that schizophrenic thinking fell back from the logical to the prelogical level:

> The regressive nature of schizophrenic thinking is confirmed by the fact that the investigation of this type of thinking proves to be identical with the assumed archaic forerunners of logical thinking. Schizophrenic thinking is relatively more concrete and active than normal thinking, not yet capable of realistic abstractions, less preparation for subsequent action and more a symbolic equivalent of action. Its concrete character is "relative" only, in so far as its concrete images do not correspond to objective realities, but are formed or influenced by the wish-fulfilling magical qualities of primitive thinking. Its active character is due to the fact that perception of stimuli and reaction to (subjective elaboration of) stimuli are interwoven with each other again.

Hence, in this view, the sway of the primary process and the failure of repression leads many schizophrenic patients to express ideas and wishes that other people deeply repress because of their forbidden or unacceptable nature.

Bowers (2) has suggested that acute psychotic experiences have three main determinants. First, that certain aspects of psychotic experience are governed by an altered state of consciousness so that a certain form may be seen to be held in common by acute psychoses and other altered states. He includes experiences of heightened awareness, intensification of sensory experience, alteration in the sense of self, externalization of conflict, and invasion of perceptual and cognitive modalities among those factors that are state determined. The second group of determinants of structure in the psychotic experience that he proposes are idiosyncratic and reflect the individual's psychology, history, and intra-psychic conflict. These factors determine the particular content of psychosis. Finally he postulates that the life events and developmental challenges faced by the individual determine the time of the psychotic episode. This model allows for the presence of biological predisposition to an altered state of consciousness which can be triggered by psychic conflict and, as Bowers indicates, suggests a psychosomatic relationship in the psychoses and is a useful conception that integrates both biological and psychological elements.

Psychotic states may be roughly grouped into two major categories, the affective psychoses and the schizophrenias. Despite intensive research and a plethora of theories, the aetiology and pathogenesis of the functional psychoses remain unknown. Exclusive biological or psychological theories have typified an unfortunate dualistic tendency that has often obscured the complexity involved in understanding the nature of psychosis. Even reaching consensus on what constitutes schizophrenia, for instance, has been elusive. The diagnosis of schizophrenia has been defined by various criteria, then the term itself has become reified, as if schizophrenia were one "thing" or "disease" when, in fact, all that the term represents is a description of a cluster of symptoms which have no clear prognostic or definitional implications by themselves.

Rieder (6) in a perceptive analysis of this issue shows how the confusion surrounding the definition of schizophrenia begins with Emil Kraepelin who, at the turn of the century, distinguished manic-depressive psychosis from dementia praecox (our modern-day schizophrenia), a nosological distinction that, in general, has stood the test of time. Kraepelin was an astute observer and his naturalistic descriptions of the phenomenology of psychotic states have never been surpassed. It should be noted, however, that the idea that a patient's psychotic speech might have an underlying meaning and not merely be gibberish was alien to Kraepelin.[1] Kraepelin's account of dementia praecox included a gloomy prognostic factor—in his view the patient would inevitably deteriorate over time as the illness ran its inexorable and malignant course. This confounded his nosology since clinical experience showed that it was not invariable that the patient deteriorated. Indeed many did so, but others became symptom-free. Eugene Bleuler, in 1903, jettisoned the element of an inevitably deteriorating course and coined the term schizophrenia to describe a clinical entity based on a symptom picture without prognostic elements built in. These symptoms included disturbances of affect and thinking together with the presence of hallucinations and delusions. As Rieder has noted, Bleuler, in turn, also engendered confusion by not confining himself solely to symptoms and he introduced gratuitous concepts of aetiology together with the idea that the disease could be diagnosed when there was little or no currently observable symptomatology. To compound the diagnostic problem further, Pope and Lipinski (8) have demonstrated that a patient suffering from manic-depressive illness can present during the acute manic phase all the classic Bleulerian symptoms of schizophrenia including hallucinations, delusions, and a florid thought disorder.

While the delineation of manic-depressive psychosis as a clinical entity has been reasonably well established, considerable argument over what constitutes "real" schizophrenia still reigns. This confusion undoubtedly reflects the fact that there is no one "disease" of schizophrenia and, as was suggested by Bellak (9) and others some time ago, there is a schizophrenic syndrome which, in all likelihood, embodies a heterogeneous group of disorders. As a syndrome, it probably represents a final common pathway for a number of disorders whose aetiology and pathogenesis may be quite different from one another. This heterogeneity has resulted in chaos in research efforts, since positive psychological or biological findings in any one subgroup may not be generalizable to others and, at present, we have no way of determining homogeneous subgroups within the syndrome. The determination of homogeneous subgroups within the schizophrenic syndrome is one of the most critical issues facing clinical researchers in the field of schizophrenia. As a consequence the search for biological "markers" that will delineate specific subgroups has been a central focus of much schizophrenia research.

Given the fact that schizophrenia remains an enigma, Strauss and Carpenter (10) have recently posited a sophisticated interactive developmental systems model, one which does justice to the multiple variables involved in predisposition to, onset of, and outcome of the disorder. The virtue of their conception is that it is multidimensional and represents a method of organizing information relevant to understanding the interaction of the many factors, social, psychological, developmental, and biological, that are involved in the onset and perpetuation of the schizophrenic syndrome and it stands in favourable contrast to a simplistic solely biomedical or psychological conception.

It is likely that schizophrenia will eventually be shown to be a group of discrete disorders some of which are characterized by considerable genetically determined biological predisposition in which precipitating and sustaining environmental factors are necessary to give rise to the syndrome while others may be found to be primarily a consequence of intrapsychic and interpersonal stress without prominent biological loading. Our current inability to predict outcome will undoubtedly yield eventually to a greater understanding of the relative importance of these factors in different subtypes of the syndrome. This in turn, will lead to a clearer therapeutic approach to the patient. For the moment, clinicians must function on an empirical basis utilizing the range of therapeutic interventions, both somatic and psychological, at their command. Psychological understanding of the meaning of the disorder in a particular individual and the ability to use the patient's capacity for attachment to others in a therapeutic manner must always remain prominent in treatment efforts.

The need for such attachment and the accompanying fear was poignantly expressed by a schizophrenic patient (11, p. c1):

Can I ever forget that I am schizophrenic? I am isolated and I am alone. I am never real. I play-act my life, touching and feeling only shadows. My heart and soul are touched, but the feelings remain locked away, festering inside me because they cannot find expression. . . . Recently, my mind has played tricks on me, creating The People inside my head who sometimes come out to haunt me and torment me. They surround me in rooms, hide behind trees and under the snow outside. They taunt me and scream at me and devise plans to break my spirit. The voices come and go, but The People are always there, always real. . . . Life for most schizophrenics is a nightmare full of fears and doubts about oneself and reality; they have a distorted view of that most profound question of how they relate to the world around them. Boundaries become unclear and other people are frightening and not to be trusted. Thus, the very thing which could bring relief—closeness to other people—is shunned as something horrible and dangerous. For this reason it is absolutely essential to have someone to depend on, to draw the schizophrenic out of his jungle of terrors and eventually into the less frightening world of reality. . . . One of the hardest issues for me to deal with has been trust. My mind has created so many reasons to fear the real world and the people in it that trusting a new person or moving to a new level of trust with a familiar person presents a terrifying conflict that must be hammered out over and over until I can find a way to overcome my fears or in a few cases give up the battle, even if just for the time being. The intensity of this conflict makes it hard to build relationships. It's hard for the family to help. It's difficult for them to understand the nature of the disease. Therapy with schizophrenics can go on for years before a level of trust is built up sufficiently for the patient to use his therapist as a bridge between the two worlds he is confronted with. For me, each new experience of trust adds to a new dimension to my life and brings me that much closer to living in reality.

Freud's publication of the Schreber case in 1911 (12) was a landmark in psychoanalytic contributions to psychosis. As Strachey (13) notes, the importance of this case history for psychoanalysis is not confined to the light it sheds on the problem of paranoia for, in addition, it was a forerunner of Freud's seminal metapsychological papers on narcissism and repression and his classic "Instincts and Their Vicissitudes."

The subject of the case study, Daniel Schreber, was a noted jurist in Saxony who, in 1893, was promoted to president (*Senatspräsident*) of the Superior Court of Appeals in Dresden. Shortly thereafter, he developed a psychotic illness which resulted in his hospitalization for nine years. During the latter part of this period Schreber began to write a book recounting the subjective experience of his illness which, to the dismay of his family, he published in 1903, though not without some considerable censorship being imposed on the manuscript.

This book (1) is a remarkable document that vividly captures the horror and phantasmagoric quality of psychosis. Freud used this as his psychoanalytic case material for a study of paranoia since, in his words (12, p. 9), "we cannot accept patients suffering from this complaint, or, at all events, we cannot keep them for long, since we cannot offer treatment unless there is some prospect of therapeutic success.'' It is clear that Freud did not feel that psychoanalysis had much to contribute to the therapy of psychosis in contrast to what it might reveal concerning the processes of psychotic experience, in particular delusion formation.

Schreber's first episode of mental illness occurred in 1884 and he spent six months in a clinic run by Paul Flechsig, a distinguished German neuropsychiatrist. His symptoms then were mainly of a hypochrondriacal nature. He made a complete recovery but, shortly after his appointment as *Senatspräsident* in 1893, he had the idea while waking up one morning ''that after all it really must be very nice to be a woman submitting to the act of copulation'' (1, p. 63). By the end of 1893 he had been forced to return to Flechsig's clinic for further treatment. He became increasingly psychotic believing that he was dead and decomposing and that his body was being handled in all manner of revolting ways. Gradually delusional ideas developed that he was in direct communication with God and that he was living in another world. Simultaneously, he began to believe that he was being persecuted, most prominently by Flechsig, whom he called ''a soul-murderer'' (1, p. 75).

In 1894 he was transferred to another asylum and by 1900, though still actively delusional, he petitioned the court system to obtain his discharge and by 1902 he was successful in this quest. Weber, his physician in the second asylum, noted in 1899:

The culminating point of the patient's delusional system is his belief that he has a mission to redeem the world and to restore mankind to their lost state of bliss. He was called to this task by direct inspiration of God. . . . The most essential part of his mission of redemption is that it must be preceded by his transformation into a woman. . . . But neither he nor the rest of mankind can regain the life beyond except by his being transformed into a woman (a process which may occupy many years or even decades) by means of divine miracles. He himself, of this he is convinced, is the only object upon which divine miracles are worked, and he is thus the most remarkable human being who has ever lived on earth—Every hour and every minute for years he has experienced these miracles in his body, and he has had them confirmed by the voices that have conversed with him. During the first years of his illness certain of his bodily organs suffered such destructive injuries as would inevitably have led to the death of any other man: he lived for a long time without a stomach, without intestines, almost without lungs, with a torn oesophagus, without a bladder, and with shattered ribs, he used sometimes to swallow part of his own larynx with his food, etc. But divine miracles (''rays'') always restored what had been destroyed, and therefore, as long as he remains a man, he is altogether immortal. These alarming phenomena have ceased long ago, and his ''femaleness'' has become prominent instead. This is a matter of a process of development which will probably require decades, if not centuries, for its completion, and it is unlikely that anyone now living will survive to see the end of it. He has a feeling that enormous numbers of "female nerves" have already passed over into his body, and out of them a new race of men will proceed, through a process of direct impregnation by God. Not until then, it seems will he be able to die a natural death, and, along with the rest of mankind, will he regain a state of bliss. In the meantime not only the sun, but trees and birds, which are in the nature of bemiracled residues of former human souls, speak to him in human accents, and miraculous things happen everywhere around him (12, pp. 16–7).

Freud noted that Schreber's fantasy of being transformed into a woman, which required emasculation, was of a primary nature and appeared during the incubation period of his illness and was a part of his delusional system that persisted after his discharge from Weber's asylum. Freud also observed that Schreber exhibited a mixture of reverence and rebelliousness in his delusional ideas concerning God, with whom Schreber believed he had a special exalted relationship. Freud noted (12, p. 32) two main changes produced in Schreber by his illness:

Before it he had been inclined to sexual asceticism and had been a doubter in regard to God; while after it he was a believer in God and a devotee of voluptuousness. But just as his reconquered belief in God was of a peculiar kind, so too the sexual enjoyment which he had won for himself was of a most unusual character. It was not the sexual liberty of a man, but the sexual feelings of a woman. He took up a feminine attitude towards God; he felt that he was God's wife.

Freud postulated that there was an essential psychogenetic relation between the two principal elements of Schreber's delusions—his transformation into a woman and his favored relation to God.

Because of the intensity of Schreber's relationship with Flechsig, his initial gratitude for Flechsig's curing him of his earlier (1884) illness, and the radical transformation this feeling underwent during his psychosis to the point where Flechsig became his persecutor, "the soul-murderer," Freud concluded that the exciting cause of Schreber's illness was an outburst of homosexual libido, that the object of this libido was Flechsig and that Schreber's struggles against the libidinal impulse produced the intrapsychic conflict which gave rise to his symptoms. Freud observed (12, p. 48) that the replacement of Flechsig by God in his delusions enabled Schreber to find a psychotic solution for his conflict:

It was impossible for Schreber to become reconciled to playing the part of a female wanton towards his doctor; but the task of providing God himself with the voluptuous sensations that He required called up no such resistance on the part of his ego. Emasculation was now no longer a disgrace; it became "consonant with the Order of

Things," it took its place in a great cosmic chain of events, and was instrumental in the re-creation of humanity after its extinction. "A new race of men, born from the spirit of Schreber" would, so he thought, revere as their ancestor this man who believed himself the victim of persecution. By this means an outlet was provided which would satisfy both of the contending forces. His ego found compensation in his mega-lomania, while his feminine wishful phantasy made its way through and became acceptable.

Freud further concluded that the feminine fantasy which aroused such conflict in Schreber had its origins in his infantile longings for his father and older brother. His transference feelings for his brother appeared in his delu-sions concerning Flechsig and his feelings for his father in his delusions concerning God. The negative Oedipus complex is thus the core of Schreber's illness and its delusions. Freud postulated (12, p. 57) that the exciting cause of the conflict that manifested itself in the feminine wishful fantasy was due to the privation that Schreber suffered in not being able to have children:

His marriage, which he describes as being in other respects a happy one, brought him no children; and in particular it brought him no son who might have consoled him for the loss of his father and brother and upon whom he might have drained off his unsatisfied homosexual affection. . . . Dr. Schreber may have formed a phantasy that if he were a woman he would manage the business of having children more suc-cessfully; and he may thus have found his way back into the feminine attitude towards his father which he had exhibited in the earliest year of his childhood. If that were so, then his delusion that as a result of his emasculation the world was to be peopled with "a new race of men, born from the spirit of Schreber"—a delusion the realization of which he was continually postponing to a more and more remote future—would also be designed to offer him an escape from his childlessness. If the "little men" whom Schreber himself finds so puzzling were children, then we should have no difficulty in understanding why they were collected in such great numbers on his head: they were in truth the "children of his spirit."

In the third section of his case study, Freud developed his theory of the mechanism of paranoia, noting (12, p. 59) "that what was characteristically paranoic about the illness was the fact that the patient, as a means of warding off a homosexual wishful phantasy, reacted with delusions of persecution." Hence a defence against a homosexual wish was seen to be at the center of the conflict which underlay paranoia. He postulated that failures in psychosexual development between the stages of autoerotism, narcissism, and homosex-uality predisposed the individual to paranoia when a regressive flow of libido occurred in response to libidinal frustration. The mechanism of projection was adumbrated to explain how internal perceptions were replaced by external perceptions. Projection was seen to be at the heart of the paranoiac's symptom formation. For Freud all the common forms of paranoia could be represented as contradictions of the single proposition: "I (a man) love him (a man)" and this is contradicted by "I do not love him—I hate him," which was transformed by projection into "He hates (persecutes) me, which will justify me in hating him." As Freud stated (12, p. 63) "and thus the impelling unconscious feeling makes its appearance as though it were the consequence of an external perception: 'I do not love him—I hate him, because he persecutes me.' Observation leaves room for no doubt that the persecutor is some one who was once loved."

Freud also provided (12, p. 70) a compelling explanation for the experience of the end of the world which is common in acute psychotic states:

The patient has withdrawn from the people in his environment and from the external world generally the libidinal cathexis which he has hitherto directed on to them. Thus everything has become indifferent and irrelevant to him, and has to be explained by means of a secondary rationalization a being "miracled up, cursorily improvised." The end of the world is the projection of this internal catastrophe; his subjective world has come to an end since his withdrawal of his love from it.

Freud made an important postulate that the formation of delusions "is in reality an attempt at recovery, a process of reconstruction" (12, p. 71). This penetrating idea of the restitutive and self-reparative function of delusion formation has found support in biological studies of psychosis wherein the production of adrenocortical hormones (a physiological measure of stress) are at extremely high levels during the onset of acute psychosis but drop rapidly with the appearance of delusions in the patient (14).

At the conclusion of the case study Freud made the prophetic comment (12, p. 79): "It remains for the future to decide . . . whether there is more truth in Schreber's delusions than other people are as yet prepared to believe." The subsequent research by Niederland (15) on Schreber and his father showed that indeed there were kernels of personal historical truth embodied in Schreber's delusions.

Schreber's father was a physician and educator who achieved considerable contemporary fame through the publication of numerous works devoted to his theories of child rearing, theories he applied in practice to his son. Niederland noted (15, p. 50) that "the main body of Dr. Schreber's educational system is condensed in his oft-repeated advice to parents and educators that they use a maximum of pressure and coercion during the earliest years of the child's life. . . . At the same time, by subjecting the child to a rigid system of vigorous physical training and by combining methodical muscular exercises with measures aimed at physical and emotional restraint, both bodily and mental health will be promoted.'' To this end Dr. Schreber invented and constructed bizarre apparatuses with bolts, body straps, and iron bars which, when the child was placed in them, enforced mechanical restraint. As Niederland noted (15, p. 56), throughout the elder Schreber's works ''there are minute inflexible instruction for the child's total behaviour including its orderliness and cleanliness.'' Corporal punishment for the slightest transgression was an integral part of this regimen. The overtly sadistic elements of this ''system'' and his obsession with ''cleanliness'' are apparent. Niederland correctly inferred that Dr. Schreber's fanatical crusade was directed against the ''horror'' of masturbation which he believed made children stupid and dumb, vulnerable to mental and physical disease, and led to impotence and sterility.

The father, following a head injury at age fifty-one, became ill and died at fifty-three. Niederland noted that the son became psychotic at the age of fifty-one and initially his chief complaints were about softening of the brain and imminent death. Niederland concluded that Schreber's struggle both for and against identification with his father was a central theme of his memoirs. Just as the elder Schreber's writings had a crusade-like quality of reforming and strengthening the human race through stringent child-rearing practices, so too the son's memoirs can be seen to bring ''blessed knowledge'' to mankind that will transform human beings. Niederland shows (15, p. 60) that the

bizarre ideas in the son's delusional system appear to be derived from the introjected paternal image and constitute archaic elaborations of certain paternal characteristics and procedures as experiences introjected early in life and later ''released'' in the memoirs by the son. The introjection of his autocratic father's methods re-emerge as delusional or hallucinatory entities in the son's archaic regression and he records them in a number of autobiographical, relevant, but otherwise obscure passages throughout the memoirs. Many of the divine miracles of God affecting the patient's body become recognizable, shorn of their delusional distortions of what they must originally have been modeled on: the infantile, regressively distorted image of the father's massive, coercive, as well as seductive manipulations performed on the child's body.

Grotstein (16, p. 380) has suggested that ''when Schreber became Senatspräsident at 51 he was stepping into his father's shoes of success and of his illness at the same time.'' Thus his identification with his father and his oedipal fear of success combined with the fantasy of the retaliating paternal imago were the psychodynamic precipitants for his psychosis.

By juxtaposing the father's writings with the son's memoirs, Niederland convincingly correlated the son's delusional productions with his actual childhood experiences at the hands of his father. There is, thus, a realistic core, a kernel of "historical truth" metaphorically expressed in Schreber's delusional material.

Interestingly, Freud anticipated such findings. In his paper "Constructions in Analysis" (17, p. 267) he wrote:

I noticed that true hallucinations occasionally occurred in the case of other patients who were certainly not psychotic. My line of thought proceeded as follows. Perhaps it may be a general characteristic of hallucinations to which sufficient attention has not hitherto been paid that in them something that has been experienced in infancy and then forgotten returns—something that the child has seen or heard at a time when he could still hardly speak and that now forces its way into consciousness, probably distorted and displaced owing to the operation of forces that are opposed to this return. And, in view of the close relation between hallucinations and particular forms of psychosis, our line of thought may be carried still further. It may be that the delusions into which these hallucinations are so constantly incorporated may themselves be less independent of the upward drive of the unconscious and the return of the repressed than we usually assume. In the mechanism of a delusion we stress as a rule only two factors: the turning away from the real world and its motive forces on the one hand, and the influence exercised by wish-fulfilment on the content of the delusion on the other. But may it not be that the dynamic process is rather that the turning away from reality is exploited by the upward drive of the repressed in order to force its content into consciousness, while the resistances stirred up by this process and the trend to wish-fulfilment share the responsibility for the distortion and displacement of what is recollected? This is after all the familiar mechanism of dreams, which intuition has equated with madness from time immemorial.

This view of delusions is not, I think, entirely new, but it nevertheless emphasizes a point of view which is not usually brought into the foreground. The essence of it is that there is not only method in madness, as the poet has already perceived, but also a fragment of historical truth; and it is plausible to suppose that the compulsive belief attaching to delusions derives its strength precisely from infantile sources of this kind.

The Schreber study was written well before Freud developed the dual-instinct theory and the enormous role played by aggression in paranoia is not acknowledged by him until 1923 (18), by which time he had developed his structural theory of the psychic apparatus. Freud commented (18, p. 43) that love was often accompanied by hate and that "in persecutory paranoia the patient fends off an excessively strong homosexual attachment to some particular person in a special way; and as a result this person whom he loved most becomes a persecutor, against whom the patient directs an often dangerous aggressiveness." An ambivalent attitude is present from the beginning toward the loved object and the transformation of love into hate takes place by "a reactive displacement of cathexis, energy being withdrawn from the erotic impulse and added to the hostile one" (18, p. 44). This aspect of paranoia and the important role of aggression and its vicissitudes is examined by Bak in his paper "Masochism in Paranoia" (chapter 6).

In a further development of psychoanalytic theories of paranoia Fenichel (5, p. 430) astutely observed that

like elements of the body, one's mental characteristics, too, may be projected onto the persecutor. This occurs not only in the projection of the hatred which is basic for the delusion; certain definite attitudes and expressions, which are ascribed to the persecutor, also correspond to traits of the patient and especially often to demands of the patient's superego. The persecutor, then, observes and criticizes the patient; the persecutors themselves represent projections of the patient's bad conscience—the projection of the superego is most clearly seen in ideas of reference and of being influenced. The patient feels that he is being controlled, observed, influenced, criticized, called upon to account for himself, and punished. The voices he hears utter criticisms of him, usually referring to his sexual activities which are depicted as dirty or homosexual. The patient hears himself reproached for his homosexuality and pregenital tendencies, just as severe parents might have talked to their naughty child.

This important observation of Fenichel's—the projection of the superego and its appearance in auditory hallucinations and delusional ideas is often encountered in the psychoses, not only in the schizophrenias, but in the affective psychoses as well. John Perceval in his account of his psychosis (4, pp. 46–47) wrote the following which captures the condemnatory, retributional aspects of superego projection:

The voices informed me that my conduct was owing to a spirit of mockery and blasphemy having possession of me—I was usually addressed in verse; and I was made to know that there were three degrees of hell; with the last of which among the worms, the moles, and the bats, I was often threatened. One day, when my head was towards the right-hand corner of the bed, and I was lying on my back across it, with my feet tied to the left-hand bed-post at the bottom; I imagined I was being examined before the tribunal of the Almighty; an act of disobedience provoked the Almighty to cast me with a thunderbolt to hell, and the holy counsellors supplicated him to do so. An awful pause followed; I seemed removed to the gates of hell; and a stroke of lightening appeared to pierce the air on my right, but it did not strike me; for then the reason of my disobedience on earth, and the mystery of my sinfulness was revealed to me; and in a disconsolate state of mind, as one about to enter on a solitary and everlasting stage of suffering, I complained to myself that if I had but known these things before, and had I had but another trial allowed to me on earth, I hoped I might have done my duty. The voice I attributed to my Saviour recorded my thoughts aloud, as if he had staid by me to the last, and overheard me, saying, he says so and so. And I imagined it was agreed upon, that I should be tried again in this life upon earth.

The appearance of Melanie Klein's influential internal object relations theory in the 1930s marks the next major psychoanalytic contribution to the psychology of psychosis. Klein's theories were inspired by her clinical work with children and severely disturbed adults. While her theory has been severely criticized for both its anthropomorphism and the telescoping of childhood psychosexual development into early infancy, her concepts have appealed to many clinicians who work with psychotic patients since they provide a compelling explanation for some of the extreme psychological phenomena encountered in psychotic states. Segal (19, p. 3) notes that Klein "was led to see that the child's object relationships extend far into the past, right back to a relationship to part-objects such as the breast and the penis, preceding the relationship to the parents as whole people." These anlage of later object relations are thought by some clinicians to make their reappearance in states of ego disintegration exemplified by the psychoses.

The conflict between aggression and libido was felt by Klein to be especially intense in the early stages of development and it was her contention that anxiety was more a function of the arousal of aggression than libido and that defences were erected primarily against aggression and anxiety. Klein's emphasis on the centrality of aggression stands in contrast to classical psychoanalytic theory which gives prominence to the libido. As Segal has observed, Melanie Klein saw that little children, under the spur of anxiety, were constantly trying to split their objects and their feelings and trying to retain good feelings and introject good objects, while expelling bad objects and projecting bad feelings. Klein placed great emphasis on the importance of symbol formation in the development of the ego and she noted that in psychosis it is symbol formation itself which is affected. According to Klein, destructive fantasies concerning the mother's body during the height of oral ambivalence, arouse anxiety and the child displaces interest in the mother's body through symbolization to the outside world. Klein felt that sadistic fantasies developed towards both parents. Segal summarized this (19, p. 6):

The more sadistic are his phantasies towards the parents, and the more terrifying therefore the images of them, the more he feels compelled to keep these feelings away from his good parents and the more he tries to introject again those good external parents. Introjection of bad figures however cannot be avoided. Thus in the early stages of development the infant would introject both the good and the bad breasts, penises, mother's body and parental couple. He tries to deal with the bad introjects which become equaled with faeces by anal mechanisms of control and ejection.

Klein described a developmental unfolding of the child in which this defense mechanism of splitting is central to the earliest phase. In what she called the paranoid-schizoid position the primary object, the breast, is split into two parts, the ideal breast and the persecuting breast. Anxiety is aroused in this stage by the fantasy that the persecutory object will get inside and overwhelm and annihilate the ideal object and the self. As Segal noted (19, p. 26) "in situations of anxiety the split is widened and projection and introjection are used in order to keep persecutory and ideal objects as far as possible from one another, while keeping both of them under control. The situation may fluctuate rapidly and persecution may be felt now outside, giving a feeling of external threat, now inside, producing fears of a hypochondriacal nature." Schreber's hypochondriacal and paranoid symptoms could be interpreted as regressive manifestations of this paranoid-schizoid position for Klein felt that the fixation points of psychosis were to be found in the earliest months of infancy.

The paranoid-schizoid position is followed by the depressive position in Klein's developmental schema. The mother is now recognized as a whole object as opposed to previous part-object and split-object relationships. In the depressive position the central anxiety for the child is the fear that his destructive impulses will destroy the whole object upon whom he is totally dependent. Klein viewed manic defences as occurring in response to the depression the infant may feel when he fantasizes he has destroyed the object on whom he is dependent. Manic defences deny any feeling of dependence and oppose psychic reality through fantasies of omnipotence with its accompanying elation.

Internal good and bad objects, the splitting of objects, self and object fragmentation, the projection of the bad object, the massive anxiety engendered by destructive aggressive fantasies; these are all Kleinian concepts that have considerable explanatory power for some of the phenomenology encountered in the psychoses and later theoreticians such as Jacobson and Kernberg in their work with psychotic and borderline states acknowledge their debt to Klein. The raw appearance of primitive infantile elements in the symptoms of psychosis is disputed by classical psychoanalysts, however, who do not see psychotic fears, fantasies, and thoughts as emerging naked from the unconscious, but view them merely as manifest content, albeit exaggerated, whose latent meaning can only be determined by obtaining associative material. Nonetheless, Klein's theory, in some ways the ultimate depth psychology, speaks powerfully to clinicians engaged in the daunting task of psychotherapeutic work with psychotic patients.

It has often been noted clinically that the onset of an acute psychotic episode may be heralded by a state of confusion and acute anxiety which is then replaced by the psychotic individual's sudden ''understanding'' of the ''meaning'' of the experience. This ''understanding'' may include the belief that the person has been chosen to be God's agent, if not the Messiah, and a conviction that knowledge hidden from others is now in his or her grasp. This sense of noesis is often accompanied by a state of exultation and a feeling of being in direct communion with God.

A representative account of such an episode is to be found in Morag Coate's (20, p. 21) description of the onset of her psychosis:

I got up from where I had been sitting and moved into another room. Suddenly my whole being was filled with light and loveliness and with an upsurge of deeply moving feeling from within myself to meet and reciprocate the influence that flowed into me. I was in a state of the most vivid awareness and illumination. What can I say of it? A cloudless, cerulean blue sky of the mind, shot through with shafts of exquisite, warm, dazzling sunlight. In its first and most intense stage it lasted perhaps an hour. It seemed that some force or impulse from without were acting on me, looking into me; that I was in touch with a reality beyond my own; that I had made direct contact with the secret, ultimate source of life. What I had read of the accounts of others acquired suddenly a new meaning. It flashed across my mind, ''This is what the mystics mean by the direct experience of God.''

Analogous experiences are seen in episodes of religious conversion where the individual is not psychotic, consistent with Bowers's postulate that the psychotic state of consciousness has some elements in common with other altered states. For instance, St. Augustine (21, p. 164) wrote the following:

Our conversation had brought us to this point that any pleasure whatsoever of the bodily senses, in any brightness whatsoever of corporeal light, seemed to us not worthy of comparison with the pleasure of that eternal Light, not worthy even of mention. Rising as our love flamed upward to that Selfsame, we passed in review the various levels of bodily things, up to the heavens themselves whence sun and moon and stars shine upon this earth. And higher still we soared, thinking in our minds and speaking and marvelling at Your works: and so we came to our own souls, and went beyond them to come at last to the region of richness unending, where You feed Israel forever with the food of Truth; and there life is that Wisdom by which all things are made, both the things that have been and the things that are yet to be. But this Wisdom itself is not made: it is as it has ever been, and so it shall be forever; indeed ''has ever been'' and ''shall be forever'' have no place in it, but it simply is, for it is eternal.

This description of St. Augustine's may be compared with John Custance's (22, p. 45) description of his psychosis:

From the first the experience seemed to me to be holy. What I say was the Power of Love—the name came to me at once—the Power that I knew somehow to have made all universes, past, present and to come, to be utterly infinite, an infinity of infinities, to have conquered the Power of Hate, its opposite, and thus created the sun, the stars, the moon, the planets, the earth, light, life, joy and peace, never-ending. . . .

In that peace I felt utterly and completely forgiven, relieved from all burden of sin. The whole infinity seemed to open up before me, and during the weeks and months which followed I passed through experiences which are virtually indescribable. The complete transformation of "reality" transported me as it were into the Kingdom of Heaven. The ordinary beauties of nature, particularly, I remember the skies at sunrise and sunset, took on a transcendental loveliness beyond belief. Every morning, quite contrary to my usual sluggish habits, I jumped up to look at them, and when possible went out to drink in, in a sort of ecstasy, the freshness of the morning air.

I feel so close to God, so inspired by His Spirit that in a sense I am God. I see the future, plan the Universe, save mankind; I am utterly and completely immortal; I am even male and female. The whole Universe, animate and inanimate, past present and future is within me. All nature and life, all spirits, are co-operating and connected with me; all things are possible.

In both accounts, the feeling of being transported beyond the self to a new realm, together with the affect of ecstasy and a heightened state of awareness, is the same.

Such elevated mood states are characteristic of mania. Typically, elation and euphoria may accompany the hyperexcitability, racing thoughts, flight of ideas, and irritability of the manic patient. An increased sensitivity to stimuli both external and internal is a central part of the manic process. The dramatic therapeutic response of many manic patients to lithium carbonate is highly suggestive of an underlying neurotransmitter disturbance. Certain psychological mechanisms, however, in the exaggerated pathological state of mania, are laid bare, as is true in general in the psychoses wherein extreme pathology provides insight into normal as well as pathological mental functioning.

The psychological nature of mania was examined by Freud (23) in "Group Psychology and the Analysis of the Ego." He compared sleep and mania because they held in common the disappearance of a part of the personality— in sleep the ego disappears, rejoining the id, while in mania the superego disappears, rejoining the ego. Lewin (24) in his important monograph "The Psychoanalysis of Elation" extended and developed this thesis. For Lewin, mania could be compared to sleep if it was seen to resemble the dream of a small child with its playful wish fulfillments, in essence the dream life of the narcissistic pleasure ego. Lewin further saw both sleep and mania as the result of an intrapsychic fusion with the breast at nursing. He viewed elation as "a sleep equivalent guarded by a type of censorship that is created particularly to employ the defense mechanism denial'' (24, p. 101).

Oral eroticism was thus considered by Lewin to be the major psychological component of manic-depressive illness. Three central fantasies which he called ''the oral triad'' were the manifestation of this unconscious orality— the wish to devour, the wish to be devoured, and the wish to go to sleep. All three had their origins in the nursing situation wherein the physiological need to eat and to sleep became psychological wishes. He acknowledged that the middle element of the triad, the wish to be devoured is not obviously evident in the nursing situation and was a construction, based on inference (24, p. 104): ''that the nursling 'wishes to be eaten' means merely that toward the end of the act of suckling, and with the gradual approach of sleep, the infant has certain perceptions and experiences of yielding, relaxing, and falling that leave a string of mnemonic impressions, and that later on these memories and experiences serve as a nucleus for the cluster of ideas of being eaten in various forms.'' The wishes of the oral triad may ''assume fantastic disguises and coloring'' in the manic patient (24, p. 137).

In the ecstatic state Lewin felt that ''the breast is condensed psychologically with the superego, a deathless one with which the ego identifies itself, so that it can participate in its immortality . . . along with the active devouring fantasies goes the sense of yielding to the deathless figure, relaxing into it, and ultimately joining it in sleep or a sleeplike state.''

Lewin provided (24, p. 148) a clinical example of this in the words of a hypomanic patient:

At orgasm, I melt into the other person. It is hard to describe, but there is a certain oneness, a loss of my body in the other person, as if I were part of him without my individual identity, yet in him part of a larger whole. At other times, I am the dominant individual and he the lost one, so that I become the perfect whole. It is something like aligning one's self with a great cause like Christianity or woman's suffrage, a complete loss of the self in them. . . . When he seemed to enter me I gained his attributes, for example, his aesthetic taste, which was better than mine. It seemed as if I absorbed the beauty he made me aware of. It was a substitute for having it. . . . For a man to take a woman's breast in his mouth at orgasm makes the sexual act mutual and simultaneous.

Ecstatic mood states relive the nonverbal experience of union at the breast. Lewin suggested that the ideas that have become differentiated as sleep, death, immortality, heaven, and the oceanic feeling all spring from the matrix of subjective experience that is found following nursing. For Lewin (24, p. 182) ''the happy mood of the manic is a repetition. It is subjectively valid and real to the one who experiences it, because it relives a primary, real, happy feeling. In the actual content of ideas of manics, besides the experience of the breast, are included the later events of childhood which themselves in some way repeat or revive the nursing situation or may themselves have been falsified by it.''

Psychoanalytic contributions to an understanding of psychosis, while at times prone to a reductionist tendency concerning theories of aetiology, have had the singular virtue of taking the patient's subjective experience and individual psychological history as their source material. As such, they provide an avenue into the psychological understanding of the meaning of the symptoms of the disorder for any one person together with insight into why a psychotic episode should occur at a particular time. Advances in biological research will ultimately explicate the disturbances in neurochemistry that underly some of the schizophrenias and affective psychoses. Such advances, however, will not vitiate psychological understanding of these crippling disorders, but will be complementary to them and will enhance the development of a rational therapy of the psychoses leading to a true biopsychosocial treatment that does justice to the complexity inherent in psychotic illness.

NOTE

1. R. D. Laing (7, pp. 29–31) provides an illuminating account of the likely meaning of a patient's behavior and speech while being publicly interviewed by Kraepelin.

REFERENCES

1. MacAlpine, I., and Hunter, R. A. (eds. & trans.) Daniel Paul Schreber. *Memoirs of My Nervous Illness.* Dawson & Sons. London, 1955.
2. Bowers, M. B. *Retreat from Sanity.* Penguin Books. Baltimore, 1974.
3. Freud, S. "The Loss of Reality in Neurosis and Psychosis." *Standard Edition,* vol. 19.
4. Bateson, G. (ed.) *Perceval's Narrative: A Patient's Account of His Psychosis, 1830–1832.* William Morrow. New York, 1974.
5. Fenichel, O. *The Psychoanalytic Theory of Neurosis.* W. W. Norton. New York, 1945.
6. Rieder, R. O. "The Origins of Our Confusion About Schizophrenia." *Psychiatry,* vol. 37: 197–208, 1974.
7. Laing, R. D. *The Divided Self.* Penguin Books. Baltimore, 1961.
8. Pope, M. G., Jr., and Lipinski, J. F. "Diagnosis in Schizophrenia and Manic Depressive Illness." *Archives of General Psychiatry,* vol. 35: 811–28, 1978.
9. Bellak, L. (ed.) *Schizophrenia: A Review of the Syndrome.* Logos Press. New York, 1958.
10. Strauss, J. S., and Carpenter, W. T., Jr. *Schizophrenia.* Plenum. New York, 1981.
11. *The New York Times.* March 18, 1986.

12. Freud, S. "Psychoanalytic Notes on an Autobiographical Account of a Case of Paranoia." *Standard Edition*, vol. 12.

13. Strachey, J. Editor's note to Freud, S. "Psychoanalytic Notes on an Autobiographical Account of a Case of Paranoia." *Standard Edition*, vol. 12: 5.

14. Sacher, E. J., Kanter, S. S., Buie, D., Engle, R., and Mehlman R. "Psychoendocrinology of Ego Disintegration." *American Journal of Psychiatry*, vol. 126: 1067–78, 1970.

15. Niederland, W. G. (ed). *The Schreber Case*. Quadrangle/New York Times Book Co., 1974.

16. Grotstein, J. S. "The Schreber Case: A Reappraisal." *International Journal of Psychoanalytic Psychotherapy*, vol. 10: 321–82, 1984.

17. Freud, S. "Constructions in Analysis." *Standard Edition*, vol. 23.

18. Freud, S. "The Ego and the Id." *Standard Edition*, vol. 19.

19. Segal, H. *Introduction to the Work of Melanie Klein*. Basic Books. New York, 1973.

20. Coate, M. *Beyond All Reason*. J. P. Lippincott. New York, 1965.

21. St. Augustine. *Confessions*. (Translated by F. K. Sheed). Sheed & Ward. New York, 1943.

22. Custance, J. *Wisdom, Madness and Folly*. Pellegrini and Cudahy. New York, 1952.

23. Freud, S. "Group Psychology and the Analysis of the Ego." *Standard Edition*, vol. 18.

24. Lewin, B. *The Psychoanalysis of Elation*. W. W. Norton. New York, 1950.

PART I

THE PHENOMENOLOGY OF PSYCHOSIS

The fantastic and bizarre symptoms often experienced by psychotic patients have begged for psychological explanation especially in light of what appears to be the naked appearance of primary-process thinking and the breakdown of normal defence mechanisms such as repression. A psychoanalytic theory of the phenomenology of the psychoses can be constructed without simultaneously advancing a general theory of aetiology and given the paucity of confirmed scientific data concerning the latter such a position would appear to be prudent. Even within the psychoanalytic theory of psychotic phenomenology, however, considerable controversy reigns and two opposing viewpoints have been asserted.

Freud (1) postulated that the pathological process of schizophrenia was a consequence of a shift of libidinal energies from their investment in representations of objects to an investment in representations of the self. Hence the symptoms that reflect the break with reality are consequences of a decathexis of the world of objects which no longer seem real to the afflicted individual. The hypercathexis of the self leads to hypochondriasis and delusions of grandeur. Finally, paranoid delusions are the result of the recathexis of object representations in what Freud viewed as a restitutional attempt. The concept of decathexis of objects provided an explanation for the bizarre language used by schizophrenics and Freud (2) suggested that there was a decathexis of the unconscious representation of the object itself while simultaneously there was a hypercathexis of the word presentation and words were then treated as if they had been things. Because of their inability to cathect representations of objects, Freud felt that psychotic patients could not develop transference relationships. Thus, for Freud, in at least one stage of his thinking, the differences between the psychoses and neuroses were qualitative in nature and the symptoms of psychosis were not parallels, writ large, of the symptoms seen in the neuroses. As London demonstrates, however, he was quite inconsistent in this view and at times favoured a unitary view of the psychoses which placed them on a continuum with the neuroses.

Arlow and Brenner (3) proposed a revision of the psychopathology of the psychoses which abandoned Freud's concept of libidinal decathexis and re-cathexis. They suggested that mental representations of objects can be, and are, well cathected in the psychoses and that since transference phenomena do occur in schizophrenia, the shift in libido economy postulated by Freud is fallacious. They proposed that the differences between the neuroses and psychoses are quantitative, not qualitative. They applied this thesis to delusions and hallucination in the following manner (3, p. 10):

We suggest that delusions and hallucinations may be explained as follows within the conceptual framework of the structural theory. In either case a fantasy has resulted from the patient's inner conflict, whether that conflict is over instinctual wishes, self-punitive demands, or both. Whatever other defensive mechanisms may be involved in the formation of the fantasy, e.g., repression, projection, denial, etc., there is among the ego's defences a regressive alteration of reality testing. The ego's ability to dis-tinguish between external reality and the particular fantasy in question is impaired in order to avoid or minimize the development of anxiety. Thus the fantasy appears real to the patient. Instead of being experienced as a daydream, it is experienced as a delusion or hallucination. What determines whether it is one or the other is the presence or absence of sensory elements in the fantasy. If there are such elements, the result is a hallucination. If there are none, it is a delusion.

Utilizing the structural theory, they felt that in the psychoses, just as in the neuroses,

in the presence of intrapsychic (structural) conflict, a danger situation arises in which the ego is threatened by anxiety. In order to fend off overwhelming anxiety, the ego institutes a set of defensive maneuvres. The purpose of the maneuvres is to master, to diminish or to contain the anxiety. The ego tries to accomplish this by arranging different kinds of compromises between the conflicting forces of the mind. Of the many forms of compromise formation which may eventuate under these circum-stances, the most important ones for us in the present context are formation of symp-toms, distortion of character and severe inhibitions (3, p. 10).

Retaining the thesis that the differences between the psychoses and the neuroses are quantitative they conceded that instinctual regression tends to be more pronounced and severe in the psychoses, that conflicts over aggression are more frequent and that disturbances of ego and superego functioning are much more severe than in the neuroses. They also postulated that ego weak-nesses, arising out of developmental traumata, might be responsible for the severity of disturbance seen in the psychoses.

Freeman (4) criticized the view that identical mechanisms of symptom formation occur in both the neuroses and psychoses and that it is principally the ego defect in psychosis which differentiates them. He stated (4, p. 414):

There are similarities in the initial stages (of psychosis and neurosis) consisting of efforts at repression. These fail, but the failure in psychosis is on a much more massive scale. There is the irruption of repressed drive-representations which have a primary-process quality. From this point on the mechanisms are entirely different. In neurosis the repressed contents are dealt with by means which hold the drive-derivatives back from direct expression, simultaneously giving them a partial outlet in the symptoms. In psychosis projection and hallucination alter the aim and object of the drive-representations which have emerged from repression. The cathexis of these representations allows for their becoming a new (psychotic) reality for the patient-the phase of re-cathexis.

London, in two papers in this section, reviews and critically assesses the two theories of schizophrenia in order to develop a psychoanalytic theory specific for the disorder. He traces the complex, at times contradictory, and ultimately unresolved, nature of Freud's thought on psychosis and proposes a theory of the psychopathology of schizophrenia based on an inability to organize and sustain mental object representations. In this thesis disturbed reality integration in schizophrenia is secondary to disturbed mental object representation and schizophrenic behaviors are reactive to a psychological deficiency state rather than a psychologically motivated behavior in response to intrapsychic conflict.

The next paper in this section is Victor Tausk's "On the Origin of the 'Influencing Machine' in Schizophrenia." Following the original publication, this paper rapidly attained the status of a classic. Tausk first introduced the important concept of loss of ego boundaries in schizophrenia and greatly extended Freud's original work on delusion formation.

Freeman's paper presents clinical material which he views as substantiating Freud's original thesis of the process of schizophrenia involving a shift of libidinal energies from their investment in representations of objects to an investment in representations of the self. Though Freeman feels that the unconscious conflicts which initiate symptom formation in the neuroses do not differ materially from those conflicts which precipitate psychotic states, he contends that there is a radical difference in the defensive reactions which ensue and that the regression in the latter is qualitatively different. For Freeman the restitutive psychotic reality with its delusion formation is also a form of adaptation defending the individual against the dread of internal catastrophe and complete disintegration, hence the tenacity of the psychotic individual's belief in his delusional system which protects him from this horror.

Searles, in his paper on the sources of anxiety in paranoid schizophrenia posits that the single most basic threat to the paranoid schizophrenic person is the fear that he will cease to exist as a human individual. For the paranoid patient there is also the fear that he will be reduced to only part of a person, most often a genital. This latter insight of Searles's represents an intriguing extension of Tausk's analysis of the meaning of the delusion of the influencing machine as a projection of the psychotic individual's whole body which is unconsciously fantasized as a genital.

Bak's paper examines masochism in paranoia and convincingly demonstrates how paranoia is, in fact, delusional masochism.

Edith Jacobson, more than any other psychoanalyst, attempted to integrate object-relations theory with classical psychoanalytic theory. Continuing this effort in her paper in this section, she contrasts the pathological mechanisms of identification in manic-depressives with that of schizophrenics and provides a convincing psychoanalytic confirmation of the original descriptive nosological distinction between the psychoses made by Kraepelin.

REFERENCES

1. Freud, S. "Psychoanalytic Notes on an Autobiographical Account of a Case of Paranoia." *Standard Edition*, vol. 12.
2. Freud, S. "The Unconscious." *Standard Edition*, vol. 14.
3. Arlow, J. A., and Brenner, C. "The Psychopathology of the Psychoses: A Proposed Revision." *International Journal of Psychoanalysis*, vol. 50: 5–14, 1969.
4. Freeman, T. "The Psychopathology of the Psychoses: A Reply to Arlow and Brenner." *International Journal of Psycho-analysis*, vol. 51: 407–15, 1970.

1. An Essay on Psychoanalytic Theory: Two Theories of Schizophrenia. Part I: Review and Critical Assessment of the Development of the Two Theories

Nathaniel J. London

THE PROBLEM OF UNITARY THEORY

Sound theory remains well rooted in the observations it serves to organize and the investigative goals it serves to define. One of the obstacles to any sound theory is the dilemma as to whether it has been over-extended or under-extended. The usual tendency is toward a dialectic of unitary and multiple theories: first one and then the other in ascendancy in the advance of science. The trend in this dialectic usually favours multiple theories in the progression toward increasing specialization. Such advances are also dependent on the creative capacities of those scientists, like Sigmund Freud, who can bring together a wide range of observations into a single theoretical framework. Freud's ambitions and extraordinary capacity for synthesis also led him to err in the direction of over-extended or over-synthesized theories, a tendency which he recognized and often corrected. In fact, he cautioned against using psychoanalysis as a general psychology (1914*a*, p. 50).

An orientation toward psychoanalytic metapsychology as a unified and cohesive theory of human behaviour favours over-extended theorizing. A proper focus on factors specific to one or more behaviours but not to others tends to become obscured. This essay is orientated toward a different view of psychoanalytic metapsychology: not as a unified theory but as a group of interrelated but separable theories derived from a common focus of investigation (intrapsychic) and primarily from a common method (the psychoanalytic situation).[1]

Psychoanalysts have special reason to favour unified theory. While the *focus* of psychoanalysis is on subjective inner experience, the *scope* of psychoanalysis emphasizes the interrelatedness of all aspects of human behaviour. Psychoanalytic theory and practice involve establishing connexions between seemingly unrelated behavioural phenomena and organizing the data according to different metapsychological points of view (Rapaport & Gill, 1959). The 'scientific elegance' of psychoanalytic theory not only lies in its ability to organize extremely complex data, but derives from the *actual* interdependence of human experiences as revealed by psychoanalysis. It is well known that efforts to segment psychoanalytic theory, i.e. to emphasize one aspect rather than another, may have the effect of undercutting basic concepts. For example, an emphasis on 'ego psychology' may be used, not as a differentiated area of psychoanalytic study, but rather as a dismemberment of psychoanalytic knowledge in the service of a denial of psychosexual development. This essay is orientated toward specifying psychoanalytic propositions rather than segmenting them; toward defining investigative goals rather than building unified theories.

THEORY OF SCHIZOPHRENIA

The psychoanalytic theory of schizophrenia is pre-eminently suited to illustrate this point, and this essay will be devoted entirely to this subject. Freud's *Classical Theory* of schizophrenia is an example of his tendency to oversynthesize. The Classical Theory may be separated into two theories, which I shall term the *Unitary Theory* and the *Specific Theory*.[2] Both theories have undergone considerable elaboration and documentation since Freud's pioneering work. They appear to be incompatible. The more familiar *Unitary Theory* is focused on *intrapsychic motives* common to neurotic as well as schizophrenic behaviours. It strives to understand schizophrenia in terms of factors common to all human experience. Whatever its merits, the Unitary Theory has been granted undue consideration in order to maintain a unified theory of psychosis *and* neurosis. The *Specific Theory* is orientated toward factors considered unique to schizophrenic behaviours, distinguishable from intrapsychic motives, and which interfere with developing and sustaining mental representations. This theory, which has been most succinctly formulated as 'decathexis of the mental representations of objects', appears more promising for research in schizophrenia. Yet the Specific Theory has been formulated in too restrictive a fashion. The available evidence of schizophrenic behaviour not only points to a disturbance in the representation of objects but extends to many aspects of mental representation.

I first recognized incompatible trends in Freud's Classical Theory of schizophrenia during a survey of his writings. However, the formulation of a Unitary Theory and a Specific Theory, as developed in this essay, will involve more than a dissection of Freud's Classical Theory. The two theories correspond to two major contemporary orientations toward schizophrenia which are formulated in various ways by different authors. I have organized the Unitary and Specific Theories in order to clarify the differences between these two orientations. There are serious differences in the organization of data, in investigative approaches and goals as well as in clinical therapeutic interventions. For example, in a given instance, a psychoanalyst may communicate or defer communicating psychodynamic understanding to his patient, depending on his theoretical orientation.

The differences in these psychoanalytic orientations toward schizophrenia have not been formulated in theoretical language which allows for fruitful scientific dispute and resolutions. Arlow & Brenner's (1969) proposed revision of the psychopathology of the psychoses is a noteworthy effort to clarify one side of the argument. Unified and cohesive psychoanalytic theory has proved frustrating to psychoanalytic investigators in the area of schizophrenia. It is difficult to compare the findings of different authors insofar as they have tended to use individualized theoretical formulations. This essay may be viewed as an attempt to develop a psychoanalytic theory specific for schizophrenia, consistent with, but separable from, other psychoanalytic theories. In pursuing this attempt, I have found it necessary to reconsider basic psychoanalytic issues, such as the theory of instinctual drives, the theory of mental representation and the problem of reality integration. Perhaps the development of a more widely acceptable psychoanalytic theory of schizophrenia may not only be helpful to investigations in this area but the study of schizophrenia may be more effectively applied to understanding basic psychoanalytic concepts. To further this end, I shall first review and critically assess the development of the two theories in the context of Freud's writings. Part II (see chapter 2) consists of a reformulation of the Specific Theory in terms of current psychoanalytic theory and current knowledge of schizophrenic behaviours.

INTRODUCTION TO THE TWO THEORIES OF SCHIZOPHRENIA

While I believe that the phenomenology of schizophrenia is far from being fully explored, there is an extensive body of knowledge about this clinical entity (or entities), much of which has derived from psychoanalysis. Both the Unitary and Specific Theories are designed to account for the same body of knowledge about schizophrenic behaviours, but neither theory purports to account for their aetiology.

The *Unitary Theory* consists of the following propositions:

1. There is a continuity between schizophrenic behaviour and all other psychological states. This aspect of the Unitary Theory—the *continuity concept*—is not unique to psychoanalysis and is supported by many authors working from different vantage points, e.g. Freud (1917*b*, p. 421), Burton (1961), Kubie (1967) and Arlow & Brenner (1969). Schizophrenic behaviour is considered a more severe disturbance than neurotic behaviour. It is distinguished from neurotic behaviour in degree but not in kind (Arlow & Brenner, 1969).

2. The theory of schizophrenia is conceptually subordinated to the theory of *intrapsychic conflict and defence*. Accordingly, schizophrenia is primarily viewed as an *unconsciously purposive behaviour* derived from the interplay of intrapsychic drives and defences. Yet schizophrenia is also partly viewed as a *psychological deficiency state* derived from a developmental disturbance early in the formation of object relations (narcissism). The traumatic developmental factors considered to favour the development of schizophrenia are considered the same as those favouring neurotic development, except that they are more severe and perhaps occur earlier in life. Within this theory, there is the implication that anyone may develop schizophrenia given a certain degree of unmanageable intrapsychic conflict.

Arlow & Brenner (1969) reformulated the Unitary Theory in a way that brought the theory up to date with contemporary psychoanalysis and also sharpened the differentiation from the Specific Theory. They held that mental object representations are well cathected in schizophrenia. They maintained that schizophrenics may develop

the same fundamental process which can be recognized in the transference of neurotic patients, i.e. the displacement on to the image of the analyst of instinctual cathexes originally invested in infantile objects.

Typical schizophrenic delusions, hallucinations, hypochondriasis and megalomania were explained in terms of conflict and defence. They proposed that the *psychodynamics* of hypochondriacal symptoms are 'identical with the structure of the conversion symptoms of hysterical patients'. The increased severity and unique aspects of schizophrenic symptoms were attributed to ego weakness, regression of ego functions, and a preponderance of conflicts over aggressive impulses in schizophrenia as opposed to the preponderance of libidinal conflicts in neuroses.

The *Specific Theory* consists of the following propositions:

1. Schizophrenic behaviour is unique and separable from other behaviours

for investigative purposes. This position is maintained even though schizophrenic behaviour occurs in association with other behaviours and it may be difficult at times to distinguish schizophrenic from non-schizophrenic phenomena.

2. Among the many clinical features considered unique for schizophrenia, limitations in the capacity for transference are emphasized.

3. All formulations of schizophrenia are subordinate to a concept expressed as 'withdrawal of cathexes from the mental representations of objects'. Schizophrenic behaviour is accordingly viewed as reactive to an 'internal catastrophe' (cathectic withdrawal). In other words, the varied symptomatology of schizophrenia is considered an adaptation to a psychological deficiency state (cf. Wexler, 1971).

The concept 'cathectic withdrawal' has never been thoroughly defined because of serious conceptual problems, and because the referent phenomenology is not yet fully understood. Nevertheless, it remains as a central concept. The observations from which it has been derived are mutually understood among psychoanalysts and utilized in theoretical writings and clinical practice. The extent to which this concept is seriously valued is exemplified by Novey (1958, p. 66):

> What we describe as psychosis is a disturbance in the internal operations of the ego; the disturbance between ego and reality is only secondary . . . What the patient experiences as real or unreal depends on the character of his investments in his internal objects, and fragmentation of these investments may or may not be manifested by evident changes in social behaviour. Where such fragmentation is severe, we are entitled to speak of it as psychosis.

CRITICAL REVIEW OF FREUD'S THEORIES OF SCHIZOPHRENIA

Freud explicitly and consistently applied the libido theory and its derivative theories of intrapsychic conflict and defence to schizophrenia in order to develop a unified theory for schizophrenia and neuroses (appendix 1). However, as much as he sought a unified theory for schizophrenia and neuroses, Freud was equally preoccupied with a search for a specific theory and actually formulated one.

The Unitary Theory

As early as 1895 (Draft H), Freud described the defence mechanism of *projection* in paranoia—a distortion of reality due to defensive externalization of inner conflicts. He succeeded brilliantly in his two earliest publications on psychosis (1896, 1911) in establishing the usefulness of the psychodynamic viewpoint to understanding symptom formation in schizophrenia. The significance of the theory of intrapsychic conflict to passive homosexuality in paranoia, as described in the Schreber study, was particularly convincing. With this impressive evidence, Freud developed a theory of schizophrenia as a purposive behaviour organized around instinctual drive cathexes and sexual conflicts. He did this according to the same sequential formula which had proved so accurate in the neuroses: intrapsychic conflict—anxiety—a defensive struggle—regression to a preexisting fixation. The only difference from the theory of neuroses consisted in fixation to a developmental phase early in the formation of object relations (narcissism) and a different mode of defence (1911, 1917*b*, 1924*b*). Freud was uncertain about defence in schizophrenia until he described the conflict between the ego and the external world (1924*b*). He then described *disavowal* as a specific defence—that schizophrenics disavow mental representations of outer reality for the same reasons that neurotics repress instinctual demands (1924*b*). Under the Unitary Theory, withdrawal of instinctual drive cathexes ('decathexis') was considered a means of defence common to neuroses and schizophrenia.

The Specific Theory

Freud did not easily embrace the notion of a continuity between neuroses and schizophrenia. Among his outstanding contributions to the study of schizophrenia,[3] he established the differential diagnosis of psychotic states from neuroses. He excluded the treatment of schizophrenics from the psychoanalytic method because he considered the disturbance in thinking and in object relations such as to preclude the use of free association (1911, p. 9) and the development of transference (1917*b*, p. 447). He also emphasized a different form of the reaction to danger in schizophrenia (appendix 2) and the prevalence of primitive thoughts and imagery (appendix 3). He questioned whether instinctual drives were primary determining factors in schizophrenia or were secondary to some disturbance in perceptual or cognitive functions (appendix 4).

The development of the Specific Theory in Freud's writings is extremely complicated, involving six successive definitions for 'decathexis'. He vacillated between an intrapsychic focus ('internal catastrophe') and an environmentalist focus (social withdrawal) in accounting for disturbances in 'reality'.

In addition, he kept linking his specific ideas about schizophrenia to a primary determining role for drives and conflicts as in neuroses (Unitary Theory). Freud began with the roots of a specific theory (1911, p. 69). Drawing upon delusions of the 'end of the world', he considered schizophrenic alienation from the environment related to an 'internal catastrophe'—or, in Schreber's words, 'a profound internal change'. The details of such an 'internal catastrophe' were not made clear but it was linked to the Unitary Theory in being explained by a withdrawal of libidinal drives (*first definition of 'decathexis'*). For his *second definition of 'decathexis'* (1911, p. 71), Freud shifted from an 'internal catastrophe' to an environmental focus. Abraham (1908) had drawn upon schizophrenic states of indifference and apathy to emphasize a withdrawal from (external) objects. Freud similarly emphasized schizophrenic alienation from external reality to define 'decathexis' now as a 'detachment of libido from people—and things—that were previously loved'. Libidinal drives were treated at this point as an aspect of social interest rather than as intrapsychic motivating forces.[4] Abraham and Freud did not have access to what has subsequently been learned about schizophrenic indifference to the environment: namely, that it is not primary, that it is favoured by certain environmental factors such as 'hospitalism', and that it may recede with relatively simple treatment measures without essentially modifying the schizophrenic disturbance. Because this early formulation has been mistaken as the sum and substance of the 'decathexis' theory, evidence for the reversibility of schizophrenic indifference has been mistakenly used to refute the theory as well as Freud's assertion that schizophrenics fail to establish transference. Freud, however, was immediately dissatisfied with his emphasis on social withdrawal, noting that the formulation failed to distinguish comparable neurotic withdrawal states.

Freud's *third definition of 'decathexis'* (1911, pp. 71–2) was an intricate *tour de force* which still began with an environmental focus. He described libidinal withdrawal from the environment as a common first step in both psychosis and neurosis. Asserting that repression was the second step in the formation of neuroses, he attempted to define a defence comparable to repression and specific for schizophrenia—an attempt which occupied him for many years. Again following Abraham (1908), Freud suggested that the withdrawn libido is redirected on to the ego in schizophrenia (ego hypercathexis); thus reestablishing a narcissistic state and accounting for megalomania, hypochondriasis and (1914*b*, p. 84) anxiety. Furthermore, he proposed that delusions and hallucinations were 'restitutional' symptoms designed to recapture the lost (external) object world. Freud was uncertain as to whether the gross disturbances in reality integration observed in schizophrenia could be explained in this way by the libido theory (1911, pp. 73–4). Jung, who was generally critical of Freud's libido theory, had claimed that the ego hypercathexis theory 'would result in the psychology of an ascetic anchorite, not in a dementia praecox' (Freud, 1914b).[5] Freud agreed that social withdrawal could not be explained directly by a withdrawal of sexual drives. He returned to his original intrapsychic focus on an 'internal catastrophe' to assert a primary determining role for libidinal drives.

For his *fourth definition of 'decathexis'* (1914b, p. 74), Freud specified that, in neuroses, the withdrawn libido is redirected to fantasy objects. A failure to cathect fantasy objects in schizophrenia, as now advanced by Freud, was a further step in explaining the 'internal catastrophe'. This point was also one of a series of critical steps in establishing the focus of psychoanalysis on subjective mental experience, in differentiating intrapsychic tension (instinctual drives) from social interest, in distinguishing (intrapsychic) object relations from 'interpersonal relations', and so differentiating psychoanalysis from sociology. Freud continued to specify the 'internal catastrophe' in his *fifth definition of 'decathexis'* (1915b, p. 203), when he presented the first metapsychological statement of what I term the Specific Theory. He now described 'decathexis' of the 'unconscious presentation of the object'. This hypothesis extended the disturbance in schizophrenia to basic aspects of object representation and so defined a psychological deficiency state. Freud seriously questioned whether he had now proposed a process radically different from intrapsychic defence (appendix 5). It seems clear that Freud was concerned that this proposal did not fit a unified theory for schizophrenia and neuroses, and he considered rejecting this specific theory (1917a, pp. 225, 235). At the same time, he studied primitive object relations in melancholia (1917c), a work which has enriched our understanding of 'decathexis of object representations' in schizophrenia. The significance of the Specific Theory has been further developed by others. The crucial point that disturbances in reality integration are secondary to a primary 'internal catastrophe' was never specifically stated by Freud. In later writings Freud continued to define 'decathexis', according to the Unitary Theory, as a defence mechanism, as well as to assert a continuity for schizophrenia and neuroses (appendix 6). In a *sixth definition of 'decathexis'* (appendix 7), he reversed the deep intrapsychic focus of decathexis from '*Ucs.* presentations'. He returned to a position close to the early environmentalist focus, applying 'decathexis' to representations close to perceptions of external reality. Specifically, he applied 'decathexis' to the 'internal world', defining 'internal world' at this point as a copy of the external world (1924*a*, p. 150). *'Decathexis' and the two theories*. In advancing a theory of cathectic withdrawal from the *'Ucs.* presentation of the object', Freud used a definition for 'decathexis' different from the one used in the Unitary Theory. This definitional confusion presents serious problems for psychoanalytic theory. 'Decathexis', as it is applied in the Unitary Theory, refers to an instinctual drive vicissitude or a defence mechanism. This terminology derives from Freud's use of 'instinctual drives and their cathexes' to indicate intrapsychic motivating forces. Such usage belongs to the drive organization of memory and the theory of intrapsychic conflict (Freud, 1900, pp. 565–7, 598–600). 'Decathexis', as it is applied in the Specific Theory, refers to a basic disturbance in mental representation (psychological deficiency state). 'Decathexis', in this sense, derives from Freud's use of the term 'cathexis' to indicate quantitative factors responsible for developing and sustaining mental representations. It belongs to the controversial theory of 'psychic energy' as well as to Freud's significant contributions to the organization of memory (Freud, 1900, pp. 538–44).

The double definition of 'decathexis' described here is at the heart of the theoretical problem for this essay and provides one justification for separating Freud's Classical Theory into a Unitary and a Specific Theory. The double definition derives from an earlier fusion or confusion of two main lines of Freud's work. One main line of inquiry, involving behavioural motivation, began when Freud recognized the importance of sexuality in development and behaviour from his clinical studies of hysteria. This discovery was developed and elaborated over a period of years into the crucial role of intrapsychic motivating forces—termed instinctual drives—in purposive behaviours (e.g. intrapsychic conflicts). So long as one assumes a clear conceptual distinction between mind, body and environment, then these intrapsychic motivating forces must be mental representations (Freud, 1915*a*, p. 122) derived from the internalization of tension and need states.[6] Instinctual drives, according to this definition, ultimately derive from the memory traces of stimulation external to the mental apparatus, i.e. from physiological stimulation (Freud, 1915*a*: '. . . the demand made upon the mind for work in consequence of its connection with the body'), shaped by environmental experiences, and nurtured by the mental representations of whatever physiologically instinctive responses are innate to the human condition.[7] The other main investigative line began with Freud's study of language development (1891, pp. 77–8) and

led to the organization of memory and the development of mental representations. Through his neurophysiological speculations in the Project (1895b),
Freud came to organize his formulations of memory and mental representations around hypothesized superordinate quantitative factors—'psychic energies'. Whatever these superordinate factors may be, they are as much responsible for developing and sustaining instinctual drives and drive derivatives
(according to the definition of instinctual drives above) as they are responsible
for object representations.

Freud attempted to fuse these two theories—instinctual drives and psychic
energy—as early as the Project (1895b, p. 379). In 'The Interpretation of
Dreams' (1900, pp. 565–6) he brought the two theories together by attributing the development of object relations to frustrated drives. Since then, instinctual drives and psychic energy have been considered synonymous.
Freud's confusion of these two distinct investigative lines resulted, in my
view, in an over-simplification of the organization of memory and an over-
extension of the theory of instinctual drives. I would have to go beyond the
limits of this essay to properly discuss and document this assertion, but the
reader should understand that the subject is pertinent to the theory of schizophrenia. Through an earlier confusion of the theory of instinctual drives with
the superordinate psychic energy theory, Freud was able to define 'decathexis' as a defence mechanism (Unitary Theory) and alternatively as a disruption of mental representations (Specific Theory).

CRITICAL ASSESSMENT

The Unitary Theory

I contend that the Unitary Theory is orientated more toward advancing a
unified psychoanalytic position than toward an optimal research strategy. This
point may be supported by the following considerations of instinctual drives,
anxiety and defence.

Instinctual Drives. Prior to formulating the structural theory, Freud advanced a conflict theory for schizophrenia in terms of a primary *determining*
role for libidinal drives. Other authors have maintained this orientation in
different formulations of drive theory. Hartmann (1953, p. 185) classified
'decathexis' among instinctual vicissitudes rather than as a defence. Arlow &
Brenner (1969) emphasized a preponderance of conflicts involving aggressive
drives. Kleinian analysts emphasize Freud's death instinct (Segal, 1964).

Segal (1970) has suggested, with good reason, that Freud most probably would not have used the 'decathexis' concept if he had developed his theory of schizophrenia after he developed the death instinct hypothesis. While I disagree with these authors, all of them have drawn upon well-documented evidence. Primitive as well as higher level tension and need states are clearly involved in schizophrenic behaviours. Further understanding of such evidence is needed for psychoanalytic progress in schizophrenia. For example, the special relation of passive anal homosexuality to paranoia remains essentially unexplained. The difficulty with 'the *Unitary Theory* is that it is orientated toward proving a *primary determining* role for instinctual drives in schizophrenia similar to neuroses. The result is a research strategy which obscures investigating the unique ways in which drives may be involved in and affected by the schizophrenic thought disorder.

Anxiety. The subject of anxiety is well suited to illustrate the problem presented by a theory devoted to establishing a continuity between schizophrenia and neuroses. In his last contribution to schizophrenia, Freud (1924*b*) discussed the reaction to danger along the lines of neurotic anxiety (signal anxiety and the defensive process). From the outset (1911), however, he seriously questioned the *form* of the reaction to danger in schizophrenia as opposed to the neuroses. He did this by defining hypochondriasis in paranoia as a primitive reaction to danger (appendix 2). This is different from Arlow & Brenner's (1969) unitary view of hypochondriasis as a compromise formation derived from intrapsychic conflicts.

Our current knowledge indicates that there are reactions to danger observed in schizophrenia which differ from the neurotic anxiety response in both *form* and *function*.[8] Schizophrenics typically show reactions to danger which are not observed in neuroses—such as hypochondriasis and bizarre states of panic and excitement. These states appear to be intimately and concretely involved in primitive object relations (Rosenfeld, 1958). Furthermore, such reactions to danger typically appear reactive rather than anticipatory. The clinician thinking along the lines of the Unitary Theory will ascribe the absence of anticipatory anxiety in a schizophrenic subject to *defensive denial*. Such an orientation makes it difficult to consider the more likely possibility that decompensations in schizophrenic behaviour do not provide the kinds of advance subjective warning typical of impending neurotic disturbances. Pious (1961) has described sudden shifts in the level of organization of schizophrenic behaviour ('nadir events') which cannot be explained in terms of anticipatory anxiety.

Defence. Freud took his stand in favour of a primary role for defence, despite one critical reservation (appendix 5). His position is vulnerable to criticism on three counts: (1) it assumes an over-extended orientation to intrapsychic determinism, (2) its claim to account for primitive thoughts and imagery is questionable, and (3) its claim to account for disturbances of 'reality' is tenuous. Let us consider these three points.

1. Intrapsychic Determinism. In attributing 'decathexis' to the defensive process, Freud defined the disturbance in object relations in schizophrenia entirely as an unconsciously purposive behaviour (cf. Schafer, 1968*a*). This is an attractive orientation for psychoanalysts. It is even attractive for some schizophrenics who gain hope and a heightened sense of personal responsibility from the idea that their disturbed behaviour is designed to avoid some painful realization or consequence. For other schizophrenics, such an orientation, particularly when relentlessly pursued by the analyst, may become intolerably frustrating, confusing or even terrifying.

   In my view, research strategy for schizophrenia is hampered by an excessive intrapsychic determinism implicit in the Unitary Theory at least as much as it is by anti-psychoanalytic theories which avoid, minimize or scotomatize the evidence for unconsciously motivated determiners. There is no proof that schizophrenic behaviour is unconsciously motivated to avoid some painful conflict; there is only proof that schizophrenics have unconscious motives. Wise men may argue endlessly whether *ego-splitting* or *disavowal* are primitive defence mechanisms (Unitary Theory) or whether these tendencies represent an inability to maintain intrapsychic structure and organize reality (Specific Theory). Both positions may be correct. Since passive experiences tend to be reenacted in the service of defence, a disturbance in ego integration or reality integration may gain some measure of representation and appear as defensively motivated *ego-splitting* or *disavowal*. Many aspects of schizophrenic experience (deficiency state) appear to be reenacted in this way. The defensive use of schizophrenic language is the most familiar example. The Unitary Theory, being organized to prove that *all* aspects of schizophrenic behaviour are defensively motivated, is paradoxically ill-equipped to conceptualize such important defence motives.

2. Primitive Thoughts and Imagery. Freud found it difficult to reconcile the primitive thinking characteristic of schizophrenia with his insistence on the continuity of neurosis and psychosis (appendix 3). He accounted for primitive thinking descriptively in terms of regression to primary process thinking (by analogy with dreaming). The contents of schizophrenic thought (e.g. hallucinations and delusions) were considered purposive attempts to reconstitute the lost object world. As the Unitary Theory has developed in psychoanalysis, primitive thought and imagery in schizophrenia have come to be ascribed to a failure of a hierarchical system of defences. Such a position makes a defensive system exclusively responsible for higher mental organization. It is a hypothesis which strengthens the Unitary Theory but merits careful questioning. Loewald (1965), for example, has suggested that such thought disturbances indicate a fragmentation of internalizations rather than a failure of defence.[9]

3. Disturbances of 'Reality'. Freud attributed disturbances of reality to a specific defence mechanism: *disavowal*. Disavowal is a difficult theoretical concept. It ignores the 'internal catastrophe' and over-simplifies the problem of reality integration in schizophrenia. Schizophrenics repress as well as deny, they 'adhere to reality' as well as disavow it (cf. Jacobson, 1967, pp. 18–20).

Freud must have realized that he had over-simplified matters, because he continued to study *disavowal* in a particularly interesting way. He related the concept to splitting of the ego in the defensive process in fetishism (1940*b*) and schizophrenia (1940*a*). In finally turning to the problem of ego-splitting, Freud returned to the issues posed by Janet much earlier. Janet (1903) had emphasized a weakening of associative links (*abaissement du niveau mental*), referring to the gross discontinuities of behavioural integrations in schizophrenia. Some aspects of this evidence, as they pertain to reality integration, present problems for the theory of defence. Schizophrenics may experience a range of disparate reality integrations; may shift from one to another, often with bewildering rapidity; or even maintain more than one simultaneously. A clearer understanding of whatever is meant by 'ego-splitting' might help explain the puzzling shifts in reality integration observed in schizophrenia as well as the peremptory quality of certain reality integrations. Peremptory thought in schizophrenia has been attributed, in terms of the Unitary Theory, to the effects of uncontrolled drives (Rapaport, 1958). To my own view, this clinical phenomenon is distinguishable from problems of impulse control and is as yet unexplained.

Shifts in reality integration are related to levels of integration in schizophrenia—a subject which has become more timely as our descriptive knowledge has increased. Schizophrenics may assume behavioural integrations which appear typically neurotic, psychopathic or normal, except that they are extremely rigid and unstable. Similarly, as Jacobson has described (1967), schizophrenics may develop integrations based on involvements with work, with groups, or patterned interactions with others (such as a life of homosexuality), which are also extremely unstable. It is almost too easy to explain this evidence by defence theory: that these integrations are in the service of defence against narcissistic regression, and reflect the continuity of schizophrenic behaviours with a hierarchy of defences which stabilize successive levels of personality development both structurally and genetically. In contradiction of this defence theory, clinicians also consider these integrations to be essentially schizophrenic. They differ in psychodynamics from the non-schizophrenic behaviours they mimic and *protect* against an actual danger of psychosis rather than defend against the anticipated danger (anxiety) of psychic helplessness (uncontrolled drives). The matter is as yet unsettled: is it defence or deficiency state? A theory is needed which can at least encompass these alternatives.

The Specific Theory

This theory, expressed in condensed fashion by Freud as a withdrawal of cathexes from the 'unconscious presentation' of objects, is known today as *decathexis of the mental representations of objects*. I have asserted that this theory holds more promise than the Unitary Theory for further psychoanalytic investigation of schizophrenia. In order to support such an assertion, it would first be necessary to clarify the definitions of mental representations, of object representations, and of 'decathexis' as applied to the Specific Theory. It would also be important to clarify whether the hypothesized 'internal catastrophe' is necessarily limited only to object representations or is more extensive. Supporting evidence should be collected to indicate that an 'internal catastrophe' is primary to disturbed reality integration in schizophrenia. Finally, some way must be found, within the Specific Theory, to account for intrapsychic motives, i.e. for drives and defences. In Part II of this essay, I shall reformulate the Specific Theory within the framework of these considerations (see chapter 2).

SUMMARY AND CONCLUSIONS

I have distinguished two main psychoanalytic theories of schizophrenia which I have termed the Unitary Theory and the Specific Theory. They appear incompatible with each other, yet both derive from Freud's Classical Theory of schizophrenia. They correspond to two main contemporary orientations toward schizophrenia. Freud favoured the Unity Theory for the same reason that he developed it: in order to provide a unified theory for schizophrenia and neuroses. I have critically assessed the primary roles assigned by the Unitary Theory to instinctual drives, anxiety and defence and conclude that the theory fails to encompass present knowledge of schizophrenic behaviours. I submit that, at this point in the development of psychoanalysis, pursuit of a unified and cohesive psychoanalytic theory is an unwise research strategy. I recommend, instead, that psychoanalytic metapsychology be viewed as a group of interrelated but separable theories. I maintain that the Specific Theory ('decathexis of the mental representations of objects') holds more promise for the psychoanalytic study of schizophrenia. I have noted that the term 'decathexis' is defined differently in the Unitary and Specific Theories. This double definition is based on ambiguities in the definition of instinctual drives and their cathexes. I have separated the definition of instinctual drives as intrapsychic motivating forces from their definition as superordinate 'psychic energies' responsible for developing and sustaining mental representations. This distinction helps distinguish the two theories of schizophrenia and will provide a basis for reformulating the Specific Theory in Part II of this essay.

APPENDIX

Significant Quotations from Freud's Writings

1. 'As early as 1897 . . . I was then already aiming at a libido theory of the neuroses, which was to explain all neurotic and psychotic phenomena as proceeding from abnormal vicissitudes of the libido' (1914a, p. 29). In a more exuberant mood, Freud hoped that the 'libido theory could celebrate its triumph all along the line from the simplest "actual" neuroses to the most severe alienation of the personality' (1917b, p. 430).

2. 'I shall not consider any theory of paranoia trustworthy unless it also covers the hypochondriacal symptoms by which the disorder is accompanied. It seems to me that hypochondria stands in the same relation to paranoia as anxiety neurosis does to hysteria' (1911, p. 56, n. 3).

'A failure of this psychical mechanism gives rise to the hypochondria of paranoia and this is homologous to the anxiety of the transference neuroses' (1914b, p. 86).

3. 'Paranoia decomposes just as hysteria condenses. Or rather, paranoia resolves once more into their elements the products of the condensations and identifications which are effected in the unconscious' (1911, p. 49).

Freud focused on clinical evidence that schizophrenia expresses a great deal 'which is repressed in neurosis and revealed only by psychoanalysis' (1915*b*, p. 197).

4. In his terminology of that era, Freud phrased the question in terms of a primary role for 'ego-cathexes' (1911, p. 75) or ego interests (1917*b*, p. 430).

5. 'As regards schizophrenia . . . a doubt must occur to us whether the process here termed repression has anything to do with the repression which takes place in the transference neuroses. The formula that repression is a process which occurs between the systems *Ucs.* and *Pcs.* (or *Cs.*), and results in keeping something at a distance from consciousness, must in any case be modified, in order that it may also be able to include the case of dementia praecox and other narcissistic affections. . . . The most superficial reflection shows us how much more radically this attempt at flight, this flight of the ego, is put into operation in the narcissistic neuroses' (1915*b*, p. 203).

6. 'If it lay with our plan to go more deeply into dementia praecox, I would show you that the process which detaches the libido from objects and cuts off its return to them is closely related to the process of repression and is to be looked upon as its counterpart. . . . The conflict seems to be the same and to be carried on between the same forces . . . the concepts we arrive at during our study of the transference neuroses are adequate in helping us find our way about in the narcissistic neuroses . . . at bottom the field of phenomena is the same' (1917*b*, p. 421).

7. '. . . what the mechanism, analogous to repression, can be by means of which the ego detaches itself from the external world. This cannot, I think, be answered without fresh investigations; but such a mechanism, it should seem, *must*, like repression, comprise a withdrawal of cathexes sent out by the ego' (1924*a*, p. 153).

NOTES

1. Other methods of investigation include modifications of the standard psychoanalytic situation, longitudinal studies, psychoanalytic biography, etc.
2. Freeman (1970) has presented an excellent and well-documented defence of Freud's Classical Theory in reply to Arlow & Brenner's (1969) revision of what I term the Unitary Theory. He did not, however, deal with the theoretical problems which are the focus of this essay.
3. It is worth recalling, in this context, how explicitly Bleuler (1911, p. 1) acknowledged the importance of Freud's contribution in the introduction to his monograph redefining dementia

praecox as schizophrenia: 'An important aspect of the attempt to advance and enlarge the concepts of psychopathology is nothing less than the application of Freud's ideas to dementia praecox.'

4. It is likely, given Abraham's later contributions to the study of object relations, that both he and Freud already held an intrapsychic focus which they were not yet able to conceptualize. Freud and Abraham were already collaborators when Abraham prepared his 1908 paper, as they remained throughout the period of Freud's publications on psychosis. Freud's contributions to this subject were strongly influenced by Abraham, who was considerably more experienced in clinical work with psychotics.

5. The subtheory of 'ego hypercathexis' is not essential to either the Unitary or the Specific Theory. It was recently rejected on clinical and theoretical grounds by Schafer (1968b) and Arlow & Brenner (1969), and defended by Freeman (1970). Whatever merits this theory may have for understanding the transitions from narcissism to object love, it is based on a clinical observation (egocentrism) which is not crucial for schizophrenia. Freud proposed a hypercathexis of self-representations (or possibly ego functions) at the expense of object cathexes, while our present knowledge of schizophrenia indicates that self and object representations (as well as related ego functions) share a common fate in reverting to forms less differentiated from each other.

6. At the same time, Freud also defined instinctual drives as a concept 'on the frontier between the mental and the somatic'—a definition which fails to distinguish drives from physiological stimulation.

7. In psychoanalytic metapsychology, the distinction between structure (representational element) and function is not yet clear. Whether or not one may justifiably conceptualize an intrapsychic *function* is a profound riddle beyond the scope of this essay. It is a subject at the heart of the problem raised by an understanding of instinctual drives (representational elements) as intrapsychic motivating forces; the subject of a psychic apparatus which can initiate stimulation.

8. The form of neurotic anxiety derives from memories of infantile experiences of helplessness in danger situations (traumatic states). The function of neurotic anxiety is usually anticipatory. It is evoked as a signal in the service of anticipating, evaluating and responding to potential danger.

9. I cannot do justice to Loewald's hypothesis, which has influenced but extends beyond the views expressed in this essay. It should be noted that Loewald was not referring to a fragmentation of object representations but to a more basic 'differentiation of ego structure'.

REFERENCES

Abraham, K. (1908). The psycho-sexual differences between hysteria and dementia praecox. In *Selected Papers on Psycho-Analysis*. London: Hogarth Press, 1949.

Arlow, J. A. & Brenner, C. (1969). The psychopathology of the psychoses: a proposed revision. *Int. J. Psycho-Anal.* **50**, 5–14.

Bleuler, E. (1911). *Dementia Praecox or the Group of Schizophrenias*. New York: Int. Univ. Press, 1950.

Burton, A. (ed.) (1961). *Psychotherapy of the Psychoses*. New York: Basic Books.

Freeman, T. (1970). The psychopathology of the psychoses: a reply to Arlow and Brenner. *Int. J. Psycho-Anal.* **51**, 407–15.

Freud, S. (1891). *On Aphasia*. New York: Int. Univ. Press, 1953.

Freud, S. (1895a). Draft H. In M. Bonaparte *et al.* (eds.), *The Origins of Psychoanalysis*. New York: Basic Books, 1954.

Freud, S. (1895b). Project for a scientific psychology. Ibid.
Freud, S. (1896). Further remarks on the neuropsychoses of defence. III: Analysis of a case of chronic paranoia. S.E. 3.
Freud, S. (1900). The interpretation of dreams. S.E. 5.
Freud, S. (1911). Psycho-analytic notes on an autobiographical account of a case of paranoia (dementia paranoides). S.E. 12.
Freud, S. (1914a). On the history of the psychoanalytic movement. S.E. 14.
Freud, S. (1914b). On narcissism: an introduction. S.E. 14.
Freud, S. (1915a). Instincts and their vicissitudes. S.E. 14.
Freud, S. (1915b). The unconscious. S.E. 14.
Freud, S. (1917a). A metapsychological supplement to the theory of dreams. S.E. 14.
Freud, S. (1917b). Introductory lectures on psychoanalysis. S.E. 16.
Freud, S. (1917c). Mourning and melancholia. S.E. 14.
Freud, S. (1924a). Neurosis and psychosis. S.E. 19.
Freud, S. (1924b). The loss of reality in neurosis and psychosis. S.E. 19.
Freud, S. (1940a). An outline of psycho-analysis. S.E. 23.
Freud, S. (1940b). Splitting of the ego in the process of defence. S.E. 23.
Hartmann, H. (1953). Contribution to the metapsychology of schizophrenia. In Essays on Ego Psychology. New York: Int. Univ. Press, 1964.
Jacobson, E. (1967). Psychotic Conflict and Reality. New York: Int. Univ. Press.
Janet, P. (1903). Les Obsessions et la psychasthénie. Paris: Alcan.
Kubie, L. S. (1967). The relation of psychotic disorganization to the neurotic process. J. Am. psychoanal. Ass. 15, 626–40.
Loewald, H. W. (1965). On internalization. (Unpublished manuscript.)
Novey, S. (1958). The meaning of the concept of mental representation of objects. Psychoanal. Q. 27, 57–79.
Pious, W. L. (1961). A hypothesis about the nature of schizophrenic behaviour. In A. Burton (ed.), Psychotherapy of the Psychoses. New York: Basic Books.
Rapaport, D. (1958). A historical survey of psychoanalytic psychology. In Collected Papers of David Rapaport. New York: Basic Books, 1967.
Rapaport, D. & Gill, M. M. (1959). The points of view and assumptions of metapsychology. Ibid.
Rosenfeld, H. (1958). Some observations on the psychopathology of hypochondriacal states. Int. J. Psycho-Anal. 39, 121–4.
Schafer, R. (1968a). The mechanisms of defence. Int. J. Psycho-Anal. 49, 49–62.
Schafer, R. (1968b). Aspects of Internalization. New York: Int. Univ. Press.
Segal, H. (1964). Introduction to the Work of Melanie Klein. New York: Basic Books.
Segal, H. (1970). Personal communication.
Wexler, M. (1971). Schizophrenia: conflict and deficiency. Psychoanal. Q. 40, 83–99.

2. An Essay on Psychoanalytic Theory: Two Theories of Schizophrenia. Part II: Discussion and Restatement of the Specific Theory of Schizophrenia

Nathaniel J. London

In Part I, I surveyed Freud's Classical Theory of schizophrenia to show that it may be separated into two theories. These two theories have been developed as the main psychoanalytic theories of schizophrenia today. The Unitary Theory, as I have termed it, emphasizes a continuity between schizophrenia and neuroses, both viewed as intrapsychically motivated or purposive behaviours determined by instinctual drives and defences. Within the Unitary Theory, 'decathexis' refers to the defensive process, disturbances in 'reality' are considered defensively motivated by means of the mechanism 'disavowal', and transference in schizophrenia is considered fundamentally the same as in neuroses. Freud developed and favoured the Unitary Theory in order to provide a unified psychoanalytic theory for neuroses and psychoses. I maintained that this theory has failed to provide a satisfactory research strategy for schizophrenia, precisely because it is orientated more toward a unified and cohesive psychoanalytic theory than toward the unique phenomena of schizophrenic behaviours. I supported this assertion in a critical assessment of the roles assigned by the Unitary Theory to instinctual drives, anxiety and defence as primary determiners of schizophrenic behaviours.

What I have termed the Specific Theory emphasizes schizophrenic behaviours as unique psychological deficiency states. The focal point for the psychological deficiency, first described by Freud as an 'internal catastrophe' and later as libidinal withdrawal from the 'unconscious presentation of the object', is described in contemporary language as 'decathexis of the mental representations of objects'. Within the Specific Theory, 'decathexis' refers to a basic disturbance in mental representation, disturbances in 'reality' are considered secondary to the primary disturbance in mental representation ('internal catastrophe'), and the capacity for transference among schizophrenics is considered limited. In contrast to the Unitary Theory, the Specific

Theory has not been systematically and comprehensively developed in the psychoanalytic literature. Yet the concepts of the Specific Theory are mutually understood among psychoanalysts and are regularly used in clinical practice and theoretical writings. In order to present the Specific Theory as a worthy alternative to the Unitary Theory, I shall first discuss basic definitions involved in the theory and then review supporting evidence.

DEFINITIONAL CONSIDERATIONS

Instinctual Drives and Their Cathexes

In Part I (see chapter 1) I distinguished between two definitions implicit in Freud's theory of instinctual drives which allow a definition of 'decathexis' within the Unitary Theory different from the use of 'decathexis' within the Specific Theory. Both definitions are pertinent to the Specific Theory, but in different ways. According to one definition, instinctual drives and their cathexes are intrapsychic motivating forces involved in purposive behaviours (e.g. intrapsychic conflicts). I further limited the definition of intrapsychic motivating forces to Freud's definition of them as mental representations (Freud, 1915, p. 122) derived from the internalization of tension and need states. This is the definitional basis for the term 'decathexis' within the Unitary Theory. In Freud's second definition, instinctual drives are 'psychic energies': superordinate factors responsible for developing and sustaining mental representations. This is the definitional basis for the term 'decathexis' within the Specific Theory. In this essay I shall limit the definition of instinctual drives and their cathexes to the first definition—to those aspects of mental representation which serve as intrapsychic motivating forces. Some other means should be found to formulate a superordinate disturbance in mental representation indicated in the Specific Theory by the term 'decathexis'. In order to formulate this central concept of the Specific Theory, it is first necessary to reconsider the definitions of mental representation and mental object representation.

The Scope of Mental Representations

A systematic metapsychological definition of mental representation is only now being developed in psychoanalytic writings (cf. Beres & Joseph, 1970). I offer the following for consideration and use in this essay: *Mental representa-*

tion refers to the mental organization of memory traces; memory traces deriving from experiences involving internal and external stimulation and the responses of the stimulated subject. Mental representation is a theoretical concept which serves to organize complex observations of subjective experience so as to delineate a specifically mental sphere of behaviour, i.e. to maintain a differentiation of mind and body as well as a differentiation of mind and environment. This concept emphasizes that the building blocks of mental organization comprise an internalization of experiences of the subject in interaction with his internal and external environments. *Mental representation* is not the only way that the building blocks of mental organization may be conceptualized. Piaget's concept of 'schemata' (1954) is an equally valid overlapping formulation. Piaget's 'schemata' conceptualize the internalization of patterned interactions from the viewpoint of the observer. *Mental representation* organizes related observations, in a uniquely psychoanalytic way, from the viewpoint of the subject and his inner experience.

A formulation of schizophrenic behaviour limited only to the mental representation of objects rests on shaky theoretical ground. Life experiences are internalized—not objects! The idea that objects are internalized comes from a confusion of incorporative fantasies with the process of internalization. The life experiences which concern us consist of interactions with people involving many subjective and objective responses. The memory traces of life experiences are internalized in terms of images, thoughts and feelings—the elusive data of psychoanalysis. The *psychoanalyst-observer* identifies object representations from this data in order to classify and organize it. He may use the same data to identify instinctual drives and other representational elements. In subjective experience, distinctions between drive and object are inconstant and complex.

We tend to forget that many aspects of experiences with people—elements inextricably linked to object representation—are also representations. The wishes, motives and reactions so central to psychoanalytic study—instinctual drives, defences, affects, signal anxiety—all of these fall under the definition of mental representations. They all derive from the internalization of life experiences. If one overlooks this important consideration, one is apt to assume a simplistic view that representation involves only a reconstitution of the environment in subjective mental life. The many ways in which memory traces of life experiences become encoded, organized and reorganized constitute the area of psychoanalytic study. The entire body of psychoanalytic observations establishes the fact that mental representations involve far more than a replica of life experiences. Mental life is organized such that mental representations need not bear any one-to-one relation to the memory traces from which they derive nor to the ongoing experiences to which they remain linked. It is only as a matter of convenience that certain mental representations are designated by their internal or external perceptual referents (e.g. objects or representations of time and space). The relation of mental representations to external stimulation refers to the problem of reality integration; the comparable relation to internal stimulation refers to the mind-body problem; and the psychoanalytic study of mental representation refers to both of these and more. The category of mental representations reflects the *integrations* of stimulation achieved by the mind. Such an emphasis on integration is implicit in Freud's (1915) definition of instinctual drives in terms of pressure, aim, source and object; so that *instinctual drive* serves not only as a representational concept (referring to intrapsychic motivating forces) but also as the most basic among psychoanalytic integrative concepts. That the terms *instinctual drive representative* and *object representation* are commonly used interchangeably typifies such an integrative view in psychoanalysis.

In view of the foregoing discussion, it is difficult to imagine a disruption of object representations without comparable effects upon the related drives, defences, affects—even upon the representations of time and space. It is appropriate to reconsider the phenomena of schizophrenic behaviours to determine whether the disturbance is limited to object representation or involves all aspects of representation.

Mental Object Representations

The term 'mental object representation'[1] is used in two ways which must be distinguished (Brierley, 1939; Schafer, 1968): as a phenomenological-experiential concept or as a metapsychological term. As a phenomenological concept, *object representation* refers to specific imagery, recollections and other subjective experiences involving a person or thing (Schafer, 1968). As a metapsychological concept, *object representation* refers to an assessment of the overall level of intrapsychic organization and integration of objects in a given individual, determined by the observer on the basis of a wide range of direct and indirect evidence which may or may not include specific imagery or recollections.[2] I shall use *mental object representation* as a metapsychological term in restating the Specific Theory and designate specific imagery when appropriate.

As metapsychological terms, *object representations, object relations* and *object constancy* are prominent in psychoanalysis because they emphasize the importance for mental development of the internalization of experiences with emotionally significant persons. Object representation, in contrast to Freud's more specific reference to the '*Ucs.* presentation of the object', is an inter-systemic concept subject to metapsychological analysis, according to Waelder's (1930) principle of multiple function, into its id, ego and superego aspects. The concept is not focused on representations close to perceptions of referent environmental figures.[3] It refers to a complex representation of experiences with emotionally significant persons such as to provide an integration of the drives, perceptions, affects, related memories, and fantasy elaborations of such experiences. In psychoanalysis, such representations are considered to be organized around 'instinctual' experiences (tension and need states) and the (primarily visual) perceptions of emotionally significant persons. Perhaps what is meant by a 'well-cathected' object representation may be defined by the following criteria: (1) significance (for mental development and mental organization); (2) stability (constancy); (3) internalization (differentiation from perceptions of environmental figures); (4) discrimination (details and organization, differentiation of self and object representations from each other); (5) integration with internal stimulation (drives); and (6) integration with external stimulation ('reality', including external objects and their displacement substitutes).

A parallel concept of self representations has been formulated to account for the subject as well as the object in the mental representation of experiences. The category of self representations (e.g. as formulated by Schafer, 1968) is particularly pertinent to the theory of schizophrenia. In order to simplify this essay, I shall assume that any discussion of mental representations will also, where appropriate, include self representations.

Reformulation of 'Decathexis'

I suggest discarding the term 'decathexis' from the theory of schizophrenia, in order to better formulate the concept it designates. Arlow & Brenner (1969) have soundly dropped the term from the Unitary Theory. They designate specific defences rather than use such a general term for defence. Since I have limited the definition of instinctual drives and their cathexes to the area of mental representation, the use of 'decathexis' to indicate a superordinate disturbance of mental representations is confusing.

Schur (1966) provided a means to reformulate the Specific Theory, although his interest was in non-schizophrenic behaviours where experiences fail to gain mental representation (like primal repression). He emphasized that the need to withdraw from excessive stimulation (e.g. a source of pain and danger) 'has not achieved in the course of evolution the degree of internalization which is the basis for an instinctual drive. There is no motivational force to seek an object in order to withdraw from it'. Schur proposed the following solution: Mental functioning is regulated by both the pleasure and unpleasure principles. The *pleasure principle*, linked biologically to approach responses, is specifically involved in the regulation of instinctual drives. It regulates the 'need to recreate by action or by fantasy the experience of satisfaction through the elimination of drive tension'. The *unpleasure principle*, linked biologically to withdrawal responses, is evolutionally and ontogenetically a more primitive regulatory principle. It applies to the

necessity to withdraw from excessive stimulation impinging on the mental apparatus from the outside, where 'outside' implies both outside the organism and outside the mental apparatus. Eventually this necessity *extends to the withdrawl from the memory traces of such stimulation* (italics mine).

Schur's discussion of the unpleasure principle appears to describe the regulation of mental representations in schizophrenia as developed in this essay.

According to the foregoing considerations, I suggest that the following be substituted for 'decathexis' with respect to the Specific Theory: *a disturbance in the capacity to organize memory traces into mental object representations and to sustain mental object representations (as already defined). It is rooted in developmental factors which are superordinate to the development of instinctual drives, is linked biologically to withdrawal responses, and is regulated by the unpleasure principle* (Schur, 1966). Intrapsychic conflicts and defences are significant among other factors which may alter the capacity of the ego to organize stimulation and so precipitate a disturbance in mental representation. Whether the pattern of withdrawal may gain some measure of representation so that the ego may initiate an episode of schizophrenic behaviour, as seems to occur in some schizophrenics, would not invalidate this formulation.[4]

REVIEW AND DISCUSSION OF EVIDENCE SUPPORTING THE SPECIFIC THEORY

Mental Object Representations

Psychoanalytic research in schizophrenia over the past 60 years has revealed, mapped out, and extensively documented consistent evidence of a disturbance in object representation. Such evidence may be roughly classified as follows.

1. *Primary process imagery and mechanisms* designated as archaic or primitive involving *introjects, identifications* and *incorporative phenomena* are prominent among schizophrenics. These behaviours, when observed in schizophrenics, are characterized by a disturbance in reality integration (links to experiences with real persons obscure) as well as drive integration. According to the Unitary Theory, these phenomena represent a defensive genetic regression to early infantile levels of object relations. According to the Specific Theory, these phenomena are reactive to an inability to organize and sustain mental object representations.

2. Observations indicating an undifferentiated state of self and object representation have been designated by various authors as fusion of self and object (Jacobson, 1954), symbiosis (Mahler, 1952) and projective identification (Segal, 1964). This body of data, which is overwhelming in its consistency and sound documentation, constitutes an unforeseen and outstanding psychoanalytic contribution to the study of schizophrenia. According to the Unitary Theory, symbiotic object relations indicate regression to a developmental phase preceding the achievement of separation-individuation. According to the Kleinian group, aspects of the same data are conceptualized as 'projective identification' and organized to formulate characteristic primitive defence mechanisms. The Specific Theory holds that the crucial determiners of these undifferentiated representations rest outside of the defensive process.

3. Impairment in the *constancy* of self and object representations, a point which strongly supports the Specific Theory, is prominent in clinical assessments of schizophrenic behaviour. To my knowledge, the evidence to support such an important conclusion is yet to be systematically collected and assessed. Some of the evidence is indirect, consisting of the extreme reactions to separation of schizophrenics under certain conditions. The direct evidence involves disturbances in *evocative recall* and related behaviours. The most familiar examples occur when schizophrenic subjects attempt to recall or anticipate some person or experience, only to be inundated by grotesque and terrifying imagery. Such confusion of objects with primitive drives is the opposite of 'decathexis' and at least indicates what Fraiberg (1969) has termed impaired autonomy of evocative recall from drives. However, there is considerable evidence pointing to an even more profound disturbance in evocative recall: not only is the image of the object or the self replaced by bizarre drive representations, but it is not available (e.g. Giovacchini, 1969). Aspects of this category of evidence were used by Freud when he first formulated the theory of cathectic withdrawal: that the 'end of the world' delusions were expressions of an 'internal catastrophe'. Freud was referring to delusional

experiences of unreality and estrangement in which the self or aspects of the environment are reported as empty, drained, hollow or destroyed. These profound disturbances in reported imagery with respect to past, present or anticipated situations are generally accompanied by confusion, disorientation, terror and panic. Pious's (1961) formulation of 'emptying' with respect to the 'nadir event' in schizophrenic behaviour is based on evidence pertinent to this point.

Arlow & Brenner (1969) presented a clinical example of a negative hallucination which may serve to illustrate differences in the Unitary and Specific Theories with respect to *object constancy*. They described a patient who, in the course of a quarrel with his wife, experienced an impulse to kill her. At that moment, he looked at her face. It appeared to be sectioned radially like a pie. Successively, in clockwise fashion, the segments of his wife's face were obliterated until it appeared blank and without content. At that moment the patient became intensely hungry and drank some milk. Soon his anger was gone. For a while, he treated his wife as if she did not exist, but became friendly toward her again after a few days.

According to Arlow & Brenner, the patient was spared the anxiety connected with controlling the impulse to kill his wife. He acted in keeping with an inner fantasy that she was indeed dead. Thus both defence and wish-fulfilment were combined in a negative hallucination. The Specific Theory would focus on the incident from a different viewpoint, a focus which would allow more possibilities. A disturbance in the mental representation of the wife would be considered the primary factor leading to the negative hallucination. It would not be taken for granted that an aggressive impulse evoked in the violent quarrel precipitated the disturbance in object representation, although that would be a possibility. Some other event may have been the precipitating factor, and it is even possible that the violent quarrel was his initial reaction to a disturbance in representation (primitive aggression in reaction to object loss). In any case, when he looked at his wife's face he experienced a sense of (delusional) unreality and the sectional negative hallucination provided a delusional expression for the experienced 'internal catastrophe' (loss of evocative recall); perhaps with an associated incorporative fantasy (drinking the milk). I wish to emphasize that the psychodynamic explanation offered by Arlow & Brenner is a possibility under the Specific Theory, but not the only possibility. The decisive point is that the Unitary Theory would regard conflict and defence with regard to an aggressive impulse as the primary factor and the Specific Theory would regard the disturbance in object constancy as the primary factor.

Other Representations

I have noted above that instinctual drives, defences, affects and signal anxiety may all be conceived as *representations* on the same metapsychological level of abstraction as the object representations to which they are inextricably linked. Of course, the concept of a regressive alteration of drives, defences, etc. in schizophrenia is a familiar psychoanalytic concept—formulated in the Unitary Theory as a defensive regression of specific ego functions. However, it is timely to try to progress beyond the descriptive value of the concept of ego functions and attempt to specify the complicated thought processes involved. Our present knowledge of schizophrenia indicates that drives, defences, affects, the reaction to danger and representations of time and space all undergo the same shift to primitive undifferentiated forms so familiar to us with respect to object representations. It is at least worth considering that such shifts may be *identical* with the disturbance in object representations and derive from a common mechanism apart from the defensive process. Perhaps disturbances in object representations have been highlighted because they appear in concrete imagery and are therefore more obvious to the observer. However, a shift in the reaction to danger from a level of signal anxiety to one of hypochondriasis is just as clear and dramatic as any of the observations about object representations. The same is true of an abrupt shift from erotic excitement to primitive rage. There are disturbances in the constancy of drives as well as of objects. In certain schizophrenic behaviours, the subject is particularly vulnerable to physiological stimulation because the drive is not available to organize the stimulation. An extreme example of this was an acute catatonic patient who reported repeated dribbling seminal emissions without erection and a blank fantasy. At the other extreme, it is not unusual to find cases with severe disturbances in drive organization and no apparent disturbances in physiological sexual functioning. A radical disturbance in the representation of affects is well known among analysts and is well expressed by the following quotation from Jacobson (1967):

In view of the deterioration of superego and ego, it is altogether questionable whether in certain types of schizophrenia, or at certain stages of the illness, we can speak in ordinary terms about the patient's emotional attitudes, as though the libidinal and destructive drive impulses would always find the same affective expression as in normal persons' feelings and feeling qualities. Even when psychotics show emotional reactions, these are frequently difficult to understand, and such terms as 'love' and 'hate' may have a very different meaning to them than they do to us. For this reason, the therapist's empathy with psychotic patients is put to such severe tests.

Assessment of the role of aggressive drives in schizophrenic behaviours is difficult. Since drives tend to be as undifferentiated as object representations, it is hard to distinguish libidinal and aggressive components. Also, in clinical practice it is hard to distinguish the withdrawal response (of the Specific Theory) from aggressive drives. In fact, the death instinct hypothesis, unlike the Specific Theory, unites the withdrawal response and aggression in a single concept. In fairness to such a view, there is evidence to indicate that the withdrawal response does gain some measure of representation in schizophrenic behaviours, so that it may be initiated by the ego in the service of aggression.

Representations of space and time in schizophrenic states also merit careful consideration. Gross distortions in spatial orientation and time perception are common. Pious (1961) has described disturbances in the patterning of incoming stimuli in schizophrenic behaviours as follows:

Each behavioural state has its characteristic organization of perception and, therefore, its own state of consciousness. Perceptual qualities undergo extensive alteration. Changes in discrimination determine what is to be excluded and included. Intensity is altered so that what may be ordinarily subliminal is perceived, dim lights may appear very bright, whispers may be heard as echoing roars, and the like. I believe that at some of the very archaic levels one sensation may be replaced by another, as visual for auditory, etc. Proprioceptive and kinaesthetic perceptions are equally involved.

Reality Integration

The 'reality issue' in schizophrenia is usually discussed in terms of *reality testing* (an ego function), *reality* being designated either as mental representations of reality (internal reality) or 'external reality'. In order to look more deeply into the mechanisms of reality testing, I ask the reader to bear with me and accept a different terminology. I shall refer to *reality* exclusively as an aspect of mental representation, and focus on the variable and reciprocal patterning of environmental stimulation into mental integrations of 'reality' (cf. Loewald, 1951). Such patterning derives from elements both inside and outside the mental apparatus and may be termed 'reality integration', i.e. reality integration is here defined as the integration of mental representations with environmental stimulation.[5]

The hypothesis that disturbed reality integration in schizophrenia is secondary to disturbed mental representation is consistent with a view that mental representations or the 'inner world' are involved in crucial regulating or modulating functions (Freud, 1923; Hartmann, 1939; Rapaport, 1957*a*, pp.

696–8). I should like to review briefly some aspects of such modulation. Let me recall that 'representing' signifies far more than encoding a replica of the external world. *Mental representation* involves a special psychoanalytic orientation toward the symbolic process in terms of an emphasis on internalization of experiences. 'Representing' means that life experiences (in all their biological and sociological complexities) become integrated, reconstituted and re-enacted at various levels of abstraction and according to different patterns of organization; through the medium of different psychological behaviours (the range of primary and secondary process thought), in ways that endow these experiences with meaning and purpose. This means that man is able to profit from experience in ways unavailable to lower animals. While lower animals respond to new experiences with prepatterned 'instinctive' responses to stimulation, man is also able to call upon his inventory of representations (integrations of past experiences) to modify and enrich his reactions and responses. In this way, mental representations are involved in modulating the course of human behaviour and endow it with all that is implied by the concept 'ego autonomy' (Rapaport, 1957b). Associative channels allow rapid and efficient access to the inventory of representations and the memories of experiences from which they derive. Disturbances in such access involve the psychodynamic viewpoint and intrapsychic conflict.

If one were to compare a representational system to an immeasurably complex computer program, then the ego could be considered to have a computer-like access to organizations of past, present and future modalities, to representations over a range of primary and secondary thought processes, to organizations of memories according to different integrations of reality, and, through displacement, to a range of possibilities for drive organization. Such access to representations allows for the complexity of the human organization of stimulation in subjective experience and adaptive response.

The radical disturbance in mental representations proposed by the Specific Theory should lead to drastic limitations on the capacity to respond to stimulation far beyond those imposed by countercathectic forces. Let us consider the evidence which may support such a conclusion.

The most dramatic evidence of disturbed reality integration in schizophrenia consists of the 'break with reality'. In such instances, reality testing (Hartmann, 1953) may be disturbed insofar as: (1) perceptions may be obscured by a profusion of primitive imagery, (2) thoughts and images may be undifferentiated from perceptions, and (3) peremptory reality integrations may be assumed in which stimulation is organized into rigid patterns (e.g. paranoid) to the degree that the capacity for 'objectivity' is impaired.

I shall organize further evidence around a striking apparent paradox in observations of schizophrenic behaviours. It is commonplace among schizophrenic subjects, including those who develop breaks with reality, to find evidence of an exaggerated but highly 'accurate' organization of the environment—an excessive dependence on environmental stimulation (cf. Frosch, 1966, 1970). Both the 'break with reality' and 'adherence to reality' have been formulated within the Unitary Theory as results of intrapsychic defence. However, not only the 'break with reality' but also the environmental dependence have been understood as adaptations to object loss. I understand such an adaptation in the following way. A schizophrenic subject searches and scans his environment to provide patterns for the organization of stimulation normally provided by a stable representational system in integration with immediate experience. When this attempt succeeds, the result is a reality integration which may appear to attain a high level of organization, but which is inefficient and brittle.[6] The schizophrenic subject has used an organization of the environment which is not backed up by that complex organization of past experience which we call a stable representational system. The environment, being limited by the dimensions of time and space, cannot provide the consistency, the symbolic condensations or the range of patterns afforded by a representational system. When the environmental patterning fails to organize ongoing experience, then the chaotic behavioural disturbances characteristic of acute schizophrenia ensue. Restabilization occurs around organization of a more primitive and concrete reality integration and a coordinate restriction of the range of organized stimulation. The foregoing view of schizophrenic regression as a change in the organization and integration of environmental stimulation is consistent with a view that disturbances in the symbolic process limit the capacity to handle stimulation (cf. Kubie, 1953). If differs from a formulation in terms of a defensive 'disavowal' of reality (Freud, 1924).

Jacobson (1967), in describing how certain schizophrenics turn to reality to prevent psychotic breakdown, pointed out the paradox between such observations and Freud's formulation of schizophrenia in terms of disavowal of reality. Such a conclusion could not have been too apparent to Freud. The evidence available to him, based on observations made outside of a therapeutic involvement, indicated that schizophrenics tend to reject their environment in favour of delusions and hallucinations. Their remoteness, isolation and stubborn peremptory adherence to delusions indicated an exaggerated and bizarre pseudo-autonomy from the environment which Freud formulated as a 'restitutional' adaptation. Freud did not have available to him the body of

knowledge of schizophrenic behaviours drawn from the treatment situation—
of schizophrenics whose alienation becomes tempered by being accepted, at
least partly understood, and offered hope by means of a therapeutic alliance.
Work with such patients has shown that the schizophrenic 'break with reality'
must be qualified. At least it is incumbent upon us to look more deeply into
what we mean in asserting that the ego's capacity for reality testing is impaired.

I wish to emphasize that preoccupations with accuracy in perception are
just as characteristic of schizophrenia as preoccupations with regressive imagery. Accordingly, Freud's formulation of a purposive 'disavowal' of reality in
schizophrenia is inexact. Schizophrenic subjects often show evidence of a
characteristic hypervigilance. While such hypervigilance may be formulated
in conflict terms (attention to reality as a defence against anxiety-laden delusional thoughts), it is also understood as an effort to maintain an orientation in
space, time and identity. In schizophrenic concrete thinking,[7] attention to
reality may take the extreme form of a preoccupation with verbal perceptions
rather than the significance of the words. Such was the evidence used by
Freud to deduce that the primary disturbance in schizophrenia rested with
mental representations ('*Ucs.* presentations') rather than perceptions. Similar
attention to reality, at less concrete levels of schizophrenic thinking, may be
observed in the evidence that certain schizophrenics are particularly gifted at
assessing aspects of social reality without the 'myths' or 'hypocrisies' which
obscure the observations of most people. Social myths and even 'hypocrisies'
involve the internalization of culture and are part of the representational
system (Parsons, 1952; Novey, 1955; Lidz *et al.*, 1957). It is not surprising
that a schizophrenic subject, being deficient in such representations, may have
a desperate need to assess social reality accurately and may perceive aspects
of the environment with an accuracy achieved by others only with great effort.
Such capacities belong to what may be termed 'schizophrenic realism'. The
schizophrenic character, Aston, in Pinter's play *The Caretaker*, provides a
classic example of such realism. His view of the environment is stark, clear
and parsimonious, but also rigid, lacking in nuances and affectless. It is well
known in clinical work that schizophrenic patients tend to say precisely what
they mean, whether referring to internal or external events and perceptions—
an achievement often hard won with neurotic patients who are more likely to
be uncertain in describing the subtleties and variations in their experiences.
The treatment relationship with schizophrenics may, for long periods of time,
tolerate serious misunderstandings on the part of either patient or analyst, only

to founder over some specific detail. The detail will prove essential for a given level of reality integration. Such a brittle reality integration, anchored at specific points with no margin for error, places a heavy burden on the analyst and is responsible, in my view, for exaggerations in the assertion that schizophrenic patients are particularly prone to elicit 'countertransference distortions'. Frequently, the creative achievement of getting beyond one's highly synthesized reality integration to tune in on a specific issue for a schizophrenic patient is misinterpreted as overcoming a countertransference problem. The dependence on the environment in schizophrenia may be observed with particular clarity in the context of the treatment relationship.

The 'Mental Image'

The schizophrenic patient's mental image of the analyst has been found to have unusual significance in many instances. This observation has been well described by Wexler (1952), Cameron (chapter 10) and Pious (1961). This 'mental image', which is concrete and vivid, is considered to be a primitive incorporation directly bound to the person and personality of the analyst. According to Pious, the mental image

acts to soothe, comfort, scold and protect the schizophrenic, and consoles him in his loneliness and distress. It sets limits for him in his daily life and lends its strength to the threshold (against psychological deprivation). As his strength increases, its ministrations become fewer and finally leaves him on his own.

The mental image may be inconstant, subject to many vicissitudes from beatification to terrifying distortions, or blend in with other archaic representations. It is usually derived from perceptions of the analyst (e.g. face or voice) but may be selected from some substitute such as a photograph or painting in the analyst's office. The image appears in times of need both in the absence of the analyst and in his presence. Difficulty in evoking the image, or its appearance in a grossly distorted form, is associated with a shift to a more primitive level of behaviour. While the image may be sustained over periods of time without contact with the analyst, it is commonplace for schizophrenic patients to require such contact to sustain and verify the image. The mental image appears to reflect a primitive mental representation in the absence of the organization and integration required for a state of object constancy. There is a degree of object constancy insofar as the image can be evoked in the absence of the analyst. Presumably, the mental image fades away when a level of object constancy is consolidated, although more evidence is needed to establish this point. The Specific Theory helps organize observations about the mental image; while a theory which holds that objects are 'well-cathected' in schizophrenia or that disavowal of reality is a primary mechanism interferes with such investigations.

Transference

The discovery that selected schizophrenic patients may establish an intense therapeutic alliance was once held to refute Freud's assertion that transference is not possible in schizophrenia. Recent distinctions between therapeutic alliance and transference (Zetzel, 1956b; Tarachow, 1962; Greenson & Wexler, 1969) have reopened the question. Whether or not an 'analysable' transference may be developed in psychoanalytic work with schizophrenics remains today an unresolved and controversial issue. What is not controversial is substantial evidence that schizophrenic subjects are prone to develop certain characteristic reactions in the treatment relationship which differ from the transference reactions of neurotics. This evidence is perhaps the most important among the observations supporting the Specific Theory.

Typically, schizophrenic patients who develop a therapeutic alliance become unusually dependent on the person, personality and responses of the analyst (i.e. on the reality integration of the therapeutic alliance) to a degree which interferes with the development of transference. The 'adherence to reality' is too intense to allow the regressive shifts required for transference. I refer here to a need for help in maintaining and consolidating a given level of reality integration (Knight, 1953). I also refer to efforts to use the analyst as a substitute for (internal) object constancy—the most dramatic evidence for which pertains to the 'mental image' noted above. Finally, it is commonplace for a schizophrenic subject to draw upon the analyst's responses in quite concrete ways to consolidate a sense of identity.

The most striking evidence for the nature of reality integration in schizophrenia derives from observations of patients subjected to that stimulus deprivation, characteristic of the standard psychoanalytic situation, designed to foster the development of transference. Under these circumstances, schizophrenic patients, instead of developing a transference reaction, are prone to react with a 'break with reality'—a shift to increasingly primitive reality integrations characteristic of acute psychosis. In these reactions to the psychoanalytic situation, it is far from clear to me what criteria would distinguish a 'transference psychosis' from a 'psychotic therapeutic alliance' (cf. Searles, chapter 9). A subjective distinction between transference and therapeutic alliance, which is available or potentially available to non-schizophrenic analysands, tends to become blurred among schizophrenics. However, the question of transference in schizophrenia need not be settled in a formulation of the Specific Theory. What is pertinent to the Specific Theory is that, in the psychoanalytic situation, reactions occur with schizophrenic subjects which highlight a dependence on a therapeutic alliance to maintain object constancy and reality integration.

Developmental Factors and the Specific Theory

In addition to noting Freud's concept of narcissism (1914), a developmental issue central to all psychoanalysis as well as the theory of schizophrenia, special mention should be made of Tausk's (chapter 3) brilliant contribution, 'The Origin of the "Influencing Machine" in Schizophrenia'. This paper paved the way and anticipated later psychoanalytic contributions to the developmental issues in schizophrenia. Here, Tausk first formulated the concepts of *identity* and *ego boundaries*, and explored the normal development of self and object representations from undifferentiated anlage. The main point for consideration in this essay is whether, or to what degree, pathology recapitulates ontogeny as it so clearly does in defensive regression in the neuroses. There is no doubt that detailed observation on thought processes, and particularly on the means of representation of objects, by two generations of psychoanalysts since Tausk's fundamental work has not only enriched our knowledge of schizophrenic thinking but has also provided a valuable stimulus and framework for considering the development of the normal preverbal child. Psychoanalytic studies of early developmental factors have not been so conclusive with respect to schizophrenia as with neuroses. Of course, analytic work with schizophrenics abounds with influences of the past on the present. It is not infrequent that, despite the difficulties in establishing genetic points with schizophrenics, traumatic childhood experiences can be related to a given patient's preoccupations and symptomatology in ways that further the treatment. However, in my view, the most convincing evidence so far available for the influence of childhood environmental factors on the development of schizophrenia has not come from clinical psychoanalysis and studies of the transference with schizophrenic patients, but from family studies in investigations such as those of Lidz *et al.* (1965) and Singer & Wynne (1965). In summary: (1) An understanding of developmental factors is essential for analytic work with schizophrenic patients. (2) While developmental links can readily be noted in the object relations of schizophrenics, considering schizo-phrenic object relations as a genetic regression to preverbal childhood remains a tenuous hypothesis. Since intense rebirth wishes are so prevalent among schizophrenics, these patients are particularly prone to welcome and 'confirm' reconstructions of preverbal childhood in ways that are spurious and irrelevant to establishing the point.

RESTATEMENT OF THE SPECIFIC PSYCHOANALYTIC THEORY OF SCHIZOPHRENIA

1. The Specific Theory of schizophrenia in psychoanalysis considers schizo-phrenic behaviours to be reactive to a psychological deficiency state rather than a psychologically motivated behaviour in response to intrapsychic con-flict (as in the Unitary Theory) or a learned behaviour.

2. *Primary Area of Intrapsychic Disturbance.*[8] Schizophrenic behaviours involve a disturbance, variable in degree, in the capacity to organize memory traces into mental object representations and to sustain mental object repre-sentations (as defined earlier). This disturbance is rooted in developmental factors which are superordinate to the development of instinctual drives, is linked biologically to withdrawal responses, and is regulated by the un-pleasure principle (Schur, 1966). The evidence upon which this formulation is based is considered unique to schizophrenic behaviours, so that schizophrenia is considered to differ qualitatively from psychoneurotic behaviours (although the occurrence of mixed states is not ruled out).

3. *Extended Formulation.* It is appropriate to extend the Specific Theory to include all aspects of representation, even though further research may suc-ceed in pinpointing the disturbance in schizophrenia to a more specific area.[9] There is ample evidence that the intrapsychic disturbance extends not only to include self representations but to include representations such as instinctual drives, defences, affects, signal anxiety, and even representations of time and space. All of these representational elements are inextricably linked to object representation, all of them being aspects of the internalization of experiences with emotionally significant persons.

4. *Reality Integration.* The disturbance in mental representation limits the capacity to regulate or modulate somatic and environmental stimulation. Ac-cordingly, schizophrenic subjects are particularly vulnerable to insufficient or

excessive stimulation. To the degree that mental representations are disturbed, reality integration (as defined above) tends to be rigid, unstable, and excessively dependent on environmental perceptions. For this reason, assessments of reality integration in schizophrenic subjects may reveal paradoxical findings: schizophrenics may show an excessive dependence on the environment and/or excessive disruption of reality testing. In either case, disturbed reality integration is considered secondary to the disturbance in representations.

5. Transference. Freud's assertion that schizophrenics are incapable of transference has been neither proved nor disproved, but further study of the question requires a distinction between transference and non-transference aspects of the analytic relationship. From the viewpoint of the Specific Theory, obstacles to the development of transference arise to the degree that object representations are impaired as well as to the degree that there is excessive dependence on environmental stimulation in terms of the person, personality and responses of the analyst.

6. Intrapsychic Motives (Drives and Defences). If the Specific Theory is to encompass our knowledge of schizophrenia, it must account for the area of intrapsychic conflict. I believe the problem may be resolved by considering determiners of the experiment of nature we call schizophrenia as independent, dependent and intervening variables (Rapaport, 1960, pp. 66–72). The Unitary Theory holds instinctual drives as the independent variable in schizophrenia and neuroses. The Specific Theory holds a disturbance in mental representation (deficiency state) as the independent variable. In that case, intrapsychic motives may serve in the Specific Theory as both dependent and intervening variables—in the following ways.

Dependent Variables. Instinctual drives and defences, which are aspects of mental representation, undergo a fate similar to object representations—tending toward primitive and undifferentiated levels of organization. The means of expression and resolution of intrapsychic conflicts is profoundly affected by the level of drive and defence organization in any given behaviour. Further understanding of primitive drives and defences at various levels of schizophrenic organization is needed. I have suggested that aspects of schizophrenic experience are internalized (gain representation) and are reenacted in the service of defence. This is responsible for confusion in distinguishing certain expressions of drive or defence from manifestations of the deficiency state.

Intervening Variables. Instinctual drives and defences are characteristic of the human condition; and no less so for schizophrenics to the degree that mental development has progressed. There are wide differences among schizophrenics in drive development, cognitive development and character formation, each with its own constellation of motivational factors. Intrapsychic conflicts may precipitate a disturbance in the organization of mental representations in a person predisposed to schizophrenia, but there is no evidence that conflicts are the only factors precipitating schizophrenic behaviours. Evidence for the resolution of conflicts by standard psychoanalytic technique with certain schizophrenic patients is an important finding, but one which makes only a modest contribution to the difficult theoretical and therapeutic problems presented by this illness.

7. Developmental Regression. The issues of regression and fixation are as cogent to the Specific Theory as to the Unitary Theory. However, the primitive object relations observed in schizophrenia are considered secondary to the impairment of representations noted above. These primitive representations are considered genetically linked to early phases of development, but the degree to which they indicate infantile representations re-evoked through genetic regression is considered a speculative and unresolved question.

CONCLUSIONS

In this essay I have been as much concerned with psychoanalytic theory as with the problem of schizophrenia. The schizophrenia problem is the best example of a tendency to overextend crucial psychoanalytic concepts in the service of maintaining a cohesive unified theory. I believe it is timely to view psychoanalytic metapsychology as a group of interrelated but separable theories, derived from a common investigative focus (intrapsychic) and primarily from a common method.

Two main psychoanalytic orientations toward schizophrenia may be separated out from Freud's intricate Classical Theory. The Unitary Theory considers schizophrenic behaviours to be unconsciously purposeful in response to intrapsychic conflicts. The Specific Theory considers schizophrenic behaviours to be unique psychological deficiency states resulting from 'decathexis' of the mental representations of objects. Freud strongly favoured the Unitary Theory despite serious doubts and reservations. However, he never distinguished the two theories and applied 'decathexis' to both. In order to clarify these two theories and reformulate the Specific Theory, I have reconsidered the definitions of instinctual drives and mental representations.

The definition of instinctual drives should be limited to mental representations, derived from the internalization of tension and need states, which serve as intrapsychic motivating forces. Freud defined instinctual drives and their cathexes differently in formulating the Specific Theory. Here they indicate factors ('psychic energies') responsible for developing and sustaining mental representations. Whatever these factors may be, they are superordinate to the concept of instinctual drives as defined above. In fact, such factors are responsible for developing and sustaining instinctual drives. Because of these theoretical considerations, and in view of the available evidence, the Specific Theory should be extended to include not only a disturbance in object representation but also to involve such representations as drives, defences, affects, signal anxiety, and representations of time and space. In so extending the Specific Theory, I have cautioned against reifying these theoretical classifications of mental representations. Mental representation is a special—an especially useful—psychoanalytic concept designed to formulate the organization of memory: the internalization of life experiences as building blocks of mental organization. The disturbances of mental representation observed in schizophrenia interfere with the regulation or modulation of stimulation and result in impaired reality integration.

The Unitary and Specific Theories, as now formulated, appear to be incompatible, but neither theory can be proved or disproved at the present time. I contend that the Unitary Theory imposes comprehensive psychoanalytic theory on the data. The Unitary Theory asserts an essential continuity between schizophrenic and neurotic behaviours. Such an assertion, while possible, strains our available knowledge of these mental states so disparate in phenomenology and likely aetiologies. The Unitary Theory also considers intrapsychic conflict and defence as primary determiners (the independent variable) of schizophrenic behaviours. The Specific Theory is focused on a deficiency in mental representations (the independent variable), treating conflict and defence as both dependent and intervening variables. I have suggested that some aspects of schizophrenic experience (deficiency state) gain mental representation and are used in the service of defence. The Specific Theory offers a scientific strategy focused on factors specific and unique to schizophrenia, and for that reason provides a better means to explore the intrapsychic motives so central to the Unitary Theory. Finally, the Specific Theory is consistent with all of the serious aetiological hypotheses concerning schizophrenia, be they nature or nurture, physiological or cultural.

ADDENDUM

A Note on the History of the Use of the Two Theories

Freud's (1911) psychodynamic formulations of intrapsychic conflict in the study of Schreber excited interest in psychoanalytic study of schizophrenia in a powerfully convincing way. On the other hand, his caveat about the schizophrenic's inability to establish transference or free-associate served to discourage the application of psychoanalytic methods to this group of mentally ill. Tausk, working within Freud's framework, succeeded in advancing the understanding of the mechanisms of schizophrenic behaviour and relating these mechanisms in more specific ways to normal developmental phases. By this time (1919; see chapter 3), no one seriously interested in understanding thought processes in schizophrenia could dispense with the psychoanalytic contribution. However one may assess the merits of the Unitary Theory today, there is no doubt that it had tremendous heuristic value in decoding many of the enigmatic productions of schizophrenics. Psychoanalytic interest in schizophrenia was intensified, under the leadership of Federn (1952), by the discovery that schizophrenics are capable of establishing a treatment alliance (or capable of 'transference', as it was then and still is frequently erroneously conceptualized). At this point, the psychoanalytic study of schizophrenia came to a fork in the road. One road led to the application of the standard psychoanalytic method and the Unitary Theory to schizophrenic patients. In some instances, this led to chaotic treatment situations. Some analysts found schizophrenic patients *submitting* to interpretations and confused this with working with them (Greenson, 1971, personal communication). Specific problems of applying psychoanalytic techniques and theory to such patients had to be clarified by such contributions as Knight's (1953). More significantly, certain psychoanalysts found they could work with select schizophrenic patients along conventional lines, or with occasional modifications or 'parameters', with highly successful results. These analysts are likely to be the ones who draw upon their own successful experiences to support the Unitary Theory and view schizophrenia on a continuum with neurotic behaviour. However, it is also clear that most psychoanalysts are extremely cautious or avoid applying the psychoanalytic method in unmodified form to schizophrenics, and those who do so have contributed little over the years to advancing our understanding of this difficult clinical condition. The other fork in the road led to a relatively small band of clinical investigators (such as Federn, 1952; Sullivan, 1962; Fromm-Reichmann, 1952; Sechehaye, 1951; as well as Wexler, Pious and Searles), who, working more loosely within the psychoanalytic framework, devoted themselves to extensive psychoanalytic work with schizophrenics. I also include in this group Klein and her followers such as Segal and Rosenfeld, who work within their own definition of classical analytic technique. It is this group which has made the most significant contributions to the study of schizophrenia, both with regard to clinical technique and with regard to mapping out the vicissitudes of the archaic thought processes and object relations characteristic for schizophrenia.[10] This group never had an easy time with psychoanalytic orthodoxy for a number of reasons, including, in my view, the fact that no coherent mutually agreed psychoanalytic theory of schizophrenia has yet been developed. Some of the problems may be made more explicit by considering two specific investigators.

1. Harry Stack Sullivan's (1962) application of psychoanalysis to the study of schizophrenia led to difficult theoretical and clinical problems. It seems clear to me that Sullivan came to reject the psychoanalytic concept of transference because the concept, as defined at that time, failed to distinguish between treatment alliance and analytic transference proper. Instead, Sullivan (1947) advanced an interesting descriptive concept (parataxic distortion) which provided a framework for organizing schizophrenic problems of reality integration within the treatment relationship, but dispensed with the appropriate psychoanalytic focus on inner experience. Similarly, Sullivan achieved an original and creative appreciation of the special problems created by schizophrenic dependence on the environment in terms of the treatment context and the environmental factors in child-rearing. Unfortunately, he was unable to reconcile these important findings—which are fully accepted among psychoanalysts today—with his concept of psychoanalysis. The result was that he shifted to an increasingly environmentalist position ('interpersonal relations'). Furthermore, consistent with the continuity concept, his findings with respect to schizophrenia were extended to the neuroses, leading to an environmentalist school ('neo-Freudian') and a rupture with organized psychoanalysis which has yet to be healed.

2. Melanie Klein and her followers, in following an orientation entirely

opposite to Sullivan, have encountered similar theoretical problems as well as a serious break with their psychoanalytic colleagues. The Kleinian theory of schizophrenia is a literal application of Freud's original Classical Theory. According to this theory, the disturbance in object relations is considered primary and all aspects of schizophrenic object relations are considered motivated by drives and defences. The problems of Kleinian theory have been well reviewed elsewhere (Zetzel, 1956*a*; Kernberg, 1969). I simply assert that it is unsound research strategy to reduce all the complexities of schizophrenic object relations to the motives of intrapsychic conflict and, in the long run, it must lead to serious therapeutic limitations. Nevertheless, in my view the Kleinian school has made important contributions to the understanding of schizophrenic object relations, to clarifying primitive levels of intrapsychic conflict, and to therapeutic approaches to these issues. I have emphasized Sullivan and Klein in this essay, because both of them have made outstanding contributions to the psychoanalytic study of schizophrenia, yet the work of both has been confused and obscured by inadequate theory leading to serious breaches within organized psychoanalysis. Their important findings in respect of schizophrenia have been extended to the neuroses by some of their followers (an application of the 'continuity concept') in ways that have fostered clannish movements within psychoanalysis and obscured scientific advances which could derive from their contributions. The history of the psychoanalytic study of schizophrenia has resulted in impressive and creative achievements—far more than I can indicate in this essay—but it has also been marred by serious theoretical controversies. I believe it is a mistake to over-emphasize the role of personalities and politics in understanding these controversies, and so to neglect the fact that they have been based on serious and valid theoretical problems.

NOTES

1. While the concept *mental object representation* is implicit in Freud's works, the first comprehensive definition was offered by Sterba (1947). Its significance has been clarified and discussed by Novey (1958), Sandler & Rosenblatt (1962), Schafer (1968) and Fraiberg (1969).
2. In order to clarify the difference between object representation as a subjective phenomenon or as metapsychological concept, consider the following. It is not too unusual, in the course of analytic work, to uncover intense wishes for merger or fusion with another person as expressed through dreams, fantasies, etc. These fantasies of fusion of self and object do not necessarily indicate that the analysand in question functions on a level of undifferentiated self and object representations. On the other hand, it is entirely possible for an analyst to

conclude, on the basis of extensive direct and indirect evidence, that a given individual functions on a level of symbiotic object relations even without specific reports of imagery involving fusion of self and object.

3. Beres & Joseph (1970) have accounted for the deep intrapsychic focus of mental representations by defining them as 'unconscious organizations' with conscious derivatives. Their view merits serious consideration.

4. Schur did not apply his distinction between the pleasure principle and the unpleasure principle to schizophrenia. Rather, he applied it to the traumatic neuroses. If the Unitary and Specific Theories can be brought together, it might be done by finding a bridge between schizophrenia and traumatic neuroses. Much of the above definition could apply to traumatic neuroses, but the following distinction should be particularly noted: In traumatic neuroses, the memory traces of specific experiences fail to gain mental representation, influencing but not disrupting the basic integration of self and object representations. In schizophrenia, the basic integration of self and object representations is disrupted.

5. Following Schur (1966), it would be accurate to consider such integration as involving all stimulation external to the mental apparatus, thus including somatic stimulation (internal environment).

6. In differentiating schizophrenic behaviour from the behaviour of the normal child, it might prove useful to consider differences in the 'protective stimulus barrier' (Freud, 1926). I believe that a careful survey of the control of stimulation (not only in terms of inborn thresholds but also as thresholds which gain representation and have their own maturational and developmental sequences) would reveal that schizophrenic subjects are more vulnerable to excessive or insufficient stimulation than the normal child.

7. Schizophrenic concrete thinking differs from other forms of concrete thinking, particularly insofar as it may coexist with an excellent capacity for abstraction (Lidz et al., 1957).

8. I refer to a 'primary area of disturbance' advisedly, and avoid reference to any 'mechanism'. Freeman (1970) has cautioned that schizophrenic behaviours involve all areas of mental functioning. It is easy to assemble evidence to assert that a primary mechanism for schizophrenia rests in specific ego functions, cognitive functions, drive development, or even mental representations. I feel overwhelmed that the psychoanalytic investigator has more overlapping theoretical tools at his disposal than well-organized data. I believe that the psychoanalytic data concerning schizophrenia may be organized in terms of mental representation, that many aspects of schizophrenic behaviour appear secondary to the representational disturbance, and that a focus on mental representation may serve a useful research strategy.

9. This theoretical statement is not intended to be an aetiological formulation, nor to prejudge whatever hereditary, physiological or environmental factors may ultimately prove aetiologically significant. My personal opinion that disturbances in parental care are sufficient to inhibit the development of mental representations and will eventually prove the decisive aetiological factor in most or all cases of schizophrenia is not relevant to this essay.

10. It is appropriate to add to this group the contributions from child analysis made by Mahler (1952), in formulating the symbiotic phase of development.

REFERENCES

Arlow, J. A. & Brenner, C. (1969). The psychopathology of the psychoses: a proposed revision. *Int. J. Psycho-Anal.* **50**, 5–14.

Beres, D. & Joseph, E. D. (1970). The concept of mental representation in psychoanalysis. *Int. J. Psycho-Anal.* **51**, 1–9.

Brierley, M. (1939). Problems connected with the work of Melanie Klein. In *Trends in Psycho-Analysis*. London: Hogarth Press, 1951.

Federn, P. (1952). On the treatment of psychosis. In *Ego Psychology and the Psychoses*. New York: Basic Books.

Fraiberg, S. (1969). Libidinal object constancy and mental representation. *Psychoanal. Study Child* **24**.

Freeman, T. (1970). The psychopathology of the psychoses: a reply to Arlow and Brenner. *Int. J. Psycho-Anal.* **51**, 407–15.

Freud, S. (1911). Psycho-analytic notes on an autobiographical account of a case of paranoia (dementia paranoides). *S.E.* **12**.

Freud, S. (1914). On narcissism: an introduction. *S.E.* **14**.

Freud, S. (1915). Instincts and their vicissitudes. *S.E.* **14**.

Freud, S. (1923). The ego and the id. *S.E.* **19**.

Freud, S. (1924). The loss of reality in neurosis and psychosis. *S.E.* **19**.

Freud, S. (1926). Inhibitions, symptoms and anxiety. *S.E.* **20**.

Fromm-Reichmann, F. (1952). Some aspects of psychoanalytic psychotherapy with schizophrenics. In E. B. Brody & F. C. Redlich (eds.), *Psychotherapy with Schizophrenics*. New York: Int. Univ. Press.

Frosch, J. (1966). A note on reality constancy. In R. M. Loewenstein *et al.* (eds.), *Psychoanalysis: A General Psychology*. New York: Int. Univ. Press.

Frosch, J. (1970). Psychoanalytic considerations of the psychotic character. *J. Am. psychoanal. Ass.* **18**, 24–50.

Giovacchini, P. L. (1969). The influence of interpretation upon schizophrenic patients. *Int. J. Psycho-Anal.* **50**, 179–86.

Greenson, R. R. & Wexler, M. (1969). The nontransference relationship in the psychoanalytic situation. *Int. J. Psycho-Anal.* **50**, 27–39.

Hartmann, H. (1939). *Ego Psychology and the Problem of Adaptation*. New York: Int. Univ. Press, 1958.

Hartmann, H. (1953). Contribution to the metapsychology of schizophrenia. In *Essays on Ego Psychology*. New York: Int. Univ. Press, 1964.

Jacobson, E. (1954). Contribution to the metapsychology of psychotic identifications. *J. Am. psychoanal. Ass.* **2**, 239–62.

Jacobson, E. (1967). *Psychotic Conflict and Reality*. New York: Int. Univ. Press.

Kernberg, O. F. (1969). A contribution to the ego-psychological critique of the Kleinian school. *Int. J. Psycho-Anal.* **50**, 317–33.

Knight, R. P. (1953). Management and psychotherapy of the borderline schizophrenic patient. In R. P. Knight & C. Friedman (eds.), *Psychoanalytic Psychiatry and Psychology*. New York: Int. Univ. Press, 1954.

Kubie, L. S. (1953). The distortion of the symbolic process in neurosis and psychosis. *J. Am. psycho-anal. Ass.* **1**, 59–86.

Lidz, T., Fleck S. & Cornelison, A. (1965). *Schizophrenia and the Family*. New York: Int. Univ. Press.

Lidz, T. *et al.* (1957). Transmission of irrationality. In *Schizophrenia and the Family*. New York: Int. Univ. Press, 1965.

Loewald, H. W. (1951). Ego and reality. *Int. J. Psycho-Anal.* **32**, 10–18.

Mahler, M. S. (1952). On child psychosis and schizophrenia: autistic and symbiotic infantile psychoses. *Psychoanal. Study Child* **7**.

Novey, S. (1955). Some philosophical speculations about the concept of the genital character. *Int. J. Psycho-Anal.* **36**, 88–94.

Novey, S. (1958). The meaning of the concept of mental representation of objects. *Psychoanal. Q.* **27**, 57–79.

Parsons, T. (1952). The superego and the theory of social systems. In *Social Structure and Personality*. New York: Free Press, 1965.

Piaget, J. (1954). *Play, Dreams and Imitation in Childhood*. New York: Norton, 1951.

Pinter, H. (1961). *The Caretaker and The Dumb Waiter*. New York: Grove Press.

Pious, W. L. (1961). A hypothesis about the nature of schizophrenic behaviour. In A. Burton (ed.), *Psychotherapy of the Psychoses*. New York: Basic Books.

Rapaport, D. (1957a). A theoretical analysis of the superego concept. In *Collected Papers of David Rapaport*. New York: Basic Books, 1967.

Rapaport, D. (1957b). The theory of ego autonomy: a generalization. *Ibid.*

Rapaport, D. (1960). The structure of psychoanalytic theory: a systematizing attempt. *Psychol. Issues*, monogr. 6.

Sandler, J. & Rosenblatt, B. (1962). The concept of the representational world. *Psychoanal. Study Child* **17**.

Schafer, R. (1968). *Aspects of Internalization*. New York: Int. Univ. Press.

Schur, M. (1966). *The Id and the Regulatory Principles of Mental Functioning*. New York: Int. Univ. Press.

Sechehaye, M. A. (1951). *Symbolic Realization*. New York: Int. Univ. Press.

Segal, H. (1964). *Introduction to the Work of Melanie Klein*. New York: Basic Books.

Singer, M. T. & Wynne, L. C. (1965). Thought disorder and family relations of schizophrenics. IV. Results and implications. *Archs gen. Psychiat.* **12**, 201–12.

Sterba, R. (1947). *Introduction to the Psychoanalytic Theory of the Libido*. New York: Nervous & Mental Disease Monographs.

Sullivan, H. S. (1947). *Conceptions of Modern Psychiatry*. Washington: Wm. Alanson White Psychiatric Foundation.

Sullivan, H. S. (1962). *Schizophrenia as a Human Process*. New York: Norton.

Tarachow, S. (1962). Interpretation and reality in psychotherapy. *Int. J. Psycho-Anal.* **43**, 377–87.

Waelder, R. (1930). The principle of multiple function. *Psychoanal. Q.* **5** (1935), 45–62.

Wexler, M. (1952). The structural problem in schizophrenia: the role of the internal object. In E. B. Brody & F. C. Redlich (eds.), *Psychotherapy with Schizophrenics*. New York: Int. Univ. Press.

Zetzel, E. R. (1956a). An approach to the relation between concept and content in psychoanalytic theory. *Psychoanal. Study Child* **11**.

Zetzel, E. R. (1956b). Current concepts of transference. *Int. J. Psycho-Anal.* **37**, 369–76.

3. On the Origin of the "Influencing Machine" in Schizophrenia

Victor Tausk

I

The following considerations are based upon a single example of the "influencing machine" complained of by a certain type of schizophrenic patient. Although in this particular case the structure of the machine differs materially, to the best of my knowledge, from all other varieties of apparatus of this sort, it is hoped that the present example will nevertheless facilitate psychoanalytic insight into the genesis and purpose of this delusional instrument.

My example is a variant—a very rare variant—of the typical influencing machine. The objection can of course be made that it is rash to draw general conclusions from the study of a single case, and that generalizations, to be regarded as scientifically valid, should be based on a larger mass of material. My justification is that I have simply not encountered any further case material in support of my conclusions, and that to the best of my knowledge psychiatric literature contains no descriptions of individual cases of the influencing machine phenomenon, such as would make my paper superfluous. There exist only general descriptions of the apparatus, and its regular features and functions are given only as perfunctory clinical illustrations. Clinical psychiatry, interested only in general descriptions, lays no stress upon the significance of individual symptoms for the study of the dynamics of psychoses. Psychiatry has not hitherto sufficiently investigated the origin, the meaning, and the purpose of a symptom, because, not employing the psychoanalytical method, it does not even postulate such problems. Yet in principle, it is permissible to derive general conclusions from exceptional types. Variants and mixed forms stimulate inquiry into general types. The conformity of typical cases may have the ultimate effect of an impenetrable barrier, while a deviation from type, on the other hand, may be a window in the wall through which a clear view is to be obtained.

Deviations from the rule and ambiguous types compel the assumption that a given phenomenon may be of diverse origin. It is only when an unexpected departure from the accustomed occurs that one feels the necessity of investigating the uniformity which had previously characterized the phenomenon or at least had seemed to do so. Inquiry into extraordinary causative factors has often stimulated inquiry into those ordinarily encountered.

It is to be hoped only that the example taken as a basis for the following conclusions will prove to justify them, and that the origin and significance of this variant example have been correctly conceived and formulated.

II

The schizophrenic influencing machine is a machine of mystical nature. The patients are able to give only vague hints of its construction. It consists of boxes, cranks, levers, wheels, buttons, wires, batteries, and the like. Patients endeavor to discover the construction of the apparatus by means of their technical knowledge, and it appears that with the progressive popularization of the sciences, all the forces known to technology are utilized to explain the functioning of the apparatus. All the discoveries of mankind, however, are regarded as inadequate to explain the marvelous powers of this machine, by which the patients feel themselves persecuted.

The main effects of the influencing machine are the following:

1. It makes the patients see pictures. When this is the case, the machine is generally a magic lantern or cinematograph. The pictures are seen on a single plane, on walls or windowpanes, and unlike typical visual hallucinations are not three-dimensional.

2. It produces, as well as removes, thoughts and feelings by means of waves or rays or mysterious forces which the patient's knowledge of physics is inadequate to explain. In such cases, the machine is often called a "suggestion-apparatus". Its construction cannot be explained, but its function consists in the transmission or "draining off" of thoughts and feelings by one or several persecutors.

3. It produces motor phenomena in the body, erections and seminal emissions, that are intended to deprive the patient of his male potency and weaken him. This is accomplished either by means of suggestion or by air-currents, electricity, magnetism, or X-rays.

4. It creates sensations that in part cannot be described, because they are strange to the patient himself, and that in part are sensed as electrical, magnetic, or due to air-currents.

5. It is also responsible for other occurrences in the patient's body, such as cutaneous eruptions, abscesses, and other pathological processes.

The machine serves to persecute the patient and is operated by enemies. To the best of my knowledge, the latter are exclusively of the male sex. They are predominantly physicians by whom the patient has been treated. The manipulation of the apparatus is likewise obscure, the patient rarely having a clear idea of its operation. Buttons are pushed, levers set in motion, cranks turned. The connection with the patient is often established by means of invisible wires leading into his bed, in which case the patient is influenced by the machine only when he is in bed.

However, it is noteworthy that a large number of patients complain of all these ailments without ascribing them to the influence of a machine. Many patients consider the cause of all these alien or hostile sensations of physical or psychic change to be simply an external mental influence, suggestion or telepathic power, emanating from enemies. My own observations and those of other authors leave no room for doubt that these complaints precede the symptom of the influencing apparatus, and that the latter is a subsequent pathological development. Its appearance, as many observers state, serves the purpose of an explanation for the pathologic changes that are felt as alien and painful and dominate the patient's emotional life and sensations.

According to this view, the idea of the influencing machine originates in the need for causality that is inherent in man; and the same need for causality will probably also account for the persecutors who act not through the medium of an apparatus but merely by suggestion or by telepathy. Clinical psychiatry explains the symptom of an influencing machine as analogous to the ideas of persecution in paranoia (which, it is known, the patient invents in order to justify his delusions of grandeur), and calls it *"paranoia somatica"*.

However, there is a group of patients that dispenses completely with any gratification of the need for causality, and complains simply of emotional changes and strange apparitions within the physical and psychic personality, without the intervention of a foreign or hostile power. It is particularly declared by some patients that their visions are not foisted upon them in any way but that, to their great astonishment, they simply see them. There also occur other strange sensations for which there is no evidence of an originator, especially, for instance, the complaint of a loss or change of thoughts and feelings, without the thoughts or feelings being "drained" from them or "foisted" upon them; and of a similar nature are complaints of a change of sensations in the skin, face, and extremities. This group of patients does not complain of influences originating from a foreign, hostile force, but of a feeling of inner estrangement. They become strange to themselves, no longer understand themselves: limbs, face, facial expression, thoughts, and feelings, have become estranged. These symptoms clearly are part of an early stage of dementia praecox, although they may also be observed in advanced stages as well.

In some cases it may be stated with certainty, and in others with strong probability, that the sense of persecution originates from the sensations of change accompanied by a sense of estrangement. These feelings of persecution are ascribed to a foreign, personal interference, "suggestion", or "telepathic influence". In other cases, the ideas of persecution or influence may be seen entering into the construction of an influencing apparatus. It is necessary to assume, therefore, that the influencing apparatus represents the terminal stage in the evolution of the symptom, which started with simple sensations of change. I do not believe that heretofore the entire sequence in the development of the symptom could have been studied completely from a single case. But I have observed the connection between at least two stages (of which I shall present an example later), and I have no hesitation in maintaining that under especially favorable circumstances it may be possible to observe the entire series of developmental stages in a single patient. Meanwhile, I am in the position of the observer of plasmodia who notes various pathological forms in the blood cells as developmental stages of a continuous cycle of growth, although he is never able to observe in any one blood corpuscle more than a single phase.

Recognition of the various symptoms as stages of a unified developmental process is rendered difficult not merely by inaccurate observation but by other factors as well. Patients conceal single stages behind secondary and correlative symptoms—each patient in accordance with his morbid disposition. Changes of feeling are covered up by a simultaneously or consecutively produced psychosis or neurosis belonging to another clinical group, such as depression, mania, paranoia, compulsion neurosis, anxiety hysteria, or amentia; and these clinical pictures, advancing to the foreground, conceal from the observer the more subtle elements in the development of the delusion of reference. It is, besides, very likely that in many cases not every stage of development reaches consciousness, and that one stage or another runs its course in the unconscious and thus leaves gaps in the conscious psyche. Finally, depending upon the rapidity of the pathological process and upon the individual disposition, some of the stages may be missing altogether.

Ideas of reference in schizophrenia develop equally with or without the influencing apparatus. In but one case (at the Belgrade Neuropsychiatric

Division) have I been able to observe electrical currents in the absence of the influencing apparatus to which those are usually ascribed—in the absence, in fact, of any hostile powers whatsoever.

This observation was made in the case of a thirty-four-year-old man, Josef H., an inmate of insane asylums at frequent intervals throughout his life. He felt electrical currents streaming through him, which entered the earth through his legs; he produced the current within himself, declaring with pride that that was his power! How and for what purpose he did this he refused to disclose. Upon discovering these currents in himself for the first time, he was (he admitted) somewhat astonished, but he soon came to the conclusion that this manifestation had a special significance—that the currents served a mysterious end, regarding which he refused any information.

I shall now cite another instance, a singular case of *"paranoia somatica"*, having, as will later be seen, a significance of its own in substantiating the developmental process which I have assumed. The same example has already been cited by Freud in another connection. Miss Emma A. felt herself influenced by her lover in a singular manner; she maintained that her eyes were no longer properly placed in her head but were entirely twisted out of position, and this she attributed to the fact that her lover was an evil, deceitful person who twisted eyes. At church one day she suddenly felt a thrust, as if she were being moved from her place, which had its cause in the fact that her lover disguised himself,[1] and that he had already ruined her and made her as evil as himself.

This patient did not merely feel herself persecuted and influenced; hers was a case of being influenced by identification with the persecutor. If we take into consideration the view held by Freud and myself that in object-choice the mechanism of identification precedes the cathexis proper by projection, we may regard the case of Miss Emma A. as representing the stage in the development of the delusion of reference preceding the projection (namely, on to a distant persecutor in the outer world). The identification is obviously an attempt to project the feelings of the inner change on to the outer world. It constitutes a bridge between the feelings of an inner change without external cause and the attribution of these changes to the power of an external person, a kind of intermediary position between the feeling of self-estrangement and the delusion of reference. This rounds out especially well, and substantiates psychoanalytically, the concept of the development of the symptom, up to its crystallization in the influencing machine. We are here concerned with the discovery, or rather the invention, of a hostile object; but for the intellectual process it is unimportant whether the objects observed are hostile or friendly, and the psychoanalyst, at least, will certainly have no objection to the equating of love and hate in this instance. Among the illustrations that may be given of the various forms or stages of the delusion of reference, the case of Staudenmayer (whose autobiography was presented before the Vienna Psychoanalytic Society some years ago) may be mentioned.

Staudenmayer—who, if I am not mistaken, was declared to be a paranoiac and is at any rate considered to be one by me—described his sensations during his bowel movements from the beginning of the movement to its conclusion, and attributed every single peristaltic motion coming to his awareness to the activity of special demons allegedly located in the intestines and entrusted with the performance of each separate motion.

We may now summarize and describe schematically the phenomena that in some cases appear to be produced by the influencing machine and that in other cases occur without it.

1. We note, first, simple sensations of inner change, in the beginning devoid of, and later accompanied by, a sense of estrangement, without awareness of an originator. The sensations are of changes in the psychical and physical functions within various parts of one's own body. In many cases this stage of the illness probably occurs at a very early age, before puberty. Since at this age no exact reports can be obtained on inner conditions, and since, in addition, pathological changes are not infrequently compensated by infantile peculiarities of character, such as naughtiness, aggressiveness, concealed fantasies, masturbation, seclusiveness, dullness and so forth, this stage either remains unrecognized or else is misnamed. It is only at puberty, when special adjustments to the environment are required of the individual, who is compelled to relinquish all crude expressions of his abnormality, that the illness comes to the surface; it is at this time, too, that further development of symptoms is stimulated.

2. Feelings of inner change in the form of abnormal sensations, with awareness of an originator,—in this instance the patient himself (case Josef H.).

3. Feelings of inner change accompanied by awareness of an originator, who, although existing within the patient, is nevertheless not the patient himself (case Staudenmayer).

4. Feelings of inner change accompanied by hallucinatory projection of the inner occurrence to the external world, without awareness of an originator; at first, feelings of estrangement are not present, but later on they appear (seeing pictures).

5. Feelings of inner change accompanied by awareness of an external originator as a result of identification (case Emma A.).

6. Feelings of inner change accompanied by projection of the inner occurrence to the outer world and belief in an originator produced by the paranoid mechanism (causing pictures to appear, influencing by suggestion, hypnotism, electricity, producing or draining off thoughts and feelings, effecting bodily motions, weakening potency, producing erection, seminal emissions, and so forth).

7. Feelings of inner change attributed to the workings of the influencing machine manipulated by enemies. At first, the enemies are usually unknown to the patient and only vaguely discerned by him; later on he is able to make them out, knows who they are, and enlarges their circle after the pattern of the paranoid conspiracy. Similarly, the patient is at first completely unable to explain the construction of the influencing apparatus, but familiarizes himself with it gradually.

Having solved the relation between ideas of reference and the influencing apparatus, we may proceed to an examination of the latter without reference to its effects.

It is not necessary to discuss the magic lantern which produces pictures or images, because its structure harmonizes perfectly with the function attributed to it, and because it does not reveal any error of judgment beyond the fact of its nonexistence. This rational superstructure is absolutely impenetrable. We must, at the start, use structures less solidly built, the walls of which reveal gaps through which it is possible to look inside.

(a) The ordinary influencing machine has a very obscure construction; large parts of it are completely unimaginable. In cases where the patient believes he understands the construction of the apparatus well, it is obvious that this feeling is, at best, analogous to that of a dreamer who has a feeling of understanding, but has not the understanding itself. This characteristic may be discovered whenever an accurate description of the apparatus is demanded of the patient.

(b) The apparatus is, as far as I know, always a machine; and a very complicated one.

The psychoanalyst cannot for a moment doubt that this machine must be a symbol—a view recently emphasized by Freud in one of his lectures, in which he stated that the complicated machines appearing in dreams always represent the genitalia. Having studied machine dreams analytically over a long period of time, I can fully confirm Freud's statement; I may add, moreover, that the machines always stand for the dreamer's own genitalia and that the dreams are of a masturbatory character. I can state further that these dreams are dreams of escape, of the type described in my paper on alcoholic delirium.[2] In this paper it is shown that whenever an urge to masturbate, or rather a readiness to ejaculate semen, leads to a dream fantasy which is favorable to discharge, another fantasy is hastily substituted, by means of which a new state of inhibition is induced momentarily, and the ejaculation of semen is made difficult if not impossible. The dream reacts to the repudiated wish for discharge with a successive alteration of symbols.

The machine dream possesses an analogous mechanism, except that the introduction of single components of the machine is not accompanied by the simultaneous disappearance of the other components for which they are substituted, the new components being simply added to the old ones. This is how the hopelessly complex machine originates. In order to strengthen the inhibition, the symbol has been made complex, instead of being displaced by another one; but the result is the same. Each complexity draws the attention of the dreamer to himself, rouses his intellectual interest, reciprocally weakens his libidinal interest, and effects in this manner inhibition of instinct.

In machine dreams the dreamer awakens, more often than not, with his hand on his genitalia, after having dreamed of manipulating the machine. It may, therefore, be assumed that the influencing apparatus is a representation of the patient's genitalia projected to the outer world, analogous in origin to the machine in dreams. The frequent complaint of the schizophrenic that the apparatus causes erection, drains off semen, and weakens potency only confirms this view. At any rate, the analogy of the symptom to a dream production, as well as the accessibility of the symptom to psychoanalytic dream interpretation is a step beyond the rationalizations and the demand for causal connections that underlie the usual clinical interpretation of the influencing machine in schizophrenia. I can now present my example, which will not only strengthen our hypothesis, but will enlarge it materially.

The patient is Miss Natalija A., thirty-one years old, formerly a student of philosophy. She has been completely deaf for a great number of years, due to an ulcer of the ear, and can make herself understood only by means of writing. She declares that for six and a half years she has been under the influence of an electrical machine made in Berlin, though this machine's use is prohibited by the police. It has the form of a human body, indeed, the patient's own form, though not in all details. Her mother, likewise the patient's male and female friends, are also under the influence of this machine or of similar machines. Of the latter she gives no explanation, describing only the apparatus to which she herself is subjected. She is certain that for men there is a masculine machine representing the masculine form and for women a female one. The trunk (torso) has the shape of a lid, resembling the lid of a coffin and is lined with silk or velvet. Regarding the limbs two significant explanations are given. At the first interview she described them as entirely natural parts of the body. A few weeks later these limbs were not placed on the coffin lid in their natural form, but were merely drawn on it in two dimensions, in the position they would occupy in the natural state of the body. She cannot see the head—she says that she is not sure about it and she does not know whether the machine bears her own head. She has practically nothing to report about the head. The patient does not know definitely how this machine is to be handled, neither does she know how it is connected with her; but she vaguely thinks that it is by means of telepathy. The outstanding fact about the machine is that it is being manipulated by someone in a certain manner, and everything that occurs to it happens also to her. When someone strikes this machine, she feels the blow in the corresponding part of her own body. The ulcer (lupus) now present on her nose was first produced on the nose of the machine, and some time later the patient herself became afflicted with it. The inner parts of the machine consist of electric batteries, which are supposed to represent the internal organs of the human body. Those who handle the machine produce a slimy substance in her nose, disgusting smells, dreams, thoughts, feelings, and disturb her while she is thinking, reading, or writing. At an earlier stage, sexual sensations were produced in her through manipulation of the genitalia of the machine; but now the machine no longer possesses any genitalia, though why or how they disappeared she cannot tell. Ever since the machine lost its genitalia, the patient has ceased to experience sexual sensations.

She became familiar with the apparatus, about which she had previously heard, through all kinds of occurrences, especially through conversations among people, that is, through auditory hallucinations. The man who utilizes the apparatus to persecute her, her rejected suitor, a college professor, is prompted by jealousy. Very soon after she had refused his courtship she felt that he was trying by means of suggestion to bring about a friendship between his sister-in-law, her mother, and herself, his obvious purpose being to use this influence to make her accept him. When, however, suggestion failed, he subjected her to the influence of the machine; not only she herself but also her mother, her physicians, her friends, all those who had her welfare at heart, came under the influence of this diabolical apparatus, with the result that the physicians submitted a mistaken diagnosis to her, the apparatus deluding them into diagnosing other ailments than those with which she was afflicted. She could no longer get along with her friends and relatives, arousing everyone's animosity, and feeling compelled to run away. It was impossible to obtain any further details from the patient. On her third visit she became inaccessible and only stated that the analyst, too, was under the influence of the apparatus, that he had become hostile to her, and that they could no longer understand each other.

This case provides a definite reason for believing that the influencing machine represents a stage in the development of a symptom which can also appear without this stage, as a delusion of reference. The patient clearly stated that her persecutor had recourse to the apparatus only when his attempt to influence her by suggestion failed. The fact that she seems to have previously heard about the machine is also enlightening. This vague recognition obviously awakened in the patient old familiar sensations that she had experienced before she was subjected to the apparatus; this is analogous to the well-known fact that persons in a state of infatuation have the feeling of having always known the beloved one—in reality they are merely rediscovering one of their old libidinal imagos. We shall hear later in how remote a past she had first experienced sensations similar to those caused by the influencing apparatus.

The peculiar construction of the machine substantiates our assumptions to a great extent, especially with regard to the significance of the machine as a projected symbol of the genitalia. We may add that the apparatus represents not only the patient's genitalia but obviously, her whole person. It represents the projection of the patient's body on to the outer world. At least, the following results are unquestionably obtained from the patient's report: the apparatus is distinguished above all by its human form, easily recognized despite many non-human characteristics. In form it resembles the patient herself, and she senses all manipulations performed on the apparatus in the corresponding part of her own body and in the same manner. All effects and changes undergone by the apparatus take place simultaneously in the patient's body, and *vice versa*. Thus, the apparatus loses its genitalia following the patient's loss of her genital sensations; it had possessed genitalia for as long a period as her genital sensations had lasted.

Applying the technique of dream interpretation to this case, it may be said that the patient's inability to provide any detailed description of the head of the apparatus, and especially her inability to decide whether it was her own head or not, proves conclusively that it is her own head. We know from analytic observations that the person not recognized in a dream is actually the dreamer himself. In my analysis of the *Dream of the Clinic*,[3] it was clear that the dreamer meant herself when she dreamt of a person whose head she could not see.

A further detail in the description of the apparatus—namely, that the lid is lined with silk or velvet—may substantiate this opinion. Women very frequently describe in such terms the feelings evoked by caressing their own skin. That the intestines appear in the form of batteries is only of slight significance here, although it will assume a profounder meaning later on. This superficial interpretation may be associated with the information given directly or indirectly to school children to the effect that the viscera resemble a very complicated machine. In our case the tendency seems to be towards a verbal interpretation of this infantile conception. This conclusion regarding its ontogeny is arrived at with the help of the description given by the patient of her influencing apparatus.

At the very beginning the patient reported that the limbs of the apparatus appeared in their natural form and position. Several weeks later, she declared that the limbs were drawn on the lid. This is obviously a manifestation of the progressive distortion undergone by the apparatus, which, consequently, eventually loses all human characteristics and becomes a typical, unintelligible, influencing machine. First the genitalia, then the limbs are eliminated in this process. The patient, to be sure, is unable to report how the genitalia are removed. She states, however, that the limbs are removed in the following manner: they lose their three-dimensional human form and flatten to a two-dimensional plane. It would not have been surprising if after a lapse of several weeks, the patient had declared that the apparatus did not possess any limbs at all. Nor would it have been astonishing had she stated that the apparatus had never had any limbs. A failure to recall the developmental stages of the apparatus has obviously the same significance as that of forgetting the origin of dream pictures. It is not too bold a conclusion to draw that the coffin lid of the machine is a product of such successive distortions and that originally it had represented a human being—namely, the patient herself.

Psychoanalytic experience brings to light the causative factors in such distortion. Underlying every distortion of a psychic phenomenon there is a defense mechanism which has as its aim the protection of the conscious ego against the appearance or reappearance of undisguised fantasies. The patient obviously seeks not to recognize herself in the influencing machine and therefore in self-protection she divests it of all human features; in a word, the less human the appearance of the delusion, the less does she recognize herself in it. The origin of this rejection will be examined later.

When the influencing machine of Miss Natalija A. first came to my attention, it was in a special stage of development; I was fortunate, moreover, in observing the machine in the process of development as concerned the limbs, and also in obtaining specific information from the patient herself regarding the genitalia. I assume that this process will end with the production of the typical influencing apparatus known to clinical observation, but I cannot affirm that this apparatus will pass through all the stages of development to the very end. It is very possible that it will stop at a middle point, without proceeding further.

III

In the meantime, we may consider a second hypothesis that may have suggested itself to the reader. It must be taken into consideration that, notwithstanding all that has been said above, the influencing machine of Miss Natalija A. may be merely an inexplicable exception to the general rule. The complex, unintelligible machine as fantastically described and interpreted by other patients would perhaps first have to be studied and defined before an explanation of Miss N.'s influencing machine could be undertaken. For want of other material at hand to substantiate our hypothesis, except the machine dream, we shall start with the assumption that the influencing apparatus is a projection of the patient's genitalia. In presenting this second hypothesis together with, or in lieu of, the first, I realize how much indulgence is exacted of the reader, and I should not be surprised if I were reproached with levity or legerdemain. I myself was unpleasantly surprised to discover that this second hypothesis was probably as valid as the first, and that in consequence both became improbable or worthless, since their content differs and each leads to quite a different theory. Fortunately, another theory suggests itself which brings into immediate harmony both interpretations of the influencing apparatus. This problem will be touched upon again towards the end of this paper.

Attention may be called now to a symptom in schizophrenia, which I have named "loss of ego boundaries". This symptom is the complaint that "everyone" knows the patient's thoughts, that his thoughts are not enclosed in his own head, but are spread throughout the world and occur simultaneously in the heads of all persons. The patient seems no longer to realize that he is a separate psychical entity, an ego with individual boundaries. A sixteen-year-old patient in the Wagner-Jauregg Clinic indulged in gay laughter whenever she was asked for her thoughts. Catamnesis revealed that for a long while when being questioned, she had believed I had been jesting; she knew that I must be familiar with her thoughts, since they occurred at the same time in my own head.

We are familiar with this infantile stage of thinking, in which a strong belief exists that others know of the child's thoughts. Until the child has been successful in its first lie, the parents are supposed to know everything, even its most secret thoughts. Later on, in the event that the child has been caught lying, this conception may be formed again, now caused by the feeling of guilt. The striving for the right to have secrets from which the parents are excluded is one of the most powerful factors in the formation of the ego, especially in establishing and carrying out one's own will. The developmental stage observed in the above-mentioned case falls into this period, in which the child does not yet sense this right to privacy and does not yet doubt that the parents and educators know everything.[4]

The symptom with the content that "thoughts are given to them", the patients deduce subsequently from their belief that others know their thoughts. This must be attributed to the infantile impressions originating in an earlier period in life, when the child knows nothing through its own efforts but obtains all its knowledge from others: how to make use of its limbs, its language, its thoughts. At that period all is "given to" the child, all joy and all sorrow, and it is difficult to evaluate what share the child itself has in its accomplishments.[5] The sudden discovery that it is able to accomplish a task without the help of others is greeted by the child with a great deal of surprise and excitement. It is probable, therefore, that this symptom represents a regression to this particular stage of infancy. But this special period of infancy presents a problem: How far back does it go? What causes the formation of the ego and, as a reaction to the outer world, the ego boundaries, and what arouses the realization of individuality, of self, as a distinct psychical unit?

Theoretically we cannot assume that the ego begins to take form earlier than the time of object finding. The latter comes with gratification and renunciation of instinctual drives, whereas an awareness of the outer world, independent of the infant's drives and desires, is established only gradually. It is hardly possible that the sex instincts should have a greater influence upon the development of this awareness than the drive to be nourished. To be sure, the sex instincts will soon take on a special significance which must not be underestimated. But for the time being, it should be stated that there is a stage when no objects of the outer world exist, and therefore there is no realization that one has an ego. At that period there nevertheless exist desires and drives, and a specific urge to obtain mastery over whatever stimulates the sex organs is observable. The developmental stage that precedes the stage of object finding has been recognized as that of *identification*. This became evident from the analysis of neurotics, in whom the inability to obtain possession of objects of gratification, or to reach goals of pleasure, was seen to be due to their identification with the objects. The neurotic himself simply stands for what attracts him in the outer world; he has not found his way to the outer world and, therefore, is unable to develop an adequate ego in his stunted, exclusively libidinal relationships. This peculiar organization of libido has been termed narcissistic. The libido in such cases has been directed towards the neurotic's own personality; it is attached to his own ego and not to the objects of the outer world. Observations and theoretical considerations, especially those of Freud, have led to the assumption that this libido organization characterizes the beginning of psychical development, the "objectless" period, and that, at any rate, this libido organization must be considered a correlate, if not a cause, of the "objectlessness". This organization of libido corresponds also to the stage of intellectual development in which the person considers all the sensory stimuli he receives as endogenous and immanent. At this stage of development the psyche does not yet perceive that intervals of time and space exist between the object from which the stimulus emanates and the sensory response.

The next stage of development is then that of an outward projection of the stimulus and the attributing of this stimulus to a distant object, hence a stage of distancing and objectivation of the intellect, and along with this a transfer of libido to the discovered, or rather, self-created, outer world. As a safeguard to this psychical achievement, and as a kind of critical authority for objectivation, there is evolved at the same time the faculty of distinguishing between objectivity and subjectivity, an awareness of reality, which enables the individual to recognize his inner experiences as distinct from the outer stimuli— in other words, to regard inner experiences as internal and not to confuse them with the objects of sensory response.

This correlative developmental process, however, is apt to meet with inhibitions. There are inhibitions from the intellectual side, or as we say, from the ego—the chief weapon of which is the intellect—and there are inhibitions that arise from the transference of libido in various stages of development, and with various results depending upon the relation of the ego to the libido. These points of inhibition are called, after Freud, fixation-points. In most cases the factor that causes ego disturbances, seems to lie in lesions of the libido. Thus, it is clear from Freud's interpretation that paranoia is a reaction to repressed homosexuality. The prohibition against finding an object for the homosexual drive, which results in an inhibition of the transference of homosexual libido organization, should be recognized as originating from within and remaining within. This projection is a defensive measure of the ego against the renounced homosexual libido that emerges with onrushing force out of repression. Libidinal inhibition leads to intellectual inhibition, which may be manifested in impaired judgment, or in insanity. An internal psychical process due to displacement and projection is mistaken for an external one, which leads to more or less marked "affective weakness of judgment", with the accompanying reactions of the psyche quantitatively and qualitatively determined by the morbid process.

We may say that in the case of an impaired libido organization, the ego finds itself facing the task of mastering an insane outer world, and hence behaves insanely.[6]

In the neuropsychoses that usually appear in later life, with a history of previous relative psychic health, it is not difficult to observe that the impairment of the ego is caused by an impairment of the libido. However, in cases of psychosis that develop gradually and insidiously, beginning with earliest infancy, we may assume not so much a successive impairment of libido and ego as a correlative inhibition, primarily, of the entire development of the individual. The one group of instinctual drives does not develop normally, and this is paralleled by an arrest of the functions of the other group of drives and by a simultaneous development of secondary relations, which are to be regarded as attempts at self-cure and at adaptation to the functional disturbance by means of compensations and overcompensations. Furthermore, there occur regressions on the part of functions which have developed normally but which, whenever there is a marked discordance between the diseased and the normal portions of the psyche, abandon their normal level and retreat, for the purpose of adaptation, to the lower level of the impaired functions. During this retreat, there may arise various temporary or permanent symptom formations of different clinical types; and from these develop all mixed psychotic formations. The existence of these partial processes and their great variety with regard to levels of regression at a given moment requires careful consideration. In considering inhibitions of instinctual drives we must constantly keep in mind that all inhibited drives are capable of being transformed into, or being discharged as, anxiety. To quote Freud, "It may be said that, in a certain theoretical sense, symptoms are formed only in order to forestall an otherwise inevitable development of anxiety."

IV

We have learned from Freud that the projection of the homosexual libido in paranoia is to be regarded as a defensive measure of the ego against an inopportune and socially reprehensible sexual urge pressing from the unconscious. Is it possible to regard the projection of the patient's own body in the case of Miss Natalija as an analogous situation? Naturally, the projection would have to subserve the defense of that libido which belongs to the patient's own body, and which has become either too extensive or too inopportune in its demands for the patient to be able to tolerate it as her own. It is also necessary to assume that this projection pertains only to the libido of the body and not to the libido of the psychic ego, as well, that, moreover, the libido of the psychic ego[7] has facilitated the defense against the bodily libido because it was, so to speak, ashamed of it. That a projection mechanism has been chosen for the purpose of defense—a mechanism belonging to the primary functioning of the ego in the process of object finding—gives us reason to believe that we are here dealing with a libido position which is coëval with the beginnings of intellectual object finding and which is achieved either by regression or by the persistence of a vestigial phenomenon (*Resterscheinung—Freud*), which has been for years and up to the onset of the illness effectively compensated or concealed. In regressions, however, there is always an effort to reach the formerly uninhibited libido positions. In paranoia, regression reaches a stage when homosexual object choice has not yet come under the prohibition of the ego and there is free homosexual libido which is only later subjected to repression at the behest of the cultural demands of the ego.

The libido directed towards a person's own self, which the ego tries to get rid of by projecting its own body, naturally, is characteristic of a period when it was still free from conflict with the demands of other love-objects. This period must coincide with the developmental stage of the psyche in which object finding still occurs within the individual's own body, and when the latter is still regarded as part of the outer world.

I am intentionally differentiating between object choice and object finding. By the former, I mean only libidinal cathexis; by the latter, the intellectual awareness of this cathexis. An object is *found* by the intellect, and *chosen* by the libido. These processes may occur either simultaneously or in sequence, but for my purpose they are to be regarded as distinct.

The projection of one's body may, then, be traced back to the developmental stage in which one's own body is the goal of the object finding. This must be the time when the infant is discovering his body, part by part, as the outer world, and is still groping for his hands and feet as though they were foreign objects. At this time, everything that "happens" to him emanates from his own body; his psyche is the object of stimuli arising in his own body but acting upon it as if produced by outer objects. These disjecta membra are later on pieced together and systematized into a unified whole under the supervision of a psychic unity that receives all sensations of pleasure and pain from these separate parts. This process takes place by means of identification with one's own body. The ego, thus discovered, is cathected with the available libido; in accordance with the psychic nature of the ego, narcissism develops; and, in accordance with the function of individual organs as sources of pleasure, autoeroticism results.

But if the psychoanalytic theories previously employed are correct, this object finding within one's own organs, which can be regarded as parts of the outer world only by projection, must be preceded by a stage of identification with a narcissistic libido position,[8] and it is necessary to assume two successive stages of identification and projection.

The projection which participated in the object finding within one's own organs would, then, be the second phase of the preceding stage, although the part that depends upon the postulated identification has still to be discovered.

I am, then, assuming the evidence of these two successive phases of identification and projection in object finding and object choice within one's own body.

I do not run counter to psychoanalytic conceptions in contending that the individual comes into the world as an organic unity in which libido and ego are not yet separated, and all available libido is related to that organic unity, which does not deserve the name "ego" (i.e., a psychical self-protective organization) any more than does the cell. In this situation the individual is equally a sexual and an individual being, simultaneously performing ego and reproductive functions, like the cell that takes nourishment up to the time when it divides. This stage of the newly born child is biological up to the time of conception, but must be regarded as psychological from the time when—at an indeterminable stage of foetal life—cerebral development takes place.

From the point of view of libido, we may say that the newly born child is a sexual being. I am in accord with Freud's assumption that the individual's first renunciation is the renunciation of the protection of the mother's body imposed upon the libido and accompanied by that expression of anxiety, the birth-cry. However, once this first trauma is over and no discontent arises to bring the infant into a clash with himself and with the environment, he is in complete possession of his own libido and knows nothing of the outer world, not even that part of the world which he will soon discover within himself. It is this stage of identity that precedes the first projection for the purpose of object finding within one's own body. This stage did not come about because of that psychic activity which may be called identification, but is present from the beginning. Nevertheless the result is the same as in actively established identity—absolute self-satisfaction, no outer world, no objects. Let us designate this stage as the innate narcissistic one. In this situation the libido is directed outward, first cathects the subject's own body by the indirect way of projection, and returns by way of self-discovery to the ego. In the meantime, the ego has undergone a decided alteration under the influence of these first psychic stirrings, which one may call experience, and is now again cathected by libido. Let us call this stage, acquired narcissism. The latter finds a considerable quantity of innate narcissism already present and is superimposed on it. The condition of innate narcissism normally remains attached for all time to the organs and their functions, and is in constant conflict with the various further stages of ego development which, with the assistance of anxiety and judgment, take place under the aegis of all the faculties that have been gradually acquired in the meantime. The struggle is carried on, at first, chiefly in the sphere of excretory functions and of the autoerotic sources of pleasure, since these are the spheres that give rise to the greatest difficulties in the individual's relation to the environment. Nevertheless, we must definitely understand that throughout life the ego develops with constant shiftings in the narcissistic libido position, that man in his struggle for existence is constantly compelled to find and recognize himself anew, and that the acquisition of narcissism is immanent in culture and is conceivable only on the basis of intact inborn narcissism that serves as a source of nourishment and regeneration. This constant struggle centering about the self occurs in various degrees in relation to various instinctual drives; it concerns homo-and hetero-sexuality and every libido component in different degrees at different times, and provokes various reactions, compensations, superstructures and eliminations. These secondary psychical formations then enter again into combination and produce insoluble dynamic, qualitative, relative and modal relations, resulting in a great variety of character types and symptoms. The development both of the ego and of the libido—so far as concerns either alone or in their relation to each other—may become arrested and may set up goals of regression at as many points as there are primary, secondary, tertiary (etc.) factors of relationship and development. The entire problem is further complicated by the elements of time and space and so made insoluble. Let us suppose that the projection of one's own body is a pathological repetition of that psychical stage when the individual was endeavoring to discover his body by means of projection. It would not be too much to say that just as the projection in normal primary development has been successful because the innate narcissistic libido position had to be renounced under the attack of outer stimuli, so also pathological projection takes place because there has developed an accumulation of narcissistic libido analogous to the primary narcissism, though here anachronistic, regressive or fixated, but resembling it in character in so far as it isolates the individual from the outer world. Hence, projection of one's own body may be regarded as a defense against a libido position corresponding to the end of fœtal existence and the beginning of extrauterine development. Freud, indeed, has not hesitated to declare, in his *Introductory Lectures*, that psychological problems are to be traced back to intrauterine existence.

These considerations may be used as a starting point for the explanation of various schizophrenic symptoms. Is it not possible that catalepsy, *flexibilitas cerea*, corresponds to the stage when man senses his own organs as foreign, as not belonging to himself, and as being dominated by an outside force? A similar instance is the symptom of having one's limbs moved by someone. This symptom reproduces especially well the situation in which one's own body becomes strange and, so to speak, part of an outer world dominated by outer forces. May we not say that catatonic stupor, which represents a complete rejection of the outer world, is a return to the uterus? May not these severest catatonic symptoms be the ultimate refuge of a psyche that has given up even the most primitive ego functions and has retreated *in toto* to the fœtal and nursing stages, because it cannot use in the present state of its libido even the simplest ego functions that maintain the relation to the outer world? The catatonic symptom, the negativistic stare of the schizophrenic, is nothing else than a renunciation of the outer world expressed in "organ language". Does not also the "nursing reflex" in the terminal stages of general paralysis indicate such a regression to infancy?[9]

The psychic correlate of *flexibilitas cerea* and of that stage in which man regards himself as a part of the outer world, lacks consciousness of his own volition and of his own ego boundaries, is the feeling that everyone knows and is in possession of the thoughts of the patient. In the period here duplicated pathologically there are indeed no thoughts, but even thoughts are subjected, as already stated above, to the same process of being regarded at first as coming from the outer world before they are accounted among the functions of the ego. Thoughts must first be assimilated into the consciousness of ego-unity before they can be an automatic ego-function; and this cannot occur before the intellect has advanced to the stage of memory perceptions. Freud has taught that this, too, is a later process, and that it is preceded by the stage of hallucinations of memory pictures, that is, a stage when the perceptions actually appear in the outer world and are not regarded as internal occurrences. Moreover, this stage of hallucinatory perceptions, in itself representing a kind of objectivation, object finding and object choice, also belongs to the first period of life. The regression, of course, does not occur equally in all psychical faculties and relationships. The capacity for thinking with memory perceptions is still intact, but the libido is already degraded to the nursing stage and sets up a relation with the thinking faculty as it exists. The consciousness of personality has been lost, and this loss is shown in the patient's inability to locate his intact psychical inventory. The patient who declares that his thoughts and feelings are in all people's minds merely declares, in words and concepts derived from the memory-reserve of a later developmental stage, that his libido finds itself at the stage when it is still identical with the outer world, still has no ego-boundaries set up against the outer world, and his libido is now compelled therefore to renounce the normal intellectual object relations in so far as these depend upon the degraded libido position.

These feelings and this mode of expression depend upon the intactness of the psyche's ability to operate with memory perceptions. This faculty, too, may undergo regression.[10] In this case the patient hallucinates. The libido has retreated behind the stage of identification, the intellect no longer knows how to establish a relation to the outer world, even by means of identification. The psyche is approaching closer and closer to the mother's womb.

Furthermore, may not perhaps "picture-seeing in planes" represent a stage of the development of the visual sense still earlier than the hallucinatory stage?

V

I have stated that narcissistic self-discovery and self-choice repeat themselves with every new acquisition of the ego, to this effect, that, under the guidance of conscience and judgment, each new acquisition is either rejected, or cathected with libido and attributed to the ego. Let us call this narcissism, psychic narcissism, and let us contrast it with the organic narcissism that guarantees in the unconscious the unity and functioning of the organism. There is nothing new in calling attention to the great dependence of physical health, and even of life itself, upon what is called love of life, or in the reminder that one can actually die of a "broken heart", and that university professors emeritus often die soon after they have been absolved of their duties, even when they have previously been in the best of health. They die, not of old age, but because they lose the love of life when they can no longer perform the duties they have loved. Freud tells of a famous musician who succumbed to his illness because of the discontinuance of his creative work.

We must assume that the libido flows through the entire body, perhaps like a substance (Freud's view), and that the integration of the organism is effected by a libido tonus, the oscillations of which correspond to the oscillations of psychic narcissism and object libido.[11] Upon this tonus depends the resistance to illness and death. Love of life has saved many a man who was given up by physicians as incurable.

Whenever there occurs an influx of organic narcissism to a given organ as a site of predilection,[12] there may also occur a consciousness of organ relations and organic functions which in normal life are relegated to an unconscious and vegetative rôle. Analogously, objects cathected by psychic narcissism and object love come to consciousness wherever the cathexis has reached a sufficient degree of strength. This influx of libido directs attention to the organ and provides the consciousness of a transformation of the organ or its functions, i.e., the feeling of estrangement. This is the mechanism described by Freud as hypochondria. This influx of libido is followed by the turning away of the ego from the organ pathologically overcharged with libido, or from its functions; that is, by estrangement.[13] This is to be considered a defensive measure against the anxiety associated with hypochondria. The feeling of strangeness is a defense against libidinal cathexis, no matter whether it concerns objects of the outer world, one's own body, or its parts. Of course, the estrangement does not cause the giving up of the unconscious libido position. The estrangement is not a destructive force but merely a denial of the pathological cathexis; it is an instance of the ostrich tactics of the ego, which may be very easily reduced *ad absurdum*, and which must ultimately be supplanted by other or more effective measures of defense.

When, in paranoia, the feeling of estrangement no longer affords protection, the libidinal drive towards the homosexual object is projected on to the latter and appears, by a reversal of direction, as aggression towards the loving one (the patient himself) in the form of a sense of persecution. Strangers become enemies. The enmity is a new and more energetic attempt at protection against the rejected unconscious libido.

The narcissistic organ libido in schizophrenia may undergo a similar transformation. The estranged organ—in our case, the entire body—appears as an outer enemy, as a machine used to afflict the patient.

We are, then, compelled to distinguish three principal stages in the history of the "influencing machine":

1. The sense of internal alteration produced by the influx of libido into a given organ (hypochondria).

2. The feeling of estrangement produced by rejection, whereby the pathologically altered organs or their functions are so to speak denied and eliminated as something alien to the wholly or partially sound organs and functions accepted by the ego.

3. The sense of persecution (*paranoia somatica*) arising from projection of the pathological alteration on to the outer world, (a) by attribution of the alteration to a foreign hostile power, (b) by the construction of the influencing machine as a summation of some or all of the pathologically altered organs (the whole body) projected outward. It is to be noted that among these organs the genitals take precedence in the projection.

The assumption of an influx of libido into specific organs in the physiological sense of the word should receive proper consideration. On the basis of this assumption transient swellings of organs often observed in schizophrenia without inflammation and without an actual œdema may be interpreted as equivalents of erection, produced like erections of the penis and clitoris by an overflow of secretion resulting from libidinal charging of organs.[14]

VI

It is not at all surprising that the hostile apparatus is handled by persons who to an objective observer cannot but appear as love objects—suitors, lovers, physicians. All these persons are associated with sensuousness, deal with the body, and demand a transfer of libido to themselves. This is what actually occurs in normal situations. But the narcissistic libido, whenever too strongly fixated, cannot but regard this demand made by love objects as inimical, and looks upon the object as an enemy. It is to be noted, however, that another group of love objects—mother, the patient's present physician, close friends of the family—are not counted among the patient's persecutors but among the persecuted, compelled to share his fate in being subjected to the influencing machine. In contrast to paranoia, the persecuted and not the persecutors are organized into a passive conspiracy, and this conspiracy is of passive nature. Of this phenomenon the following explanation may be offered:

It is noteworthy that the persecutors are all persons who live at some distance from the patient, whereas the persecuted belong to the closest circle of acquaintanceship and—including the physicians who are imagos of the father and hence also family members—represent a kind of constantly present family. Now, the family members are those love objects who because of their presence from the beginning of the patient's life are subjected to the narcissistic object choice by identification. To these persons our patient still applies this form of object choice in so far as she subjects them to her own fate, identifying herself with them. Normally, the demand for transfer of libido with respect to members of the family is not felt either as requiring the overcoming of any great distance or any substantial sacrifice of narcissism. In establishing an identification with these persons the patient follows a well-trodden path, which does not appear sufficiently inimical to the patient to force her to revolt against the cathexis of these objects and to regard them as hostile. It is different with lovers and suitors. These threaten a narcissistic position with their substantial demands for object libido and are, therefore, repulsed as enemies. The fact that these persons are spatially distant evokes a feeling of distance on the part of the libido. The transfer of libido *par distance* is felt as an extraordinarily strong demand for the acknowledgment of an object position, as a demand for self-denial. This also holds for normal conditions. Spatial distance separating the beloved threatens the object libido; it even leads people ultimately to withdraw themselves and give up the object. To have to love at a distance is a difficult task, only unwillingly performed. Our patient, however, cannot simply give up her love objects in a normal way, because she has not cathected them normally. To those demanding much from her she can only react with the paranoid mechanism; to those demanding less, only with identification. I do not know why the persons who work the influencing machine are in my observations exclusively male. This may be due to faulty observation or to chance. Further investigations must clarify this point. However, that heterosexual objects can appear as persecutors in contradiction to Freud's theory of the exclusively homosexual genesis of paranoia, may be explained by the fact that the influencing machine corresponds to a regressive psychic stage in which the important distinction is not between the sexes but between narcissistic and object libido, and every object demanding a transfer of libido is regarded as hostile irrespective of its sex.

VII

After this long digression—which, I hope, will not be regarded as super-fluous—we may return to the question of how even the ordinary, clinically familiar, influencing machine in its typical form can be a projection of the patient's body, as was true in the case of Miss Natalija. The answer should not be difficult to discover. If we do not want to assume that the machine has been established by successive substitutions of the parts of the patient's idea of his own body picture (''*wie Fuchs aus alopex*''),[15] and if we make use, instead of the genitality of the machine, as previously established, to explain the typical influencing machine, we may avail ourselves of the following considerations:

The regression of libido to the early infantile stage determines the re-transformation of the meanwhile genitally centralized libido into the pregenital stage, in which the entire body is a libidinal zone—in which the entire body is a genital. Such fantasies are also found in cases of narcissistically strongly cathected, sexually extremely infantile, neurosis. I have myself observed such cases. The fantasy originates in the intrauterine (mother's body) complex and usually has the content of the man's desire to creep completely into the genital from which he came, refusing to content himself with any lesser satisfaction. The entire individual is in this case a penis. Further, the road of identification with the father (the penis of the father) is overdetermined in the symptom formation of male patients. The symptom is also to be conceived as regression to a stage of diffuse narcissistic organ libido and is in most cases associated with genital impotence. The genital, too, is renounced.[16] The same situation is revealed by the lack of genitalia in the influencing machine of Miss N. The intrauterine fantasy and the identification[17] with mother probably find expres-sion in the dome-like lid of the trunk which perhaps represented the patient's mother during pregnancy. The enclosed batteries are perhaps the child, which is the patient herself. The fact that the child is equated with the batteries, that is, with a machine, lends further support to the supposition that the person feels himself to be a genital, and this all the more because the machine's lack of genitalia stands for the pregenital—in a certain sense, non-genital stage.

The construction of the influencing apparatus in the form of a machine therefore represents a projection of the entire body, now wholly a genital.

The fact that the machine in dreams is nothing but a representation of the genital raised to primacy in no way contradicts the possibility that it is in schizophrenia a symbol of the entire body conceived as a penis, and hence a representative of the pregenital epoch. The patient has indeed not lost the ideational content of his past life. The picture of the genital as a representation of sexuality has been retained in the psychical apparatus. It is therefore used as a means of representation, a mode of expression, a language in which phenomena existing prior to this means of expression are communicated. Here the genital is merely a symbol of a sexuality older than the symbolism and than any means of social expression. The picture, then, is in the language of the later genital period nothing but: "I am sexuality". But the context is, "I am wholly a genital". This test has of course to be translated into the language suited to the actual libido conditions.

It is possible that the ordinary influencing apparatus in the form of the machine owes its existence simply to the fact that its early stages were not formed gradually, because the pathological process seized too precipitately upon remote phases of existence. It is also possible that the early stages were not noticed by observers and not reported by the patient, or not recognized and evaluated as early stages. Thus the connection between the influencing apparatus of Miss N. and the ordinary influencing machine has been lost to science.

But the contradiction between the two concepts—on the one hand, that the machine form of the influencing apparatus originated through successive distortions of the influencing apparatus that represents the projection of the body, and, on the other hand, that the machine form of the influencing apparatus represents, like the machine in a dream, a projection of the genitalia, is now abolished. The evolution by distortion of the human apparatus into a machine is a projection that corresponds to the development of the pathological process which converts the ego into a diffuse sexual being, or—expressed in the language of the genital period—into a genital, a machine independent of the aims of the ego and subordinated to a foreign will.[18] It is no longer subordinated to the will of the ego, but dominates it. Here, too, we are reminded of the astonishment of boys when they become aware for the first time of erection. And the fact that the erection is shortly conceived as an exceptional and mysterious feat, supports the assumption that erection is felt to be a thing independent of the ego, a part of the outer world not completely mastered.

NOTES

1. This patient's words, "Sich verstellt"—taken literally, mean "moves himself from one place to another".

2. Tausk, Victor: *Zur Psychologie des alkohol. Beschäftigungsdelir.* Int. Ztsch. f. Psa. III, 1915.
3. Published in Int. Ztsch. f. Psa. II, 1914. P. 466. Miss N. dreams: I am seated on an upper bench in the surgical amphitheatre. Below a woman is being operated on. She lies with her head towards me, but I cannot see the head, as it seems to be concealed by the lower benches. I see the woman only from her chest down. I see both thighs and a heap of white towels and linens. I see nothing else clearly.
   Analysis of the dream reveals that the dreamer sees herself as the woman operated on. A few days before the night of the dream, the dreamer called on a young physician who made advances to her. On this occasion she was reclining on a couch. The physician raised her skirts and while he operated ''below'', she perceived the heap of white underclothes overhead. Just as much as she saw of herself in this situation, she sees of the woman in the dream, and the woman's head in the actual situation. According to Freud, the ''woman without a head'' in a dream represents the mother. The basic reason for this interpretation will not be discussed here, but will be treated in another section of this paper.
4. This would fall into the period before the first successful lie, which occurs very early in infancy. Lies fabricated in the first year of life are nothing unusual; they can be observed especially in children who resist the regular elimination of bodily wastes when, by means of grimaces, gestures and inarticulated words, they mislead the training person into believing that they have had satisfactory evacuation. The educator who allows herself to be deceived by the child must ultimately look to divine guidance in order to keep the child within the truth, when the latter, to gain forbidden pleasure, begins to enjoy the practice of lying. Very soon the time arrives when recourse to the highest authority of omniscience becomes necessary. The introduction of the omniscient God in the educational system becomes, indeed, a necessity, since, de facto, children learn to lie from parents and upbringers, who by misrepresentations and unkept promises make the child obey and teach him to disguise his true purposes. In order to safeguard the success of education, teachers cannot but transfer the power of omniscience to God—an authority which they themselves have abandoned. The incomprehensible nature of this deity precludes the possibility of practicing deception on him. Nevertheless, many children do not submit even to this authority, continually test their God with regard to his omniscience, and not infrequently actually succeed in unmasking him as a phantom of the dethroned parental, specifically paternal, power.
5. In the discussion of this paper at the Vienna Psychoanalytic Society, Freud emphasized that the infant's conception that others knew its thoughts has its source in the process of learning to speak. Having obtained its language from others, the infant has also received thoughts from them; and the child's feeling that others know his thoughts as well as that others have ''made'' him the language and, along with it, his thoughts, has, therefore, some basis in reality.
6. The cases in which inhibition endangers the intellect primarily are to be attributed to dementia.
7. The projection of the libido position of the psychic ego produces the symptoms of simple paranoia, the mechanism of which was discovered by Freud. In what follows we shall omit from consideration the fact that ego-libido is necessarily homosexual in its strivings, that is, attracted by the sex which the ego itself represents. We shall describe briefly only one mechanism, which appears to be out of harmony with object-libido and which is exemplified by the symptomatology of our patient, Miss Natalija.
   The patient reports: After she had rejected her suitor, she felt that he suggested that her mother and she strike up a friendship with his sister-in-law, so that the patient might be more amenable to a later proposal on his part. What appears here as suggestion on the suitor's part is nothing more than the projection of the patient's own unconscious inclination to accept the

proposal of marriage. She had rejected the proposal not without inner conflict and had vacillated between accepting and rejecting her suitor. She gave realization in action to the rejection, while she projected her inclination to accept the proposal on to the object of her conflicting desires and made it appear as the sensory effect of an influence on the part of the object, or in other words as her symptom.

The patient was ambivalent towards her suitor, and projected one side of the conflict, the positive libidinal one, while manifesting in action the negative side, the rejection, because this procedure was in conformity with her ego. The choice, which in this instance has projection as its outcome, may in other cases be the reverse one. Here I am merely calling attention to the mechanism of partial projection of ambivalent tendencies.

A special contribution to the subject of the projection mechanism, which also made me aware of this principle, was made by Dr. Helene Deutsch in her discussion of this paper at the Vienna Psychoanalytic Society. A schizophrenic patient had the feeling that her friends always laid down their work when she herself began to work and that they sat down whenever she stood up; in brief, that others were always performing the opposite of what she herself was doing. The patient merely felt this; she could not possibly see it, since she was blind. Dr. Deutsch regarded the symptom as a projection of one or two tendencies present in every one of her patient's actions—namely, the tendency to do and the tendency not to do. This interpretation was confirmed by cases presented by other discussers. On this occasion Freud proposed the formulation that it is ambivalence that makes the projection mechanism possible. Once expressed, this thesis appears self-evident. It has a corollary in another contention of Freud's, to the effect that ambivalence produces repression. This has as its natural consequence the formulation mentioned, above, since only what is repressed is projected, in so far as boundaries between the unconscious and the conscious still obtain. The entire problem furnishes special justification for Bleuler's term "schizophrenia".

The present paper shows how, albeit unconsciously, I had been demonstrating Freud's formulation.

8. Freud has already indicated in his paper on the Schreber biography, that the libido in schizophrenia is located at a stage even earlier than autoeroticism. I arrive at the same conclusion by a different route, and I take the liberty of presenting this fact as proof of the correctness of Freud's contentions.

9. Many patients are actually aware of this regression to infancy and to the embryonic stage—the latter, though, only as a threat of further illness. A patient said to me: "I feel that I am constantly becoming younger and smaller. Now I am four years old. Shortly, I shall get into diapers and then back into mother."

Dr. Helene Deutsch, during the discussion of this paper, reported the case of a thirty-one-year-old female schizophrenic who wet and soiled her bed and stated as her justification that "they were making a baby of her".

On the same occasion Freud, referring especially to the influencing machine of Miss Natalija, and to the interchangeability of sexuality and death, called attention to the significance of the mode of burial of Egyptian mummies. To place the mummy in a case resembling the human body suggests the idea of the return to "mother earth", the return to the mother's body in death. Freud's reference shows how as a compensation for the bitterness of death, men take for granted the bliss of existence in the uterus. The fantasy of return to the uterus is, then, an atavistic one, a preformed fantasy, and as such it may be added to the "primal fantasies" postulated by Freud. This fantasy appears symptomatically in schizophrenia as the pathological reality of the regressing, disintegrating psyche. The mummy returns to the mother's body by physical, and the schizophrenic by psychical death. (*"Mutterleibsphantasie"*—an expression, as far as I know, first used by Gustav Grüner.)

10. For further discussion of this subject, see Freud: *Metapsychologische Ergänzung zur Traum-*

lehre. Int. Ztsch. f. Psa. VI, 1916/1917. (Translated in *Coll. Papers* IV, 137–152.) This work appeared while the present paper was in proofs. I am pleased to be able to refer to the many points of agreement between my contentions and Freud's in his paper, of which I had no knowledge at the time.

11. Melancholia is the illness, the mechanism of which consists in the disintegration of psychic narcissism, in the renunciation of love for the psychic ego. Melancholia, in pure culture, is the paradigm of the dependence of the organic upon the psychic narcissism. The separation of libido from the psychic ego, i.e., the rejection and condemnation of the *raison d'être* of the psychic person, brings with it the rejection of the physical person, the tendency to physical self-destruction. There occurs a consecutive separation of the libido from those organs which guarantee the functioning and the value of the physical individuality, a separation by means of which the organs' function is impaired or given up. Hence appetite is lost, constipation occurs, menstruation ceases, and potency is lost—all as a result of unconscious mechanisms. This failure of function is to be traced to the destruction of the respective organic libido positions which are essentially vegetative, i.e., unconscious; it is thus to be strictly differentiated from the conscious, deliberate suicidal tendency expressed in refusal of nourishment or in activities inimical to life.

Melancholia is the persecution psychosis without projection; its structure is due to a specific mechanism of identification. (Further discussion on this point in my paper *Diagnostische Erörterungen auf Grund der Zustandsbilder der sogen. Kriegspsychosen.* Wiener med. Wochenschrift XXXVII-XXXVIII, 1916. While this paper was in proof, Freud's article *Trauer und Melancholie* [translated in *Coll. Papers* IV, 152–173] appeared, to which I refer in this connection.)

12. This involves the Freudian principle of the erotogenicity of organs, that is, of the erotogenic zones.

13. Dr. Otto Pötzl suggested on a certain occasion (I do not remember whether it was in connection with a thesis of his own or as an addendum to theories of others) that the catatonic stare is an expression of the patient's inability to apportion his motor impulses disintegrated by the split of his volition into agonistic and antagonistic elements, so that a purposeful action may again be performed.

Pötzl's conception is in harmony with the psychoanalytic theory that the regressive narcissistic libido undergoes a pathological division with the cathexis of the individual functions of the psyche and the organs, so that the agonistic and antagonistic portions of the purposefully directed antithetical pair of forces are brought into the reach of awareness by the disturbance of the equilibrium between their respective libido quantities and are deprived of automatic functioning. This would be a special case of hypochondria and estrangement related to the antithetical pairs of forces with their respective specific consequences.

Pötzl's view does not contradict the assumption that the outer world may be eliminated as a result of regressive narcissistic libido, and it actually allows the application of the theory of hypochondria to further special points in the psycho-physical make-up of men. Pötzl's concept even suggests the hypothesis that there was in the life of man a period—a not definitely determinable one, it is true, and perhaps only potential—in which the activity of the antagonistic pair of forces was still automatic and had to be discovered and learned by the person himself as if from an alien outer world. This period may well be present in ontogenesis only as an "engram" of phylogenetic stages which comprised the origin of the now complex motor organs from the simplest, single-tracked active formations. Regression in schizophrenia would then be traceable to those "engrams" of the oldest era of the race, and the theory would demand that these phylogenetic traces of function retain their capacity for being reactivated. We must not shrink from this hypothesis. It provides us with another idea to use in investigating problems in schizophrenia: perhaps this remarkable disease consists in just this—that the phylogenetic vestiges of function retain in many individuals an extraordinary capacity for being reactivated. Psychoanalysis would have to make room for this conception, since psychoanalysis has already in many instances uncovered the roots of symptoms in the history of the species. From this it may perhaps be possible, via ontogenesis, to proceed to an explanation of the mysterious "electrical currents" complained of by patients. This par-æsthesia may once have been a sensation that accompanied the first nerve and muscle functions. It is perhaps a reminiscence of the sensation of the newly born being who enters the strange air of the external world out of the comfortable covering of the mother's womb, or for whom the latter is replaced by its first garments. The bed he first lay in, is perhaps that one which comes to the patient's consciousness when he feels himself, while lying in bed, electrified by invisible wires.

14. These psychological assumptions are strongly supported from the organological standpoint by a report made some years ago by Fauser at Stuttgart on the presence of sexual secretion in the blood of dementia præcox patients, as demonstrated by Abderhalden's dialytic method. New and important findings in this connection are to be expected from Steinach's experiments. When the present paper was completed, there appeared in the Münchner mediz. Wochenschrift, No. 6, 1918, under the title *Umstimmungen der Homosexualität durch Austausch der Pubertätsdrüsen* ("Transformations of Homosexuality by Exchange of Puberty Glands"), a very interesting and significant article by Steinach and Lichtenstern, which realized these expectations. After the completion of this paper there also appeared in the Internationale Zeitschrift f. ärztl. Psa. Volume IV, 1917, an article by S. Ferenczi, *Von Krankheits- und Pathoneurosen* ("Disease- or Patho-Neuroses", in *Further Contributions to the Theory and Technique of Psychoanalysis*, p. 78–89. London, 1926) in which the assumption of the libidinal cathexis of individual organs in the sense above described appears to be applied with notable success.

15. "Like fox from alopex"—a student parody on etymological derivations consisting of the stringing together of rhyming and nearly rhyming words.—TRANSLATOR.

16. This renunciation of the genitalia is felt by the male schizophrenic as a loss of virility, which is "drained off" from him, or else as a direct transformation into a woman, corresponding to the infantile notion of boys that there is only one kind of genital, namely their own, and that those of women are the result of castration and really represent a loss of the genital. The castration complex is often combined with the infantile identification of semen with urine resulting from urethral eroticism. I have observed an attack of castration anxiety while catheterizing a schizophrenic who refused to empty his bladder. He maintained that I was practicing coitus with him by means of the catheter and that I had emptied him of all his semen. Thus his retention of urine appears as a refusal to yield semen, representing his virility. The patient's playing with excrement is explicable by the narcissistically rooted conception that fæces and urine are parts of the body. Coprophagia is not inhibited by the thought that the excreta are nothing else than the body from which they come.

17. The proof of this identification derived from symbolic language has already been given in the dream of "the woman without a head", footnote, page 532.

18. Indeed, the machines produced by man's ingenuity and created in the image of man are unconscious projections of man's bodily structure. Man's ingenuity seems to be unable to free itself from its relation to the unconscious.

4. Narcissism and Defensive Processes in Schizophrenic States

Thomas Freeman

The purpose of this paper is to examine once again the processes of defence in schizophrenic states and their relationship to the various forms of mental activity which underlie the clinical phenomena. The concept of defence was introduced by Freud (4) as a result of his study of dreams and psychoneurotic symptoms. In both groups of phenomena he described the unconscious mental conflict which occurs between instinctual wishes on the one hand and ethical and moral standards on the other. As long as the defensive forces maintain the upper hand dreams adequately protect sleep and anxiety does not become a source of distress in waking life. However, once the defences have become inadequate anxiety leads to further measures which end in symptoms. The model upon which symptom formation is based is that of the dream. Both are compromises between conflicting forces and their mental representation is such as to keep their real significance unconscious.

Psychoneurotic symptoms are the equivalent of unconscious mental conflicts. Can the same be said for the signs and symptoms of schizophrenic reactions? One method of studying this problem is to examine the defensive processes which occur in these classes of mental illness and observe their relationship to the symptom complex. However, the relationship of symptoms to the repressed in schizophrenic states is only one aspect of a more general question. This concerns the manner in which the defences interact with the mental processes which lead to the cognitive disturbances and to the other signs which are characteristic of this group of diseases. It is this topic which will be the principal subject matter of this paper.

CLINICAL MATERIAL

I

The first patient is a nurse of 21 years old who was admitted to hospital on account of the sudden appearance of psychotic symptoms. She announced that she was due to be married (quite untrue) and that she was being desexualized by machines in the operating theatre. When she arrived in hospital the latter ideas had disappeared, but she had developed an extreme form of egocentrism which was characterized by the conviction that everything that happened was of special significance. During interviews it was noted that she was slow and dreamy in her behaviour. Her flow of talk was punctuated by pauses and halts. She had to be encouraged to talk. She rarely kept to the subject in hand and wandered along apparently irrelevant series of associations.

The first excerpt from this patient's material is derived from an interview which took place about four months after admission to hospital. At this meeting she was quiet and withdrawn, showing her usual disinclination to communicate. It is important to add that at this particular time the patient's statements were being recorded in a notebook. Half way through the session she interrupted her silence by saying that she was thinking about the drug Largactil (Chlorpromazine). She was asked what made her think of this drug. She said the three R's—reading, writing and arithmetic. As this did not clarify the matter she was again asked the same question. This time she explained that she split the word into three parts, Larg . . . Act . . . Til.

The first part of the word was associated with the three R's, the second with 'putting on an act', and the third with the till in the hospital canteen. The matter was clarified further by the recognition that she had been looking at a container of Largactil tablets. Her associations revealed, however, that this was not the sole determinant for the selection and communication of this particular idea. With encouragement she was able to reveal her concern about the recording of her utterances and her belief that the doctor was putting on an act specially for her benefit. With this she was able to disclose that she believed that all the doctors, nurses, and patients were acting special parts.

This material illustrates the patient's reactions to anxiety aroused by the interview situation. At this period the transference was due to a displacement from the patient's grandfather, who was stern and severe. Unlike the psycho-neurotic patient she was unable to find a substitutive expression for the pre-conscious transference thoughts in some apparently indifferent series of remarks.

The second illustration reveals some of the patient's delusional ideas. She believed that her uncle, friends, and a former headmaster were influencing events in the ward with a special purpose relevant to herself. She explained that statements on the radio and television and other significant events had convinced her that the ultimate aim of these 'helpers' was to reunite her with her father, whom she had not seen since early childhood. She went so far as to say that one of the doctors was 'training' her by means of special signs to become a ship's nurse so that she could travel to the Far East where her father was living.

Following this she complained that the coughing of other patients troubled her. When asked why, she said it made her think of Plymouth and father. The elucidation of this strange reply was as follows. While knitting in the ward somebody coughed. 'Ply' was a reference to a type of wool, and 'mouth' had to do with coughing—hence Plymouth. As a small child she had spat—again the mouth—at father; thus the association Plymouth and father. There was a possibility that the stimulus for this series of associations was the interviewer's coughing. If this was so, then an element of transference was buried in these communications.

II

A review of this material permits the elaboration of the following hypothesis. The interview situation described in the first excerpt led to an outbreak of anxiety following upon the development of a predominantly superego transference. As in the neuroses, anxiety acted as a signal, leading to the initiation of defensive processes. The major defence was regression, affecting both the instinctual drives and the ego organization.

When the clinical phenomena are examined they can be divided into two groups: first, disturbances of cognition resulting from ego regression, and second, data which can be regarded as the result of narcissism. The cognitive abnormalities are to be located principally in the spheres of the thought and perceptual processes. The patient's announcement that she was thinking of Largactil was the result of a displacement of cathexis from preconscious fears about the interview situation to an apparently irrelevant verbal idea. In this instance displacement acts as a defence, as it would in a neurotic or healthy individual. The difference between the two lies in the selection of the verbal idea and in the manner in which it was manipulated. The choice of idea, apparently selected at random from a host of visual percepts, was determined by contents already active in the patient's mind. The fragmentation of the word and its numerous associations—the interviews, the person of the physician, and the delusional ideas—reveal the extensive degree of condensation which this verbal idea allowed. In this respect the relationship of the verbal idea—Largactil—to the preconscious thoughts can be compared to that which exists between the manifest content of a dream and the latent dream thoughts.

In the second illustration condensation and displacement operated to conceal from both patient and doctor certain preoccupations which caused anxiety. In both examples the patient was unable to continue a train of thought to its conclusion. Such sequences of thought were interrupted by visual and auditory percepts, the causes of which could sometimes be discovered. On other occasions it was anxiety which disrupted the thought sequence. As in the material presented, these pauses were followed by associations with little connexion with what went before. Only through questioning could the connecting links be found which eventually led to the preconscious thoughts.

The phenomena which can be categorized as narcissistic comprise those ideas whose content consisted in the belief that she was the centre of special activities. These activities were referred to by the patient in her statement that everyone was acting. Reference has been made to her belief that one particular doctor was training her to be a ship's nurse. Associated with this delusional idea was the further notion that the hospital ward was organized like a ship. The number of beds added up to the number of letters comprising the name of a shipping line, and the behaviour of the nurses and patients was as if they were on a boat. She revealed that she had the feeling that the officers of this shipping line with whom she identified the medical staff were arranging a marriage for her with a captain of the self-same line.

In this case the delusions consisted of wishful phantasies which had assumed reality for the patient. The narcissistic regression explained the omnipotence of thought which enabled her to believe that her wishes were in fact coming true. These delusional ideas served to protect the patient from the painful thought that in fact she was without immediate prospects of marriage, and in this respect the defence of reversal was operative. The delusions also served to explain the strange happenings which she was experiencing and which could be attributed to the extreme degree of egocentricism (narcissism). The content of the delusions was taken from phantasies derived from the Oedipus complex.

Delusions with a similar type of wish-fulfilling content were also observed in a chronic schizophrenic patient who asserted (i) that he was the only living Saint; (ii) that he was a famous poet; (iii) that he had sacrificed his girl friend on account of (i) and (ii). These delusions served as a defence (reversal) against the knowledge that he was not saintly (owing to guilt over masturbation), that he was a very mediocre poet, and lastly, that the girl friend had given him up.

In both patients the ego regression and the regression to narcissism called out new psychical formations—the delusions—in order to restore some form of adaptation to the world of objects and simultaneously to banish the pain of disappointment. In the case of the young nurse continued activity of the superego interfered with these wish-fulfilments by leading to anxiety and guilt. It was this superego pressure that initiated the series of phenomena described in the first excerpt. The regression which took place did not lead, as it occasionally does, to the dissolution of the superego or to an extensive disruption of the ego organization. The latter was limited to a partial break-through of the primary process, leading to a cognitive state reminiscent of that which occurs in sleep and permits the construction of dreams.

III

The second case is that of a woman of 40 who, until the present time (1962), has been in hospital for a period of nine years. Her illness began quite suddenly. She was married, with two children, and her husband was an engineer in the oil industry. They had been living in Persia until political crises led to the evacuation of the families of British employees of the oil company. Some months later the patient's husband also returned to the United Kingdom. After they resumed life together the patient began to accuse her husband of infidelity. There was reality in these reproaches, and eventually her husband went off with another woman. It was reported that she had become increasingly lethargic and disinterested. She neglected the house and the children; she was forgetful and self-preoccupied. When she was admitted to hospital she continually criticized her husband. She complained of feeling vaguely unwell, but apart from this no obvious psychotic symptomatology was apparent for some weeks. Gradually evidences of thought disorder, hallucinatory experiences, and inappropriate affect were obtained. The diagnosis of schizophrenia was made. Insulin coma treatment had no effect upon the condition.

During her long stay in hospital this patient's behaviour has been characterized by alternating phases of withdrawal and of restless aggressiveness. In the latter phases she complained that other patients, medical and nursing staff were interfering with her body, brain, and identity. Physically she was generally thin and pale. A typical example of her thought content is as follows: 'That's not me' (looking at herself in the mirror). 'They put me inside people while I'm sitting on a chair. That's not me . . . dirty face, dirty teeth, dirty brain, dirty thoughts. Animals take you, that's what they do.' When asked what she meant by this she said 'They put me in T.V. A big crocodile took a man in the swamp' (this was a reference to a film on television the day before) . . . 'it took me. The face said it was taking me even though I was sitting. I had a bad night last night. I went to sleep with someone else's head. That's what they do to me . . . I don't like Miss X' (another patient), 'she puts dirty thoughts in my mind. She rams in Eastern thoughts and things that appear on T.V. They can see everything that goes on in me. I'm a fool. I go on sitting. I don't want to be taken sexually because I'm not made right. It's a trick of the mind, I can't take, it's only afterwards I know.'

In the restless phases she would march up and down the ward shouting abuse at patients and staff. The following excerpt illustrates the disturbance in form and content of her thought processes: 'They are dirty, Persian Oil and Glasgow Royal.' She came to a halt and fixed her eyes on a picture—a print of 'The Man in Armour'. She shouted out at the picture 'You are dirty, getting inside me'. She lifted the picture from the wall and smashed it on the floor. When asked why she had done this she said 'I will not take the responsibility of that, it was you. The doctor is to blame in Glasgow Royal. Glass is a mere detail.' Later she added 'I will not be responsible, they are playing different parts, I'm never me.' When the incident was discussed with her later she appeared to be very pleased with herself and could not stop laughing. She said 'I like the man in the picture'. 'I like his appearance.'

In order to structure the situation and thus obtain material which might throw light on the immediate cause of the disturbed phases the nurse in the ward began to have daily discussions with the patient. These discussions were regularly reported and their content assessed. The nurse/patient relationship extended over a period of three to four months and then had to be terminated.

When the daily meetings began the patient was menstruating. She was noisy, abusive, and the content of her thought followed the lines described above. Typical of this phase was the statement 'Oil is behind it all'. With the cessation of her menses she became progressively quieter and was easier to contact. She was, however, still resentful of her hospitalization and she remained forgetful and generally inconsistent in behaviour. After about a month there were signs that some form of relationship between patient and nurse was developing. Not only was she more co-operative, but she said to another nurse, 'I know you, nurse, I like you, you brought me up here from Ward 3.'

She remained in this positive quiescent phase for several weeks. She told the nurse all about her husband's infidelity and how he had gone off with another woman. She emphasized that this woman had been much cleverer than she and very much better educated. These revelations were followed by a period of depression. She sat with closed eyes. When asked why she did this she said 'There's nothing for me to see, there's nothing for me.' She refused to wash and comb her hair. This phase passed, and she seemed much better. She said to the nurse 'You are a nice girl . . . sometimes I am nice, sometimes they are pleased with me.'

Her better period did not last long. She was disappointed by a visitor not arriving, and the next day was aggressive and difficult. She refused to eat, saying 'I do not require to eat food. They are inside me eating the food.' The more aggressive she became, the more persecuted she felt from both internal and external sources. She repeatedly announced that her husband left her because of the other woman's education and intelligence. Some days later she said 'I wish I had been educated to be a nurse or something.'

The disturbed phase continued throughout and after the next menstrual period. She continued to be preoccupied with education. She said 'I read so I can be educated like a nurse. You see I'm not educated in skins and hair and things like that.' Gradually she quietened down, but within a week or two she began to show obvious hostility to the nurse. She shouted angrily 'You won't get away with this much longer, I will see to that'. The next day she was in a similar mood. She had the following outburst: 'You can't make me a nurse, it's a dirty profession.' Later she added 'You are my slave—you are a big black slave and I'm a lady—don't forget that . . . you can't make me a nurse.'

IV

A review of the material suggests that an initial positive attachment to the nurse was replaced by jealousy, envy, and rivalry. In order to clarify the transference situation which developed it is important to point out that the patient had predominantly positive feelings towards the ward doctor who had had occasional interviews with her in earlier months. It was clear from what she said that she identified the doctor with her husband and the nurse with the other woman. She believed that her lack of intelligence and education led to the doctor's being interested in the nurse and thus as uninterested in her as had been the case with her husband. She wanted to be intelligent and educated, and to be as fortunate as the nurse. The penis envy in this woman was intense, and this envy had been displaced to the intellectual sphere. She had in fact married a man who was comparatively well educated and came from a social class higher than her own. Both he and the ward doctor could be regarded as narcissistic object choices—and more specifically the longed-for penis. Her early childhood environment must have predisposed towards this penis envy, because she was the only girl in a family of five. The 'castration' problems were to be seen in her disturbance at menstruation, which she periodically denied. The menses enhanced the crushing sense of inferiority which was already present.

The disappointment, envy, and jealousy led to hate which turned the patient's relationship with the nurse from positive to negative. However, this was not all. The hate was countered by regression. This regression affected the ego and also the instinctual basis of object relationships. With regard to the former there was a disruption of the self-representations, the patient no longer having any assurance about her own identity. The thought processes fell under the sway of the primary process, as in the examples given above. The statement 'Oil is mental' was a condensation product which contained hostile thoughts against her husband, the doctor, and everything associated with her unhappy life experiences. Perceptual processes were also involved. She could not discriminate herself from other objects, nor could she discriminate the perception of one object from another. This was clear in the example of the television programme to which she referred.

The ego regression also led to a breakdown of the counter-cathexes directed against the drives. She attempted to deal with this by projection—'They put dirty thoughts in my mind' or 'They make me lie down on a couch and put a pillow under my hips' (this was the position she adopted in intercourse with her husband). These ideas and concomitant auditory hallucinations led to outbursts of hate; in this she identified with the aggressor. Many of these libidinal outbursts were as frequently homosexual as heterosexual in their origins. The latter could be traced to her attachment to the ward doctor. Finally the ego regression led to a loss of body boundaries—a state akin to primary identification.

The regression affecting the instinctual basis of object relations led to a backward movement going far beyond the pathological narcissistic state which is to be observed in all psychotic reactions. Nevertheless her narcissism was obvious, as in the case when she referred to the nurse as a slave. The regression could be thought of as extending to the auto-erotic phase where objects no longer exist. In this case such an auto-erotic fixation was only temporary, and then the patient regained some form of object relationships. In this respect the object cathexis may have been the expression of restitutional tendencies.

As the patient's material indicated, the restitutional measures undertaken—the defences—were as follows. First projection and denial—by these means she ignored the origin of her feelings and wishes and thus attributed them to objects outside herself. Second, by a special form of regression—topographic regression—painful memories and the verbal representation of drives were given a hallucinatory quality. Ideas and memories were converted into auditory and visual percepts. An instance of this was the hallucination which commanded her to lie on the couch in a coital posture.

V

It is of particular interest to compare the defensive manoeuvres of this patient with those of a female psychoneurotic patient under similar conditions. A psychoneurotic patient in psychoanalytic treatment may develop a transference relationship identical with the one described above. Rivalry, envy, and jealousy based upon penis envy may occur with no less intensity. What defences would operate here? The transference hate and the phantasies through which it finds representation may be repressed. Alternatively this hatred may be defensively introjected into the superego, leading to depression of mood and self-criticism. A further possibility is the displacement of the hatred and the envy on to a figure outside the analysis—acting out in the transference. At no time, however, would the defence take the form of a serious ego and instinctual regression. The neurotic patient would not abandon object cathexes. The absence of an instinctual and ego regression and the retaining of objects would appear to be the decisive difference between the pyscho-neurotic reaction on the one hand and the schizophrenic patient on the other.

VI

Clinical phenomena of the type presented above support the theory that in schizophrenic states regression must be considered the principal defensive process. The regression inevitably leads to a reinstatement of a narcissistic position following upon the withdrawal and reinstinctualization of object cathexes. A regressive trend may also affect the ego organization and lead to a further series of clinical manifestations. In the first patient the ego defect was expressed in the area of the thought processes, although there was some evidence of a disturbance in perceptual processes as well.

The ego regression may have other consequences, as in the case of a 40-year-old paranoid schizophrenic woman who insisted that she was tortured by genital sensations. She believed that these sensations were not hers, but those of unknown men. She said that male genitals were literally inside her, and that the men were continually masturbating. At other times she believed that a woman was stimulating the man's penis. She further maintained that she could tell the kind of man it was from the sensations. Sometimes he was black, at other times thin, and sometimes fat. These beliefs could be correlated with the physician who was in charge of her case; in fact a black doctor, a thin and a fat doctor had looked after her on different occasions. At a later time she announced while in a state of 'narcissistic union' with one physician that the man whose genital was inside her was 'extremely brainy'.

Apart from the genital experiences the patient believed that she was the recipient of all the suffering in the world. If a woman was ill with chest pain she had chest pain; if another was in labour she experienced her labour pains. This patient's grandiosity revealed itself in numerous ways. When angry with a doctor she told him that those who went against her always ended in serious trouble, and she cited instances of this. She insisted that she was no ordinary patient, and her identification with Christ was clear in her assertion that she was born to bring peace to the world and as a result had to bear the sufferings of humanity.

In this case the ego regression led to alterations in the self-representations and to a loss of the boundaries of the self. Projection and denial enabled the patient to rid herself of the masturbatory conflict and assisted in the construction of her delusional ideas. It is possible to imagine that the weakened functional capacity of the ego boundary enabled her to introject a phantasy penis into the self-representation and thus deny castration anxiety. However, this process of introjection merely led to an intensification of the paranoid delusion. Such a defence, however, would have been impossible without a serious injury to the ego boundary.

An interpretation of this kind helps the clinician to understand why patients like this show such extreme resistance against gaining insight into the irrational nature of their beliefs. The resolution of the delusion would lead to a situation where the patient was brought face to face with the anxiety (due in these last two patients to phallic conflicts and castration fear) which had led to the regression in the first place. Here the economic point of view must be taken into account. It must surely be the flood of instinctual (de-neutralized) energy which can neither be discharged nor assimilated which eventually leads to the narcissistic regression and to ultimate delusion formation. Reduction of the level of instinctual tension can lead to the disappearance of the delusions. This indeed may be the mode of action of chlorpromazine and the phenothiazine group of drugs.

PROCESSES OF DEFENCE IN SCHIZOPHRENIC STATES

I

The unconscious conflicts which initiate symptom formation in the neuroses do not differ materially from those conflicts which precipitate schizophrenic reactions. The difference lies in the defensive reactions which ensue. In the former anxiety leads to a series of defensive manoeuvres, and sometimes to a regression from the oedipal to the preoedipal phase. In the latter the regression is of a completely different order.

It is instructive at this point to recall Freud's (5) classification of the phenomena which he conceptualized under the term 'regression'. First he distinguished between regression as it applies to the instinctual drives—in the biological sphere—and regression as it affects the ego organization. Second, he isolated three different categories of regression. Topographical regression is the process whereby cathectic changes lead to the replacement of verbal ideas by visual images as occurs in dreams. Temporal regression is the type of regression which may occur in cases of hysteria. Childlike behaviour and affective responses predominate during the acute phases of such illnesses alongside rational thought processes and complete insight into the fact of being ill. Transference neuroses are also instances of temporal regression. Finally formal regression is the process whereby differentiated mental processes are replaced by primitive means of mental representation.

The defence concept is the keystone of psychoanalytical psychopathology. In the neuroses there is ample opportunity to observe the operation of defence mechanisms activated by an almost wholly intact ego. Identifications, for example, are resolved into the appropriate object relations through the medium of the transference. Defence in psychotic reactions, however, is complicated by the fact that the very organization which initiates the defence is seriously injured by the disease process. This means that the types of defensive process available to the ego organization and their performance will alter in accordance with the extent of the psychotic process (2). Defensive processes in the early phase of a schizophrenic illness might be expected to differ in both their form and aims from those operative in the later and chronic stages of the disease.

In his first formulations of schizophrenia and paranoia Freud (6) suggested that the decisive factor is the regression of libido. This regression followed upon the withdrawal of libidinal cathexes from objects in the real world and from the intrapsychic object representations. The return of these cathexes to the self leads to a pathological narcissistic state in which the self is flooded with libidinal (instinctual) energy. In Freud's (6) view the first stages of the disease (the detachment and withdrawal of cathexes) occur silently. It is only the attempt to recathect the object world (restitutional phase) which leads to the major signs and symptoms of the disease.

Freud (6) proposed that the regression to narcissism was characteristic of paranoia. The projection mechanism had the function of defence and led to the construction of the persecutory delusions. In the case of schizophrenic states he suggested that the regression went beyond the narcissistic position and was located in the phase of autoerotism—a state prior to the beginnings of the self. In this hypothesis of a regression to autoerotism he was acknowledging the defects in ego functioning which are characteristic of the disease. He went on to propose that in schizophrenic states the restitutional tendency was due not to projection, as in paranoia, but to a hallucinatory mechanism, that is, the conversion of ideas and memory traces into visual and auditory percepts. This process was to be observed in the second case quoted above. Freud's hypothesis can therefore explain the frequent combination of persecutory delusions and other schizophrenic symptoms—the hallucinations and thought disorder.

In an early paper Freud (7) pointed out that the differences in symptomatology which are encountered in schizophrenic states can be accounted for by the extent of the libidinal detachment. He referred to the fact that the mental organization may not be wholly affected by the disease process. Thus three sets of phenomena can be discerned in the clinical picture: first, those representing what remains of the normal personality; second, those representing the detachment of the libido from objects; and third, those representing the trend towards recovery. If Freud's formulation is described in contemporary economic terms (9) the concept of libidinal withdrawal and detachment would be replaced by the withdrawal and detachment of neutralized object cathexes. This implies a simultaneous deneutralization of these cathexes with a return to their original instinctual quality. A similar de-neutralization would occur within the ego.

In the cases quoted certain phenomena were considered to result from an instinctual regression. This regression to narcissism comprised the principal defence against superego and ego anxiety. Other defence mechanisms can also be identified, amongst which could be listed displacement, denial, reversal, projection, and introjection. All these processes, however, occurred secondarily to the regression to narcissism. Other phenomena resulted from varying degrees of ego regression.

In the neuroses the aim of defence is to remove from consciousness all trace of the phantasies and wishes which have caused anxiety. The symptoms can be traced to these phantasies, and it is usually easy to observe the imprint of the repressed content upon the form and content of the symptoms. What is the position in schizophrenic reactions? Can a similar relationship be found between the repressed contents and the form and content of the psychotic symptoms?

The role of defence in the early phases of a schizophrenic illness can only be evaluated whenever there is a clear understanding of the different mental processes which are operative in the initial stages (Freud's phase one) of the disease. The regression to narcissism following upon withdrawal of object cathexes has two important results. First, it leads to a heightened egocentrism which is combined with a sense of omnipotence and omniscience. Magic thinking—omnipotence of thought—is characteristic of this state, and 'end of the world' delusions are to be frequently observed. Second, the heightened narcissism results in a pathological bodily sensibility. Some insights are provided into the strange and terrifying experiences which occur in the primary phase of schizophrenic reactions by chronic patients. When these patients have regained their capacity for verbal communications, as sometimes occurs, they report all manner of disturbances in the awareness of the body. In 1943 Bychowski (1) reported a number of clinical examples of this type. These upsets may affect the head or the trunk. Sometimes these patients will complain of having left their bodies or having disappeared. These bodily sensations are usually accompanied by disorders of visual perception. Other people have changed in appearance or they have disappeared—even rising up in the air before the patient's eyes. Associated with these phenomena are the world destruction phantasies and the loss of the capacity to differentiate oneself from objects. It is instructive to observe this constellation of phenomena—generally associated with the early phase of the disease—occurring in a patient whose illness is of many years standing. Sexual excitations may also reach a high level of intensity and become a source of serious distress to the patient, as occurred in the second case quoted above.

The ego is also affected by regression, but here it is important to consider the possibility that not all the clinical manifestations are necessarily due to regression. This distinction between regressive and non-regressive phenomena is even more pertinent in the second (restitutional) phase of the illness. There is a danger of regarding all the clinical data in schizophrenic reactions as being nothing more than the result of a regression to early phases of infantile development. Many years ago Schilder (12) sounded a cautionary note regarding this perhaps understandable tendency in psycho-analytical theorizing. Katan (10) has pointed out that there is no evidence to support the hypothesis that a psychotic reaction in adult life is based upon an infantile psychosis. This distinction which Katan makes is also reflected in his theory that the symptoms of the prepsychotic period are of a different order from the symptoms of the psychosis proper. In his opinion the patient while in the prepsychotic phase is still trying to regain the world of objects, but once the illness has developed this trend ceases, and is replaced by a preoccupation with the newly-created psychotic reality.

The breakdown of the ego resulting from regressive and non-regressive changes leads to a series of alterations in the functional level of attention, conceptual thinking, perceptual processes, and memory. The failure of countercathexes may lead to a breakthrough of the primary process. In the initial phase of the disease (Freud's phase one) the ego organization, although weakened, may still exploit the appearance of the primary process for defensive ends. This occurred in the first patient. Condensation and displacement were employed to conceal anxious thoughts just as they would in the dream. Behind the verbal idea 'Largactil' lay the wishes, fears, and phantasies which were to find a representation in the delusional ideas.

Visual and auditory hallucinations can be explained on the basis of a topographic regression. Wishes (drive-cathected ideas) are activated, but instead of their finding expression in phantasies they are experienced as percepts. This process probably occurs in both schizophrenic and non-schizophrenic psychoses. In the latter it is not uncommon to find that the patient hallucinates visually and auditorily the presence of a loved object, or of the therapist if the patient is in a treatment relationship.

The vast majority of hallucinatory phenomena are, however, more complicated than this. This complexity arises from the fact that the wishes which are aroused lead to anxiety and thus to the intrusion of defensive measures. In the second case quoted above the patient accused the others in the ward of throwing her husband and children at her. When asked to explain, she said the other patients were throwing pictures of her husband and children. She did not want this, as it was too painful. She had not seen them for many years. These visual hallucinations, it may be hypothesized, were the result of a wish to be once again with her family. The cathexes underlying these wishes awakened memories which were experienced as visual percepts. The patient denied their origin in herself and projected them because of their painful quality.

In other cases the superego enters the situation as a result of the anxiety and guilt which the drives arouse. This was particularly clear in another patient who hallucinated scenes of rape and violence. In this case the memory traces of parental intercourse were revived as percepts. In the second patient to whom reference was recently made the voices which told her to adopt a coital posture were also reacted to with rage and anger. A further patient who looked upon her doctor as her chief (sexual) persecutor complained bitterly that she was forced to endure a tingling sensation on her thigh because he was continually masturbating. These tactile hallucinations reinforced her delusional system.

Hallucinatory phenomena may be closely integrated with the remainder of the psychotic reality or they may be merely sporadic isolated experiences. In the former instance they are undoubtedly part of the restitutional process—the attempt to re-cathect objects. The hallucinatory experiences, however, derive their cathexes from dammed-up instinctual energy. They are essentially drive-cathected ideas—memory traces associated with heightened instinctual tension. Such hallucinations are therefore treated by the patients with the same condemnation as they apply to the drives themselves. In this respect these hallucinations comprise a form of the 'return of the repressed', Katan (11) has pointed out the economic function of hallucinations and their discharge function.

Hallucinations, whether auditory or visual, can be classified in two ways. First, according as they are or are not closely tied to the remainder of the psychotic reality, or are apparently independent and autonomous phenomena. In the former instance they must be regarded as fundamental aspects of the restitutional process. In the latter they may still represent the relationship to objects which have not yet been abandoned (de-cathected). Secondly, hallucinations may be classified according as they are or are not derived from forbidden wishes. If this is so the superego influence is apparent, and defensive processes such as denial and projection can be seen to be operative. It may be worth while to make these distinctions, as it would enable hallucinations to be differentiated in both the withdrawal and restitutional phases of schizophrenic illnesses.

In Freud's phase one the defence has the aim of ridding consciousness of the conflicts that provoke anxiety. The breakdown of stable counter-cathexes directed towards the instinct drives and the environment results in the employment of primitive defensive measures, amongst which may be numbered displacement, condensation, topographic regression, and projection. By such means a patient can hide his anxious and guilty thoughts from both himself and others. In this respect the defensive aim does not differ appreciably from that of the psychoneurotic patient. The clinical manifestations can be traced back to the conflict situation. The question is whether or not the same process holds good for the delusions and other signs of the established schizophrenic case.

II

Delusions and hallucinations are the outcome of restitutional processes. The newly-constructed psychotic reality consumes the cathexes which were previously directed to real objects. Through projection, denial, and often reversal the patient is able to ignore both the nature and origin of his drives on the one hand and superego reactions on the other. The content of the delusions and hallucinations can generally be related to the conflicts which participated in the precipitation of the illness. In as far as the conflicts are disowned, the delusions represent a form of defence analogous to the psycho-neurotic symptom. It is important, however, to recall that the delusion is not created by projection or denial. There are delusions in schizophrenic states which are not in any way related to projection. The content of such delusions comprises ideas of grandeur and omnipotence. While the content of these grandiose delusions can be regarded as serving a defensive function, it is nevertheless based upon the pathological narcissism which followed upon the instinctual regression. The fact that delusions do not always have a persecutory content indicates that the process of delusion formation should be considered apart from the content which it comprises.

Once the delusions and hallucinations are established, little effort is made to conceal the nature of the conflicts and phantasies which were associated with the onset of the illness. In this aspect the schizophrenic manifestations differ entirely from psychoneurotic symptoms, where the main purpose of defence is concealment of the repressed from consciousness. This difference is probably due to the failure of repression and other stable counter-cathexes in schizophrenic states. The preservation of the psychotic reality, however, ensures a continued repudiation of these openly expressed libidinal and aggressive phantasies. This preservation is dependent upon a continuous cathexis of new ideational material which will reinforce and strengthen the structure of the psychotic reality. Freud (8) has pointed out that this new material is derived from memory traces and from phantasies which the patient created in earlier times. It is often these phantasies which provide the main content of grandiose and wish-fulfilling delusions. Examples of this are provided by the chronic patient who believed he was a poet and also by the case of the young woman who believed she was to be a ship's nurse, at other times a ballet dancer, a model, and so on. Such material is utilized irrespective of the nature of the delusion, i.e. whether its content is grandiose, persecutory, or depressive.

In those cases where the ego is seriously damaged and the primary process makes itself apparent, verbal ideas are also utilized to consolidate the psychotic reality. Words are cathected as if they were things, and thus have a special significance for the patient. A chronic patient who began attendance at an art class presented the following clinical data. Although his work was utterly unstructured and chaotic he identified one drawing as Mickey Mouse. During this period he began to express doubts about the word 'behold' which occurred in a poem he had written before his illness. He decided to change it to 'discern'. One day he became quite anxious about using 'discern'—he wondered if he had not gone too far with Walt Disney, as the 'dis' in 'discern' belonged to Disney. Disney might get angry, and he did not want that to happen. These ideas easily fitted into his delusional system and helped to sustain it. Implicit in his communication were possible references to the art teacher and to the physician. Confrontation with this material had little meaning for him. This clinical example is quite different from that of the first case quoted above, where examination of the word 'Largactil' provided a means of enlarging the area of communication between patient and doctor.

Delusions and their associated (secondary) hallucinations cannot be regarded as regressive in nature. They are not the result of a repetition of a developmental phase, but rather are called out as a reaction to the narcissistic and ego regression. This conception has important implications for the theory which interprets the attachment of delusions and other psychotic manifestations to the psycho-analyst as indicating the presence of a transference psychosis. If transference is primarily thought of as a form of repetition, then the concept of delusional or psychotic transference become meaningless.

The psychotic reality is created not only to absorb the result of unsuccessful defence against the drives, but also to ensure a form of adaptation. The delusions and hallucinations provide a means of shoring up the ego, and threats to their status provoke anxiety. This anxiety is in the first place due to a dread of the disintegration of the psychotic reality, because with its dissolution the patient would be plunged into the mental state which ensued during the phase of cathectic withdrawal—the period of 'the internal catastrophe' as Freud (6) called it. This is perhaps the major cause of the patient's negativism in the treatment situation. At the same time this reaction of anxiety and negativism is also indirectly related to the conflicts which initiated the illness. It must be stressed, however, that this relationship is secondary to the dread of the loss of the psychotic reality.

Freud (6) pointed out that the major defence in paranoia and schizophrenic states was not the withdrawal of object (neutralized) cathexes. This process is not decisive, because it also occurs in melancholia and in severe states of depersonalization. The narcissistic and ego regression constitutes the fateful instinctual movement in those patients destined to develop schizophrenic states. This regression is certainly defensive in aim, but when the psychotic reality has achieved a permanence the defence is no longer directed against unconscious contents as in the neuroses. Repression having failed, owing to the disintegration of the ego, the repressed pours out to fill the delusions with its content. From this time on the defence is solely concerned with the preservation of the delusional system.

It is in the therapeutic situation that the purpose and aim of the defence in schizophrenic reactions can be most clearly observed. The schizophrenic patient relates to the therapist in accordance with his delusional ideas or with negativism. Prolonged psychotherapeutic contact may lead to this negativism being replaced by the delusional ideas which had formed to the reaction of the phase of withdrawal. These psychotic manifestations, displaced into the treatment situation, overshadow any of the defences which are usually encountered in the transference analysis of a psychoneurotic reaction. They will continue do do so until the patient develops the capacity for object cathexes. Once this has happened the usual ego defences make their appearance both within and outside the transference. If this favourable change does not take place, the psychotic manifestations are adhered to with even greater strength, and in such circumstances therapeutic efforts are of no avail.

This examination of defensive processes in schizophrenic states has been undertaken primarily to inquire once again into the possibility of isolating the mental processes which are operative in the different phases of the illness and in different schizophrenic syndromes. If such processes could be isolated— that is, described by means of concepts which have accepted and definite connotations—it may be possible to identify the mental processes which underlie the clinical phenomena. The distinction between different forms of hallucination, for example, has been made to illustrate the likelihood that different mental processes, with different relationships to defence, may give rise to what appear to be identical clinical phenomena.

Detailed clinical studies have already shown that the functional level of mental processes such as attention, concentration, thinking, and perception depend upon the state of the ego organization. When this is impaired the state of consciousness characterizing attention and concentration is no longer possible. The patient's state of consciousness is now characterized by a mode of cognition which has more in common with the dream state than with waking life by virtue of the prevalence of the primary process. These functional changes seem to be relatively independent of the instinctual regression to narcissism and thus of the psychotic reality (the delusions and hallucinations). An improvement in the functional capacity of the ego need not be paralleled by a resolution of the narcissistic regression. Delusions may remain unimpaired in spite of such advances in the level of the cognitive organization. However, a deterioration in cognition is often associated with an enhancement of the pathological narcissism (3).

From the standpoint of defence such observations suggest that the regression to narcissism is indeed the primary defence in schizophrenic states and that the cognitive changes are secondary to this. The clinical illustrations indicate that the cognitive deterioration and the other signs and symptoms in schizophrenic states have a defensive purpose, but the aim differs according to the phase of the disease process. The exact manner by which the cognitive changes and the symptoms come to have a defensive function is still a matter for further investigation. As Freud (8) has said, 'Elucidation of the various mechanisms in the psychoses by which the turning from reality and reconstruction of it is effected, and also of the degree of success they are able to achieve, is a task for a special psychiatry which has not yet been undertaken.' Perhaps a beginning can be made, as in this preliminary inquiry, by utilizing Freud's two-phase formulation, which offers a means of identifying different mental processes operating at different periods of the illness. An opportunity is then afforded of correlating the clinical phenomena and the underlying mental process with defensive aims.

REFERENCES

1. Bychowski, G. (1943). 'Disorders in the Body Image in the Clinical Pictures of Psychoses.' *J. nerv. ment. Dis.*, **98**, p. 54.
2. Freeman, T. (1959). 'Aspects of Defence in Neurosis and Psychosis.' *Int. J. Psycho-Anal.*, **40**, p. 199.
3. ——— (1962). 'The Psycho-Analytic Observation of Chronic Schizophrenic Reactions.' In: J. M. Tanner (ed.), *Aspects of Psychiatric Research* (Oxford: Oxford University Press).
4. Freud, S. (1894). 'The Neuro-Psychoses of Defence.' *S.E.*, **3**.
5. ——— (1900). *The Interpretation of Dreams. S.E.*, **4–5**.
6. ——— (1911). 'Psycho-Analytic Notes on an Autobiographical Account of a Case of Paranoia.' *S.E.*, **12**.
7. ——— (1914). 'On Narcissism: An Introduction.' *S.E.*, **14**.
8. ——— (1924). 'The Loss of Reality in Neurosis and Psychosis.' *S.E.*, **19**.
9. Hartmann, H. (1953). 'Contribution to the Metapsychology of Schizophrenia.' *Psychoanal. Study Child*, **8**.
10. Katan, M. (1950). 'Structural Aspects of a Case of Schizophrenia.' *Psychoanal. Study Child*, **5**.
11. ——— (1954). 'The Non-psychotic Part of the Personality in Schizophrenia.' *Int. J. Psycho-Anal.*, **35**.
12. Schilder, P. (1926). *Introduction to a Psychoanalytic Psychiatry*. (New York: Int. Univ. Press, 1928.)

5. Sources of Anxiety in Paranoid Schizophrenia

Harold F. Searles

In this description of what I have found to be the major sources of anxiety in individuals suffering from paranoid schizophrenia, I shall endeavour to demonstrate how affective phenomena and structural phenomena are interrelated. Further, although I shall have to assume, during much of this portrayal, the vantage point of the observer, whenever possible I shall discuss these sources of anxiety in terms of the patient's own subjective experience of them. This latter emphasis helps to explain the apparent paradox that I shall count, among the 'sources' of his anxiety, various ego-*defensive* phenomena. We well know that to any psychiatric patient himself, the threatening affects present themselves not undistortedly as such, but in forms modified by ego-defences which, although intendedly protective, at the same time distort his experience in a strange and frightening way.

One point I wish to make at the outset is that the paranoid individual seems rarely, if ever—except perhaps in states of panic—to feel anxiety as such. I have come to believe it pathognomonic of him that he experiences, instead, an awareness of various ingredients of his surroundings—or, less often, of things within his body—as being charged with sinister meaning, charged with malevolence toward himself. A simple example of this is to be seen in the reaction of a woman to a new room to which she had been moved, after her having spent many months in a room upstairs in the same small building. Whereas I found myself feeling, in our first interview in this new room of hers, a fair amount of anxiety which I related to the unfamiliarity of these new surroundings, she seemed entirely unaware of any such anxiety, and flatly disclaimed, when I inquired, that she felt so. She asserted that a woman has no such feelings, that a woman likes to move around and, in fact, has to, in order to keep alive. What she voiced, instead, was a threatened kind of conviction that the water in this new bathroom tasted sinister; she mentioned uneasily that some wine which a nurse had given her today tasted like 'mahogany'; and she said that she did not like being down near the earth, indicating that this would make her more vulnerable to being turned, by 'them', into a tree.

Freud (1911), in his discussion of the Schreber case, described repressed homosexual desires as being at the root of the paranoid patient's preoccupation with the persecutory figure or figures. It seems to me a more adequate explanation to think of the persecutory figure as emerging into the forefront of the patient's concern, not primarily because of repressed homosexual interest on the latter's part, but rather because the persecutory figure is that one, among all the people in the patient's current life-situation, who most readily lends himself to reflecting, or personifying, those qualities which the patient is having most vigorously to repudiate in himself and project on to the outer world. Whereas he is convinced that the persecutory figure is pursuing him— in one fashion or another pressing threateningly upon him—we find, in the course of his psychotherapy, that the state of affairs actually consists, basically, in the circumstance that his own unconscious feelings and attitudes, projected upon that other person, are pressing for awareness and acceptance into his conscious conception of himself.

He finds himself unable to renounce any concern with that other person, and reach a state of peace about the matter, for in actuality this would be tantamount to repudiating important components of himself; moreover, the other person is necessary to him as the bearer of these externalized (i.e. projected) emotions. But, on the other hand, he cannot find peace through a friendly acceptance of the persecutory figure, for this would be tantamount to accepting, into his own picture of himself, various qualities abhorrent to him. So an uneasy equilibrium is maintained, with his experiencing a gnawing, threatened, absorbing concern with the persecutory figure whom he cannot rid from his mind.

One sees this mechanism particularly clearly in those patients whose projections attach not to any real-life figure at all, but to a quite pure-culture *alter ego*. One such patient had changed his name, at the age of twelve, from John Costello to John Cousteau, evidently in an attempt to establish an identity more acceptable to himself. He came into one particular session, early in my work with him at a VA clinic years ago, shaking and perspiring visibly, and described how furious it had made him, a few days before, when at a pension examination the secretary had mistakenly called out his name as 'John Costello'. He became very worked up as he described this, saying: 'I don't like John Costello—he was a selfish stinker . . . the name sticks in my throat.' A woman who for years had the delusion that she had 'doubles' to whom she attributed all the feelings, attitudes, and behavioural acts which she had to repudiate from her concept of herself, came, in the course of our sessions, to express intense hatred of these 'doubles'. She said: 'I wish they'd fry. Somebody ought to shoot them. They're chisellers.' I commented, 'You seem to hate them at least as much as you hate psychiatrists', and she agreed. I went on: 'You seem to feel that the doubles are as much your enemy as the psychiatrists are.' She replied, vehemently: 'They [i.e. the doubles] *are* the enemy.'

Conspicuous as the defence-mechanism of projection is in paranoid schizophrenia, I have come to believe that the complementary defence, introjection, while less easily detectible, is hardly less important. The patient lives chronically under the threat, that is, not only of persecutory figures experienced as part of the *outer* world, but also under that of *introjects* which he carries about, largely unbeknown to himself, within him. These are distorted representations of people which belong, properly speaking, to the world outside the confines of his ego, but which he experiences—in so far as he becomes aware of their presence—as having invaded his self. These, existing as foreign bodies in his personality, infringe upon and diminish the area of what might be thought of as his own self—an area being kept small, also, by the draining off, into the outer world, through projection, of much affect and ideation which belongs to his self.

In the course of his psychotherapy one comes to see the extent to which these introjects threaten the self with total abolition. One woman came to express it, after many months of therapy: 'Why, I'm not even myself! . . . Those people are in my bowels and in my stomach and in my heart! . . .' On another occasion she said, with urgent anxiety: '*Who am* I? I don't have any *identity*.' For several months, when an introject of a constellation of qualities traceable to her mother held sway, she showed every indication of assuming herself to be her mother, and spoke of her siblings as 'my children'. One patient came to experience herself as a 'baggage car'; another as 'Noah's ark'. Still another experienced herself as a Trojan horse filled with a hundred people; and a man portrayed in a dream his own state of being filled with introjects: he dreamt of a man with a belly so enormous that he could scarcely move about.

A woman met me as I walked toward her building, for a therapeutic session with her, and in great agitation showed me a page in a story she was trying to read, a page on which the protagonist, 'I', was describing a conversation involving several participants. She said: 'Four men and a girl—which one is "I"?—There's William and George and Peter—maybe Peter is "I". . . . Which one is "I"?' And as we walked into the building she said: 'You've got too many people here, Dr Searles. . . . I get overwhelmed by people.' She had recently been expressing a wish to 'push people away', and would say of this or that nurse or fellow-patient, 'she reminds me of several different people'. This woman, so close to a hebephrenic state involving the loss of any continuous sense of personal identity, was attributing to these other persons her own state of personality-organization, namely that of, as one patient phrased it, a 'composite personality', comprised largely of introjects.

I have found repeatedly that the individual with paranoid schizophrenia, initially so unwaveringly certain about everything, and never doubting that his views are his very own, reaches, after years of intensive psychotherapy, a point where it becomes clear not only to the therapist, but to himself also, that nearly everything he has been saying is in actuality but an ill-understood hodge-podge of the parroted—though unwittingly caricatured and otherwise distorted—utterances of his parents and other significant persons from his childhood. He comes to reveal, at long last, precisely the confusion of a small child who has been exposed to a bewildering cacophony of parental statements and who has not found, heretofore, anyone sufficiently trustworthy and patient to help him find his way out of his confusion. Two among the patients who have reached this point, in our work together, have come to say, quite simply and seriously and trustingly, 'I don't know anything'.

Inevitably, on the path to the establishment of such a degree of trust and openness in the transference-relationship, there will be many periods when the anxiety in both participants will far exceed any mutual security they have been able to find together as yet. During these periods the unintegrated welter of emotions, memories, fantasies, somatic sensations and other perceptions, initially contained within the patient's rigidly formulated delusions, will emerge, with the result that his personality-functioning becomes chaotically fragmented—so much so, oftentimes, as to constitute a formidable threat to the therapist's own personality-organization. At such times the therapist can see to what a degree the patient's delusional formulation of his life has served as a substitute for any genuine and healthy sense of a pattern in living. The paranoid patient is not sufficiently in tune with his fellow-men; not sufficiently able to integrate the ever-flowing nature of life with its concomitants of change and growth, fulfilment and loss, birth and death; not sufficiently matured in his thought-processes to be able to distinguish the more significant from the less significant incidents and threads in his life; and not sufficiently loving and trusting to experience love as the ingredient which gives human existence cohesiveness and meaning; to be able to feel the wholeness, the genuine 'master plan', which the healthy individual comes to see in his life. I like to compare the description, in Noyes's (1951) text-book, of the process of retrospective falsification in paranoia, with the healthy realization of a true pattern in his life which the neurotic patient achieves in the later phases of a successful psychoanalysis: 'Incidents of the past receive a new interpretation and he discovers in them a significance which was not recognized when they occurred. . . .'

The fragmentation to which I refer is not different in kind from that seen in hebephrenia. Markedly varying moods, and widely disparate levels of ego-organization, may appear in rapidly changing and random sequence. The individual's perception of the world about him is jumbled up with hallucinatory phenomena and with vivid perceptions of scenes from his past. He may experience not only other people but also himself as being unwhole, a composite of bodily fragments of persons from both current life and bygone years. He may be incapable of sequential thought and speech, and may hear only fragments of what the therapist says to him. One such patient, who at the beginning of our work had shown, for years, the rigid overcontrol of feeling so characteristic of paranoid schizophrenia, went through many months of fragmentation in which, for example, she would bellow at one moment that we criminals should kill her and thus end her torture, and at the next moment would be laughing warmly; would at one moment be a monumentally arrogant woman and, the next moment, a touchingly childlike creature; and, at times when I overestimated her capacity to share an informal friendliness in our sessions, she would become overwhelmed by deeply ambivalent feelings traceable eventually to her relationship with her mother. Following one such therapeutic hour, she became savagely combative and, when the nurses were putting her into a cold wet sheet pack, she bit the breast of one of them; but only a short time later, while still in the pack, she asked another for a kiss, and this nurse, touched by this childlike request which the patient had never before made, gave her one. Her moods with me would change equally rapidly, and I can only mention in passing, here, the extreme fragmentation which occurred not only in her affective experience, but in all areas of her perceptual functioning, including that having to do with her body-image, before a healthy reintegration became established.

I find it helpful to think of this phase of fragmentation not simply under the global heading of regression—which is, indeed, one way of characterizing it—but, more specifically, as a reversal of the normal growth process of integration-and-differentiation (Searles, 1959b, c). That is, we can see normal growth, psychological as well as biological growth, to be a process of integration of previously separated *anlagen* into coherent functional structures, and, concomitantly, differentiation of functional structures into more complex patterning which provides for an increasingly wide range of discriminations and specializations of functioning. In the phase of fragmentation which I have been describing, there are phenomena not only of disintegration but also of dedifferentiation, a term introduced by Heinz Hartmann (1939) to describe the loss of already differentiated psychological functions which we find in states of regression, particularly in schizophrenia. The comparative psychologist, Heinz Werner (1940), who introduced this term independently, illuminatingly compares the states of dedifferentiation seen in schizophrenia and in brain injury, with the ego-functioning found in children and in members of so-called primitive cultures, as well as with the modes of sensory functioning found among a wide variety of lower animal species. Rapaport (1958) has extended, meaningfully, some of Hartmann's observations. Hartmann's (1950, 1956) concept that there is, already established at birth, a rudimentary ego, which tends to follow its own autonomous pattern of maturational differentiation—a process which is reversed in schizophrenia—is another concept which I have found helpful.

Thus, many of the bewildering manifestations of the paranoid patient's— or, for that matter, any other schizophrenic patient's—fragmentation can be seen to consist in such relatively obvious dedifferentiation phenomena as the loss of ego-boundaries, such that the outer world and the world within the self are mixed up, as in the phenomena of projection and introjection which I mentioned earlier; or the loss of distinction between present and past, such that persons in the present surroundings are misidentified as being persons from the past, and, contrariwise, vivid memories from the past are experienced as being perceptions of the here-and-now; or the loss of differentiation among thinking, feeling and acting, such that, for instance, the thought or feeling is reacted to as being tantamount to the deed.

But, as one studies such patients for years, one sees that the dedifferentiation is, in a subtler form, far more extensive than one had thought. One sees that the dedifferentiation of the thought processes, or to put it another way, the loss of the higher forms of ego-organization, is such that the patient has little or no realm of *fantasy* experienced as such; whenever he experiences a new combination of thoughts or mental images he immediately assumes it to be, instead, a representation of outer reality. Further, he has little or no psychological realm of *memory*, experienced as such: people about him never *remind* him of people from the past whom he then *misses*; to him these either *are* those very people, or are those people in a disguised form, or—and this is true, perhaps, of the slightly healthier patient—they are 'doing a take-off on', or as one patient put it, 'projecting', people from the past.

Further, his inability to differentiate important from trivial, intendedly communicative from non-communicative, ingredients of the world around him may account for some of his well-known *suspicion*. He may be suspicious, that is, not only for the reason that he has been hurt too often before when he has placed his trust in someone, but also because his suspicion provides his only mode of processing, of sifting out, the data from a world which is as bewilderingly complex as the adult world is to a little child. Many times I have seen this or that paranoid patient start to look utterly confused by the many words and, simultaneously, manual and other gestures coming from me, until his attention crystallized, after a brief moment or two, upon some word or some gesture, whereupon it clearly appeared that he had found his suspicion once again confirmed, had found his delusional simplification of experience adequate to pigeon-hole this new incident, and had found relief from his momentary bewilderment in face of perceptual data which his capacity for abstract thought was insufficient to enable him to integrate on any but this primitive suspicional basis.

I have been particularly interested to discover how frequently the fragmented patient is involved in a kind of literal and somaticized experience of what would be, to a healthy person with mature ego-differentiation, a *figure of speech*—a metaphor, for example—confined to the levels of thought and emotion, with at most an echo of somatic representation (Searles, 1959*a*). For example, one patient reacted to a harsh comment from me without any awareness that my comment had made her feel hurt and betrayed, but with the evident physical sensation, instead, of having been quite literally shot in the back. Upon seeing a pathetic elderly man in the nearby drug store, she remained quite unaware of the extent to which her heart had, figuratively speaking, gone out to him, as I could see in my immediately subsequent session with her; instead, she had an agonized literal experience that her heart had been torn out. Another patient, when shame and embarrassment started to emerge from repression, felt a literal, rather than a figurative, sensation of sinking through the floor. Other patients, when evidently involved in feelings of admiration or awe of me, have experienced this not as such, but as a perception of me as being gigantically tall; or, when grappling with feelings of disillusionment or contempt toward me, instead of experiencing the feeling as such, have perceived me as being a midget. They may perceive their fellow-patients, or themselves, as being not figuratively sheep-like or cow-like, for instance, but as being literally indistinguishable, perceptually, from sheep or cows, or even inanimate things. Even the earliest differentiation, in normal ego-development of infancy, that between animate and inanimate, may be lost (Searles, 1960).

Thus we see that the paranoid schizophrenic patient, when we begin working with him, is labouring under the threat not only of constellations of specific projections and introjections, but also of imminent disintegration and dedifferentiation of his whole personality-structure—such as becomes blatantly overt later on, when his delusional defences have been undermined midway along in his therapy. Our own psychodynamic understanding of this disintegration and dedifferentiation, as constituting very active (though unconscious) ego-defences of a primitive sort—whereby a part of the ego's integrity is temporarily sacrificed in the interest of personality-survival (Searles, 1959a)—cannot serve directly to alleviate the threat under which the patient himself suffers.

Usually we can detect at least a few subtle indications, even at the beginning of our contact with a relatively rigidly organized paranoid individual, that he is struggling against such disorganization of his psychological processes. The following brief portion of a psychologist's lengthy report concerning a newly admitted woman with paranoid schizophrenia, a woman who needed hospitalization but was opposed to it and whose illness was not sufficiently overt as to make possible her commitment for prolonged treatment, is reminiscent to me of various patients I have seen. After detailing at great length the many evidences of adequate personality-functioning, the psychologist says:

> I did get various definite evidences of a psychotic process going on in Mrs Bennett. In the first two hours I had with her she verbalized many rather bizarre somatic symptoms, such as a feeling that her hair had all been torn out during the stay at the previous hospital, although she said that she knew quite well that this had not actually occurred. Also, she described a feeling of 'being broken in two in the middle', indicating her abdomen. Likewise, she went into great and rather bizarre length in trying to describe some chronic lower back complaint. . . . During a subsequent hour with her, I found her to be describing her distress at being in the presence of one or another of the patients here who was knitting. She said, 'It makes me feel like wool—you know.' I could get no further elaboration about this from her.

Although this paper does not deal with therapeutic technique, I must touch upon that area in order to make an additional conceptual point concerning the paranoid patient's dedifferentiation. The beginning practitioner of psychoanalysis or psychotherapy learns, in the early years of his experience with neurotic patients, how very much of what the patient is saying has reference, at some level of awareness or unawareness, to the immediate treatment-situation itself, although the patient may be quite resistive indeed to recognizing this transference-ingredient in what he is saying. After years of practice in detecting such immediate, though usually preconscious or unconscious, referential roots in what his patients say in his presence, the therapist or analyst becomes impressed, too, with the extent to which this phenomenon enters also into ordinary conversations between individuals in daily life. For instance, A is expressing to B some strongly felt attitude concerning an absent third person, C, quite unaware that simultaneously he is revealing, to a practised ear, that he holds this attitude, in some degree, toward B as well; and B, if he does not have a practised ear, is equally unaware of this quite direct communication from A to himself. But I, at least, have come to believe that such a direct referent is nearly always present in such situations.

Such ubiquity of this phenomenon would be in line with the work of Piaget (1930), whose voluminous and meticulously detailed researches concerning normal development indicate that the establishment of ego-boundaries, far from being completed in infancy or early childhood, is still considerably incomplete as late as twelve years of age, and never reaches full completion even in adult life. He speaks of one's perception of the outer world as being distorted, even in adult life, by at least some 'adherences'—that is, projections—of ingredients which belong, properly speaking, within the boundaries of the self. Thus we might think of this circumstance which I have been describing as one in which, even among so-called normal people, A's perceptual differentiation between B and C is, at an unconscious level, not complete, such that the feelings which he is expressing about the absent person, C, may adhere to, or be directed toward, the person B who is actually in his presence.

In any case, whether or not this phenomenon occurs with such a high frequency as I myself believe it does, the paranoid schizophrenic patient may be thought of as being particularly acutely aware of this 'normal element of self-reference' in his contacts with people, when he is in the position of person B. Because his ego-boundaries are so grossly incomplete that the ingredients of the outer world, including both persons A and C, are reacted to unconsciously or perhaps even consciously as mere extensions of himself, he is very prone to hearing, in A's remarks about C, *only* that level of meaning which refers to himself, and to dismiss the significance of A's consciously intended meaning.

At this juncture I wish to note how heavy a penalty one has to pay for the use of such psychotic defences against anxiety as massive projection and introjection, disintegration and dedifferentiation. The penalty, which has no counterpart in neurosis, consists in the experience of *weirdness* suffered, for instance, by the paranoid man who, in the struggle against repressed grief, feels that his streaming tear glands are controlled by some weirdly mysterious agency outside himself; or by the woman who, projecting her violently aggressive sexual lust, feels herself to be repeatedly raped by some eery and invisible outside agency. The self-concept is constricted by so harsh a superego that the warded-off desires, in order to emerge at all, have to assume so disguised a form that the patient lives, consequently, in a nightmarishly distorted world. Data from the only quantitatively more distorted world of hebephrenic patients provide vivid examples of what I am discussing here. One hebephrenic woman, unable as yet to conceptualize her subjective unfeelingness as such, recurrently saw an eerily unhuman 'plastic man' appear, terrifyingly, at her window; another, unaware of her murderous rage as such, experienced instead an hallucination of a line of exploding teeth marching unendingly up one wall of her room, across the ceiling, and down the other side; and a hebephrenic man, whose self-concept as a little girl was repressed and projected, saw in his clothes-closet an 8- or 10-year-old girl, swimming in purple liquid, and pleaded urgently for me to rescue her.

I have become interested in trying to discern in what form, if at all, the paranoid patient experiences any awareness of his own thought-disorder and, in general, of his ego-mechanisms. It required four years of therapy for one man, for example, to become able to say, 'See, this is the way I think . . .', and to proceed to lay out before me, for our mutual investigation, his distorted ways of thinking. Prior to such a development, I believe, the patient experiences his state of more or less severe dedifferentiation of ego-functioning not as any disorder within himself, but as, rather, an indistinguishable component of the poorly delineated 'them', the anthropomorphized persecutors in his external world. One sees comparable phenomena in normal development, in the little child who, only precariously established as yet in well-differentiated modes of thought, perception, and sensation, seemingly experiences his remnants of the earlier, undifferentiated level of ego-functioning not as a truly internal threat, but rather in the form of the vaguely outlined shapes which, he is convinced, lurk behind the closed doors and in the dark corners.

Tausk, in his classic paper, 'On the origin of the "influencing machine" in schizophrenia' (see chapter 3), in which he introduced the concept of a loss of ego-boundaries, described the delusion of there being a fascinatingly compli-cated influencing machine, experienced commonly in that era by paranoid schizophrenic patients, as being in actuality a projection of the patient's own body, with the whole body being unconsciously fantasied as a genital. Since I have come to see how frequently schizophrenic patients experience abstract concepts in a concretized, and often anthropomorphized, form, I have come to believe that such phenomena as the influencing machine—which one of my patients experienced, for years, as a 'Watcher-Machine' protectively oversee-ing her daily living—represent, most significantly, the patient's own exter-nalized, and to him fascinatingly complex, ego-functioning. Modell's (1958) paper concerning hallucinations as being related more closely to ego-func-tions than to superego-functions is relevant here, and much of my clinical experience is in line with his.

If there is any single most basic threat to the paranoid schizophrenic person, it is, I believe, the threat that he will cease to exist as a human individual. This threat presents itself in various forms. There is the danger that his identity will be reduced to that of only *part* of a person—most often, a genital—rather than his being a whole person. There is the danger that his individuality may be submerged in symbiotic relatedness with the other person. There is the danger that his status in the world of his fellow human beings will be reduced to that of an animal, a dead person, or an inanimate object. And there is, finally, the danger that, in the eyes of human beings, he may cease totally to exist.

Interviews with the mothers of these people suggest some of the causative factors in the patient's unsureness that he can maintain any solid place in the emotional life of his fellow human beings. These mothers appear, so fre-quently, remarkably overcontrolled, placid—as the late Lewis Hill (1948) termed it, impervious. One mother states of the patient's father, in the most matter-of-fact tone it is possible to use: 'He died from ulcers of the stomach and cancer of the stomach and liver.' Another says, similarly dispassionately, of her son's infancy: 'There was quite an interval, at four months, when I thought he would starve to death, when he wouldn't either eat or take the bottle.'

The degree to which various of these parents disavow, whether uncon-sciously or even consciously, any blood-relationship with their child, is some-times startling. One mother, for example, in giving me an account of the background of her schizophrenic daughter, now married, commented less with scorn than with emotional detachment: 'Mrs Matthews, from a young child, was always what we called the goody girl, the Pollyanna type: tractable, obedient, of a sweet disposition; and I thought that during her childhood and adolescence I had a good contact and understanding with Mrs Matthews.' For a short time, during our lengthy session, she referred to her daughter as Alice, 'to make it easier', but soon lapsed back into using the term 'Mrs Matthews' which seemed really more in accord with the way she regarded the young woman. Several times I have been astonished to see, in the course of a patient's psychotherapy, that one or another of the parents felt that he or she had married far beneath his or her social station, to such a degree that the patient, in striving for acceptance by this particular parent, was met not only with rejection but with subtle reproach for trying to be a social climber.

Sometimes such attitudes are expressed quite openly. One mother, in telling me of her marriage, said: 'My father was violently opposed to it because he said it was worn out stock. He went to some pains to prove to me that it was stock that was on its last legs. He had done a lot of breeding of cattle', she explained—all in such a tone as to make clear that she had long ago come around to her father's way of thinking. She went on: 'There was so much T.B. and cancer in my husband's family that not only did three of my children have mental breaks, but one of his family had cancer and another one committed suicide. My side was stronger physically, stronger emotionally, stronger intellectually . . . ; but his was an old New England family', in contrast to her own Southern background. She commented, at another point, that her husband always wanted a big boat, such as one his own father had once had. 'But', she went on, 'we couldn't afford it; we had six children instead. Perhaps it would have been better if, instead of having the children, we had gotten the boat.'

The devaluation, by various of these mothers or fathers, of their child's emotions and ideas is often readily detectable. One mother said that her son, from the time he was old enough to hold a pencil in his hand, until the age of about eight, used to draw for several hours a day. 'He drew all his ideas out in the form of cartoons, little series of pictures that followed a thing through. . . . We got awfully amused at him, his odd little ideas', she commented, which reminded me of another paranoid patient's repeated references to his childhood as 'my little life'. Another mother said, of her son's graduation from a top-level preparatory school, that 'He wasn't anything', meaning that he had won no class office nor athletic award. A father, with a similarly erasing kind of scorn, said shortly, of his schizophrenic son's academic achievements, 'He's a genius; but he's no good to me being a genius in that condition', referring to the son's incomprehensible 'refusal' to apply himself to any line of work.

The mother of a very strong, and at times dangerously combative, young schizophrenic man, when asked whether her son had ever struck her, calmly replied that several times he had grabbed her hair and pulled it, and that one time—a week previously, when she had been trying to persuade him to come to Chestnut Lodge, he had slapped her face. She went on, in a rather amused way, 'I knew he would', and added that at times he had pulled her hair 'not very hard, but like a child would pull somebody else's hair. I told him', she continued with a laugh, 'that I thought it was a great improvement—''At least you don't hurt anybody when you pull my hair.'' ' A father, describing a drive he had taken with his paranoid daughter, while she had been home on a visit from the Lodge, mentioned that she had become enraged and hit his arm repeatedly, so hard that it was bruised for several days. I was astounded when he added: 'I wanted to concentrate on driving, so I acted as though nothing were happening.'

The effects of such parental responses, or lack of response, could be seen in one of my patients who, after much therapy, was able to confide to me, quite simply and resignedly, that 'nobody responds emotionally to me'. It required another patient several years of therapy to become free from her long-held, though previously unconscious, self-concept as a 'snow man in a glass'—one of those little snow men in a glass globe, with artificial snow—quite outside the realm of living human relatedness, and it was with the keenest pleasure that she finally became aware that, *I'm alive*, Dr Searles'. Another patient felt, for years, that she was a robot, and at times other types of machines, before becoming convinced that she was a human being, capable of responding emotionally and of evoking emotional responses in other human beings. Earlier, she had phrased it that her family 'used me as thing for their amusement'.

Another patient, after much therapy, said, weeping bitterly, 'I felt as though I didn't have anything that was mine, almost', and told of how, in the course of her childhood, her mother, without consulting her, had given her doll's house to a Society for Underprivileged Orphans, her doll's carriage to someone, her favourite sweater to a younger sister, and had had the girl's dog spayed; and an older sister, on going away to college, had taken as many as she desired of the patient's books, likewise without asking. A divorced woman, the mother of two small children, said of her mother that: 'If things aren't going along the way she wants them to, it is within her power to take away my financial support and take over my babies. She has threatened to cut off my financial support since I've been ill. She sold my house and she sold her house and bought a new house with room for herself, the maid, and the two babies, and', the patient ended with a hollow laugh, 'didn't leave any room for me.'

Always one can find evidence that one or both parents, during the patient's upbringing, have been so absorbed in *transference*-relatedness—traceable; that is, to unconscious elements in their own childhood relationships—transference-relatedness to various members of the marital family, including the patient, that the patient's existence in his own right receives little acknowledgement. For example, to one mother, the patient's long-deceased elder brother, an important transference-figure to the mother, was evidently still a much more alive and absorbing person to her than was her living schizophrenic son. In patients' marital family-relationships, also, one sees the same phenomenon: in a number of instances, I have found that a paranoid woman's husband is so absorbed in his relationship with their daughter, unconsciously a mother-figure to him, that the patient has come to have, for all practical purposes, no place left in his psychological life, or in the marital family-structure. Another patient said, of her childhood, that when her mother and her paternal grandmother, who lived in the home, were waging their chronic arguments, the 'tension was terrific', and 'I wasn't even given the acknowledgement of a piece of furniture in the room'.

Another woman, both of whose parents had been schizoid persons at best, and who felt convinced that she had had no single continuous home, or set of parents, said to a nurse: 'I've been in so many houses and been met with so many people behind newspapers. Either they didn't love each other or else I was to blame in some way for this. . . .' This illustrates how vulnerable is the child, who finds so little assurance of his real ability to affect other people, to the development of a conviction that he possesses some magical, inhumanly destructive, power over them. Other causes for such a self-concept lie in his uncomprehended transference significance to—and thereby power over—his parents' feelings, and in his unconscious hostility.

Out of such multiple etiological factors, one patient felt herself to be less a human being than a 'force of evil'. Another patient confided, in a troubled tone, 'I work up the other person's destructiveness against life', and in describing her previously unsuccessful treatment, said despairingly, 'I was, and still am, impervious to any influence emanating from the psychoanalyst', and likened her own imperviousness to 'cancer'. At another point, she said, 'I felt that my little girl—as much as a child needs her mother—would be happier with her father; since I am so unhappy, couldn't help infecting her . . .'. One repeatedly finds, in the course of psychotherapy with these patients, their revealing a long-standing concern lest they convey their disease to other persons, as if it were caused by germs and communicable through physical contact.

Poignantly, in a number of instances this view of the self as being unfit for the world of human beings, by reason of some ill-understood destructive effect upon one's fellow-men, has seemed to represent an effort to account for the physical isolation in which the little child lived, the deprivation in terms of physical and emotional contact with any parental figure. The quite evident anxious disorganization with which these mothers, and sometimes the fathers, have met the patient's strivings for intimacy with them, subsequent to his infancy, must be counted among the important factors in the child's develop- ing conviction that his love has a destructive effect upon human beings.

Other etiological circumstances I can touch upon only briefly. There is the parent's inability to relate to the child as being a whole person; the little son may have psychological significance for his mother or father only as a penis; and the girl may be quite literally only a pair of pretty legs, or a pair of maternal breasts, to the father or mother. Further, there is the parent's in- ability to differentiate the child clearly from his siblings, or from the parent himself or herself. One of my patients, who had two sisters, two and four years younger than herself, in one session started to reminisce, 'When I was six four and two . . .', as if she felt herself to be literally one person with her sisters. Nearly a year later she was able to describe it that her mother 'never seemed to realize that we [girls] were different from one another'. One mother commented blandly, concerning her son: 'George objects violently if I ad- dress him in the tone I use in addressing either his father or his sister. He emphasizes [in the former instance], "I'm not Dad! I'm not married to you!".' In the symbiotic relationship with the mother or father, the child is, of course, often under pressure to vicariously express the parent's unconscious feelings. One mother, who seemed largely unaware of her own very consider- able paranoid hostility, in painting a particularly malevolent picture of one among the many physicians who had, she felt, mishandled her son, com- mented approvingly that 'Eddie said he felt like killing him and for two cents he would have'. Another mother, who gave a similarly paranoid account of her daughter's experiences with a long series of previous therapists, including a terse comment concerning one, 'The man was a beast and did a bad job',

and, concerning another, an even more terse, 'I'd like his head', seemed none
the less to think of herself as a nonviolent person, and, in tracing her daughter's background for me, said of a time when the young woman had been
living with a lover: 'I lived in constant terror of what might happen that year;
both are violent people, both are filled with hate, and anything could have
happened.' It is somewhat remarkable to me that, despite such parental pressure, so many of these patients manage to avoid killing anyone.

I cannot elaborate, here, upon what might be thought of as the *internal*
causative factors in the patient's fear that he may cease to exist as a living
human individual. The resolution of these factors is invariably more difficult
for him, and for the therapist, than is the clarification of the ways in which
other persons have warped him. These internal factors, intimately related, of
course, to the external ones, include: (*a*) his wide-scale repression of his
emotions, which is one of the great causes for his feeling himself to be a dead
person, or an inanimate thing; (*b*) his unconscious denial of his dependency-
needs, such that he, regarding his therapist, for example, as being 'of no more
importance to me than that spot on the wall there', as one of my patients
phrased it, assumes, through a projection of such denial-of-dependency, that
the other person considers *him* to be next to nothing; (*c*) the externalization of
both sides of his internal conflicts, such that he feels himself to be a mere
'pawn', or 'rubber ball', buffeted about by the powerful beings upon whom
these conflicts are externalized; (*d*) emotional withdrawal from human relatedness, as an expression of hostility, so habitually, and to such an extreme
degree, that he feels himself to be, as one patient phrased it, a mere 'ghost';
and, lastly, (*e*) the clinging to the infantile view of other persons as being
omnipotent and omniscient, which is a rather effective way for one to deal
with one's feelings of guilty responsibility, but which leaves one with only the
most tenuous room for existence as a functioning and significant human
entity.

Any more comprehensive description of the etiology of paranoid schizophrenia would have to include two additional factors which I shall only
enumerate here: first, the presence of deeply repressed love-feelings in the
mother-child relationship—a factor which, as I have detailed elsewhere
(1958), is predominantly responsible for the child's introjection of the mother's submerged personality-fragmentation, and for the mother's—since she is
convinced, at a deep level, that her intimacy is destructive to the child—
becoming, early in his infancy, psychologically so aloof from him; and,
secondly, the failure of mother and child to resolve their symbiotic mode of

relatedness, a mode of relatedness which is normally found only in infancy. Their symbiosis is maintained into the patient's chronological adulthood, and those feelings, or other psychological contents, in either party which threaten the symbiosis are projected on to the world around the two. Not only such feelings as hatred and lust are projected on to the outer world, which therefore appears correspondingly threatening to the child; much of his own ego-capacities, also, being incompatible with the symbiosis with his mother, are projected on to various other figures, who are seen for a time as being larger than life, but always with eventual disillusionment. We might think of it that both the child and his mother have been unable to successfully traverse the ambivalent phase of his infancy—or, more accurately, the ambivalent phase of the mother-infant relationship, since this is a phase which, in normal development, is one of ambivalence not only for the child but also for the mother. In order to achieve true object-relatedness, as contrasted to symbiosis, this mutual ambivalence must be faced, accepted, and integrated into each person's concept of himself and of the other one.

The threat which his genital lust poses to the paranoid schizophrenic individual can be understood most meaningfully, I believe, in connexion with the structural phenomena of symbiosis, non-differentiation, and dedifferentiation which I have already touched upon. His sexual identity is poorly differentiated, and although other areas of his personality are equally poorly demarcated, the culture is particularly punitive in regard to incomplete sexual differentiation. Moreover, his own unresolved infantile omnipotence, a facet of the unresolved mother-infant symbiosis, is directly threatened by the necessity for him to accept a single sexual identity, as either male or female, and relinquish the complementary one; he cannot be wholly a man—or she, wholly a woman—without relinquishing that tenaciously held fantasied omnipotence. Further, the advent of genital lust at a time when his object-relations are at a level predominantly of symbiosis with the mother—herself poorly differentiated sexually, with a strongly, though unconsciously, phallic body-image—means that the sexual drive will be directed either toward the mother, or toward mother-surrogates, with connotations of both incest and homosexuality for the child, whether boy or girl. Another important ingredient, in the threat which lust poses for these young people, is traceable to their greatly thwarted identificatory needs; the young woman's need to identify with an adequate mother-figure is experienced as an utterly unacceptable 'lesbian tendency', and the young man's need to identify with an adequate father-figure is experienced as an equally shameful 'homosexual tendency'.

The lust, although genital in expression, actually operates, as regards its psychological significance in object-relations, upon at best an oral level—that is, the first developmental stage beyond full symbiosis—with the result that sexual intercourse is reacted to as posing the threat that one will eat, or be eaten by, the sexual partner. Most often, I think, the cannibalistic feelings which in the healthy person are relatively readily admissible to awareness, as a natural concomitant of oral needs dating back to earliest infancy, in the paranoid individual are, by contrast, deeply repressed and projected on to the other person, such that the fear is of being devoured by the other in the sexual act. With each of the paranoid schizophrenic patients who have progressed far toward health in my therapeutic experience, it has required years of therapy for them to become aware of cannibalistic desires. Prior to such a development, their view of sexual intercourse is well epitomized by this poem, composed by an intellectually brilliant and witty, but deeply paranoid, young man. This is a parody upon Edgar Allan Poe's 'Annabel Lee', and is entitled,

Miss Cannibalee

It was many and many a day ago,
  In a city you all can see,
That a maiden lived whom you might know
  By the name of Cannibalee;
And this maiden she lived with no other thought
  Than a passionate fondness for me.

I was a lad and she was a lass;
  I hoped that her tastes were free.
But she loved with a love that was more than love,
  My yearning Cannibalee;
With a love that could take me roast, or fried
  Or raw, as the case might be.

And that is the reason that long ago,
  In a city you all can see,
I had to turn the tables and eat
  My ardent Cannibalee—
Not really because I was fond of her,
  But to check her fondness for me.

But the stars never rise but I think of the size
  Of my hot-potted Cannibalee.
And the moon never stares but it brings me
  Night mares
Of my spare-rib Cannibalee;
  And all the night tide she is restless inside

Is my still indigestible dinner belle bride,
    In her pallid tomb, all rent free,
In her carnivorous sepulchre,—me.

Although such repressed emotions as hostility and lust may readily be seen, early in our work with any one of these patients, to account for some of his paranoid anxiety, as we go on with him we find that each one of the whole range of human emotions has been, in him, long repressed as constituting an equally important source of this anxiety. It may require many months for us to see how filled he is, too, with loneliness, unfulfilled dependency, and feelings of abandonment; with fear and guilt, helplessness and despair; with disillusionment and grief; with heretofore-stifled compassion and boundless love. These feelings are not easy to hear expressed, as, for instance, when a woman who, at the beginning of her therapy, has been encased for years in flintlike paranoid defences, becomes able to express her despair by saying that, 'If I had something to get well for, it would make a difference'; her grief, by saying, 'the reason I'm afraid to be close to people is because I feel so much like crying'; her loneliness, by expressing a wish that she could turn a bug into a person, so then she'd have a friend; and her helplessness in face of her ambivalence by saying, of her efforts to communicate with other persons, 'I feel just like a little child, at the edge of the Atlantic or Pacific Ocean, trying to build a castle—right *next* to the water. Something just starts to be grasped [by the other person], and then bang! it's gone—another wave.' And it is not entirely easy, either, to find oneself, in course of time, so important to, and adored by, the patient that he clearly yearns to be the ring on one's finger, sees one's face everywhere in people about him throughout the day, and finds that the days on which he has no therapeutic hour do not exist, in retrospect, for him, like so much time out of his life. But when he has become able to express any of these feelings, we can know that he is well in process of leaving his paranoid fortress, and joining the mainstream of his fellow human beings.

REFERENCES

Freud, S. (1911). Psycho-analytic notes upon an autobiographical account of a case of paranoia (Dementia Paranoides). In *Collected Papers, 3*. London: Hogarth Press (1953).

Hartmann, H. (1939). *Ego Psychology and the Problem of Adaptation*. New York: International Universities Press, 1958. (Originally published in *Int. Z. Psychoanal.* 1939.)

Hartmann, H. (1950). Psychoanalysis and developmental psychology. *The Psychoanalytic Study of the Child, 5*. New York: International Universities Press.

Hartmann, H. (1956). Notes on the reality principle. *The Psychoanalytic Study of the Child*, **11**. New York: International Universities Press.

Hill, L. B. (1948). Personal communication.

Modell, A. H. (1958). The theoretical implications of hallucinatory experiences in schizophrenia. *J. Amer. Psa. Assn.* **6**, 442.

Noyes, A. P. (1951). *Modern Clinical Psychiatry*. Philadelphia and London: W. B. Saunders. (Quote is from p. 399).

Piaget, J. (1930). *The Child's Conception of Physical Causality*. New York: The Humanities Press; London: Routledge & Kegan Paul, 1951. (First published in England in 1930.)

Rapaport, D. (1958). The theory of ego autonomy: a generalization. *Bull. Menninger Clin.* **22**, 13.

Searles, H. F. (1958). Positive feelings in the relationship between the schizophrenic and his mother. *Int. J. Psychoanal.* **39**, 569. (Reprinted in German translation, under the title, 'Positive Gefühle in der Beziehung zwischen dem Schizophrenen und seiner Mutter', *Psyche.* **14**, 165, 1960.)

Searles, H. F. (1959a). The differentiation between concrete and metaphorical thinking in the recovering schizophrenic patient. Presented at the meeting of the American Psychiatric Association, Philadelphia, 30 April 1959. *J. Amer. Psa. Assn.* **10**, 22–49, (1962).

Searles, H. F. (1959b). Integration and differentiation in schizophrenia: an over-all view. *Brit. J. Med. Psychol.* **32**, 261.

Searles, H. F. (1959c). Integration and differentiation in schizophrenia. *J. Nerv. Mental Dis.* **129**, 542.

Searles, H. F. (1960). *The Nonhuman Environment in Normal Development and in Schizophrenia*. New York: International Universities Press.

Werner, H. (1940). *Comparative Psychology of Mental Development*. New York: International Universities Press, 1957. (Originally published in German; first English translation published by Harper, 1940.)

6. Masochism in Paranoia

Robert C. Bak

Until the works of Ferenczi (*1*) and Freud gave us essential insight into paranoia, Kraepelin's point of view dominated. Kraepelin gave the classic description, delineating the symptom complex, and the bulk of the ensuing research attempted to isolate paranoia as a disease entity. With the separation of the paraphrenias from dementia præcox, the sole two remaining clinical forms of sensitive paranoia were the paranoia of jealousy and litigious paranoia. Most investigators held that the psychosis was characterogenic, originating in a specific paranoid constitution, which manifested itself in certain personality traits. The psychosis was supposed to develop under the influence of certain experiences as an exaggeration of the underlying constitution. Among the precipitating experiences were particularly emphasized injuries to the ego, such as slights, frustrated ambitions, injustices.

Freud (*2*) emerged with his brilliant genetic theory of paranoia, demonstrated by means of Schreber's autobiography. Essentially this theory states that in paranoia the ego sets up defenses against homosexuality, from which there results a regression from sublimated homosexuality to narcissism. The libido is withdrawn from the loved person, the homosexual trend ('I love him') is denied and turned into its opposite ('I hate him'), and the hatred is then projected ('because he persecutes me'). Projection undoes the withdrawal. The subsequent formation of delusions is a work of reconstruction, which carries the libido back to the object, but with a negative prefix. This ingenious theory seemed applicable to the various clinical forms of paranoia.

Clinical psychiatry took over elements of Freud's theory but in an attenuated form. Schulte (*3*) developed the 'we' theory of paranoia, translating the idea of reconstruction into Gestalt terminology. He stated that the paranoiac regains contact with the group in his delusional relations, thus 'closing the wound' of isolation. Cameron (*4*) recently, and similarly, attributed paranoid delusions to a defective development of role-taking and a relative inadequacy in social perspectives. In place of projection and reconstruction he introduced the concept of 'pseudo-community', organized by the paranoiac's reaction to his own preoccupations out of fragments of the social behavior of others. Mayer-Gross (5), paraphrasing the idea of libido withdrawal, derived persecutory delusions from the 'cooling of sympathetic emotions', which are then projected on the outside world. Kretschmer (6) in his study of the 'sensitive Beziehungswahn' stressed the sexual ethical conflict as the main factor, and derived the paranoid reaction from the interplay of character and environment: a weak sexual endowment is manifested in an 'uncertainty of instinctual drives', while psychical trauma and exhaustion serve as precipitating factors.

In psychoanalytic circles at the time of Freud's paper on Schreber, interest was mainly focused on libidinal trends and the defense against them; hence, the discovery of the rôle of homosexuality was of enormous significance for an understanding of paranoia. To this emphasis, perhaps, may be due the inadequate answer to the main and specific question, namely, why the beloved person should be transformed into a persecutor.

Stärcke (7) and van Ophuijsen (8) attempted to explain this particular vicissitude of the homosexual trend. In their valuable contributions, still dominated by the reigning interest in phases of libido development, they upheld the view that the original persecutor is the scybalum, and that the delusions of persecution are derived mainly by elaboration and symbolizations of anal sensations. But this addition to the homosexual aspect did not provide sufficient clarification.

Another factor had to be considered. The enormous rôle played by aggression in paranoia could not elude Freud very long (9). In The Ego and the Id, discussing the duality of instincts, he stated that the paranoiac does not directly transform the personal relationship from love into hate. From the start there is present an ambivalence; the transformation takes place by a reactive shifting of cathexis. The quantity of energy withdrawn from erotic trends is added to the hostile impulses.

This new important point clarified the second defensive step of the ego in paranoia. The first step is the withdrawal of love as a defense against the sexual wish. Reenforcement of hostility by the liberated energy constitutes the second step, and this second step accounts for the hatred felt for the previously loved person. The way in which this hatred is rationalized and nourished by interpretations of other persons' unconscious wishes was illuminated earlier by Freud in the article, 'Certain Neurotic Mechanisms in Jealousy, Paranoia and Homosexuality' (10). But hatred and hostility are not by any means paranoia. Therefore it seemed that somewhere in the third step of

Freud's scheme, that of the projection of the aggression, lay the secret of persecutory delusional formation.

Klein (*11*), who refers also to Róheim's (*12*) findings, believes that the fixation point of paranoia lies in the period of maximal sadism, during which the mother's body is attacked by means of dangerous and poisonous excreta. The delusions of persecution are supposed to arise from the anxiety attached to these attacks.

Nunberg (*13*) in his much-quoted paper, *Homosexuality, Magic and Aggression*, gives us a profound hint in a somewhat different direction. He describes a particular type of homosexual, in whom the sexual act satisfies simultaneously both aggressive and libidinal impulses. In this type the ego ideal is projected onto the love object, which then receives sadistic treatment in the sexual act. In paranoia the sadism is turned largely into its opposite, into masochism. This paper, following a somewhat similar line of thought, will corroborate Nunberg's view.

The patient, a man of thirty-seven, began his analysis after an acute anxiety state with depression, for which he had spent four weeks in a hospital. He improved considerably but felt the need of further help to get at the cause of his acute breakdown. A few weeks prior to his hospitalization, he had become apprehensive about his relations with his fiancée. As the wedding day approached, although he was intensely desirous of being married, his anxiety mounted. He started to examine his penis and to worry about his ordinarily well-functioning potency. With increasing panic he observed a slackening of his mental faculties. He felt as if a catastrophe impended, as if he were sitting on a volcano whose eruption would sweep him away. At this point he asked for psychiatric help and was hospitalized.

In the hospital he was preoccupied mainly with three topics. In the first place he thought that he had lost his mind, which seemed proved to him by his own difficulty in thinking and by his suicidal impulses. Second, he thought he was incapable of getting married; this it was which made him think of suicide as the only way of avoiding the prospect of remaining a bachelor and leading 'a lonely, horrid, hideous existence'. Third, he feared his nervous breakdown would be interpreted by people to be the result of some sexual aberration, and that they might spread gossip about him in this connection. This was his first definitely paranoid idea, which later turned out to be related to childhood experiences of 'being buggered' (anal intercourse).

Early in his treatment it became evident that the patient's main difficulty lay in his relation to men. Among women he was successful, especially in sexual relations, yet he had not developed any emotional tie up to the time of his engagement. His life was void of male friendships. His contacts were mainly restricted to the professional field, but even these relations proved to be very fragile. Previous to and during treatment, he got into states of anxiety which ran according to a more or less similar pattern. In most instances, he felt slighted by either of his older superiors, or by one of his rivals with whom he had had pleasant relations prior to the conflict; or he felt as though some injustice was inflicted upon him. A variation of these feelings occurred when he tried to get out of a situation in which he felt some obligation. The feeling that something was expected of him was experienced as something forced upon him. He was afraid he might be taken advantage of, 'used' and 'reduced to a mere tool'.

During a short absence from treatment he went through a typical episode which he communicated to me in a letter that gives insight into the structure and course of such a conflict.

I am writing you regarding the recurrence of my troubles. Their cause is concerned with some of my personal relationships which are in reality getting out of hand. I realize that I am abnormally conscious of and concerned with these matters. But, this consciousness and concern is part of the cycle of wanting good personal relations, of being conscious of their status, of anxiety about them and of deterioration in them, partly because of the concern.

A month ago, I moved to another building. The people were unfriendly and made no welcome and while I made some efforts to cultivate several members, I was not very successful. As a result of a strained feeling I refused to attend two of their private parties and that seems to have facilitated their resentment (which I feel, whether it exists or not). And during the course of a drinking bout indulged in by one of them, some quite serious indignities were inflicted on all members including me.

The indignities as such are a minor problem. However, other reactions are much more disturbing and are making me seriously consider drastic measures. The main reactions are: sleeplessness, marked tension and much the same feeling of "sitting on a volcano" which I have described to you. In addition, I feel ill at ease with people, noncommunicative, and the anxiety, which is apparently detectable, spoils relationships with people with whom I had previously made a considerable favorable contact.

The fear that I feel has been tremendous too, and is probably greater than I've experienced for eighteen months. As far as I can analyze it, the fear comes from the idea that I'll eventually have *to batter and beat one or more people—or be battered and beaten* [italics mine]. Some of it is from the feeling that I'll get into a physical combat and will be disgraced and "talked about" by other members of the community—disgraced because of "starting a fight" (if I win), or because of getting a licking (if I lose). Some of these aspects have tortured me day and night for a week and that means that it has been more distressing than any situation since before I stopped seeing you regularly. If one feature is most disturbing, it is the fear which may be noticeable to others and thus tends (because of that) to cause more panic.

At times like last night, I become almost panic-stricken when my mind "runs away" with all sorts of paranoid ideas. It would not be possible to name all of these, but most of them have to do with suspicion of conspiracies against me. I am moderately sure (during saner moments) that there are no conspiracies other than perhaps some small talk between the two people whom I dislike and distrust the most. I seriously suspect them of it, however, whether or not it is true.

The scene of 'indignities' referred to in the letter was truly remarkable. The patient remained seated, motionless while a drunken, boisterous person spilled beer around the room, challenging him to fight, spilling beer on him, making him soaking wet. He could neither protest nor leave. He sat there in a kind of paralyzed fascination, waiting for the assault. Only later was he overwhelmed by a desire to 'split that man's head, and ruining the reputation of the whole place in case he was not rehabilitated'.

The conflict with one individual tended to include the group of which the individual was a member (Jews, Catholics, or various nationalities). When precipitated by the transference, as a 'transitive transference' reaction (*14*) only the conflict with the group became conscious. Thus, at one time the patient felt particularly slighted by taxi drivers. They were impolite, they cut in front of him, bumped into his car, pushed him out of their way; furthermore, sailors spat in front of him, salesmen 'threw the change' in his face. He was fairly convinced in these phases that these were not chance happenings, but that they were directed against him. The reaction to these experiences was impulses of violence 'against the inferior mob or race', anxiety about them, and the desire to flee. He was on the way to developing the paranoiac pattern of the 'haunted man' whose fate is fleeing from one city to another.

Further clinical details which confirm the diagnosis of paranoia are omitted: systematization, excessive vulnerability, traces of megalomania, marked tendency to projection, ideas of reference and persecution, and litigious fantasies.

There is in the patient's history an organic factor that shaped his entire future. He was born with hypospadias. This seems to have remained unnoticed until the age of five, when he entered school. He became conspicuous through his urination: 'He can piss through a nut-hole', the boys teased him. His first name was distorted into a nickname similar to one of the vulgar expressions for the penis. They also changed his name into that of a woman. The vague notion that something was wrong became certainty when his mother said to him from an adjoining room, 'You are not quite like other boys', but avoided further explanation. The fact that she did not tell him made her appear guilty. At about the same age he agreed with his younger brother to mutual fellatio, which he performed. When the brother's turn came, he refused. This, he reasoned, occurred because his penis was unattractive. His enuresis was ridiculed by his brother and his parents. The ardent desire to be 'one of the boys', and his ostracism from the group became early realities. His envy of other boys and his hostility against them were vividly remembered. Later he heard that he was taken by his mother to several doctors, and that they might have operated on him.

He frequently examined his penis, found some scars on it, and thought they might have been caused by circumcision or by some other kind of operation. Up to an adult age, he could not decide whether the missing part of his foreskin was congenital or surgical.

A remarkable fantasy at the age of nine relates to this problem. It is probably a retrograde projection. In the fantasy he is not a child of his parents but the product of an experiment, the result of some chemical concoction. He thought he would have to go through further experiments and ordeals and probably come to a terrible end.

During puberty he became concerned with the relative enlargement of the glans penis and thought this might cause difficulty in withdrawing his penis from the vagina. From his first sexual intercourse with a prostitute he contracted gonorrhœa requiring long and painful treatments. The idea of injury done by women to the penis was thus confirmed. The evil role of women was represented in the dream:

I was incarcerated in a sort of prison. A great many people were making efforts to get me out. I finally got out. You were standing in the background.

Before the dream he had been pondering whether he should give up his affair with his current girl, a divorcee. The associations led through the links *carnis*, flesh, vulva to a memory which he was hesitant about confiding. 'It's too base and cruel', he said. As a boy of four or five he was playing with another child when they saw two dogs stuck together in coitus. They did not know quite what it was, and they chased the dogs with sticks toward a barbed-wire fence. The dogs became entangled in the barbed wire and hung suspended on the fence, their skins torn by the wire. He then got the vague idea that the dog's penis was cut off and that the bitch ran away with the male's penis inside of her.

Why he should discontinue his friendship with the divorcee became clear only later. Separation in time from her husband was not sufficient. He could not escape the feeling that the penis of the former husband was left in the wife's vagina. He had been told by his mother as a youngster that only a first marriage counts in heaven. He then visualized the second husband, roaming alone, lonely, having no place anywhere.

The notion persisted in the unconscious that woman inflicts injury on the man's penis, can tear it off and harbor it in the vagina. In the act of marriage not only his name but the man's penis is bestowed. The mother possesses the father's penis, and has power to destroy it.

The mother's treatment of the boy was total rejection. He felt he had been reared without any love at all. He could not recall any token of affection from his mother, no memory of caressing or tenderness. By contrast, the remembrance of a maid clasping him to her bosom, and the attendant feeling of her softness and warmth stood out in relief in his memory. The mother was no protection for him from his father; they presented a common front and participated in punishing the child. 'Wait until father comes home' was her repetitive admonition. Being the eldest, he saw the arrival of six children, one every second year.

Whatever the 'constitutional predisposition', the hypospadias more than paved the way to a preponderantly negative œdipus. The feminine component of his bisexuality was supplemented by his mother's harsh treatment, and by his fantasy of her threatening image. The convergence of these factors resulted in an identification with the castrating parent, the aggressive, phallic mother.

He turned to his father to be loved and appreciated by him. The father was a withdrawn, cold, strict, hard-working farmer. It was impossible to get in his good graces. The patient remembered often, with tears, how unappreciative his father was of him. As a child of six, he was helping his father gather hay. He worked diligently the whole day, and driving home from the fields he asked his father if his work that day was worth fifty cents, and if so whether he could have it. The father ignored him completely. He pleaded, and finally in desperation asked if his work was worth at least a nickel. His father brushed him off as before. The emotional cathexis of these memories was tremendous. Not being loved, and particularly not having had any physical contact as a token of love, caused him a great deal of suffering. He felt very much moved when a neighbor's son put his arms around him. He felt a strong desire to go hand in hand with his father and for many years resented that the father did not play with him and did not teach him to fight. 'Together with father' he would have been strong, powerful, and a member of the male group. But instead of the close relationship and gentle physical contact he was beaten by the father for the slightest mischief. If he got into a fight with his brothers, which they started, he was nevertheless beaten by his father, being told he was older and should know better. Sometimes he waited for hours in a cold sweat for the threatened beating. The beatings, with a stick, were ruthlessly sadistic. He was always found to be in the wrong and was never exonerated. He fantasied though, with great clarity, picking up a shovel, or getting hold of the stick and attacking his father. After one beating he vowed that when he grew up he would beat up his father.

Such powerful aggression in this helpless boy, who craved for love and physical affection, intensified his ambivalence. One part of the aggression remained in fantasy, and developed into manifold sadistic reveries. He day-dreamed, for instance, that women were stationed in stalls like racing horses. Every woman was set and alert, bent forward on her toes in the stall. The patient, the boss, was beating them using his penis as a rod. He remembered a beating in the fields, his father starting back for the house, his being left behind overwhelmed by rage and sorrow, the idea flashing through his mind, 'Now he is going back to the house to screw mother'. The patient advanced the theory that his father 'was taking something out on him' at that time. There must have been a 'lack of sexual synchronization between my parents'. He recalled vaguely that his father had some sort of 'nervous breakdown' about that time. We have noted that 'nervous breakdown' was linked in the patient's mind to sexual (anal) aberration. It becomes obvious that in the unconscious the experience of being beaten by the father became libidinized into being sexually abused by him. The yearning for affection was regressively debased into masochistic degradation. In the masochistic act, part of the sadism took a circuitous path to gratification. During prostatic treatment the patient dreamed:

I am going to the doctor for treatment. He looks like a debonair Frenchman, with a goatee. He could be a psychiatrist. The doctor starts to finger my anus, then it seems to change to intercourse. Finally I find myself dancing around in the room like a witch with a broomstick in my arse.

To get hold of the father's stick, to castrate him, is achieved when anally he incorporates the father's penis, playing the part of the castrating woman, ultimately the role of the phallic mother. The patient's pugnacity and his lifelong preoccupation with preparing himself for physical fights by 'jiu-jitsu' lessons and 'commando training' also become understandable.

The constellation in which the paranoid reaction originates, as we know from Freud, is homosexuality. One of the prominent strivings in our patient had been the ambition to be recognized, appreciated and loved by important, outstanding men. The infantile desire to gain the father's recognition was never abandoned. Before the acute phase of his illness he dreamed that he went home, resolved the differences with his father, and at the final reconciliation they both wept. In his daydreams he became the favorite son as a reward for his successes and achievements. Fulfilment of the ego ideal, and being loved according to this ideal, is a sublimation which binds large quantities of homosexual and narcissistic libido. We know, however, that relationships on this basis prove to be very fragile, undermined as they are by strong ambivalence.

In such an unstable psychological structure economic changes in the ego or in the id result in a threat to the ego, and put the ego's defenses in action. An increase in homosexual libido may be due to biological or to situational factors (seduction, frustration); however, a greater role seems to be played in the further development by injuries inflicted directly upon the ego. Slights, frustrations, and disappointments reverse sublimations and liberate homosexual libido (*15*): 'You are not a man. You should be treated as a woman.' The failure of sublimation and the direct threat of castration lead to a retreat from phallic activity and induce a masochistic regression (homosexuality) where, according to the phallic and anal-sadistic organization, the desires to be castrated, beaten, and anally abused are reactivated.

A dream illustrates this point:

> Hitler, Mussolini, and Hirohito are about to be executed, but Hirohito cannot be found. I offer to replace him. The execution looks like a decapitation. I put my head on the scaffold; they separate the scalp from my skull, and push a knife into the back of my head.

Through masochistic identification he could become the father, the powerful and loved enemy. The price he had to pay was castration (circumcision and anal intercourse).

This regression from sublimated homosexuality to masochism is an essential feature of the paranoid reaction, and constitutes the *first* defensive action of the ego. The withdrawal of love that follows is the *second* step in the defense through which the ego protects itself from the masochistic threat coming from the id. Alienation, feelings of estrangement, detachment from the previously beloved person, and free floating anxiety are the clinical corollaries of this stage. The *third* step is an increase of hostility, hatred of the love object, and the appearance of sadistic fantasies. In making the transition from love to hate the ego makes use of the displaceable energies contained in the originally ambivalent attitude. Sadism then fulfils several functions: the ego succeeds in turning passivity into activity and exploiting it as a countercathexis against masochism; furthermore, it reenforces the ego feelings (male attitude), and represents a recathexis of phallic activity. At this point mastery of the increased sadism is the primary task of the ego. That it fails is due to the interplay of several factors: weakness of the ego, masochistic fixation, and castration anxiety. The ego has to get rid of the increased tension and of the feelings of isolation, and this it manages by projecting a part of the sadism. The projection of sadism then would be the *fourth* step of defense. It is 'the paranoid mechanism proper', and it is a restitution. Projection is possible partly through the unconscious hostility of the actual and past participants and runs according to this preordained path. *In the projection of the sadism the masochism is bound to return.* The patient's preoccupation with precipitating a 'physical showdown' (being assaulted) and its ramified delusional elaborations, as being mistreated, injured, and persecuted, gratify the original masochistic desires of castration, beating, and abuse by the father. The delusion is a return of the repressed, and *paranoia is delusional masochism.*

The ego aligns itself on the side of sadism. Masochism (id) serves to reestablish object cathexis and to hinder further 'defusion'. The antagonistic hypercathexis of the two psychic agencies is an attempt to achieve equilibrium. Depending on economic factors, the outcome may be flight, murder, suicide, or subsiding of the tension and cessation of the attack. Megalomania seems to be a later development when quantities of masochistic cathexis are further withdrawn.

Omitting the individual persecutory mechanism, let us examine briefly another characteristic feature of paranoia, that of an expanding, generalized persecution by a group. The answer may be found in the family constellation, perhaps more specifically in a vicissitude of sibling rivalry. The infantile prototype of this cohesive, hostile group may be traced in the fused image of the parents, their 'common front', representing the image of the phallic mother. This concept is later widened and includes the group of siblings. In the course of development these concepts in the ego ideal are further extended but seem to preserve their fused character and highly ambivalent cathexis. By regression they undergo a masochistic transformation to which can be applied Freud's (*16*) formulation in a modified version: 'My father loves me, I am the favorite, and he beats my brothers'. The libidinal and sadistic impulse after having undergone masochistic transformation is: 'My father beats me; I am hated; they all want to beat me', and this masochistic turn seems to correspond to reality. The love object, the father, was the original persecutor. The family was aligned against the patient in a 'common front'. His schoolmates ridiculed him. He was not accepted in fraternities, and his religious group was looked down on. Here we meet some of the real elements in delusion to which Freud referred in one of his last papers, 'Constructions in Analysis'. True, to a large extent, the patient brought it on himself; but the paranoiac is not infrequently a person who has been persecuted in his past.

The sociological significance of this type of personality is well known. Our patient also turns violently against underprivileged minority groups. But once, when he witnessed a scene in which a fragile, small, Jewish-looking man was threatened with beating, he suddenly felt as if he himself were Jewish. He identifies himself with the persecuted minority on the basis of his history and on the basis of his masochistic propensity. In releasing his sadism against these groups, he not only defends himself against his own masochism, but realizes the beating fantasy through dramatization.

To what extent have these observations general validity in relation to paranoia? This case history is selected from a vast number of clinical experiences in the study of paranoid psychoses and from the analyses of paranoid personalities. We are indebted for the subtle and thorough analysis of a case of paranoia to Ruth Mack Brunswick (*17*). In addition to this we are in possession of the full infantile history of this patient described in Freud's (*18*) inimitable way in the 'Wolf-man', in 'The History of an Infantile Neurosis', and this patient's later paranoid condition, observed by Brunswick.

The paranoia that started about twelve years after the analysis with Freud centered around a hypochondriac idea. The patient felt that his nose was swollen and disfigured by a scar due to operations that were performed on it by a dermatologist (who was a substitute for Freud). He felt crippled, and ruined for life, and claimed that 'he could not go on living that way', thereby repeating his mother's words which were related to her abdominal illness. The injury to the nose was originally self-inflicted and only later treated by the dermatologist. Brunswick stated:

The patient's failure to be satisfied by his self-castration reveals a motive beyond the usual masochistic one of guilt, which, regardless of the perpetrator, would be satisfied by the act itself. The further motive is, of course, the libidinal one, the desire for castration at the hands of the father as an expression in anal-sadistic language of that father's love.' In discussing the patient's change of character, Brunswick relates it to the 'irritable and aggressive' period of childhood. 'Behind his tempers lay the masochistic desire for punishment at the hands of the father; but the outward form of his character was at that time sadistic. . . . In the present character change, the same regression to the anal-sadistic or masochistic level was present, but the role of the patient was passive. He was tormented and abused, instead of being the tormentor.' About the hypochondriac idea Brunswick wrote: 'The [childhood] fantasy of being beaten on the penis was reflected in the delusion of being injured on the nose by X [the dermatologist]'. There are many more masochistic elements in the case history, but still in the final analysis they are deprived of their due role. Brunswick derives the loss of psychic equilibrium in the patient from the flaring up of his love for the fatally ill Freud (father). This love represents a danger of castration, the love then is repressed and turned into hostility and has to be projected. It is true that the sight of the fatally ill Freud stirred up in the patient his old compassion for his father. In his childhood the sight of his sick father in a sanitarium became the prototype for his compassion for cripples, beggars, poor, and consumptive people, in whose presence he had to breathe noisily so as not to become like them. It was one of his defenses against identification with the castrated father.

We must add only some emphasis to Brunswick's analysis. Love for the ill Freud (father), which had the unconscious implication of the patient's being a 'woman', underwent regressive change into being castrated and beaten. *The homosexual object choice regressed into masochistic identification. We think that this form of regression constitutes the prerequisite of a paranoid development*, and the subsequent course in this patient also supports this assumption. In his hypochondria he consistently manœuvred to bring about his castration and at the same time defended himself against it by aggressive and litigious fantasies. This was the repetition of the sado-masochistic phase of his childhood, to which he had been thrown back partly because of a threat of castration. At that time he had been a tormentor of animals and men, but, at the same time, he indulged in fantasies of boys being beaten, and especially of being beaten on the penis. In a variation of these fantasies, 'the Czarevitch . . . is shut up in a room (the wardrobe) and beaten'. The Czarevitch was evidently himself. As we know, in hypochondriac and persecutory delusions, these fantasies find renewed expression.

A vast number of questions remains unanswered. The primary aim of this presentation has been to demonstrate the crucial role that masochism plays in the paranoid mechanism. In his paper, 'A Child Is Being Beaten', referring to the masochistic beating fantasies, Freud wrote:

'People who harbor fantasies of this kind develop a special sensitiveness and irritability towards anyone whom they can put among the class of fathers. They allow themselves to be easily offended by a person of this kind, and in that way (to their own sorrow and cost) bring about the realization of the imagined situation of being beaten by their father. I should not be surprised if it were one day possible to prove that the same fantasy is the basis of the delusional litigiousness of paranoia'.

REFERENCES

1. Ferenczi, S. On the Part Played by Homosexuality in the Pathogenesis of Paranoia. In *Contributions to Psychoanalysis*. Boston: Richard C. Badger, 1916.
2. Freud, S. *Psychoanalytic Notes Upon an Autobiographical Account of a Case of Paranoia (Dementia Paranoides)*, 1911. Coll. Papers, **III**.
3. Schulte, H. *Versuch einer Theorie der paranoischen Eigenbeziehung und Wahnbildung.* Psychologische Forschung, **V**, 1924, pp. 1–23.
4. Cameron, N. *The Development of Paranoic Thinking*. Psychol. Rev., **L**., 1943, pp. 219–233.
5. Mayer-Gross, W. *Handbuch der Geisteskrankheiten.* Spez. T. Bd. **V**, pp. 303, ff. Editor: Bumke. Berlin: Springer, 1932.
6. Kretschmer, E. *Die sensitive Beziehungswahn.* Berlin: Springer, 1924.
7. Stärcke, A. *Die Rolle der analen und oralen Quantitäten im Verfolgungswahn und in analogen Systemgedanken.* Int. Ztschr. f. Psa., **XXI**, 1935, pp. 5–22.
8. Van Ophuijsen, J. H. W. *On the Origin of the Feeling of Persecution.* Int. J. Psa., **I**, 1920, pp. 235–239.
9. Freud, S. *The Ego and the Id.* London: Hogarth Press, 1927.
10. ———. *Certain Neurotic Mechanisms in Jealousy, Paranoia and Homosexuality*, 1922. Coll. Papers, **II**, pp. 232–243.
11. Klein, M. *The Psychoanalysis of Children.* London: Hogarth Press, 1937.
12. Róheim, G. *Nach dem Tode des Urvaters.* Imago, **IV**, 1923, pp. 83–121.
13. Nunberg, H. *Homosexualität, Magie und Aggression.* Int. Ztschr. f. Psa., **XXII**, 1936, pp. 5–18.
14. Herman, I. *Die Psychoanalyse als Methode.* Vienna: Int. Psa. Verlag, 1936.
15. Freud, S. *On Narcissism: an Introduction*, 1914. Coll. Papers, **IV**, pp. 30–59.
16. ———. *'A Child Is Being Beaten'. A Contribution to the Study of the Origin of Sexual Perversions*, 1919. Coll. Papers, **II**, pp. 172–201.
17. Brunswick, R. M. *A Supplement to Freud's 'History of an Infantile Neurosis'.* Int. J. Psa., **IX**, 1928, pp. 439–476.
18. Freud, S. *From the History of an Infantile Neurosis* (1918). Coll. Papers, **III**, pp. 471–519.

7. On Psychotic Identifications[1]

Edith Jacobson

Not only in the manic-depressive but also in the schizophrenic groups of psychoses, pathological mechanisms of identification seem to play a paramount part in the psychotic symptom formation. From Freud's, Abraham's, Rado's, Klein's papers, we are familiar with the narcissistic identifications underlying the delusional ideas in manic-depressive states. But apart from the paranoid projections, the nature and functions of the identification mechanisms operating in schizophrenic processes have not been so systematically investigated.

It is a challenging task indeed to study and to compare their nature and their role in symptom formation with the corresponding phenomena in manic-depressive psychosis. The time allotted to this presentation does not permit of more than a very limited approach to the problem. May I begin with the statement that evidently, in the regressive processes induced by the psychosis, early preoedipal mechanisms of identification are revived whose general characteristics I wish to define, briefly, in contra-distinction to normal ego identification.

For this purpose I may use the term 'self-representations', in analogy to 'object-representations'. This term refers to the endopsychic concept of the bodily and mental self which, built up in the course of ego formation, normally reflects the characteristics, the state, and the functions of our conscious and preconscious ego. The term is of special value for the study of psychosis, because in these disorders the realistic representations, not only of the object world but also of the self as an integrated entity, are apt to break down and to be replaced by distorted, unrealistic, delusional concepts. In fact, the psychotic is confused about both, about the objects and his own self; a state which reminds us of the early infantile stage before the boundaries between the self and the love objects have been firmly established, a stage when the child is flooded by magic images of the object world and of his own self. At that stage the child's need to maintain his magic world and to regain union with his love objects leads easily not only to re-fusions between omnipotent paternal and maternal images, but also to a blending of such images with those of the self. Such magic union between mother and child is easily achieved when close physical contact with her is experienced. The temporary partial or total merging of self-images and love-object-images finds expression in the child's feeling that he is part of his omnipotent love objects, and *vice versa*; in his narcissistic dependence on his love objects; in his temporary belief that imitating, playing father or mother, means really being or becoming his parents. Such mechanisms precede and prepare the development of ego- and superego-identifications which arise from strivings, no longer to be one with or to be the love object, but to become *like* it in the *future*. In short, whereas the early identifications are magic in nature and lead to phantasies or even to the temporary belief that one is one with or has become the love object, regardless of reality, the ego-identifications are realistic; they promote and eventually achieve real changes of the ego, which justify the feeling that one is at least partially like the object of identification. We shall presently study the disintegration of object relations and normal ego- and superego-identifications, and their replacement by such regressively revived magic identification mechanisms in a manic-depressive and a schizophrenic case.[2]

May I introduce the case material by a brief formulation which, though it simplifies matters, may highlight in advance the different nature of the identifications in either kind of psychotic disorder. It appears that the manic-depressive, who demands continuous narcissistic supply from his love object, treats himself in his delusions of worthlessness or of grandeur respectively as if he were the bad or the good love object; whereas the schizophrenic in the prepsychotic state tends to imitate, to behave as if he were the love object and, when delusional, eventually may even consciously believe that he has become another object. Let me now briefly report two cases.

Some years ago, I treated a woman of forty suffering from her fourth depressive period. Each time, her depression had been introduced by increasing irritability and hostility towards her husband and children, which in the course of some weeks would give way to a typical depressive state with severe anxieties, retardation, withdrawal, and continuous self-accusations.

The patient came to see me in a state of transition from the first to the second stage of illness. At first she would mainly bring forward endless complaints about her husband, his inefficiency and selfishness, his aggressiveness and moral worthlessness. Quite insidiously the subject of her complaints began to change, and she herself became the centre of such attacks. One day during this phase she suddenly interrupted her alternate attacks on herself and her partner and said:

'I am so confused, I don't know whether I complain about my husband or myself. In my mind his picture is all mixed up with that of myself, as if we were the same person. Actually, we are alike only in our overdependence on each other. We cling to one another like two babies, each expecting the other to be a good mother. However, previously I have always been generous and giving, whereas he is stingy and selfish, expecting me to give myself up for him. Now, *I* want to be taken care of. Maybe this is why I have become sick. I have felt powerless to change him, but my sickness will not make him love me either.'

In this outburst my patient had disclosed the nature of her melancholic mechanisms, with an awareness that is uncommon in depressives. She had consciously perceived her impaired sense of reality and the resulting fusion and confusion between the concept of her own worthless self and the bad, devaluated image of her partner. Moreover, the patient had frankly stated to what extent her fixation at the infantile stage of magic participation in an over-valued love object had predisposed her for this regressive process.

Her pathological state had announced itself first by denunciations of her husband's character, remindful of those of a disappointed little child. However, contrary to the child's rapid change from good to bad images of his love objects, her disappointment in her partner had kindled a profound hostility which made her look at him through dark glasses only. Within some weeks, her efforts to maintain the libidinous cathexis of her love object, her fear of annihilating the 'good image' on which she depended so greatly, had turned her hostility increasingly towards herself. A pathological identification process had been induced, which one might rather describe not as an introjection of the love object into the ego but as a gradual absorption and replacement of the 'bad-husband'-image by the image of her own worthless self.[3]

During one session the patient interrupted her repetitive self-accusations by suddenly mentioning her mother. 'When I listen to my endless self-reproaches,' she said, 'I sometimes hear the voice of my mother. She was a wonderful, strong woman, but very severe and disapproving. I was as dependent on her as I am on my husband. If he were only as strong and wonderful as she was.' With her usual lucidity the patient had not only indicated that unconsciously her husband represented the mother, but had realized that her superego had become so severe through reanimation of a powerful, punitive mother-husband-image.

This points to the restitutive function of the superego changes during the melancholic period. The first-described identifications resulted in the setting up of a deflated, 'bad' love-object-image within the self-image, a process intended to maintain the libidinous cathexis of the love object. As this effort for a solution of her ambivalence conflict failed, the libidinous cathexis was increasingly withdrawn from the real love object and, eventually, from the object world in general. The patient's object relations deteriorated; her ego functions were severely inhibited and slowed up. Instead of the dissolving realistic object-representations in the ego, a powerful and indestructible, but punitive and cruel mother-husband-image was resurrected and set up in the superego which thus became repersonified and changed its functions. Contrary to that of schizophrenics, however, the melancholic superego—even though repressively personified, archaic, and highly pathological in its functions—is maintained as a psychic system and gains ever increasing strength by taking the place of the fading object-representations. In the endopsychic continuation of the struggle with the love object, the self maintains its utter dependence on the latter. It becomes, indeed, a victim of the superego, as helpless and powerless as a small child who is tortured by his cruel, powerful mother.

A manic condition may or may not follow the depression. Such a state announces the ending of the period of atonement by reunion with the love object or superego, respectively, which now changes from a punitive into a good, forgiving, omnipotent figure. The reprojection of this almighty, all-giving object-image on to the real object world re-establishes spurious object relations. The patient throws himself into an imagined world of unending pleasure and indestructible power, in which he can greedily partake, without fear. We shall presently compare these mechanisms with the magic identifications developing in a schizophrenic episode.

A brilliant girl of twenty-seven, a social science student, went into an acute catatonic episode at the time when her second marriage was going to pieces. The nature of her disease had been established beyond doubt some years before; this was her second acute breakdown. Up to the time of her first attack she had been a very ambitious girl, emotionally cold, with distinctly megalomanic, supercilious attitudes. She was forever in search of her own identity. She wished and at times believed she was a genius, an idea she shared with her schizophrenic mother.

Shortly before the onset of her acute condition, the patient had asked for an appointment. The reason for wanting to see me was her fear that her husband 'might have to commit suicide' should she desert him, as she was planning to do. Unaware of her own disturbed state, she assured me that she herself felt on top of the world except for her concern about Larry, the husband. Soon after the interview she flew into a rage, left him, and within a few hours developed a severe state of excitement. She rampaged through her hotel apartment, took a shower at two a.m., singing and making a lot of noise, etc. I rushed to her, and was easily able to establish contact and persuade her to go immediately to a sanatorium.

In the course of my talk with her, the girl—a pathetic, beautiful Ophelia clad only in a torn nightgown—pulled me down to the couch where she had seated herself. 'Let us be close,' she said. 'I have made a great philosophical discovery. Do you know the difference between closeness, likeness, same-ness, and oneness? Close is close, as with you; when you are like somebody, you are only *like* the other; sameness—you are the same as the other, but he is still *he* and you are *you*; but oneness is not two—it is one, that's horrible— horrible,' she repeated, jumping up in sudden panic: 'don't get too close, get away from the couch, I don't want to be one with you,' and she pushed me away very aggressively. Some minutes later, she became elated again. 'I am a genius,' she said, 'a genius. I am about to destroy all books on social science. I don't need them. I don't need teachers, to hell with them. I am a genius, I am a genius.' (Her husband was a social science teacher.)

When I took her in an ambulance to the hospital, she became calm, sub-dued, and depressed. 'I am dead now. Larry won't kill himself,' she said, taking out a little amulet, a tiny crab enclosed in a small plastic case. 'This is my soul,' she said, handing it to me. 'My soul is gone, my self is gone, I lost it. I am dead. Take it, keep it for me till I shall come out.' Then, in sudden panic: 'I don't want to die,' and she began to attack and to beat me, only to fall back again into her depressed mood. When we got out of the car at the hospital and I lit a cigarette, she snatched it away from my mouth, began to laugh and to smoke it herself. 'Now you can go home, I don't need you any more,' and she left in an elated mood.

This example may suffice for our purposes. The girl's acute breakdown was precipitated by conflicts with her severely compulsive husband, previously her teacher. Her object relations, prior to her episode, had in many ways resembled those of the 'as if' type described by Helene Deutsch. They were on an infintely more magic, infantile level than those of the manic-depressive patient, which were characterized by a masochistic, over-faithful clinging to her partner and which had, in general, been steady. The schizophrenic girl simply chose partners to whom she could attach her own genius phantasies and, though brilliant, changed her interests with the respective lover's or husband's. She began to throw herself into social studies after falling in love with a social scientist who had impressed her as outstanding. When he did not respond, she easily displaced her phantasies and feelings from him on to another, and then on to a third man in this field who eventually married her. In her phantasies, her lovers and their past mistresses would appear as composite figures which undoubtedly represented mixtures of infantile, omnipotent paternal and maternal images as well as projections of her own grandiose self. In dreams and even in her conscious imagery, she would easily exchange these objects or merge them with each other and with herself and attach attributes of the other sex or of both sexes on to them. Evidently these figures were fusions of split-up, infantile object-images which tended to be recomposed and distinguished only according to such organ attributes. Thus omnipotent, male-female, breast-phallus figures and castrated, breastless, injured, dead figures would be created, combining traits of various persons and of herself which lent themselves to her imagery.

The girl's episode announced itself by violent signs of open ambivalence and attacks of rage toward her husband. The final break appeared to have set in with a process of dangerous, sudden, irresistible instinctual diffusion: a situation of being enmeshed in a fatal struggle between extremely passive, masochistic strivings and severely sadistic, murderous impulses towards the love object. The patient, so far a latent schizophrenic, escaped from the intolerable conflict by a sudden break with reality and total regression to a magic, primary-process level. Her conflict found expression in the fear that either she or the love object must die or commit suicide. The tearing up of scientific books (magic murder of her husband 'in effigy'), the handing over of the amulet (symbol of her soul) to me, all this psychotic acting out reveals clearly the underlying conflict between wishful, sado-masochistic phantasies either of being destroyed by the object or of killing or having killed it.

The phantasy material of this girl prior to her episode, and of other schizophrenics as well, disclosed that the ideas of killing or being killed represent phantasies of devouring and incorporating or being devoured by the objects; phantasies with which we are familiar from M. Klein's work and Lewin's recent book on elation.

The murderous phantasies developed rapidly into delusional ideas and fears of either the object's or the patient's own imminent death. The belief in the

object's death induced, temporarily, an elated mood and megalomanic attitudes and ideas, which would quickly change to depressed states with panicky
fears of imminent death and with experiences of losing the self or of inner
death. The girl's manifest ideas at the beginning of her episode enable us to
understand the cathectic shifts and processes of identification leading to these
delusional experiences and ideas. Her philosophical elaborations described
step by step, in an almost clairvoyant way, her regressive escape from object
relationship: 'closeness', to identification: 'likeness', to magic, total identifications: first 'sameness' and eventually 'oneness', i.e. complete fusion of
self- and object-images.

In metapsychological terms, these processes may be described as follows.
Even prior to her acute episodes, the girl's reality testing had been impaired,
her concepts of the object world and of her own self distorted by the invasion
of highly irrational images into the ego and by the lack of boundaries between
the different objects as well as between the objects and her own self. The
episode announced itself by signs of increasing ambivalence and outbursts of
fury toward her husband. The breaking point, however, was reached when her
rage at him suddenly subsided as she coldly walked out on her partner.
Evidently, the cessation of affects and the assertion of 'no longer needing' the
husband were expressive of a complete withdrawal of all cathexis from the
object. Whereas the libidinous cathexis had veered away from the object to
the self, the aggression was, first, turned to inanimate object substitutes (the
books) and, with increasing catatonic excitement, more and more diffusely
discharged on the outside. Hence, a magic, total identification had taken
place: as the object-representations were dissolving, the image of the murderous, powerful object had been set up in the image of the self, a process that
found expression in megalomanic, aggressive self-expansion and the idea that
the object had died. Fear and hate of the object had disappeared; the self
threatened by the omnipotent object had been saved by the magic murder of
the object.

This state, however, was only temporary and was soon followed by the
reverse process which restored the object, though by magic destruction of the
self. Apparently the entire libidinous cathexis had now been called away from
the self-image and turned back to the object-image. A powerful, threatening
object-image had thus been resurrected at the expense of the self, an image
which during my visit became immediately attached to me. Surrender followed by panicky fears, feelings of losing the self and dying, and renewed

outbursts of rage towards me, as the murderous object, were indicative of the threatening dissolution of the self-representations which had been emptied of libido and cathected with destructive forces.

Longer periods of observation show the enormous cathectic fluidity in schizophrenics and their inability to tolerate ambivalence, which M. Klein has stressed particularly. They tend to decathect an object completely and to shift the entire (libidinous or aggressive) cathexis not only from the object to the self and *vice versa*, but also from one object to the other; furthermore, to throw all the available libido temporarily on to one object while cathecting another one or the self, respectively, with all the aggression, and to reverse these processes rapidly. In the further course of such episodes one can see how the processes of restitution succeed in resurrecting and reorganizing new, more or less fixated, delusional self- and object-representations. To go further into the schizophrenic restitution processes would overstep the boundaries of this paper. When such delusional new composite object-image units become reattached to real persons, they lead to the re-establishment of pathological, paranoid object relations. Since reality testing may temporarily still be effective in certain ego areas, relations to the outside world may then simultaneously operate on both a realistic and a delusional level.

We shall now compare these processes to the corresponding mechanisms in manic-depressives. Contrary to schizophrenics, it is characteristic of manic-depressives that the double introjection mechanisms still aim at and succeed in maintaining the situation of dependence of the self on a powerful, superior love object. This statement is in agreement with opinions previously expressed by M. Klein. In the endopsychic continuation of the conflict, in the melancholic state, the self passively surrenders to the sadistic superego as once to the love object. But even in the manic state where the archaic, punitive love-object-image or superego, respectively, turns into a loving one, its reprojection on the outside permits the self to feel part of and to feed on a highly pleasurable, good, indestructible object world. Thus the aggrandizement of the manic encompasses and depends on an illusory, grandiose world.

Comparing these mechanisms with the corresponding processes described in the schizophrenic case, we notice that this patient's grandiose, elated states as well as her states of depression and panic with fears of dying or of committing suicide are no longer the expression of conflicts of reconciliation between superego and self. In fact, schizophrenics appear to have a severe intolerance to feelings of guilt, coupled with their inability to ward off the guilt-provoking impulses by normal or neurotic defence mechanisms.

Whereas in melancholics the superego by absorbing punitive, powerful parental images gains control over the self, we may observe the opposite in schizophrenic patients: an escape from superego conflicts by a dissolution of the superego and by its regressive transformation back into threatening parental images. For such processes, the schizophrenic is evidently predisposed by his defective ego—superego formation. As in the case of the schizophrenic girl, we may find it difficult in schizoid persons to distinguish the ego ideal from their ambitious ideas and their phantasies of simply sharing the omnipotence of their love objects. The superego fears are frequently replaced by fears of omnipotent, dangerous images attached to outside persons. Instead of guilty fears and submission to a destructive superego as in melancholia, schizophrenics hence experience, as our patient did, fears of being influenced and persecuted or of being killed by murderous parental figures.

On the other hand, their grandiosity and elation, contrary to that of manic patients, is autistic in nature. Instead of feelings of owning and partaking in a world of unending pleasure, schizophrenics may show the grandiose belief of being the lonely genius who does not need the world, or of being the omnipotent, evil, or good ruler of mankind who can control, destroy, or rescue a doomed world.

In summary, we may say that in manic-depressives the regressive processes do not go so far, do not lead to total identifications, but lead up to a severely pathological conflict—or harmony—between the self and the superego, whereas in schizophrenics the deterioration of ego and superego proceeds much further; the struggle between ego and superego is retransformed into conflicts between magic self- and object-images within the deteriorating ego, whereby the self-images and the object-images may alternately dissolve and absorb each other. In so far as powerful, lasting object-images are reconstituted and reprojected on the outside world, the ego—superego conflicts change into homosexual, paranoid conflicts and fears of either killing or being persecuted and killed by outside representatives of these terrifying figures.

If I stated in advance that the manic-depressive treats himself as if he were the bad or good love object, whereas the schizophrenic behaves as if he were or even believes himself to be the object, the meaning of this difference has now become clearer. It points to the tendency and effort of the manic-depressive to submit to or reconcile with, but in any case to keep alive and to depend on, the love object. In contra-distinction to this position, the schizophrenic either destroys and replaces the object by the self or the self by the object. This difference appears to be reflected in the fact that in the schizophrenic mechanisms of imitation *of* the love object play such a paramount role, whereas all the manic-depressive needs and wants is punishment leading to forgiveness, love and gratification *from* the love object.

NOTES

1. This paper, read at the 18th International Psycho-Analytical Congress, London, July, 1953, is an abridged and modified version of the paper presented at the Symposium on Identifications held at the Midwinter Meeting of the American Psychoanalytic Association, New York, December, 1952, published under the title 'Contribution to the Metapsychology of Psychotic Identifications' (*J. of the Amer. Psa. Ass.*, **2**, 1954).
2. It is evident that much of what is to be explored in this paper relates to the findings and propositions of M. Klein and her followers.
    This is not the place to discuss the points of agreement or of differences of opinion. However, the following remarks and note 3 may contribute to the clarification of at least some terminological and conceptual differences. I am referring to M. Klein's concept of the 'introjected' versus the 'external' objects and more generally to her conception of introjection versus projection of objects.
    Commonly the idea of an introjection of objects pertains to the process of introjection of objects into the ego (the self) or the superego, i.e., to processes of identification. M. Klein, however, equates the introjection of objects on one hand with the constitution of object-images, on the other hand with superego formation, and then again with preoedipal or more mature (ego) identifications.
    I do not doubt that mechanisms of intro- and pro-jection, based on fantasies of incorporation and expulsion of objects, underlie and promote the constitution of self- and object-representations in the ego, as well as the building up of ego- and superego-identifications. This fact, however, and the common infantile roots of all these psychic formations do not justify a blurring of their decisive differences. (See also note 3.)
3. In many near-psychotic or psychotic cases where the normal boundaries between self and objects are dissolving or where the superego system is regressively repersonified, we may find symptoms and phantasies referring to 'introjected objects', sometimes to 'body introjects', such as described by M. Klein. These 'bad' introjects may be experienced as the bad, worthless part of the self, or again maintain the character of dangerous objects which threaten to destroy the self. Phantasy material of this type in small children and in psychotic adults, which it is M. Klein's great merit to have observed and described, may have tempted her not to maintain the necessary clear distinctions in her theoretical propositions (cf. note 2).
    In the use of the term projection the same difficulties arise as with regard to the term introjection. In my last paper on depression I briefly emphasized the importance of distinguishing between endopsychic object-images and external objects. Strictly speaking, we may apply the term projection whenever something belonging to the self is ascribed to an object; i.e. whenever endopsychic object-images assume traits of the self or self-images respectively, or when parts of the self (body or mind) are experienced as objects or as coming from without (as in psychotic delusions and hallucinations). The object-images on which the self has been projected thus become commonly, but need not always be, attached to real external objects. However, if we were to equate object-images in general with 'introjected objects', as M. Klein does, projection would mean the projection of 'introjected objects', alias object-images, on the external object world; i.e. would represent the simple process of attaching or transferring inner

object-images onto outside persons. To regard the process of transference as a projection appears to me wrong and contradictory to Freud's definitions, even though transference phenomena may be of a projective nature.

To summarize: In my opinion, the terms introjection and projection refer to endopsychic processes—to be observed especially in cases where the boundaries between self- and object-representations are dissolving—where either the self may be constituted in the object (projection) or the object in the self (introjection). Since these terms have been frequently misused or applied too broadly, I have refrained from employing them too freely.

REFERENCES

Abraham, K. *Selected Papers on Psycho-Analysis*. (London: Hogarth, 1927.)
Despert, J. L. 'A Comparative Study of Thinking in Schizophrenic Children and in Children of Preschool Age', *Amer. Jl. of Psychiatry*, **92**, 1940.
Deutsch, H. 'Some Forms of Emotional Disturbance and their Relationship to Schizophrenia', *Psa. Quarterly*, **11**, 1942.
Federn, P. *Ego Psychology and the Psychoses*. (London: Imago, 1953.)
Fenichel, O. 'Identification', *The Collected Papers. First Series*. (New York: Norton, 1953.)
―――― *The Psychoanalytic Theory of Neurosis*. (New York: Norton, 1953.)
Freud, A. 'A Connection between the States of Negativism and of Emotional Surrender (Hörig-keit)'. Paper read at the 17th International Psycho-Analytical Congress, Amsterdam, 7 August 1951, abstr. *Int. J. Psycho-Anal.*, **33**, 265, 1952.
Freud, S. (1914). 'On Narcissism: An Introduction', *Coll. Papers*, **IV** (London: Hogarth, 1925.)
―――― (1917). 'Mourning and Melancholia', *Coll. Papers*, **IV**. (London: Hogarth, 1925.)
―――― (1921). *Group Psychology and the Analysis of the Ego*. (London: 1922.)
―――― (1923). *The Ego and the Id*. (London: Hogarth, 1927.)
Garma, A. 'Realität und Es in der Schizophrenie', *Int. Ztschr. f. Psa.*, **18**, 1932.
Glover, E. 'Basic Mental Concepts and their Clinical and Theoretical Value', *Psa. Quarterly*, **16**, 1947.
Greenson, R. R. 'The Struggle against Identification', *J. of the Amer. Psa. Ass.*, **2**, 1954.
Harper Hart, H. 'Problems of Identification', *Psa. Quarterly*, **21**, 1947.
Hartmann, H. 'Comments on the Psychoanalytic Theory of the Ego', *The Psychoanalytic Study of the Child*, **V**. (New York: International Universities Press, 1950.)
Jacobson, E. 'Primary and Secondary Symptom Formation in Endogenous Depression'. Paper read at the Mid-winter Meeting of the American Psychoanalytic Association, New York, 16 December 1947.
―――― 'Contribution to the Metapsychology of Cyclothymic Depression', *Affective Disorders*. (New York: International Universities Press, 1953.)
Kanzer, M. 'Manic-Depressive Psychoses with Paranoid Trends', *Int. J. Psycho-Anal.*, **33**, 1952.
Katan, M. 'Schreber's Delusion of the End of the World', *Psa. Quarterly*, **18**, 1949.
―――― 'Schreber's Hallucinations about the "Little Men"', *Int. J. Psycho-Anal.*, **31**, 1950.
―――― 'Further Remarks about Schreber's Hallucinations', *Int. J. Psycho-Anal.*, **33**, 1952.
―――― 'Schreber's Prepsychotic Phase', *Int. J. Psycho-Anal.*, **34**, 1953.
Klein, M. 'A Contribution to the Psychogenesis of Manic-Depressive States' (1935), *Contributions to Psycho-Analysis*. (London: Hogarth, 1948.)
Klein, M. 'Mourning and its Relation to Manic-Depressive States' (1940), *Contributions to Psycho-Analysis*. (London: Hogarth, 1948.)

Lewin, B. D. *The Psychoanalysis of Elation*. (New York: Norton, 1950; London: Hogarth, 1951.)

Mahler, M. S. 'On Child Psychosis and Schizophrenia', *The Psychoanalytic Study of the Child*, **VII** (New York: International Universities Press, 1952.)

Mahler, M. S., Ross, J. R., and De Fries, Z., 'Clinical Studies in Benign and Malignant Cases of Childhood Psychosis (Schizophrenia-Like)', *Amer. J. Orthopsychiatry*, **19**, 1949.

Pious, W. L. 'The Pathogenic Process in Schizophrenia', *Bulletin of the Menninger Clinic*, **13**, 1949.

——— 'Obsessive-Compulsive Symptoms in an Incipient Schizophrenic', *Psa. Quarterly*, **19**, 1950.

Rado, S. 'The Problem of Melancholia', *Int. J. Psycho-Anal.*, **9**, 1928.

Reich, A. 'Narcissistic Object Choice in Women', *J. of the Amer. Psa. Ass.*, **1**, 1953.

——— 'Identifications as Archaic Elements in the Superego', *J. of the Amer. Psa. Ass.*, **2**, 1954.

Thompson, C. 'Identification with the Enemy and Loss of the Sense of Self', *Psa. Quarterly*, **9**, 1940.

Weigert-Vowinckel, E. 'A Contribution to the Theory of Schizophrenia', *Int. J. Psycho-Anal.*, **17**, 1936.

PSYCHOTHERAPEUTIC ENCOUNTERS
WITH PSYCHOSIS

The psychoanalytic treatment of the psychoses has been fraught with controversy from the beginning and many psychoanalysts have subscribed to Freud's skepticism concerning the accessibility of such patients to its methods. In an important review of the technical strategies involved in the intensive psychotherapy of schizophrenia, McGlashan (1, p. 911) noted that Freud wrote to a colleague in 1928 (2, p. 21): "Ultimately I had to confess to myself . . . that I do not care for these patients [psychotics], that they annoy me, and that I find them alien to me and to everything human. A peculiar kind of intolerance which undoubtedly disqualifies me as a psychiatrist." McGlashan speculated that this might explain some of Freud's pessimism concerning the psychoanalytic treatment of psychotic patients. McGlashan shrewdly observed that "therapists who find no fascination in or curiosity about insanity will discover schizophrenic patients unusually adept at making their lives miserable" (1, p. 911).

Freud believed that the gravity of the psychopathology in psychosis prevented the development of a transference, the *sine qua non* of psychoanalytic psychotherapy. This was a mistaken belief since transference is a natural consequence of every human relationship including that in which the psychotic patient is involved, but for the psychotic individual it may take a special form. This is addressed by Searles in his paper on transference psychosis in this section. In transference psychosis the capacity to differentiate the therapist from past objects may be lost and as Searles observes: "He is so incompletely differentiated in his ego-functioning that he tends to feel not that the therapist reminds him of, or is like, his mother or father (or whomever, from his early life) but rather his functioning towards the therapist is couched in the unscrutinized assumptions that the therapist is the mother or father." Since the schizophrenic patient has never solidly achieved a level of ego differentiation and ego integration that would allow him to experience the therapist as separate from past objects, a central goal of therapy is to facilitate ego maturation so that transference psychosis becomes transference neurosis. While acknowledging that nonpsychotic transferences may also occur in the treatment of schizophrenic patients, Searles believes this least differentiated part of the patient's ego functioning, manifesting itself in transference psychosis, is invoked in any relationship that the psychotic patient has that is as intensive as that to be found in psychoanalytic psychotherapy.

Cameron's case study proves a striking confirmation of Freud's view (3, p. 59) that "even we cannot withhold from [mental patients] something of the reverential awe which people of the past felt for the insane. They have turned away from external reality, but for that very reason they know more about internal psychical reality and can reveal a number of things to us that would otherwise be inaccessible." Cameron's paper also addresses the question of what specific elements of intensive psychotherapy may effect significant changes in the deeply disturbed patient.

Herbert Rosenfeld through a historical approach traces the modifications that have occurred in classical psychoanalytic technique in the treatment of psychotic states. He gives appropriate prominence to the pioneering work of Sullivan and Fromm-Reichmann which established interest in the United States in the use of psychoanalytically derived treatment with psychotic patients. Rosenfeld also shows how the Kleinian school, of which he is a member, subscribes to the view that direct interpretive work within the transference is possible with even the most profoundly disturbed individual.

Searles's paper on phases of patient-therapist interaction delineates the stages involved in the treatment of the psychotic patient, a model that owes much to the developmental theory of Margaret Mahler. Searles emphasizes the profound emotional demands of such work and the need for extraordinary empathy and relentless self-examination and self-analysis if it is to be successful.

Freud, with his usual searching self-scrutiny, was correct in recognizing that his abhorrence of psychotics made him ill-suited to be a therapist for them. Searles, while acknowledging the tremendous emotional strains on the therapist immersed in the treatment of a psychotic patient, embraces the Roman poet Terence's credo that "nothing human is alien to me," a posture that is mandatory if such treatment is to be entertained. As he eloquently says:

It is my experience that even the most other-wordly, even the most 'crazy', manifestations of schizophrenia come to reveal meaningfulness and reality-relatedness not only to transference reactions to the therapist, but even beyond this, as delusional identifications with real aspects of the therapist's own personality. When we come to see such meanings in the schizophrenic individual's behaviour, we come more and more to realize not only that he is now in the human fold but that, if only there had been someone all along wise and perceptive enough to know, and brave enough to acknowledge, he had never really been out of it.

REFERENCES

1. McGlashan, T. M. "Intensive Individual Psychotherapy of Schizophrenia." *Archives of General Psychiatry*, vol. 40: 909–20, 1983.
2. Schur, M. *The Id and the Regulatory Principles of Mental Functioning*. International Universities Press. New York, 1966.
3. Freud, S. "New Introductory Lectures." *Standard Edition*, vol. 22.

8. On the Treatment of Psychotic States by Psychoanalysis: An Historical Approach

Herbert Rosenfeld

During the last 50 years the psychoanalytic approach to psychosis has undergone very considerable change and at the present time there is no unified
theory of either the psychopathology or the technique of treating the psychoses. Many analysts working with psychotics have found it necessary to
alter to some extent the classical technique of analysis developed by Freud in
dealing with neurotic states; a technique which relies predominantly on the
development of transference manifestations which can be interpreted to the
patients. Freud himself thought, as I shall show later, that this technique was
unsuitable for psychotics. The work of many analysts has been influenced by
Freud's belief that psychotics do not develop a transference. However, an
increasing number of analysts have tried to develop methods with the hope
that eventually some contact with the psychotic, and with this some improvement of the psychotic condition, might be achieved.

In discussing the motives of analysts, such as Rank, who have branched off
from psychoanalysis, Freud (1933) felt that

responsibility must be laid on the intimate relations which exist in psychoanalysis
between theoretical views and therapeutic treatment.

The changes in the therapeutic approach to psychotics are certainly influenced
by the theoretical views held by the therapist and by factors in the therapist's
own personality.

A clearly defined method of approaching psychotic states is important if we
expect to do research to clarify the psychotic psychopathology rather than
concentrating on symptomatic improvement. The therapist should ask himself
whether he is inclined to change his psychoanalytic approach because he does
not understand the psychotic patient or because he believes he has arrived at a
better understanding of psychotic psychopathology, and that alterations in
technique are the outcome of his understanding.

In fact, many analysts have found that deeper understanding of psychotic psychopathology made it unnecessary to change the usual classical psychoanalytic technique to any important degree. I shall try to indicate some aspects of the theoretical background of the therapies I am describing so that the theoretical reasons for any change in psychoanalytic technique can be seen.

Modifications in analytic technique are particularly common in the approach to schizophrenics but not in work with manic-depressive patients. That is probably one of the main reasons why the number of descriptions of psychoanalytic therapy with manic-depressive patients is comparatively small compared with the extensive literature relating to the treatment of schizophrenia. In this paper, therefore, I shall concentrate mainly on the latter group.

I shall first attempt to give a picture of Freud's views relating to the treatment of psychosis. Freud made many basic contributions to the understanding of the psychopathology of the psychoses and undertook the treatment of some psychotic patients, occasionally with success. For example, as early as 1904, he reports an attempt to treat a manic-depressive patient in the symptom-free interval after the depression. However, the treatment came to an end after a few weeks when she became manic. In 1916 he reports that he had two successes in treating similar states. In 1905 he states:

Psychoses, states of confusion and deeply rooted depression are not suitable for psychoanalysis; at least not for the method as it has been practised up to the present. I do not regard it as by any means impossible that by suitable changes in the method we may succeed in overcoming this contra-indication—and so be able to initiate the psychotherapy of the psychoses.

Freud felt that analysts should limit their choice of patients to those who possess 'a normal mental condition', since in the psychoanalytic method this is used as a foothold from which to obtain control of the morbid manifestations. This links up with his later formulations that some normal ego functioning was necessary in order to begin any psychoanalytic treatment. In 1916 he explained his views in much greater detail, linking them with his developing ideas on the importance of narcissism. After discussing the withdrawal of the libido from the object into the ego as an important factor in the psychopathology of dementia praecox and also the manic-depressive states he says:

Since we have ventured to operate with the concept of ego libido the narcissistic neuroses have become accessible to us: the task before us is to arrive at the dynamic elucidation of these disorders and at the same time to complete our knowledge of mental life by coming to understand the ego.

He continues:

The ego-psychology after which we are seeking must not be based on the data of our self-perceptions but on the analysis of disturbances and disruptions of the ego. . . . But hitherto we have not made much progress with it. The narcissistic neuroses can scarcely be attacked with a technique that has served us with the transference neuroses. You will soon learn why. What always happens with them is that, after proceeding for a short distance, we come up against a wall which brings us to a stop. Even with the transference neuroses, as you know, we met with barriers of resistance, but we were able to demolish them bit by bit. In the narcissistic neuroses the resistance is unconquerable.

He continued a little later:

Our technical methods must accordingly be replaced by others; and we do not know yet whether we shall succeed in finding a substitute.

He then discussed the material available from psychotic patients with the clear intention of stimulating research into the psychopathology and treatment of narcissistic states, but the pessimistic note constantly returns, for example, in 1916 he discusses how

paranoics, melancholics, sufferers from dementia praecox remain on the whole unaffected and proof against psycho-analytic therapy,

and goes on to discuss in detail the so-called transference neurosis in order to explain the lack of success with the narcissistic neurosis:

Observation shows that sufferers from narcissistic neuroses have no capacity for transference or only insufficient residues of it. They reject the doctor, not with hostility but with indifference. For that reason they cannot be influenced by him either; what he says leaves them cold, makes no impression on them; consequently the mechanism of cure which we carry through with other people cannot be operated with them.

He then explained this lack of transference in terms of the patients having abandoned their object cathexes and the object libido having been transformed into ego libido. Sixteen years later, Freud (1933) again discussed the indications for and limitations of analytic treatment and issued a warning against over-enthusiasm about the results of psychoanalysis and now with his newer understanding of the importance of instinctual conflict he adds: sometimes

one special instinctual component is too powerful in comparison with the opposing forces that we are able to mobilize. This is quite generally true with a psychosis.

He again discussed the limitations of analytic successes due to the form of the illness and says that the field of application of analytic therapy lies in the transference neurosis. 'Everything differing from these, narcissistic and psy-chotic conditions, is unsuitable to a greater or less extent.' It would seem that between the two series of Introductory Lectures Freud had become more pessimistic about the possibilities of *analytic* treatment of psychosis. This pessimism may, however, have been connected with his increasing preoc-cupation with the problem of the relation between the suitability for analysis and constitutional excessive strength of instinct, and his awareness of the importance of the destructive (death) instinct, in severe mental illness, which he developed in greater detail in 'Analysis Terminable and Interminable' (1937). In 1940, in 'An Outline of Psychoanalysis', Freud returned again to the discussion of the treatment of psychosis now related to his greater under-standing of the psychology of the ego. He explained that the psychoanalyst has to find in the ego a useful ally so that the ego must have retained

a certain amount of coherence and some fragment of understanding for the demands of reality. But this is not to be expected of the ego of the psychotic: it cannot observe a pact of this kind. . . . Thus we discover that we must renounce the idea of trying our plan of cure upon psychotics—renounce it perhaps for ever or perhaps only for the time being, until we have found some other plan better adapted for them.

But later in the 'Outline' he added a further point to this when he described that in many 'acute psychotic disturbances there remains in some corner of the patient's mind a normal person hidden'. He then discussed 'the view which postulates that in all psychosis there is a splitting of the ego'. He said:

You may probably take it as being generally true that what occurs in all these cases is a psychical split. Two psychical attitudes have been formed instead of a single one—one, the normal one, which takes account of reality, and another which under the influence of the instincts detaches the ego from reality. The two exist alongside of each other. The issue depends on the relative strength. If the second is, or becomes the stronger, the necessary precondition for a psychosis is present. If the relation is reversed, then there is an apparent cure of the delusional disorder.

But Freud himself did not go on to apply this finding to the treatment of psychotic states (see Klein, Bion and Rosenfeld).

When one reviews Freud's contributions to the treatment of psychotic states one is impressed by his pessimism but also his obvious hope that eventually some way of approaching psychotic illness may be found. The pessimism is essentially associated with his belief that psychotics do not form a trans-ference, based on his theory that in these narcissistic conditions when object libido is withdrawn into the ego, the object presentations are completely given up. Freud attributed the extreme rigidity in resisting any change which he encountered in the psychosis to the same process: 'narcissism'. He regarded the omnipotence of the psychotic process, for example, delusions and hallucinations, as attempts at restitution designed to regain objects of the external world. But this 'object libido' was similarly found resistant to any therapeutic analysis. A third important difficulty which Freud described was the ego deficiency in psychosis which he believed made cooperation in treatment impossible. Although he formulated the important idea about the splitting of the ego in psychosis into a normal and a psychotic part this was not related by him to therapy. Freud was aware that excessive strength of instincts played an important part in psychotic states but did not discuss specific psychotic conflicts between parts of the self, such as loving and destructive parts of self, based on his theory of the life and death instincts. He regarded the main conflict in psychosis as a conflict between the ego and reality.

Abraham made very important contributions to the treatment of psychosis, particularly to the manic-depressive states. As early as 1907 he discussed the psychopathology and treatment of dementia praecox, drawing attention to the similarities of the conflicts in hysteria and dementia praecox, for example, instancing

the imaginary pregnancies which are so common in dementia praecox, and which in their psychosexual genesis are entirely similar to hysterical pregnancies.

He also states that 'obsessive ideas constitute in many cases the most prominent characteristic of the illness'. In 1908 he examined the differences between hysteria and dementia praecox and came to the conclusion that

since we have traced back all transference of feeling to sexuality we must come to the conclusion that dementia praecox destroys a person's capacity for sexual transference, i.e. for object love.

He regards 'the negativism of dementia praecox as the most complete antithesis to transference'.

In attempting to psychoanalyse them we notice the absence of transference again. Hence psychoanalysis hardly comes into consideration as a therapeutic procedure in this kind of illness.

He describes the patient's interest or longing for some objects but says if they get them, they have no effect on them. In discussing the general lack of interest in objects and the lack of sublimations, he suggests that the psychosexual characteristics of dementia praecox are the return of the patient to autoerotism and the symptoms of his illness are forms of auto-erotic sexual activity. Many of Abraham's observations, such as the preoccupation of the schizophrenic with auto-erotic masturbatory phantasies, have been confirmed by recent work.

In 1913 Abraham changed his view about the lack of transference in schizophrenia when he reported on the analysis of an undoubted case of dementia praecox, suffering from hallucinations: 'The patient during treatment soon proved himself capable of making a sufficient transference.'

In 1916 he reported on another case of dementia praecox. He said that 'a psychoanalysis can be carried out with these patients just as well as with a psychoneurotic'.

In both cases the work was facilitated on account of the abolition of many inhibitions, 'the material lies quite near consciousness and in certain circumstances is expressed without resistance'.

In 1912 Abraham reported on the investigation and treatment of six undoubted cases of manic-depressive illness and it is interesting to see how soon he began to discover transference phenomena in this group of patients. One of these cases had suffered from severe melancholia for 20 years. At the time of the report he had treated the case for only two months but

during this time no further state of depression appeared but there were two states of manic accentuation which were far milder than previously.

In another case the effectiveness of analysis was shown in a striking manner. The treatment lasted for only 40 sessions. In the sixth case the treatment could be successfully completed in six months. He commented that the treatment had a 'remarkably good result'. Six months after ending the treatment there had been no relapse. Abraham stated that it is usually extraordinarily difficult to establish a transference in these patients who have turned away from all the world in their depression, but he stressed that in one case, simply by the help of psychoanalytic interpretations of certain facts and connexions, he succeeded 'in obtaining a greater psychic rapport with the patient than he had ever previously achieved'. In another case

he was astonished that after overcoming considerable resistance he succeeded in explaining certain ideas that completely dominated the patient and observed the effect of this interpretive work. The initial improvement and every subsequent one followed directly upon the removal of definite products of repression.

During the whole course of the analysis he could most distinctly observe that the patient's improvement went hand in hand with the progress of his analysis. He commented that in those patients who have prolonged free intervals between their manic and depressive attacks, psychoanalysis should be begun during the free period. Generally speaking, Abraham, though aware of the incompleteness of his results, in this paper felt very hopeful. He said: 'It may be reserved for psychoanalysis to lead psychiatry out of the path of therapeutic nihilism.' In 1924 Abraham made further very detailed observations of manic-depressive patients. Particularly interesting and important are his comments on the patient's behaviour in the analytic situation and his reaction to the analyst's interpretations. He said, for example,

We all know how inaccessible melancholic patients are to any criticism on the part of the analyst of their ways of thought: and of course their delusional ideas are especially resistant to any such interference.

A patient once replied, when he had tried to make an interpretation, that he had not even heard him. He described the narcissistic transference in one of his patients who used always to walk into his room with an air of lofty condescension, displaying superior scepticism about psychoanalysis. In another patient this attitude used to alternate with one of chronic humility. He felt that melancholics are capable of establishing a sufficient transference to justify analysts in attempting to treat them and that important changes could not be effected in a patient until he succeeded in establishing a transference on to his analyst. He stressed, as in 1912, the patient's capacity to respond to interpretations and observed that in some cases the patient's narcissistic and negative attitudes towards certain persons, or towards his whole environment and his high degree of irritability in regard to them, diminished in a way which had never happened before.

It is interesting, therefore, that Abraham, unlike Freud, found it possible to establish a transference in manic-depressive patients and that, in spite of the strength of the patient's narcissistic behaviour during the analytic sessions, he was able to produce a change simply by means of interpretations.

There were only a very small number of analysts who attempted to treat psychoses up to 1935. Their main preoccupation was the problem of the patient's narcissism. Waelder (1925) attempted to find a theoretical and practical basis for the treatment of the narcissistic neurosis. He developed a hypothesis concerning the conditioning factors by which the psychosis comes about, or is avoided in those borderline characters in whom the phenomena of transition to the psychoses can be observed. He introduced the concept of the 'narcissistic repression', which seems, in his opinion, the basis of the withdrawal of the libido into the ego and which is also the basis of psychosis. He introduced a further concept which he called the 'union of instincts', which involves the combination of narcissism and object libido, instancing people who succeed in linking the narcissism with object libido in a manner compatible with reality which prevents the formation of pathological psychotic symptoms.

He illustrated his theory with case material. Waelder argued that if it were possible to use the libido which is flowing back into the ego at the outset of a psychotic disease in such a way that the instinct would be combined with sublimation in a manner compatible with reality, and if this union was related to object libidinal processes which are accessible to the analytic methods we might hope to be able to find a way of curing the psychosis which has already broken out. The therapeutic task in these cases he described as 'sublimation of narcissism'. In discussing the transference, Waelder pointed out that the only form of transference which can be effectively established is the narcissistic one. Waelder tried to make clear that the characteristic feature of the therapeutic intent which he advises implies an intervention into a healthy part of the personality which has not got a narcissistic fixation. He therefore depended on the existence of such a part of the personality. Practically the treatment must begin with an extremely passive period which enables the analyst to find out what the possibilities are. The analysis is maintained with the narcissistic transference and generally speaking one has to advance hand in hand with narcissism, avoiding frustration in regard to the narcissistic ideal and steadily aiming at affording narcissistic gratification compatible with reality. Waelder stressed the self-knowledge of the narcissistic patient and his capacity consciously to influence his mind:

In psychosis of the schizophrenic type, insight into the mechanism has a markedly greater power of assisting recovery than in neurosis. All self-knowledge consists in the establishing of communication between different tendencies which hitherto were cut off from one another. . . . This is a rare case in which the patient's understanding of the genesis of his illness suffices to cure him.

Waelder is one of the first analysts to speak of a narcissistic transference. This transference is apparently not used as a basis for transference interpretations but as a vehicle for the directive influence which the analyst can bring to bear upon the patient. When Waelder discusses psychotic mechanisms and tendencies cut off from one another, we are to some extent reminded of modern concepts of split off parts of the self and the interpretation of mechanisms of splitting in psychotics and borderline psychotic states which plays an important part in modern techniques of treating the psychotic ego.

In 1933 Clark contributed to the treatment of the narcissistic neurosis and psychosis. He thought that it was the narcissism which constituted the first great barrier to any therapeutic approach and possible readjustment in the narcissistic neurosis. He said (1933*a*):

In using the technique of ordinary analysis in such cases we may learn a great deal about narcissism, but we fail to help the narcissist.

He developed in this paper his theory of the narcissistic fixation and how this might be approached and overcome by psychological treatment. He observed that the narcissistic ego has not developed beyond the infantile level of need for loving protection and support and the patient is regarded as having a special individual requirement for a longer period of dependence than non-narcissistic patients. His theory is that though the narcissist may need a longer time for development, there will eventually be a tendency to step away tentatively from his withdrawn position. He believed that the therapist should fall in with the narcissistic requirements of the patient, in other words his role should be that of the 'tender, all-giving mother'. In practice, that would mean that the therapist would lend himself fully to listening to and understanding the material being presented but approach it not in terms of analytic interpretation but with emotional sympathy which would ensure the patient complete harmony. The author noted that the relationship would later assume the conditions of ordinary transference analysis but through this 'fortified technique' the ego is given a chance to resume its interrupted growth at a speed of its own choosing. At one point the author asked whether

such a passive all-giving analyst might not merely heighten the idealisations of the patient without increasing his testing of reality and his discharge of energy into sublimating activities (1933*b*).

To counteract this difficulty Clark suggested that the narcissistic identification which the analyst provides must be gradually tinctured with reality requirements. He stressed that, once the narcissistic transference is established, the procedure is very similar to that followed in the analysis of the transference neuroses.

The narcissistic shell must be broken through in order to expose the real weaknesses, the fears and dependent needs which lie behind (1933*a*).

The author gave some case material of a psychotic patient, but he did not report any significant clinical improvement by this treatment. Clark's theories and approach have many points in common with later workers interested in dealing with psychotics, such as Fromm-Reichmann's early attempts at treating schizophrenic patients and Winnicott's later theories and recommendations for approaching psychotic patients.

Waelder and Clark seem familiar with the concept of the narcissistic transference, but they are not concerned with describing the narcissistic attitude of behaviour of the patient in the analytic situation, which had been done successfully by Abraham. They both advise the analyst to change his behaviour and to fit in with the narcissistic patient's demands for love, support and satisfaction in order to create and maintain the narcissistic transference.

Stern (1938) described the transference based on the ungratified and ungratifiable narcissistic needs of his patients, who often view the analyst as godlike, omniscient and omnipotent. As a result of this they feel secure and happy in the analysis as if they were in a Nirvana, but they remain without any insight. Stern stressed that a distorted perception of the analyst is quite real to these patients. The negative transferences have to be very carefully handled. When the analyst changes in the patient's eyes into a hostile or a cruel object, the patient often comes near to a psychotic state in the transference situation. Because of the omnipotence of the good or bad imago which the analyst represents, anything savouring of criticism has a most disturbing effect on the patient, as the analyst then changes into a bad figure, and the patient easily withdraws. Stern observed that in the narcissistic transference the patient never identified himself with the analyst but only with the concept of him produced by a process of projection of his own ego ideals. He particularly emphasized the sense of omnipotence with which the patient endows both the ideally good and excessively bad imagos which he projects on to the analyst.

Cohn (1940) examined the narcissistic phenomena in the transference in greater detail. He believes that the transference in general may be regarded as a narcissistic phenomenon and he regarded the transference of the narcissistic neurosis as simply of a primitive and rudimentary type. He observed that in the narcissistic transference there is often a serious difficulty in distinguishing between subject and object, and that this problem is caused by the mechanism of projection. He relates the processes of incorporation, expulsion and projection to organic fixations, which he thinks should be made conscious because they appear magnified as long as they are not evaluated by the conscious mental apparatus. He gives a number of clinical examples of the narcissistic transference; for example, in a depressive patient the analyst was treated as if he was the patient's own stool. This was one of the reasons why he could not distinguish between himself and the analyst. During the analysis it became apparent that the patient had not only projected his faeces and his anal sensations on to the analyst but also his own penis and in this way had lost it himself. In discussing a case of schizophrenia, he described a girl who seemed only interested in a book which she was tearing into little shreds. One day she suddenly attacked the analyst violently as if she were going to try to pull him to pieces. She said to him: 'Don't leave me, I have concentrated on you entirely.' Then she dropped back into her stupor and, he adds, the analyst into his ignorance. The analyst described that he had not realized at that time that the patient had been concentrating on him and not on the book. He is now aware that there had been a transference on a very primitive level. In most of his clinical examples he stressed the use of the mechanism of projection in the narcissistic transference. The importance of the mechanism of projection and the confusion of subject and object in the narcissistic transference was stressed by many later workers with psychotic patients (Rosenfeld, Bychowski and others).

Bullard, Federn, Fromm-Reichmann and others described very intense transferences in dealing with psychotic patients. Bullard (1940) said that in the psychotic there are profound swings of transference which are in a sense similar to those of the neurotic, but so intense and so carefully concealed by a mask of indifference or hostile suspiciousness that many analysts believe that the analysis of psychotic patients is impossible. Bullard stressed overt and concealed anxiety in psychotic patients and gave details of how to deal with this problem. When these anxieties were not clearly understood and brought to the surface, they threatened the continuance of the analysis and markedly affected the existing trend of rapport. He also mentioned that the intense, often paranoid hostility of the psychotic may be indicative of anxiety and may have a defensive purpose. He gave case material to illustrate a strong negative paranoid transference in which the patient threw things at him and insisted that the analyst was torturing him. He found that even such severe negative transferences can lessen markedly when the analyst is aware of the real cause of the patient's anxieties so that the patient feels better understood. Bullard (1960) described in greater detail the analytic approach to severely paranoid patients in a hospital setting. His patients appeared to have no insight and rejected therapy at the beginning. Bullard accepted the patient's paranoid attitude as a basis for starting treatment and did not attempt to create a positive transference artificially, which he feels would be a serious drawback to effective therapy. Bullard's contributions are particularly important because in contrast to many therapists dealing with psychotics he illustrated that the negative transferences of the psychotic can be understood and analysed in a therapeutic setting.

Federn treated psychotic patients at the beginning of the century and made a very detailed contribution to the subject (1943). He found that psychotics form a transference, but this is quite unstable and he therefore employed a different method from that with neurotic patients. He emphasized that in approaching psychotic patients we should remember that these patients are accessible to psychoanalysis because first they are still capable of trans-ference; second, one part of the ego has insight into the abnormal state (but this is not a constant factor); and third, a part of the personality is still directed towards reality. The psychotic is eager to make transferences with both the healthy and the disordered parts of his ego.

The transference of the psychotic part of the personality is dangerous and can lead to aggression and slaughter as well as to deification of the object. . . . Both aggression and deification can put an end to any contact with the analyst because of deeply rooted fears.

In comparing the treatment of the psychotic and neurotic Federn said that in psychosis normal resistances have broken down and have to be re-established by psychoanalysis. In order to re-establish the resistances in the psychotic, Federn advised that one has to abandon the usual psychoanalytic technique.

First abandon free association, second abandon analysis of the positive transference, third abandon provocation of transference neurosis, because it quickly develops into a transference psychosis in which the analyst becomes the persecutor. Fourth, abandon the analysis of resistances which maintain repression. Phobias are left undisturbed because they protect against deeper fears and conflict. . . . In analysing the psychotic regression must not be increased.

He emphasized that the most important condition which should be considered in every psychoanalytic treatment of psychosis is the establishment of a posi-tive transference, which must itself never be dissolved by analysis, and an interruption of the treatment when the transference becomes negative. Mainly for this reason Federn is emphatic that no psychoanalysis of psychotics can be carried out without a skilful and interested helper, preferably a woman, to take care of the patient between sessions and particularly during periods of negative transference. In discussing the ambivalence of the psychotic and the way it shows itself in the transference Federn stressed that the analyst has to realize that ambivalence is replaced in the psychosis by two or more ego states. These split ego states alternate in their strength and with them alternate the positive and negative transference to the analyst. Federn advised that, in psychosis, the therapist should slow down and even try to stop spontaneous delivery of still unconscious mental complexes because one does not want to face any increase of the psychotic disorganization until the ego has been re-established within its normal boundaries. In his treatment of psychosis Federn relied on that part of the patient which is still in touch with reality and external objects, the remnants of the normal ego. In describing his attitude to the patient he said:

The psychoanalyst shares the acceptance of the psychotic's falsifications as realities. He shares his grief and fears and on this basis reasons with the patient. When convinced that by this procedure the patient feels himself understood the analyst presents the true reality as opposed to falsification. He then confronts the patient with his actual frustration, grief or apprehension, and connects this with the patient's deeper fears and conflicts and frustrations.

An important factor in Federn's technique is the conscious education of the patient in connexion with changes in his ego boundaries. He shows the patient, for example, that because of certain ego boundaries having lost their cathexis ideals, thoughts and memories are experienced as real and cease to be mere thinking. He stressed that the patient is able to learn to distinguish those ego boundaries with normal cathexis from those with cathexis withdrawn. He believed, contrary to Freud, that the loss of reality is a consequence of and not the cause of the basic psychotic deficiency. Federn made a detailed study of latent psychosis. He noticed that latent psychotic patients become openly psychotic during their psychoanalytic treatment. He was convinced that psychoanalysis often fosters the onset of psychotic depression and mania. In such situations he advised the immediate interruption of the free association method. He himself learnt to avoid the wakening of a latent psychosis and he became eager to take over those patients whose psychosis had been precipitated by the psychoanalysis of other analysts, and he mentioned that many patients were sent to him by former patients and by Freud himself.

Federn's contribution to the treatment of psychosis is of particular historical interest for us as he was one of the first analysts to treat psychotics with psychoanalytically orientated psychotherapy. Another point of interest is Federn's concentration of psychotherapeutic effort on the psychotic ego which he studied in detail, discussing in particular the splitting into healthy and psychotic parts, an observation which was taken up by Freud in the 'Outline'. It is interesting that Federn held the view that neither the transference psychosis nor the negative transference of the psychotic could be influenced by psychoanalytic therapy.

It will have become quite clear that Federn made no attempt to treat the psychotic part of the patient's personality. His method of treatment was devised to suppress or, as he called it, to repress the psychotic productions which were overwhelming the patient's personality. It would perhaps be more appropriate to describe Federn's treatment as an attempt to help the patient to split off and to deny the psychotic parts of the self which had temporarily overwhelmed the more healthy part of the ego. The importance of this splitting process in the apparent recovery of the psychotic has been discussed by Freud in the 'Outline'.

Up to the mid-1930s interest in the psychotherapy of the psychoses was very limited, but after about 1935 this interest increased markedly, particularly in the treatment of schizophrenia from a psychodynamic point of view. In America this stemmed largely from the work of Harry Stack Sullivan and in England from that of Melanie Klein.

Sullivan studied the interpersonal relations of his schizophrenic patients by creating a psychotherapeutic treatment unit in the Sheppard and Enoch Pratt Hospital. He found that even severely ill schizophrenic patients responded to what may be called a treatment group, where all the workers—doctors, nurses and helpers—aimed to assist the re-orientation of the schizophrenic patient towards interpersonal relations. In fact, most of the patients seemed to recover in this setting and could be discharged. In many symposia and papers Sullivan stressed the psychogenesis of schizophrenia and the capacity of schizophrenics to form a transference. He disagreed with many psychoanalytic formulations. His basic developmental theory was expressed in these words:

There is no developmental period when the human exists outside of the realm of interpersonal relatedness. From the very early post-natal stage, at which time the infant first learns to sense approval and disapproval of the mothering person by empathy, some degree of interpersonal relatedness is maintained throughout life by everyone, regardless of his state of mental health: therefore its disruption in the schizophrenic is only partial.

One of the analysts particularly inspired by Sullivan's work was Frieda Fromm-Reichmann who started her work with psychotics under his guidance and developed her technique of treatment while observing and treating severe schizophrenic patients in the Chestnut Lodge Sanatorium over a period of more than 20 years. It is interesting to observe how her assessment of the schizophrenic patient gradually made her change her technique in dealing with them. In her first paper (1939) she emphasized that the patient who later develops schizophrenia has been traumatized severely at an early period when the infant lives grandiosely in a narcissistic world of his own. In this state he feels that his desires are fulfilled as a result of his magical thinking. She thought that the early traumatic experience shortens the period of narcissistic security, which sensitizes the schizophrenic patients towards the frustrations of later life. As a result of this the patient escapes the unbearable reality of his present life by attempting to re-establish the autistic delusional world of the infant.

Fromm-Reichmann described the extreme suspicion and distrust that such a patient evinces towards the therapist who approaches him with the intention of intruding into his isolated world and personal life. It takes weeks and months of testing of the therapist until the patient is willing to accept him, but after this his dependence on the therapist is very great, though he remains extremely sensitive about it. Whenever the analyst fails the patient, it results in a severe disappointment which is experienced as a repetition of previous frustrations, and leads to outbursts of intense hatred and rage. Following these observations, Fromm-Reichmann recommended that the treatment of the schizophrenic must begin with a long preparatory period of daily interviews. As the treatment continues, the patient is neither asked to lie down nor to give free associations. Nothing matters except that the analyst permits the patient to feel comfortable and secure enough to give up his defensive narcissistic isolation and to use the physician for resuming contact with the world. The analyst's function is seen as trying to understand and to let the patient feel that he does, without attempting to prove this by giving interpretations because the schizophrenic himself understands the unconscious meaning of his productions better than anyone else. The analyst gives evidence of understanding by responding cautiously with gestures or actions appropriate to the patient's communication. Altogether she recommends as a basic rule for the treatment of schizophrenics an atmosphere of complete acceptance. It is quite clear that, in this first period of therapeutic experimenting with schizophrenic patients, Fromm-Reichmann worked with a treatment approach based on the developmental theory of narcissistic injury which is identical to the one advocated earlier by Clark and that the positive relationship to the analyst is fostered to imitate an early omnipotent magical infant-mother relationship. This fostering of the positive relationship is reminiscent of Federn's recommendation of promoting a positive transference and avoidance of frustrations leading to negative transference reactions.

In her later papers (1948, 1952, 1954) Fromm-Reichmann revised and criticized her earlier approaches. She said:

Psychoanalysts used to approach the schizophrenic with the utmost care and caution. We assumed this to be the only way of making it possible for him to overcome his deep-rooted suspicious reluctance against reassuming and accepting any personal contacts, including those with the psychoanalyst.

She now criticized this approach as this type of doctor-patient relationship addressed itself too much to the rejected child in the schizophrenic and too little to the grown-up person before his regression. She also felt that this approach of unmitigated acceptance may be experienced by sensitive adult schizophrenics as condescension or lack of respect on the part of the analyst and may be interpreted by the patient as a sign of anxiety on the part of the therapist. She now recommended that the investigation of the doctor-patient relationship and its distortions should be included in the therapeutic process. In other words, the analysis of the transference which was formerly strongly criticized was now fully recommended. She also criticized the previous cautiousness in her therapeutic endeavours; she expressed the opinion

that much valuable time had been lost by waiting too cautiously until the patient was ready to accept one or another active therapeutic intervention.

She also recommended more detailed investigation of the schizophrenic symptomatology and the schizophrenic productions: and thus follows Sullivan's direction, adding that according to him

the psychodynamics of manic illness including the schizophrenic manifestations can be understood as the result of an expression of unbearable anxiety and at the same time as an attempt at warding off this anxiety and keeping it from awareness.

In 1954 Fromm-Reichmann discussed the devastating effect of schizophrenic hostility on the patient's own personality and connected it with states of autism and partial regression.

This has led to a therapeutically helpful reformulation of the anxiety of schizophrenic patients as an outcome of the universal human conflict between dependency and hostility which is overwhelmingly magnified in schizophrenia.

She discussed the resentment or violence with which the infant and child ('the bad me', as Sullivan called it), and later the schizophrenic patient, respond to the early damaging influences of the 'bad mother' as *he* experienced her. This explains why schizophrenic patients are more concerned with their own status as dangerously hostile people than with the damage which may be done to others who associate with them. In describing the schizophrenic conflict about dependency, she discussed the tension between dependent needs and longing for freedom. The fear of closeness is tied up with anxiety about their secret hostility against persons whom they value and depend on. This, she emphasized, must be worked through in the transference.

In her paper 'Psychotherapy of Schizophrenia' (1954) she stressed the importance of the non-psychotic part of the personality, and says,

we try to reach the regressed portion of their personalities by addressing the adult portion, rudimentary as this may appear in some severely disturbed patients.

This adult part is trained to join the psychoanalyst in his therapeutic endeavours. Even in her later work Fromm-Reichmann is reluctant to use more than minimum interpretation. Her therapeutic work relied greatly on guiding and directing the patient to a dynamic understanding and insight into his illness. It is interesting that Fromm-Reichmann was able to correct her 'fallacy' of concentrating in the treatment of schizophrenia on becoming a kind of ideal mother to the regressed schizophrenic patient. In her later work she concentrated on examining the conflicts and psychotic productions of the schizophrenic patient in the transference situation which brings her work in many ways closer to the researches of analysts in England. (See Segal, Bion, Rosenfeld and others.)

Searles, another member of the Washington group of analysts, made very detailed contributions to the treatment of schizophrenic patients while working for over 13 years at the Chestnut Lodge Sanatorium. Some of his papers such as 'Dependency Processes in the Psychotherapy of Schizophrenia' (1955), were written in close cooperation with Fromm-Reichmann. He stressed that difficulties arise in the transference situation through projections. The analyst is perceived as hostile and rejecting because of the patient's own frustration and anger. He described the resistance against dependence because it means giving up phantasies of omnipotence. The patient defends himself against his dependency by projecting his dependency needs into the analyst. As a result of this he fears the therapist's demands on him and becomes competitive and contemptuous. In a later paper (see chapter 9) he described the transference problem in more detail. He believed that

the transference of the schizophrenic is expressive of a very primitive ego organisation, comparable with that which holds sway in the infant who is living in a world of part objects.

He described three tasks which the therapist should perform. First, 'the therapist must become able to function as a part of the patient.' Secondly, he must be able to foster the patient's individuation out of this level of relatedness, the level which has been described 'by Kleinian analysts as being a transference phase dominated by projective identification on the part of the patient'. The therapist's third task is to discern and make interpretations concerning the patient's now differentiated and integrated whole object. This gradually transforms the patient's transference psychosis into a transference neurosis. Searles stressed the importance of a phase of therapeutic symbiosis where he regards verbal transference interpretations as contraindicated. He explained that the patient deep in chronic schizophrenia is not able to employ or even hear verbal communications. In this phase the patient uses the analyst as his own ego and has not sufficient ego functioning to understand interpretations, and he projects into the analyst a variety of part-object transference roles, which the therapist must be able to endure and eventually enjoy. Through identification with the therapist who can endure his primitive object relations, the patient ultimately develops ego strength. In examining the transference in this symbiotic phase he said that it is astonishing to discover to what extent the patient is relating to himself or, more accurately, to a part of himself as an object. Searles does not discuss the splitting of the ego or self in detail, but his observations illustrate to what extent he has observed processes which have been described by other analysts either as narcissistic transferences or splitting and projections of part of the self into objects. He also studied the concreteness of the schizophrenic patient's thought processes which lead to transference difficulties; for example, the therapist may be experienced by the patient not as like his father or mother, but concretely as the father or mother.

Searles examined the schizophrenic transference in admirable detail and has become aware of the importance of projection and projective identification in the transference. I think, however, he is seriously mistaken in his belief that the analyst should enter into the symbiotic transference as a state of mutual dependence, in which the analyst feels as dependent on the patient as the patient on him and often expresses his feelings of love and hate quite freely to the patient. I feel that Searles, who has trained himself to make elaborate use of his countertransference feelings, is sometimes carried away by them and does not sufficiently acknowledge or recognize the patient's projected desires for a mutual relationship with the analyst which eliminates the differences between child and adult. I would regard Searles' behaviour as acting in with the patient, instead of analysing this most important conflict in psychotic patients, their difficulty in depending on an adult who is then felt to be superior, and their resentment and attempts to reverse the infant-parent relationship or attempts to seduce the analyst into a mutually dependent position or push him out of his legitimate role. In my experience this acting in does not lead to ego strengthening, but increases the existing ego weakness of the psychotic patient.

It is, of course, impossible to discuss all the contributions to the treatment of psychosis and I shall now only briefly discuss Stone's view of the psychotic transference and Edith Jacobson's work with psychotic patients. Stone (1954), in contributing to the treatment of psychotic conditions, emphasized that the transference love of the hysteric is different from the primitive phenomena of the narcissistic transference. The psychotic's transference is liable to invade or overwhelm his personality, just as his psychosis threatens to overwhelm his ego. Stone is aware that sometimes the sheer fear of the primitive intensity of their feelings forces some patients to remain detached, but where the transference does break through, insatiable demands may appear, or the need to control and tyrannize the analyst or, failing that, complete submission to him. Sometimes the transference may be literally narcissistic when the therapist is confused with the self or is like the self in all respects. He stressed both the primitive destructiveness and the need to experience the analyst as omnipotent and godlike, and he suggested that in the patient's phantasy of the analyst's omnipotence, guilt about primitive destructive aggression plays an important part. From his own experience one may speak with justification of 'transference psychosis'. In discussing the analyst's attitude, he suggested that the decisive factor is the ability to tolerate, over long periods and without giving up hope, the strains of the powerful, tormented and tormenting transference and the potential countertransference situation. It seems that Stone advised only a minimum change in the psychoanalyst's attitude, in fostering the positive transference, so that the patient would stand the strains of the hostile transference when it appeared. He did not believe that analytic treatment could be harmful in basically psychotic patients. Since he did not feel that there could be such a thing as a *latent psychotic state* liable to be uncovered. This is, of course, unlike the view of Federn. Unfortunately, Stone's views are not exemplified by clinical material.

Jacobson has contributed mainly to the treatment of manic-depressive states, but has also made an interesting contribution to the treatment of schizophrenic patients. She emphasized that, in the course of the analysis of the depressive, the analyst inevitably becomes the central love object and the centre of the depressive conflict. As the analysis progresses, the patient may develop even more serious depressive states, characterized by deep ego and id regressions. She suggested that depressives try to recover their own lost ability to love and to function through magic love from the loved object. When they fail to get such help from without, they may retreat from their love object and from the object world and continue the struggle within themselves. In her experience the treatment of the manic-depressive starts regularly in the depressive state because they usually do not come for treatment during the symptom-free interval, or in hypomanic or manic periods. The depressed patient tends to establish either an immediate, intense rapport or none. She felt there is usually an initial spurious transference success lasting many months; then there is an ensuing period of hidden negative transference with corresponding negative therapeutic reactions; and third, there is a state of dangerous introjective defences and narcissistic retreat; and finally a phase of gradual constructive conflict solution. The most difficult period in the transference relationship is when the patient lives only in the aura of the analyst and withdraws from other personal relations to a dangerous extent. The transference phantasies assume an increasingly ambivalent sadomasochistic coloring, and the author stresses particularly the patient's exhausting sadomasochistic provocations. The patient may unconsciously blackmail the analyst by playing on his guilt feelings, hoping in this way to get the longed-for responses. Failing to do so, he will try to elicit from the analyst a show of power, strictness or punitive anger, serving the alternative purpose of getting support or relief from the relentless superego pressure. She believed that in periods of threatening narcissistic withdrawal the analyst may have to show active interest in the patient's daily activities and especially in his sublimations, as she illustrates in case material. She also stressed that the depressed patient needs a more understanding attitude on the part of the analyst, an attitude which must not be confused with over-kindness, sympathy and reassurance.

In *Psychotic Conflict and Reality* (1967) Jacobson explained that her treatment of schizophrenic patients was mainly with an ambulatory type and was designed to avoid severe psychotic regression. Psychotics tend to use the external world to prevent the dissolution of their ego and superego structures. She believed that Freud's observation that psychotics give up reality and replace it by a newly created phantasy reality occurs only if reality fails to lend itself to the patients' purposes and to help them in their conflict solution. She described that if psychotic patients are able to project a bad unacceptable part of the ego into suitable external objects by a process of projective identification, they manage to remain sane as long as they can control these objects. Jacobson is aware of the regressive narcissistic nature of the patient's relations to these significant objects, and the weakness of the boundaries between the psychic representation of these objects and their own self. In describing her analytic experience with one of these patients, she said that she permitted the patient to use her as he needed and she adapted her emotional attitudes and behaviour to his wishes for warmth, or closeness or distance.

I let him 'borrow' my superego and ego, regard and treat me as his bad id and his illness: project his guilt, his faults and weaknesses into me or turn me into an ideal of saintliness he needed.

From her description it is clear that the patient not only projected his problems into her, but was acting out in the outside world significantly during this time. She said that she avoided giving him deeper interpretations of his acting out in the transference or in outside life until he himself knew that the period of danger was over. She would then use the material he had previously brought for interpretations, which at such times would be surprisingly effective. It is clear from Jacobson's description that the treatment was not used to work through the patient's early narcissistic projective identifications in the transference situation, as she was afraid of the danger of provoking a psychotic breakdown. Jacobson's method, as described here, has a great deal in common with Waelder's earlier attempts at treating the narcissistic neurosis by producing a sublimation of narcissism by linking it with object libido.

In turning now to the history of the psychoanalytic treatment of psychotic patients in England we have to consider first of all the pioneer work of Melanie Klein, who through her analysis of seriously disturbed children and adults, investigated the earliest infantile levels of development. In 1935 and 1946 she described details of the object relations, mechanisms and defences of two normal developmental phases, which she called the 'depressive position' and the 'paranoid schizoid position'. The paranoid schizoid position takes up the first four to six months of life and the depressive position follows on. The working through of these positions extends over the first few years of life. She suggested that, in the paranoid schizoid position, anxiety was experienced predominantly as persecutory and this contributed to certain defences, such as splitting off good and bad parts of the self and projecting them into objects, which through projective identification became identified with these parts of the self. This process is basic for the understanding of narcissistic object relationships. She said that if development during the paranoid schizoid position has not proceeded normally and the infant cannot, for internal or external reasons, cope with the impact of depressive anxieties which originate in the depressive position, a vicious circle arises. For if persecutory fear and correspondingly schizoid mechanisms are too strong the ego is not able to work through the depressive position. This leads to regression and reinforces the earlier persecutory fears and schizoid phenomena. Thus the basis is established for various forms of schizophrenia in later life. Another outcome may be the strengthening of depressive features, which may be the cause of manic-depressive illness later on.

Winnicott was influenced by Melanie Klein's earlier work, particularly that related to the depressive position and the manic defences. In 1945, in discussing the treatment of a dozen adult psychotic patients, he said that

no modification in Freud's technique was needed for the extension of analysis to cope with depression and hypochondria. It is also true according to my experience that the same technique can take us to still more primitive elements, provided of course that we take into consideration the change in the transference situation inherent in such work.

In referring to primitive pre-depressive relations he clearly indicated that he interprets them as they appear in the transference. By 1959 Winnicott had altered his views considerably, both in theory and in practice. He emphasized that psychotic conditions were caused by early environmental failure. He stated that

failure of the facilitating environment results in developmental faults in the individual's personality development and in the establishment of the individual's self, and the result is called schizophrenia.

As he regarded psychosis as a deficiency disease, he believed regression to the state of early infancy, which he called dependence, had now to be seen as a part of the capacity of the individual to self cure. In analysis 'regression gives an indication from the patient to the analyst as to how the analyst should behave rather than how he should interpret'. The analyst, through his behaviour, has to make up for the failure of the early environment. Winnicott's views are here identical both in theory and practice with those of Clark and Fromm-Reichmann's early experiments and recommendations (1939). In discussing the analyst's attitude to the patient during a transference psychosis, Winnicott emphasized that it is dangerous if the analyst interprets to the patient instead of waiting for the patient to discover things by himself. He feels that when the analyst is experienced through interpretation as a not-me (a separate object) he becomes dangerous because he knows too much. Fromm-Reichmann shared Winnicott's reluctance to use interpretations with psychotic patients. However, as I have pointed out, she later criticized her early tendency to maintain a very careful waiting and protecting attitude to her psychotic patients. She found this not only unnecessary but damaging because of the overemphasis on the patient's infantile helplessness.

While there were some analysts such as Winnicott and others who did not continue the application of Klein's work to the schizophrenic processes, others, such as Rosenfeld, Segal and Bion, were encouraged, particularly by her work on schizoid mechanisms, to treat schizophrenic patients by psychoanalysis.

Rosenfeld (1947) described an ambulatory analysis of a schizophrenic state with depersonalization. For some time he found the patient's narcissistic withdrawal and ego disintegration an insoluble problem until he became aware of her using certain schizoid mechanisms to defend herself against any painful feelings in the transference situation. She often lost all feelings and believed she had lost herself, experiences which could be traced to a process by which parts of her self were split off and projected into the analyst. She also had feelings of intruding inside the analyst and losing herself there, which gave rise to paranoid anxieties of being intruded by and overwhelmed by the analyst. The patient's narcissistic withdrawal had therefore been partly a defence against these paranoid fears and partly a defence against closeness because of her fears of intrusion.

In 1950 Segal made history by treating a hospitalized acute schizophrenic patient by psychoanalysis, which retained the essential features of the classical method. Even in the acute hallucinated state she interpreted the patient's defences and material with the emphasis on the negative and positive transference. In contrast to Federn, she analysed all the important resistances and interpreted unconscious material at the level of the greatest anxiety. She emphasized that progress in her patient was achieved only by making the patient aware of what had hitherto been unconscious. She found that schizophrenics often tolerate in their ego thoughts and phantasies which would probably be repressed in a neurotic, but at the same time they repress the links between phantasy and reality and these links have to be interpreted. She also illustrated that repression often referred to later infantile material of a depressive nature, while consciously very primitive archaic material was being produced in the analysis. In describing the transference at the beginning of the analysis, she stated that the patient was full of persecutory fears and he needed an unchanging good figure, which he tried to believe he had found in the analyst. However, to preserve this belief he had to use all his defences. She said:

If I frustrated him he would deny that frustration and split me into a good and bad figure. The bad figure would be introjected as hostile voices or reprojected into the hospital doctors.

At the beginning of the treatment the patient was detached from reality and unable to grasp the nature of the treatment and constantly demanded reassurance. Her aim was to retain the attitude of the analyst even without the cooperation of the patient. She said:

to achieve this I had first of all to make him accept my interpretations instead of the various gratifications he wanted. . . . I tried to show him in every interpretation that I understood what he wanted from me, why he wanted it at that particular moment. I also followed most interpretations of that kind with an interpretation of what my refusal had meant to him.

She gradually understood that the patient's constant need for reassurance was aimed at making the analyst an ally against his persecutors which were particularly related to the doctors in the hospital. She gave illustrations of how she managed to bring the negative persecutory transference, split off on to the doctors in the hospital, into the transference situation. Segal discussed the controversy as to whether the analyst should reassure the very ill schizophrenic patient in a moment of crisis and when craving for reassurance as many of the analysts whom I have quoted would do; for example, Fromm-Reichmann, Searles, Federn, Clark and Winnicott. Segal is convinced that by giving sympathy and reassurance the analyst becomes, for the time being, the good object, but only at the cost of furthering the split between good and bad objects and reinforcing the patient's pathological defences so that later the negative transference becomes unmanageable. In this paper Segal pointed out some technical difficulties in the analysis of the acute schizophrenic patients due to their concrete thinking disorder, a process which she traced to difficulties in the patient's use of symbols. As a result of this, the patient often misunderstands interpretations as they are experienced as concrete threats and actions on the part of the analyst.

In 1952 Rosenfeld described the analysis of an acute hallucinated schizophrenic patient in hospital. He stressed the peculiarity of the schizophrenic object relation (1952a):

whenever the acute schizophrenic approaches an object in love or hate he seems to become confused with this object.

He observed that the schizophrenic impulses to intrude into the analyst with positive and negative parts of the self, and the defences against this object relationship, were typical of the transference relations of most schizophrenic patients. He also discussed the role of verbal interpretations. While acknowledging the importance of the analyst's intuitive understanding of the patient's communications, he thought that the analyst should also be able to formulate consciously what he has unconsciously recognized and to convey it to the patient in a form that he can understand.

This after all is the essence of all psychoanalysis, but it is especially important in the treatment of schizophrenics, who have lost a great deal of their capacity for conscious functioning, so that without help they cannot consciously understand their unconscious experiences which are at times so vivid (1952*b*).

In 1954 Rosenfeld said that he found

that the psychotic manifestations attached themselves to the transference in both acute and chronic conditions, so that what might be called 'a transference psychosis' develops.

He stressed that, in the acute schizophrenic state, the patient tends to put his self so completely into objects (during the analysis into the analyst) that there is very little of the self left outside the object. This interferes with most ego functions, including speaking and understanding words. It also inhibits the capacity to experience relations with external objects. The patient may have difficulty in speaking and may be confused, negativistic or withdrawn as a result of the severe anxieties related to this process and he may not be able to understand ordinary conversation. Rosenfeld emphasized

if we use interpretations to approach the patient and if our interpretations touch upon his anxieties we shall get some response. There will either be a change in his behaviour or he will talk.

In this paper Rosenfeld developed the concept of the transference psychosis which had been introduced earlier by Federn (1943). However, Federn had been emphatic that the transference psychosis had to be avoided because it was unanalysable, while Rosenfeld emphasized the importance of recognizing the psychotic transference and working through it by means of interpretation.

Bion made important contributions to the psychopathology and treatment of schizophrenic patients from 1950. He emphasized that he did not

depart from the psychoanalytic procedure usually employed with neurotics, being careful always to take up both positive and negative aspects of the transference (1957).

He looked for evidence of the meaning of the patient's communication in the patient's actions and verbal communication but also in his own countertransference reaction. He investigated both the language of the schizophrenic and his disturbances in thinking. He stressed, for example, that the schizophrenic uses language in three ways: 'As a mode of acting, as a method of communication and as a mode of thought.' He clarified that the use of words and thought depended on the capacity for verbal thinking, which is often lost in schizophrenia through processes of severe splitting and projection so that the patient is only left with an embryonic capacity for it. In the analytic transference this capacity for verbal thought is often projected into the analyst, which leads both to the persecutory fears of the analyst who is believed to have taken it away, or the patient fears that he had lost it at an earlier stage of development which increases the need to regress 'to fetch it'. Lack of the capacity for verbal thought is felt by the patient to be the same thing as being insane. Bion gave a vivid picture of his analytic approach in describing the interchange of communication between patient and analyst. It illustrated the importance of the analyst's verbal interpretations in dealing with the schizophrenic's severe disturbances of speech and thought. In 1956 he contributed in greater detail to the understanding of the schizophrenic transference. He stressed the preponderance of the destructive impulses in schizophrenia, which are so great that even the impulses to love are suffused by them and turned into sadism. He also emphasized that there is a hatred of reality, as Freud pointed out, but Bion added to this the importance of the schizophrenic's hatred of internal reality and all that makes for awareness of it. Derived from these two basic difficulties there is an unremitting dread of imminent annihilation. In discussing the transference with the analyst, which he described as thin but tenacious, he said: 'The relationship with the analyst is premature, precipitate and intensely dependent.' When the patient broadens it under pressure of his life or death instincts two concurrent streams of phenomena become manifest.

First projective identification, with the analyst as object, becomes overactive with the resulting painful confusional states such as Rosenfeld has described. Second, the mental and other activities by which the dominant impulse, be it life instincts or death instincts, strives to express itself, are at once subjected to mutilation by the temporarily subordinate impulse. Driven by the wish to escape the confusional states and harassed by the multilations, the patient strives to restore the restricted relationship: the transference is again invested with its characteristic featurelessness. Oscillation between the attempt to broaden the contact and attempt to restrict continues throughout the analysis.

In 1957 he made important contributions to the therapy of schizophrenia by differentiating the psychotic from the non-psychotic parts of the schizophrenic personality. He emphasized particularly the role of projective identification in the psychotic part of the personality as a substitute for repression in the neurotic part of the personality.

The patient's destructive attacks on his ego and the substitution of projective identification for repression and introjection must be worked through.

SUMMARY

In this paper I have tried to show the main trends in the development of the treatment of the psychoses. After Freud's pessimism about the analysis of psychotic patients, due to his belief that they formed no transference, two main trends in the approach to the treatment of psychotics have appeared. There were those who believed that the narcissism of the psychotic patient presented a complete obstacle to analysis unless the analyst changed his usual analytic attitude. Analysts who held the view that the narcissism of the psychotic patient was caused by an environmental failure attempted to provide the patient with a new and better mother in the form of the analyst, to make up for the deficiency of the early environment. Exponents of this approach were particularly Clark, Fromm-Reichmann in her early period, and Winnicott in his later work. Searles' approach is closely related to this, as he recommends the analyst's intense involvement with the psychotic patient, particularly in the symbiotic phase of the analysis. Waelder and Jacobson have also altered their analytic attitude. They do not analyse the transference but maintain a predominantly positive one and use it as a vehicle to sublimate the patient's narcissism or psychosis by relating it to object libido and the external world. Federn similarly encouraged the positive transference and avoided any analysis of transference manifestations. However, he differed from Waelder and Jacobson by training the patient to repress or split off the psychotic parts of his personality. Searles and Fromm-Reichmann in her later work differ from others in this group in so far as they analyse both the negative and the positive transference.

The second group of analysts attempted to deal with the narcissism and other psychotic manifestations of the patient by the classical psychoanalytic approach with only minor changes. First came Abraham, who found that the narcissistic defences of his patients were markedly diminished by interpretations. Then Stern, Cohn, Stone and Bullard described characteristics of the positive and negative transference of psychotic patients, which they felt could be analysed by verbal transference interpretations.

Segal, Bion and Rosenfeld stressed that no change in the analyst's attitude and only minor changes in technique were necessary, and that the psychotic productions attached themselves to the transference, which could be interpreted in both its negative and its positive forms to the patient. They also relied exclusively on interpretations to deal with the serious language and thought disorder of the schizophrenic patient, and saw these difficulties as part of the malfunctioning of the psychotic ego with its disturbed relationships to both external and internal reality and objects. The development of the treatment of psychosis over the last 50 years suggests that Freud's hope that some approach to the treatment of psychosis might become possible is now justified.

REFERENCES

Abraham, K. (1907). On the significance of sexual trauma in childhood for the symptomatology of dementia praecox. In *Clinical Papers and Essays on Psychoanalysis*. London: Hogarth Press, 1955.

Abraham, K. (1908). The psycho-sexual differences between hysteria and dementia praecox. In *Selected Papers*. London: Hogarth Press, 1950.

Abraham, K. (1912). Notes on the psycho-analytical investigation and treatment of manic-depressive insanity and allied conditions. In *Selected Papers*. London: Hogarth Press, 1950.

Abraham, K. (1913). Restrictions and transformations of scoptophilia in psycho-neurotics. In *Selected Papers*. London: Hogarth Press, 1950.

Abraham, K. (1916). The first pregenital stage of the libido. In *Selected Papers*. London: Hogarth Press, 1950.

Abraham, K. (1924). A short study of the development of the libido. In *Selected Papers*. London: Hogarth Press, 1950.

Bion, W. R. (1954). Notes on the theory of schizophrenia. In *Second Thoughts*. London: Heinemann.

Bion, W. R. (1956). Development of schizophrenic thought. In *Second Thoughts*. London: Heinemann.

Bion, W. R. (1957). Differentiation of the psychotic from the non-psychotic personalities. In *Second Thoughts*. London: Heinemann.

Bullard, D. M. (1940). Experiences in the psychoanalytic treatment of psychotics. *Psychoanal. Q.* **9**, 493–504.

Bullard, D. M. (1960). Psychotherapy of paranoid patients. *Archs. gen. Psychiat.* **2**, 137–141.

Clark, L. P. (1933a). The question of prognosis in narcissistic neuroses and psychoses. *Int. J. Psycho-Anal.* **14**, 71–86.

Clark, L. P. (1933b). The treatment of narcissistic neuroses and psychoses. *Psychoanal. Q.* **20**, 304–326.

Cohn, F. S. (1940). Practical approach to the problem of narcissistic neuroses. *Psychoanal. Q.* **9**, 64–79.

Federn, P. (1943). Psychoanalysis of psychoses. In *Ego Psychology and the Psychoses*. New York: Basic Books, 1952.

Freud, S. (1905). On psychotherapy. *S.E.* **7**, 265.

Freud, S. (1916–17). Introductory lectures on psycho-analysis. *S.E.* **15–16**.

Freud, S. (1933). New introductory lectures on psycho-analysis. *S.E.* **22**.

Freud, S. (1937). Analysis terminable and interminable. *S.E.* **23**.

Freud, S. (1940). An outline of psycho-analysis. *S.E.* **23**.

Fromm-Reichmann, F. (1939). Transference problems in schizophrenics. *Psychoanal. Q.* **8**, 412–426.

Fromm-Reichmann, F. (1948). Notes on the development of treatment of schizophrenics by psychoanalytic therapy. In D. M. Bullard (ed.), *Psychoanalysis and Psychotherapy*. Chicago: Univ. of Chicago Press, 1959.

Fromm-Reichmann, F. (1952). Some aspects of psychoanalytic psychotherapy with schizophrenics. In D. M. Bullard (ed.), *Psychoanalysis and Psychotherapy*. Chicago: Univ. of Chicago Press, 1959.

Fromm-Reichmann, F. (1954). Psychotherapy of schizophrenia. In D. M. Bullard (ed.), *Psychoanalysis and Psychotherapy*. Chicago: Univ. of Chicago Press, 1959.

Jacobson, E. (1954). Transference problems in the psychoanalytic treatment of severely depressive patients. *J. Am. psychoanal. Ass.* **2**, 595–606.

Jacobson, E. (1967). *Psychotic Conflict and Reality*. London: Hogarth Press.

Klein, M. (1935). A contribution to the psychogenesis of manic-depressive states. *Int. J. Psycho-Anal.* **16**, 145–174.

Klein, M. (1946). Notes on some schizoid mechanisms. *Int. J. Psycho-Anal.* **27**, 99–110.

Rosenfeld, H. A. (1947). Analysis of a schizophrenic state with depersonalization. *Int. J. Psycho-Anal.* **28**, 130–139.

Rosenfeld, H. A. (1950). Note on the psychopathology of confusional states in chronic schizophrenias. *Int. J. Psycho-Anal.* **31**, 132–137.

Rosenfeld, H. A. (1952*a*). Notes on the psychoanalysis of the superego conflict of an acute schizophrenic patient. *Int. J. Psycho-Anal.* **33**, 111–131.

Rosenfeld, H. A. (1952*b*). Transference-phenomena and transference-analysis in an acute catatonic schizophrenic patient. *Int. J. Psycho-Anal.* **33**, 457–464.

Rosenfeld, H. A. (1954). Considerations regarding the psycho-analytic approach to acute and chronic schizophrenia. In *Psychotic States*. London: Hogarth Press, 1965.

Searles, H. F. (1955). Dependency processes in the psychotherapy of schizophrenia. In *Collected Papers on Schizophrenia and Related Subjects*. London: Hogarth Press, 1965.

Segal, H. (1950). Some aspects of the analysis of a schizophrenic. *Int. J. Psycho-Anal.* **31**, 268–278.

Segal, H. (1956). Depression in the schizophrenic. *Int. J. Psycho-Anal.* **37**, 339–343.

Segal, H. (1957). Notes on symbol formation. *Int. J. Psycho-Anal.* **38**, 391–397.

Stern, A. (1938). Psychoanalytic investigation of and therapy in the borderline group of neuroses. *Psychoanal. Q.* **7**, 467–489.

Stern, A. (1948). Transference in borderline neuroses. *Psychoanal. Q.* **17**, 527–528.

Stone, L. (1954). The widening scope of indications for psychoanalysis. *J. Am. psychoanal. Ass.* **2**, 567–594.

Sullivan, H. S. (1947). Therapeutic investigations in schizophrenia. *Psychiatry* **10**, 121–125.

Waelder, R. (1925). The psychoses: their mechanisms and accessibility to influence. *Int. J. Psycho-Anal.* **6**, 259–281.

Winnicott, D. W. (1945). Primitive emotional development. In *Collected Papers*. London: Tavistock Publications, 1958.

Winnicott, D. W. (1959–64). Classification: Is there a psycho-analytic contribution to psychiatric classification? In *The Maturational Processes and the Facilitating Environment*. London: Hogarth Press, 1965.

Winnicott, D. W. (1963). Communicating and not communicating leading to a study of certain opposites. In *The Maturational Processes and the Facilitating Environment*. London: Hogarth Press, 1965.

9. Transference Psychosis in the Psychotherapy of Chronic Schizophrenia

Harold F. Searles

After some five years of my work at Chestnut Lodge, developments in the therapy of various of my patients brought home to me the realization that even the most deep and chronic symptoms of schizophrenia are to be looked upon not simply as the tragic human debris left behind by the awesome glacial holocaust which this illness surely is, but that these very symptoms can be found to have—or, perhaps more accurately, in the course of therapy can come to reveal—an aspect which is both rich in meaning and alive, one now sees, with unquenched and unquenchable energy. That is, these very symptoms now emerge to the therapist's view as being by no means inert debris but as, rather, the manifestations of an intensely alive, though unconscious, effort on the part of the patient to recapture, to maintain, and to become free from, modes of relatedness which held sway between himself and other persons in his childhood and which he is now fostering unconsciously in current life in, most importantly, his relationship with his therapist. When the therapist sees and feels this aspect of the therapeutic situation, not only does much which has been bewildering, in his previous months or years of work with the patient, become coherently meaningful; but he senses, even more heartening-ly, how great are the patient's potential capacities for growth, capacities which are, it is now evident, far from dead, but, rather, congealed in the perpetuation of these unconscious transference-patterns of relatedness.

This realization came to me most memorably in two treatment-situations in particular, in my work with a middle-aged hebephrenic man in whom severe apathy was for years a prominent symptom, and a hebephrenic woman of about 30 who manifested, likewise for years in our work together, a degree of confusion which I often found overwhelming and deeply discouraging. I did not find it strange that a man who had been hospitalized constantly, whether on a back ward of a veterans' hospital or on a locked ward at Chestnut Lodge, for more than 10 years, should show a great deal of apathy; nor did it seem remarkable that a woman who had been hospitalized for a similar length of time, and whose records showed that she had been subjected, over the years prior to her admission to the Lodge, to approximately 140 insulin coma treatments and an indeterminate number of electroshock treatments, should be severely and persistently confused. More often than not, when I contemplated, and tried persistently to help, each of these two persons, I found solid reason to feel appalled and helpless in the face of the havoc which chronic schizophrenia, and the diverse efforts to treat chronic schizophrenia, had wrought upon these two human beings.

It therefore came as a tremendous change of view for me to hear the man, who was lying silently on his bed as usual, say one day, with a chuckle, 'If my grandmother was still alive I'd be a *real* lounge-lizard', and to find the evidence accumulating, during subsequent months and years, that his ostensible apathy was that of a person who had felt it necessary to bank the fires of his own ambitions and devote himself to staying by a grandmother, and much more importantly, before that, a psychotically depressed father, whose needs—needs to be protected from the daily cares of the world by the patient's more or less constant reassuring presence—took priority over the patient's own life as a boy and as a young man.

Now, ironically, I, who had formerly looked with dismay upon this hopeless vegetable of a patient, found myself in the position, as his transference towards me became more richly and openly elaborated, of a 'papa' to whom he reacted, with persistence and conviction, as being a mere shell of a person, a person with a long-burnt-out mind, a relic given to unpredictable moods of deep depression punctuated by explosive rages. All these qualities had marked his own illness in the preceding years, as a fuller case description would clearly show; and I do not doubt that major ingredients of his illness were originally derived from the introjection of similar qualities in his father. As his transference to me became increasingly coherent and powerful, his own personality-functioning became proportionately liberated from illness; but I must say that there were times, during the ensuing months and years, when the transference role which he not so much pinned onto me as more or less instilled into me, made me feel somewhat less than my usual robust self.

In the instance of the woman patient, it gradually became clear to me that her so deep and persistent confusion consisted basically in an unconscious and ambivalent effort, manifested with especial coherence and clarity in the relationship with me as a father in the transference, (*a*) to get me to do her thinking for her, as her father had been accustomed to doing throughout her childhood and adolescence until her hospitalization at the age of 19; (*b*) to prove me incapable of doing this—a motive which could be called, and certainly often felt to me as, a castratively hostile motive, but one which, as I shall subsequently state more fully, is at heart in the service of the patient's determination to be, and function as, an individual in her own right; and (*c*) to require me to acknowledge openly the extent of my own confusion, confusion such as had indeed been present in the father during her upbringing, and against which he erected as a defence a borderline-psychotic degree of subjective omniscience.

Despite these two therapeutic experiences, and others nearly as memorable to me, when some years later a fellow seminar-member at Chestnut Lodge raised the simple question, 'What part does transference have in this work?', I shared in the general floundering which we all, despite our analytic training and our considerable experience in the modified psycho-analytic treatment of schizophrenic patients, felt in trying to answer this question.

To be sure, we have long ago outgrown the position, in this regard, of Freud (1911*a*, 1914) and Abraham (1908), who held that the schizophrenic patient has regressed to an autoerotic level of development and is incapable, therefore, of forming a transference. Furthermore, the concept of transference psychosis, while not yet the subject of a voluminous literature, is not a new one. We have, for example, some cogent statements by Rosenfeld (1952*a*) to serve as a reliable avenue of entry into this subject:

. . . If we avoid attempts to produce a positive transference by direct reassurance or expressions of love, and simply interpret the positive and negative transference, the psychotic manifestations attach themselves to the transference, and, in the same way as a transference neurosis develops in the neurotic, so, in the analysis of psychotics, there develops what may be called a 'transference psychosis'. The success of the analysis depends on our understanding of the psychotic manifestations in the transference situation.

. . . It has been found that the psychotic manifestations attach themselves to the transference in both acute and chronic conditions, so that what one may call a 'transference-psychosis' develops. The analyst's main task in both acute and chronic schizophrenias is the recognition of the relevant transference phenomena and its communication to the patient . . .

Some of these chronic schizophrenic conditions seem often quite inaccessible until the relevant facts of the transference-psychosis are understood and interpreted . . . (Rosenfeld, 1954).

But, for a variety of reasons, it is not easy to discover this transference psychosis—or, as Little (1958) terms it, delusional transference—dimension in the patient's schizophrenic symptomatology.

To analyst and analytic student alike, the term 'transference psychosis' usually connotes a dramatic but dreaded development in which an analysand who at the beginning of the analysis was overtly sane but who had in actuality a borderline ego-structure, becomes overtly psychotic in the course of the evolving transference-relationship. We generally blame the analyst for such a development and prefer not to think any more about such matters, because of our own personal fear that we, like the poor misbegotten analysand, might become, or did narrowly avoid becoming, psychotic in our own analysis. By contrast, in working with the chronically schizophrenic patient, we are confronted with a person who has already become, long ago, openly psychotic, and whose transference to us is so hard to identify partly for the very reason that his whole daily life consists in incoherent psychotic transference-reactions, willy-nilly, to everyone about him, including the analyst in the treatment-session. Little's comment (1960) that the delusional state 'remains unconscious until it is uncovered in the analysis' holds true only in the former instance, in the borderline-schizophrenic patient; there, it is the fact that the transference is delusional which is the relatively covert, hard-to-discern aspect of the situation; in chronic schizophrenia, by contrast, nearly everything is delusional, and the difficult task is to foster the emergence of a coherent transference-meaning in the delusional symptomatology. In other words, the difficult thing in the work with the chronically schizophrenic patient is to discover the 'transference-reality' in his delusional experience.

The difficulty of discerning the transference-aspects of one's relationship with the patient can be traced to his having regressed to a state of ego-functioning which is marked by severe impairment in his capacity either to differentiate among, or to integrate, his experiences. He is so incompletely differentiated in his ego-functioning that he tends to feel not that the therapist reminds him of, or is like, his mother or father (or whomever, from his early life) but rather his functioning towards the therapist is couched in the unscrutinized assumption that the therapist *is* the mother or father. When, for example, I tried to bring to the attention of a paranoid schizophrenic woman how much alike she seemed to find the persons in her childhood on the one hand, and the persons about her here in the hospital, including myself, on the other hand, she dismissed this with an impatient retort, 'That's what I've been trying to *tell* you! What *difference* does it make?' For years subsequently in our work together, all the figures in her experience were composite figures, without any clear subjective distinction between past and present experience. Figures from the hospital scene peopled her memories of her past, and figures from what I knew to be her past were experienced, by her, as blended with the persons she saw about her in current life.

Comparably, in the instance of another paranoid schizophrenic woman, it required several years of therapy before this patient became able to remember, and give me any detailed account of, her mother, who had died shortly after the patient's admission to Chestnut Lodge, and whom I never met. She reacted to me, in the transference, in the spirit of so convinced and persistent an assumption that *I personified* one or another aspect of that mother, that it was extraordinarily difficult for me, also, to achieve a sufficient degree of psychological distance from the relatedness in order to visualize what the relationship between herself and her mother must have been, and to see the role being played, in her view of me—in her various and intense feeling-reactions to me—by a transference-magnification and distortion of various qualities which, in truth, reside in me. One of my notes, concerning a treatment-session which occurred after two and a half years of intensive therapy, includes the following comments:

> In today's hour the realization occurred to me that Susan feels hampered in moving out of the Lodge, away from me, by transference feelings from the relationship with her mother, feelings which kept her, for so many years until the advent of her overt psychosis, from leaving her mother. She brought out much material during this hour which made it plain—without her saying so explicitly—that it had never occurred to her that she might have any choice about whether to stay on at home and take care of her mother and the home, or leave and form her own life elsewhere. It was so plain that she had felt she of course must stay and take care of her mother, and that it would be unworthy, despicable, unthinkable, even to entertain thoughts of doing anything else. I've noticed for some several months that she often reacts to me as though I were an isolated person, in the backwash of life, someone she seems to feel called upon to minister to in many ways; so often, for example, she has prefaced her remarks by saying, gently, 'Dr Searles—?', as though assuming that I am preoccupied. But never till today did this transference element occur to me at all. Today it came to me with utter conviction. I have long ago felt that she was reacting to me as a condemnatory mother, a rejecting mother, a fond mother; but never before have I realized this particular element, in which I am reacted to as an elderly, lonely, desperately needful mother.
>
> She and I have not reached any consensus at all as to the fact that these feelings are partially on a transference basis, and I am not trying to push that upon her attention.

On the other hand, as I have mentioned, one of the great reasons for our underestimating the role of transference is that it may require a very long time for the transference to become not only sufficiently differentiated but also sufficiently integrated, sufficiently coherent, to be identifiable. This situation is entirely comparable with, though much more marked in degree than, that obtaining in the evolution of the relationship between neurotic patient and analyst, an evolution in which, as Glover had described with great clarity, the patient evidences, in the early phases of the analysis, *fleeting* indications of positive and negative transference in the course of development of the coherent and persistent *transference-neurosis*:

> . . . from the time we have ascertained that this transference situation [i.e., the transference-neurosis proper] is developing, everything that takes place during the analytic session, every thought, action, gesture, every reference to external thought and action, every inhibition of thought or action, relates to the transference-situation . . . (1955, p. 119).

A hebephrenic woman evidenced, for about three years following her admission to Chestnut Lodge, an extreme degree of ego-fragmentation and a bewildering lack of transference-identifiability in her chaotic behaviour both in her daily life on the ward and in her functioning during the therapeutic sessions. But gradually she developed such a degree of ego-integration that not only did our sessions come to possess, now, a quality of coherency of meaning throughout each session and a comparatively ready traceability of her reactions to childhood experiences, but also the ward staff, previously utterly unsure of where they stood with her, became able to see that she had reconstituted her childhood-family on the ward, with this person being rather consistently misidentified by the patient as being her older sister, that person being perceived as the mother, another as the long-time family nursemaid, and so on.

Another reason for the therapist's slowness in feeling the role of transference in the psycho-therapy is that when, after perhaps many months of a 'relationship building' phase of treatment during which he has found much reason to become confident that, at long last and after many painful and discouraging rejections, he personally has come to matter to this previously so-inaccessible patient, it comes as a particularly hurtful rejection to see to what a great extent the patient has been reacting to him not as a person in his own right but rather as the embodiment of some figure in the transference. One may discover that even one's physical housing, let alone one's more subtle personal feelings, is not really perceived as such by the patient. One paranoid woman, for example, used to shriek at me the anguished accusation that I had cut off my hands and grafted there the hands of her long-dead grandmother, in order that the sight of her grandmother's hands, extending from my cuffs, would tear her heart with grief and guilt about this grand-mother. For a number of years she was convinced, similarly, that the head she saw on my shoulders was not really mine, but was that of one or another person from her past. The therapist under the impact of transference of this power feels very alone indeed, with little or no confirmation of *himself* com-ing by way of any feedback from the patient.

To my mind, the most fundamental reason of all for our finding it difficult to discern, and to keep in view the evolving course of, the transference in the therapy of these patients is that the transference is expressive of a very primitive ego-organization, comparable with that which holds sway in the infant who is living in a world of part-objects, before he has built up an experience of himself, and of his mother and other persons round about him, as beings who are alive and whole and human. Transference as one sees it in the neurotic patient implies three whole persons—the patient, the therapist, and a person who figured in the patient's early life. The schizophrenic patient has never solidly achieved a level of ego-differentiation and ego-integration which will allow him to experience three whole persons, or even two whole persons, or, as yet, one whole person. The question of whether he will ever achieve such a level of ego-maturation will depend, more than anything else—in so far as the therapist's contribution is concerned—upon the latter's capacity to perform three tasks. First, the therapist must become able to function as a *part* of the patient and to permit the patient to be genuinely, at a deep level of psychological functioning, a part of himself. Secondly, he must be able to foster the patient's individuation (and, to a not insignificant degree, his own re-individuation) out of this level of relatedness, a level which is conceptualized variously by several workers in this field—by Kleinian ana-lysts (Klein *et al.*, 1955) as being a transference-phase dominated by projec-tive identification on the part of the patient; by Little (1960) as being a phase in which the patient has a heretofore-unconscious delusion of total undifferen-tiatedness with the analyst; and by most writers, including myself, as being a phase of symbiotic relatedness between patient and doctor. The therapist's third task is to discern, and make interpretations concerning, the patient's now-differentiated and now-integrated whole-object, that is to say neurotic, kind of transference-manifestations. With the achievement of the patient's individuation as a whole person and his capacity to perceive the therapist as a whole person, what was formerly in him a transference-psychosis is now a transference-neurosis.

It may be questioned whether the chronically schizophrenic person's ego-organization is, in its entirety, at every moment, and in relation to whatever person, as incompletely differentiated as my foregoing comments indicate; one recalls here the valuable papers by Katan (1954) and Bion (1957) concerning the non-psychotic part of the personality in schizophrenia. But in any event I consider it valid to conceive of the patient's *transference to the therapist* as being in the nature, basically, of a relatedness to the therapist as a mother-figure from whom the patient has never become, as yet, deeply differentiated. Furthermore, I believe that this 'sickest'—least differentiated— aspect of the patient's ego-functioning becomes called into play in *any* relationship which develops anything like the intensity that the therapeutic relationship develops.

Concerning the symbiotic phase in the therapeutic relatedness, which I cannot attempt here to discuss comprehensively, I should like at the moment merely to note how difficult it is to discern and conceptualize the transference in those situations where, however frequent they may be, it is always astonishing to discover to what an extent the patient is relating *to himself*—or, more accurately, to a part of himself—as an object. A hebephrenic woman, for example, often sounded, when alone in her room, through the closed door as though a castigating, domineering mother and a defiant child were locked in a verbal struggle in there. Another hebephrenic woman, trying to formulate an upsurge of jealousy at a time when she had just acquired some long-sought-for liberties to go unescorted into the nearby village, said, 'I guess I'm jealous of myself'; there was a peculiarly ego-splitting kind of pain in her voice as she said this, and with repercussions in me as I heard it, which is hard to convey in words. A hebephrenic man, who generally spent his sessions with me in silence and who was intensely threatened and furious whenever I started to speak, interrupted me at one such juncture with the furious command, 'Just sit there until ya catch yourself!', and later in the therapy was able to experience the same phenomenon in an unprojected form: when I inquired what he was experiencing, he replied, 'I'm playin' possum, tryin' to catch myself.' Still later on in our work, when I heard him murmuring some words which by then had become stereotyped, such as, 'Take your time . . . You don't say. . . Behave yourself . . .', and I asked, 'Who are you saying that to, Bill?', he replied, 'I'm just sittin' here echoin' myself.'

Similarly, Freud in a paper which included some data from his work with a schizophrenic patient, made the comment that ' . . . Analysis shows that he is playing out his castration complex upon his skin . . .' (Freud, 1915). Szasz (1957) has reported many instances of patients' having formed transferences to various parts of their own bodies. Furthermore, the whole of Klein's (Klein *et al.*, 1955) formulations concerning the importance of internal objects in mental functioning are relevant here.

To the extent that the patient is absorbed in reacting to a part of himself, whether a part of his body or one of his internal psychic objects, what then is the nature of the transference to the therapist who is in his presence? It is, I think, most useful to think of the transference, here, as being to the therapist as a *matrix* out of which the patient's ego-differentiation and ego-integration gradually develops, by successive identifications with this originally so un-differentiated and unintegrated, but at some level of relatedness truly external, transference 'object'.

In an earlier communication (1960, p. 352) I reported a hebephrenic woman's saying apprehensively, in clear reference to me, 'There's a weird doctor around here that doesn't make sense to me. He's metal—he's [looking uneasily at the walls of the room] everything.' I asked, 'Wooden?', thinking of the wood on the walls of her room in which we were sitting. She nodded agreement and added, 'He's everywhere'. Later in the therapy, as I have detailed elsewhere (see chapter 11), both participants' anxiety, and retaliatory hostility, in the symbiotic phase of the transference have become sufficiently resolved for each to experience the other as comparably omnipresent, com-parably pervading one's whole existence; no longer, however, is this felt as a malignant, threatening and constricting presence, but rather as a benign and nurturing one.

The British analysts who embrace Klein's theoretical concepts have written more than anyone else about transference psychosis and its therapeutic man-agement. Their approach is based upon her concept of projective identifica-tion. The most relevant of her views are to be found in her paper of 1946, 'Notes on Some Schizoid Mechanisms':

> I have often expressed my view that object relations exist from the beginning of life, the first object being the mother's breast which is split into a good (gratifying) and bad (frustrating) breast; this splitting results in a division between love and hate. I have further suggested that the relation to the first object implies its introjection and projec-tion, and thus from the beginning object relations are moulded by an interaction between introjection and projection, between internal and external objects and situa-tions . . .
>
> . . . With the introjection of the complete object in about the second quarter of the first year marked steps in integration are made . . . The loved and hated aspects of the mother are no longer felt to be so widely separated, and the result is an increased fear of loss, a strong feeling of guilt and states akin to mourning, because the aggressive

impulses are felt to be directed against the loved object. The depressive position [in contrast to the earlier, above-described paranoid position] has come to the fore . . .
. . . in the first few months of life anxiety is predominantly experienced as fear of persecution and . . . this contributes to certain mechanisms and defences which characterize the paranoid and schizoid positions. Outstanding among these defences is the mechanism of splitting internal and external objects, emotions and the ego. These mechanisms and defences are part of normal development and at the same time form the basis for later schizophrenic illness. I described the processes underlying identification by projection [i.e., projective identification] as a combination of splitting off parts of the self and projecting them on to another person . . .

Rosenfeld, a follower of Klein who has contributed several highly illuminating papers concerning schizophrenia, writes (1952a),

. . . I have observed that whenever the acute schizophrenic patient approaches an object in love or hate he seems to become confused with this object. This confusion seems to be due not only to phantasies of oral incorporation leading to *introjective* identification, but at the same time to impulses and phantasies in the patient of entering inside the object with the whole or parts of his self, leading to '*projective* identification'. This situation may be regarded as the most primitive object relationship, starting from birth . . . While projective identification is based primarily on an object relationship, it can also be used as a mechanism of defence: for example, to split off and project good and bad parts of the ego into external objects, which then become identified with the projected parts of the self. The chronic schizophrenic patient makes ample use of this type of projective identification as a defence . . .

In another paper, he presents detailed clinical data which serve to document the implicit point, among others, that whereas the schizophrenic patient may appear to have regressed to such an objectless auto-erotic level of development as was postulated by Freud (1911a, 1914) and Abraham (1908), in actuality the patient is involved in object-relatedness with the analyst, object-relatedness of the primitive introjective- and projective-identification kind. For example, Rosenfeld concludes his description of the data from one of the sessions as follows:

. . . The whole material of the session suggested that in the withdrawn state he was introjecting me and my penis, and at the same time was projecting himself into me. So here again I suggest that it is sometimes possible to detect the object-relation in an apparently auto-erotic state.
. . . only at a later stage of treatment was it possible to distinguish between the mechanisms of introjection of objects and projective identification, which so frequently go on simultaneously (1952b).

We find, among the writings of the Kleinian analysts, a number of interesting examples of delusional-transference interpretations, in all of which the keynote is the concept of projective (or introjective) identification. For instance, Rosenfeld writes at one juncture (1952a),

The patient himself gave the clue to the transference situation, and showed that he had projected his damaged self containing the destroyed world, not only into all the other patients, but into me, and had changed me in this way. But instead of becoming relieved by this projection he became more anxious, because he was afraid of what I was then putting back into him, whereupon his introjective processes became severely disturbed. One would therefore expect a severe deterioration in his condition, and in fact his clinical state during the next ten days became very precarious. He began to get more and more suspicious about food, and finally refused to eat and drink anything . . . everything he took inside seemed to him bad, damaged, and poisonous (like faeces), so there was no point in eating anything. We know that projection leads again to re-introjection, so that he also felt as if he had inside himself all the destroyed and bad objects which he had projected into the outer world: and he indicated by coughing, retching, and movements of his mouth and fingers that he was preoccupied with this problem . . . I told him that he was not only afraid of getting something bad inside him, but that he was also afraid of taking good things, the good orange juice and good interpretations, inside since he was afraid that these would make him feel guilty again. When I said this, a kind of shock went right through his body; he gave a groan of understanding, and his facial expression changed. By the end of the hour he had emptied the glass of orange juice, the first food or drink he had taken for two days . . .

In another paper (1954) Rosenfeld writes, concerning his work with an acutely schizophrenic girl who was intermittently overwhelmed with confusion and unable to speak,

. . . She then looked at me for quite a time and said: 'Why do you imitate me?' I interpreted that she had put herself into me and that she felt that I was her and had to talk and think for her. I explained to her that this was the reason why she felt so shut in when she came to my house and why she had to escape from me. She was now looking much more comfortable and trusting, and said: 'You are the world's best person'. I interpreted that because she felt I was so good she wanted to be inside me and have my goodness.
. . . Following the interpretations that the patient felt she was inside me, she was able to extricate herself out of me which lessened her confusion. She then became more aware of me as an external object and was able to talk . . .'

Bion (1956) defines projective identification as

. . . a splitting off by the patient of a part of his personality and a projection of it into the object where it becomes installed, sometimes as a persecutor, leaving the psyche from which it has been split off correspondingly impoverished.

The following brief example of his use of verbal interpretations comes from his work with a schizoid man:

. . . As the silence continued I became aware of a fear that the patient was meditating a physical attack upon me, though I could see no outward change in his posture. As the tension grew I felt increasingly sure that this was so. Then, and only then, I said to him, 'You have been pushing into my insides your fear that you will murder me'. There was no change in the patient's position but I noticed that he clenched his fists till the skin over the knuckles became white. The silence was unbroken. At the same time I felt that the tension in the room, presumably in the relationship between him and me, had decreased. I said to him, 'When I spoke to you, you took your fear that you would murder me back into yourself; you are now feeling afraid you will make a murderous attack upon me.' I followed the same method throughout the session, waiting for impressions to pile up until I felt I was in a position to make my interpretation. It will be noted that my interpretation depends on the use of Melanie Klein's theory of projective identification, first to illuminate my counter-transference, and then to frame the interpretation which I give the patient.

It seems to me that the above instances of verbal transference-interpretations can be looked upon as one form of intervention, at times effective, which constitutes an appeal-for-collaboration to the non-psychotic area of the patient's personality, an area of which, as noted previously, both Katan (1954) and Bion (1957) have written. But, particularly among long-hospitalized chronically schizophrenic persons, we see many a patient who is too ill to be able to register verbal statements; and even in the foregoing examples from Rosenfeld's and Bion's experiences, it is impossible to know to what extent the patient is helped by an illuminatingly accurate verbal content in the therapist's words, or to what extent that which is effective springs, rather, from the feelings of confidence, firmness, and understanding which accompany these words spoken by a therapist who feels that he has a reliable theoretical basis for formulating the clinical phenomena in which he finds himself.

In trying to conceptualize such ego-states in the patient, and such states of relatedness between patient and doctor, I find of additional value the concepts presented by Little in her papers, 'On Delusional Transference (Transference Psychosis)' (1958) and 'On Basic Unity' (1960):

. . . a neurotic can recognize the analyst as a real person, who for the time being symbolizes, or 'stands-in' for his parents . . .
Where the transference is delusional there is no such 'stand-in' or 'as-if' quality about it. To such a patient the analyst *is*, in an absolute way, . . . both the idealized parents and their opposites, or rather, the parents deified and diabolized, and also himself (the patient) deified and diabolized . . .
The transference delusion hides a state in the patient which he both needs and fears to reach. In it subject and object, all feeling, thought, and movement are experienced

TRANSFERENCE PSYCHOSIS   189

as the same thing. That is to say there is only a *state of being* or of experiencing, and no sense of there being a *person*; e.g., there is only an anger, fear, love, movement, etc., but no person feeling anger, fear or love, or moving. And since all these things are one and the same, there is no separateness or distinction between them. It is a state of undifferentiatedness, both as regards psyche and soma, experienced as chaos.

To reach this state is a terrifying thing, as it means losing all sense of being a person, and all sense of identity. The patient who reaches it becomes for the moment only a pain, rage, mess, scream, etc., and is wholly dependent on the analyst for there being anywhere a person who feels or acts. There is in fact, identification with the analyst of primary kind, but the patient cannot be aware of it.

This state has to be reached so that the unreality of these identities can be recognized, but the reaching of it is felt as utter annihilation—hence the need to maintain the delusion in the transference . . .

[Concerning] the state of undifferentiatedness which the delusion hides . . . The terms 'primary identification' and 'primary narcissism' to my mind do not fit it, nor does 'paranoid-schizoid position'. I would rather describe it as a state of primordial undifferentiatedness, or of *basic unity*, in which a primitive identification might be said to be included. What I want to convey is that the undifferentiatedness is absolute, in both degree and extent. Nothing exists apart from anything else, and the process of differentiation has to start from scratch (1958).

Little not only takes issue with various of the Kleinian theoretical concepts, but stresses the importance of physical movement and contact in helping to resolve the delusional transference:

Rosemary has never sorted herself out from her sister Joyce, who is 2 years older. All childhood happenings, ideas or feelings are told of the entity 'we'; ('We did this, We hated that'). She and Joyce are indivisible; she 'never feels a person', but is often 'two people', and sometimes 'half a person'. At the beginning of a session she frequently doesn't 'know how to begin' . . .

. . . Rosemary was functioning separately on at least two different levels, and I am understanding the separateness as being due to a failure of fusion, rather than to the action of a splitting mechanism . . .

Throughout her analysis she has continued to be paralysed with terror, and unable to find any starting-point other than something happening in me. . . . Her silence and immobility can remain total for weeks on end, and only when I show signs of life in some explicit way (for anything merely implicit is useless) can she begin to tell me what has been going on . . .

In the light of this idea of absolute identity between patient and analyst I think we have to reconsider our ideas of such mental mechanisms as projection, introjection, condensation, displacement, and all that Freud included in the term 'dream work'.

. . . we can see here how what we have considered to be condensation becomes instead a regression to the primordial undifferentiated state. Similarly, . . . what appeared to be projective identification turned out to be an assertion of absolute identity with me (1960).

I have worked with patients so deeply dedifferentiated that only after several years of intensive therapy did they become able to distinguish between an 'outside' and an 'inside'. Until such a development has occurred, one may find Little's formulations helpful in approaching the patient; subsequently, the formulations of Klein and her followers, which imply both a far higher degree of psychic structure (differentiation) and a far greater reliance upon verbal interpretations, are in my experience oftentimes pertinent. It is not a matter, I believe, of our having to choose between irreconcilable theoretical concepts, but rather to determine in which phase of the patient's ego-development each is more useful for us.

FOUR VARIETIES OF TRANSFERENCE PSYCHOSIS

Transference psychosis—or, in Little's (1958) phrase, delusional transference—may be defined as any type of transference which distorts or prevents a relatedness between patient and therapist as two separate, alive, human and sane beings. In what follows here, I shall present a variety of examples of such transference, examples which I have encountered in my clinical work and each of which I consider useful as being typical of clinical situations with one patient after another. The theoretical framework which I shall use as a vehicle for presenting clusters of these typical situations is one of which I feel much less than sure; but, beyond providing some presentational coherence, it represents the clearest theoretical integration of these seemingly dissimilar clinical phenomena which I have thus far been able to formulate. I should explain also, by way of prefacing these descriptions, that any one patient will be apt to show, over the course of treatment and perhaps in any one therapeutic session, all four of the different varieties of transference psychosis which I shall describe.

(I)

Transference-situations in which the therapist feels unrelated to the patient. In these situations, the therapist may find the patient reacting to him as being an inanimate object, an animal, a corpse, an idea, or something else not essentially human and alive. I have included many examples of such situations in my monograph on the role of the nonhuman environment in normal development and in schizophrenia (1960), and here I shall merely enumerate a few sample-situations which are not described there. My present understanding of such situations is that they are genetically traceable to the part-object world of infancy and very early childhood—the era during which the child has not yet achieved a differentiation between animate and inanimate, between human and nonhuman, in the surrounding world and in himself, and has not yet built up, through accumulated part-object relatednesses, an image of himself and of his mother as whole and separate objects. I have termed the phase of therapy in which such transference-relatedness—or 'unrelatedness'—predominates the 'out-of-contact phase' (see chapter 11), and have indicated that the early-life era which is etiologically pertinent is that from which, as Mahler (1952) describes it, autistic childhood psychosis stems, as contrasted with the developmentally later symbiotic childhood psychosis; the former type found, by Mahler, in the child who had never become firmly involved in the mother-infant symbiosis typical of later infancy and early childhood in healthy maturation, and the latter type found by her in the child who had become involved in a symbiotic relationship with the mother, but had never outgrown this mode of relatedness.

The patient's misidentification of the therapist is a typical clinical situation in point here, in addition to the varieties mentioned in my monograph. One paranoid schizophrenic man, reared as a devout Catholic, would attend Mass at the local church each Sunday, and then when I arrived for the Monday hour he would regularly misidentify me as a priest; this he would do with a degree of certainty which I found quite uncomfortable, despite my soon coming to realize that, in all probability, he was thus repressing, through this delusional misperception of me, feelings of disloyalty to his church which were aroused by his receiving treatment—however unwillingly—from a psycho-analyst, a situation to which he thought his church adamantly opposed, and one to which his deceased mother had been in any case unswervingly hostile.

The transference-position of one who is continually and at times bizarrely misidentified can be a very stressful position for the therapist to endure. One hebephrenic woman misidentified me continually, for months on end, as a succession of dozens of different persons from her past, such that I found the lack of confirmation of myself, as I know myself, to be almost intolerable. I have already described the paranoid woman who used to shriek with anguish and condemnation, while gazing over at my hands, that I had cut off the hands of her grandmother and fastened them onto myself in order to turn a knife in her heart; and who upon innumerable occasions reacted to my head as being, not my own, but the decapitated and grafted-on head of one or another person she had known. On one occasion she said to a nurse, 'Even your voice can be changed by wiring to sound like the voice of a person that I know'. She once declared to me, with chilling conviction, her certainty that I was a machine sent to kill her; and, at another time, that I was a woman who had killed my husband and was about to kill her, likewise.

Similarly, the delusional transference may consist in the patient's feeling misidentified by the other person. A paranoid woman, when responded to fondly and at length by a nurse who had known her for a long time, confided, as the nurse reported it, that 'she felt when I was talking to her that I was actually talking to a third person outside her window'. This 'third person' she said was 'angels' . . . A spinster, when in one therapeutic session I tried to promote our mutual exploring of sexual conflicts which were emerging from repression in her, protested, 'Why do you talk to me like that, Dr Searles?'; sometimes this was said with a warm, pleasurable laugh, but at other times in such a way as to make clear that she felt, as she said, 'uncomfortable'. At one such point she seemed to go completely out of contact and, when I asked her what she was experiencing, she replied, 'You make me uncomfortable when you talk like that, Dr Searles.' I asked her how she felt I talked and she replied, 'As if I were an old married woman.' I then asked her if she felt I was not talking to *her* on such occasions, and she agreed. I then suggested that naturally enough she felt removed from the situation, and she agreed with this also. There were a number of similar occasions when she behaved as though not psychologically present in the situation, evidently feeling totally misidentified by me, when my remarks were too widely at variance from her own self-concept.

In much the same vein are the instances of a patient's misidentification of himself, such that, in the instance of one paranoid woman, she assumed for many months that she was her own mother, and her children were not the two actual children I knew to be hers but were, rather, her three adult siblings. This had an utterly literal reality for her, quite beyond any figurative implications apparent enough to an observer; so, for weeks on end, I felt quite cut off from the person I knew her to be. Another paranoid woman would, one might say, literally become her mother at times of increased anxiety; another way of saying it is that a pathogenic introject derived from her mother would take over and dominate her behaviour and her sense of identity, such that one could only wait at such times for her paranoid tirades to run down until that which one knew as her real self became accessible and able to hear one's comments. The hebephrenic woman I have already mentioned, who in each hour misidentified me as being dozens of different persons from her past, from the movies, and so on, misidentified herself just as continually. On rare occasions she would ask, pathetically, if I had seen Louise (her own name) lately; it had evidently been a long time since she had seen herself, even fleetingly. Even this rare use of her own name was an indication that she felt more nearly in touch with herself than she usually did.

Also to be mentioned in this same category of phenomena are instances where the patient reacts to the therapist, in the transference, as being but one among his myriad hallucinations, or as possessing even less reality than do the hallucinatory figures. A childless hebephrenic woman, when I would come into her room, would experience me as '1500 men' who were interfering with her relationship with her daughter. It appeared that she was misidentifying herself as being her mother, and was experiencing herself-as-a-child in the form of the hallucinatory daughter outside herself, a hallucination towards which she was far more absorbed in attempted relatedness than she was with the hallucinatory men into which her perception of me devolved. In another instance later on she explained, exasperatedly, while ripping her clothes—a symptom of hers which, for many months, was maddeningly and discouragingly difficult to control—that she was trying to 'get through' me as, she made clear, the personification of her father, in order to 'reach my mother' experienced by her, apparently, as an hallucinatory presence in the room apart from either of us. In the instance of a hebephrenic man, for months I felt reacted to by him as being no more than part of the woodwork, a mute and non-participative onlooker to his lively interactions with a group of hallucinatory figures in the room—a group which, as the months wore on, assumed more coherence and identifiability as his childhood family. Later on there was a phase during which I felt that he now registered me in his awareness as comparable with, and invested with something like as much feeling as, the hallucinatory figures with which he had for so long been immersed, and now I found myself feeling competitive with, and often jealous of, his hallucinations. Still later I reached a point where I felt sure that I mattered to him far more than did his hallucinations, so that whenever he began to hallucinate I could readily see this as subsidiary to—that is, as an unconscious defence-mechanism related to some event in—his relatedness with me as a real person.

Another form of psychotic transference which causes the therapist to feel strikingly unrelated to the patient is that in which the patient is reacting to *him* as being psychotic. Hill has noted that

. . . Sometimes it is quite striking that the patient comes to believe that the doctor is thoroughly psychotic, quite in the fashion in which he himself has been psychotic . . . (1955, p. 206).

In my experience, this is an integral part of the transference-evolution seen over the course of therapy with chronically schizophrenic patients. Each such patient has had at least one parent who evidenced borderline schizophrenic ego-functioning, if not openly psychotic behaviour, during the patient's childhood, and it will then be in the nature of his unfolding transference to his therapist that he will come to regard the therapist, convincedly and, in many instances, for months on end, as being emotionally inaccessible (out of contact), delusional, and given, perhaps, to unpredictable and potentially murderous outbursts. Hill describes it that it is thus, in the schizophrenic patient's view, that at the end of his treatment

. . . He is good, and the badness is left with the doctor. Even the illness is left with the doctor . . . (1955, p. 206).

In earlier papers I have given detailed examples of this form of delusional transference, and have emphasized the need for treatment to be pursued far beyond this phase, until the craziness has been well resolved, rather than simply left in this projected form upon the therapist (1959a, see also chapter 11). But here I wish simply to note how important it is that the therapist be able to endure the explicit emergence of such a transference on the part of the patient, towards him. Bion makes some interesting comments concerning— by contrast—the etiological significance of the patient's projection of his own *sanity*, which help to highlight this point concerning the necessary transference-evolution:

I spoke of Melanie Klein's picture of the paranoid-schizoid position and the important part played in it by the infant's phantasies of sadistic attacks on the breast. Identical attacks are directed against the apparatus of perception from the beginning of life. This part of his personality is cut up, split into minute fragments, and then, using the projective identification, expelled from the personality. Having thus rid himself of the apparatus of conscious awareness of internal and external reality, the patient achieves a state which is felt to be neither alive nor dead . . .

Projective identification of conscious awareness and the associated [i.e., consequent] inchoation of verbal thought is the central factor in the differentiation [in any one schizophrenic person] of the psychotic from the non-psychotic personality . . . (1956).

. . . patients will use the mechanism of projective identification to rid themselves of their 'sanity'. If the analyst appears by his conduct to condone the feasibility of this, the way is open to massive regression . . . I am absolutely in agreement with Maurits Katan [1954] in his views on the importance of the non-psychotic part of the personality in schizophrenia (1955).

The therapist who cannot endure the patient's reacting to him as insane—who cannot stand the projection of the insane part of the personality upon him, but who unwittingly fosters and as it were insists upon the patient's projection of his own sanity upon him—cannot succeed in helping the patient to distinguish between the sane and insane ingredients of the patient's own personality, and in helping him to resolve the insanity.

These considerations have shed, for me, additional light upon the psychodynamics at work in the borderline or schizoid patient who is described by Helene Deutsch (1942) and Annie Reich (1953) as relating to others in an 'as if' fashion—as if he were experiencing a deep emotional involvement, when he is really incapable of relating except on the basis of a primitive identification of an imitative sort, traceable to his superficial identification with a narcissistic mother. I find that the nascently genuine emotionality is kept under repression in such a patient, originally out of a need to shield his mother from such real and spontaneous emotion. Comparably, I find it typical of borderline patients in general that not only their emotionality but their ego-perceptions in general are held subjectively in great doubt, and hence their sense of reality is impaired, for the reason that one's parent—or, in the therapy-session, the therapist—must be spared from the reality of those perceptual data which the patient *tends* to see or hear or otherwise sense full well and accurately; but in the transference he has reason to doubt that the therapist-mother or -father can stand exposure to it, by reason of the near-psychotic narcissistic brittleness of ego-functioning which he attributes to the therapist, traceable to his experience with such a narcissistic mother as Deutsch and Reich describe.

Thus in the treatment sessions the patient tends to feel 'like a bull in a china shop', as various patients have expressed it, severely constricted in thought and feeling with, perhaps, their psychic productions taking shape, in their own view, only fuzzily like indistinct images on a TV screen. One of my patients regularly prefaces, or immediately afterwards tries to undo, her most penetrating observations, concerning either myself or her parents or whomever, with the apologetic statement, 'I know I'm crazy . . . '. Another borderline woman patient at the Lodge, who shows a remarkably accurate perceptiveness as to what is going on in me, as indicated by either verbal or non-verbal communicational nuances, regularly gives me a way out of facing the reality of these by qualifying her comments with 'I sort of got the impression just then that . . .' or 'It seemed to me as if . . .', or 'I don't know, but I just had the thought that . . . '. I now understand a little better why a schizoid patient whom I treated years ago once went to the extent of putting it that, 'A sort of a half an idea just crept into my unconscious: . . . '. On the basis of a lifetime of experience with an extremely brittle mother, he was, as I now realize in retrospect, putting it thus tentatively on the assumption that I could not stand more direct exposure to the thought-and-feeling which he was conveying. These matters do not involve, I wish most strongly to emphasize, merely forms of communication on the patient's part; they extend into, and to a high degree permeate, his subjective experience, his perceptual functioning in general, so that he may feel quite out of touch indeed with thoughts and feelings which, in the transference, he unconsciously senses to be too threatening to the parent-therapist.

Brodey's (1959, 1961) papers, reporting his observations and theoretical formulations concerning the family therapy of schizophrenia, have been very helpful to my discovering the transference-meanings which I have just mentioned. Brodey describes how greatly the schizophrenic patient's awareness of reality is constricted by reason of a need to be attentive to the mother's inner workings, and he says that, for example,

> . . . One patient while psychotic seemed alive, vibrant, and was most discerning in her relationship with the mother; but she was psychotic and her behaviour unpredictable to the extreme. As she moved from this position back to what would be called by the mother 'reasonableness', she returned to being a puppet dancing with every movement of her mother's hand with lifeless accuracy . . . (1961).

(II)

The second category of *instances of transference psychosis* is that comprising those situations *in which a clear-cut relatedness has been established between patient and therapist, and the therapist therefore no longer feels unrelated to the patient; but the relatedness is a deeply ambivalent one.* My theoretical concept of such situations is that the transference-evolution has unearthed that era of the patient's ego-development in which the mother-infant symbiosis had come to possess too high a degree of ambivalence for him to have been able to follow the healthy sequence from identification with mother to the subsequent establishment of successful individuation; the ambivalence had been too intense for him to develop an integrated ego, and his ego-development had been turned, instead, into a defensive autism which left him vulnerable to the later development of schizophrenia. Thus, in the transference-evolution to the therapist, he deeply hungers for, and must have if he is to become born as a real person, a symbiotic relatedness with the mother-therapist which is comparatively free from ambivalence—a phase analogous to the preambivalently symbiotic phase of the healthy mother-infant relationship. But he fears this, too, as being equivalent to the annihilation of himself, or the mother-therapist, or both.

Such theoretical concepts have been arrived at largely empirically, 'after the fact' as it were, emergent from the accomplishment of difficult clinical work.

I worked with a luxuriantly and most persistently delusional paranoid woman, for example, for four years before discovering, in the course of the next few months, two of the transference-determinants (various additional ones became clear to me in later years of the therapy) which had been forming the fountainheads of all her so bewildering delusions. I consider it significant that these revelations of the nature of the transference came to light only after her previously tenacious fear and hostility had given way to a considerable degree of positive feeling in the transference.

One of these approximately concomitant revelations came to light in an hour in which she said, with a striking amount of fondness, in reference to the female therapist who had worked with her at a previous hospital, 'If I had that doctor to talk to every day, I could even tolerate life here at Chestnut Lodge.' She went on to describe this therapist in terms strikingly similar to those she had applied, over the years, to 'my so-called mother'. What emerged in essence, during this hour and over the subsequent few months, was a revelation of the intense loyalty she had felt, all along, towards the earlier therapist, such that I now understood in retrospect why, over these four difficult years, in her loud defiance of and manifold resistance to therapy, she would often loudly proclaim that she was 'upholding the standards of the medical profession'. She had been upholding what she believed, with an incredible degree of confusion and distortion, to be the standards of Doctor X, the former therapist, who was so little differentiated, in her perception, from her own mother.

Actually, both her mother and Doctor X were remembered by her as being multiple figures, of varying sexual identities. I felt little inclination to be critical of the former therapist, for every critical implication which the patient's words bore towards that therapist, she had long made, and for a long time would yet make, towards me also, during periods when I was, for her, such a mother-figure—or, more accurately, such mother-figures—in the transference.

To return to my point here, I wish simply to emphasize what a revelation it was for me to see how greatly, for her, any positive feeling towards me, any achieved bit of collaboration in the therapy with me, conflicted with her sense of loyalty to the former therapist, and, by the same token, to what a great degree her discouragingly persistent delusions comprised, *en bloc*, a formidably massive effort to fend me off so that she could preserve her loyalty to the former therapist, in turn so transparent a screen for her own mother who, as her father told me and as I found abundantly documented in the events of the transference-relationship, 'loved to dominate' the patient as a child and demanded the patient's loyalty to her views, no matter how conflictual, divergent, self-destructive, nonsensical, and simply crazy those views in fact were.

The other of these concomitant revelations can perhaps be best conveyed by quoting my notes concerning an hour approximately two months following the hour alluded to above:

The work with her has gone extremely well, and very collaboratively, again ever since about 12 March [three weeks ago]. In today's hour she was dressed in a very cute dancecostume, looking both very cute in a small-girl way and very seductive in a mature-woman way, with many flirtatious raisings of her skirt as she dissertated about theology, philosophy, and the complex workings of the world in general. Very early in the hour she accused me, in an unstinging way, of having 'lustful', 'erotic' desires. It actually was, much of the time, a quite anxious hour for me, with my feeling that she and I were interacting at two quite separate levels: (1) debating (she was doing the great bulk of it); and (2) a nonverbal sexual level, what with her sexy posturings and skirt-liftings. My discomfort consciously related to my feeling that the sexy business on her part was dissociated; so I felt, as it were, alone in having to deal with it. But late in the hour I chided her lightly, telling her, 'You've been giving me a difficult time, prancing around in that outfit looking cute as can be, and accusing me of having lustful, erotic desires.' She laughed in a pleased way; so I guess her own erotic feelings can't be too heavily repressed at the moment.

But there was an additional very significant development in this hour; it became more apparent to me than ever before—I've seen it before but never realized the influential strength of this particular dynamism—that she not only loves to debate actively (which I've long known) but that she almost certainly greatly misses, unconsciously, the probably hours-long debates she used to have with her mother—at least I'm pretty sure it was her mother [confirmed by abundant data subsequently in the therapy]. She herself always refers to it as 'they' who used to say so-and-so; she was quoting to me, during this hour, much of the debates they used to have—quoting what she used to say and then telling me what 'they' used to say. The point of all this is that today I realized, better than before, that all this delusional thinking, *en bloc*, provides a *way of relating* which she greatly enjoys, a way of relating which I'm very inclined to think characterized a relatedness with her mother which she greatly misses, unconsciously. It became quite clear to me today that her behaviour is not oriented towards any satisfactory *resolution*, contentwise, of the arguments, the debates. As I told her, I feel that she would say that a tree is a dog, if necessary, to start a good argument; I said this in a friendly way, feeling friendly. I feel sure that she does not realize the dynamics of this as yet.

In the final section of this paper I shall discuss the matter of *interpretations* of transference-psychosis. At the moment, I wish to note that one of my great difficulties in the work with this woman had to do with my susceptibility to being drawn into arguing with her delusional utterances. On innumerable occasions I could no longer sit silent while the most basic tenets of my concept of reality were being assaulted, not merely by the content of her words but by the tremendous forcefulness of her personality; on these occasions, the preservation of my sanity demanded that I speak. On other occasions, I would argue in an effort to rescue her from a degree of delusional confusion which was, on such occasions, indubitably genuine and indescribable here; to say that a tree is a dog would be only the tiniest measure of her confusion at such times. On still other occasions, when her anxiety was much less and there was little of any urgent helplessness or threatening domineeringness on her part, she would simply make it irresistible fun to argue with her.

No matter in what spirit the arguments ensued, they always served, for her, as a way of simultaneously relating me, emotionally and psychologically, to herself and yet keeping me safely separate from herself, outside herself. These arguments were so difficult to deal with successfully in the therapy because they were the expression of her ambivalently-symbiotic relationship with her mother. She needed so much for us to be psychologically one person—an experience which had not been successful in her early relationship with her mother—and yet, for very good reasons in her history, she felt that this would amount to the annihilation of both of us. The subsequent months and years of the therapy included a clear-cut preambivalently—that is, relatively non-ambivalently—symbiotic phase, the culmination of which she experienced as literally becoming born; but at this phrase which I am describing, her arguing—and my reciprocal arguing—represented a mutual deferring of that phase. She held it off partly by the defence-mechanism of arguing; others of my patients have shown other types of defences used for the same purpose.

It is significant that this woman came to describe, eloquently and feelingly, how intensely exasperating she used to find it when her older brother—who for a long time in her treatment she insisted was 'my mother'—'got into my mind' in the course of arguments between them, rather than, as I would put it, maintaining his position in outer reality. She clearly conveyed how utterly helpless she would feel on such occasions, when she would experience him as a physical presence 'in my mind', where, so her words and gestures conveyed, she could not get her hands on him, and therefore could not reach him.

A hebephrenic woman came to express her ambivalently-symbiotic relatedness, or one might say her need for, and avoidance of, symbiosis, in a way more primitive than the arguing of which the paranoid woman I have just described was capable. She came to maintain for years, on the one hand, a demeanour of stony and silent antagonism toward me, seeming genuinely not to see me much of the time; yet on the other hand this demeanour would be interlarded with moments when she would make urgent pleas for oneness with me. Her history indicated that her relationship with each of her parents had been, until she became overtly psychotic in her early twenties, ambivalently symbiotic in nature. A note made concerning an hour in the sixth year of our work, at a time when I had become comparatively free from enmeshment in an ambivalently symbiotic relationship with her—at a time when I had come to feel, with predominant relief but with some guilt and concern, that I had 'fallen out of love with her'—suggests something of her striving to regain the symbiosis with me:

The work with Ellen continues to show, most prominently, her making clear her ambivalent effort to achieve, and to avoid, a symbiotic relatedness with me as a representative of her father. It seems to me of late that, because of my sense of separateness from her which is so much greater than that of a few years ago, her emphasis is mainly on the efforts to achieve [i.e., to regain] such a relationship.

Thus, for example, in yesterday's hour she indicated her doubt that she could survive if I stepped out of the room for a moment to get a cup of coffee, which I did. I cannot overemphasize how poignantly she expresses this kind of anxiety, such that in retrospect I am not surprised that I had such tremendous difficulty in going ahead years ago and functioning freely in the face of her anxiety and pleas in this direction [i.e., pleas for symbiosis].

This woman had once confided in me, 'My father lives when he gives to me', and the years of our therapeutic collaboration provided abundant evidence that one of the major aspects of her delusional transference to me was as a father whose own life demanded the perpetuation of a symbiotic relationship wherein he 'gave' incessantly to her, 'solicitously' lived her life for her, and so on.

(III)

The third category of *instances of transference psychosis* are those *in which the patient's psychosis represents, in the transference, an effort to complement the therapist's personality, or to help the therapist-parent to become established as a separate and whole person.* These clinical situations, which appear quite diverse, all represent the patient's living out, in the transference, of the difficulty he has had since early childhood with a parent who has not proved strong enough, on his or her own, to accept the resolution of a symbiotic relationship which should have predominated only in the patient's infancy and early childhood. Because the parent is able to relate *only* symbiotically to the child, the child is given to feel that the resolution of the symbiotic mode of relatedness will mean the death of the parent, and his own potentially individual self is thus experienced by the patient as an inherently murderous self. The anxiety defended against by the schizophrenic symptomatology may be looked upon as springing from the simultaneous conviction that (a) the desperately-needed symbiotic experience (no matter how formulated, or incapable of formulation, in the patient's mind) is tantamount to death as an individual, the erasure of individuality; and (b) the goal of fully-achieved individuation is seen as equivalent to the murder of the parent.

These are far from being simply delusional notions on the patient's part, without any basis in reality. I have been struck, for instance, with the highly significant circumstances in which fatal or near-fatal cardiovascular accidents, quite beyond the much more frequent upsurges in anxiety of sometimes psychotic proportions, have occurred among parents of recovering schizophrenic patients. Several such incidents have occurred in the families of patients with whom I have been working; but this statistically insignificant sampling grows to sobering proportions when one sees it supported by similar incidents which have occurred in the course of my 14 years of work at Chestnut Lodge, in the collective experiences of, in cumulative total, perhaps 50 therapists who have worked with hundreds of patients here, over the years. Such patients have had much solid historical reason to sense their own growth-impulses as being inescapably murderous in nature, and therefore as being necessary to contain at all costs.

Comparatively early in my experience here, in my work with a catatonic young woman, I came to see that one of the determinants of various kinds of helplessness on her part consisted in an unconscious effort to promote her father's becoming a man; her persistent hope evidently was that he would find himself as man in the course of rescuing her from the situation in which she was floundering. This determinant became clearly revealed in the unfolding of her transference to me, and evident to both of us; the working through of her disappointment in her father, in this connexion, was one of the solid achievements in her therapy. Since then, I have found the same unconscious 'motive' in various other schizophrenic patients, in one form or another.

A 45-year-old hebephrenic woman, for example, given for years to maddeningly fragmented and semi-audible speech, and equally maddening physical contrariness and unmanageability, came eventually to make clear that this represented, in the context of the transference-relationship to me as a father, her effort to promote my making myself more firmly delineated, as it were— more explicit, more decisive, more firm. I had met her father, who died of a coronary occlusion a few months after her entry into intensive psycho-therapy at the Lodge, and I had found him to be a remarkably inscrutable man. She had evidently found him so, too, and she made clear, in the transference, that she had found him to be, as well, a maddeningly indecisive person, who had as it were driven her out of her mind with his tantalizing indecisiveness and his crushingly disappointing failure to see things through. As she once put it, he 'always gave up two-thirds of the way up the mountain'; their symbiotic relatedness had consisted in her regarding him, overtly, as an adored pal, with whom she hiked, played tennis and golf, went horseback riding and sailing, and shared her experiences (by detailed subsequent reports) with boy friends whom she always compared unfavourably with him. They also played musical instruments together.

In the transference relationship, I early found that she was trying not simply to seduce me sexually, but was trying to get me to become a man by having intercourse with her. Once, for example, she wiggled her bare buttocks at me suggestively and, when I failed to make the apparently-desired response, she quickly began showing increasing exasperation and said to herself, with great annoyance, 'Charlie [her father's nickname, which she generally used in referring to him and often used in referring to me] never did know how to play the bass clef!'

But comparable realizations on my part, concerning other manifestations of this same motive of father-building in the transference, were arrived at only with the greatest of difficulty. It was only after several years that I discovered that one of the major determinants of her deeply schizophrenic mode of communication, which as I say was maddeningly fragmented and semiaudible, consisted in an effort on her part, an evidently genuinely unconscious effort, to foster my declaring myself, delineating myself, through my responsive efforts at filling in and clarifying which this mode of speech tended powerfully to evoke from me. Such schizophrenic speech tends to function in a way analogous to a Rorschach test, inviting the therapist's own projective self-revelations. Similarly, it was only after years of the most maddeningly indecisive and unmanageable behaviour on her part, whether during attempted walks in the hospital grounds with me or with various other personnel members, or when asked to perform any physical act, however ostensibly simple, that I realized that *her* extreme indecisiveness represented, in part, her effort to promote the other person's (in the therapeutic sessions, my) becoming decisive through his or her eventually becoming completely out of patience and cutting through all indecisiveness in the situation by a furiously impatient and unequivocal command.

Other more verbal and better integrated patients have come to make clear that their delusional utterances represent, in part, an effort to get the therapist to make clear where he stands—to determine how crazy or how sane he is, to find out what is his view of the people and events and things with which the patient is concerned. It has often come to me as not only a useful but also as an amusing realization to discover that my supposedly delusional, confused patient is now involved in trying the delusions upon me for size, or is otherwise involved in doing a kind of mental status examination of me. Recently a long-hebephrenic and genuinely disoriented woman murmured haltingly to me, 'What's the date?', and I started patiently to tell this poor benighted soul the date, when I suddenly realized that, from her view, it was I whose psyche was in question, and that she was trying cautiously to discern whether *I* knew the date. Space does not allow for an attempt to document conclusively that this is what her seeming disorientation, earlier in our work quite genuine indeed, had come to mean; all I can ask is that one does not forget that this is what one's patient may be doing with one. When this dimension of the transference-relationship comes into view, it comes to one's attention that an astonishing number of bits of behaviour on the patient's part are interpretable in this light, as being evidence of a persistent, unending watchfulness for, and when opportunity affords itself, a brief and covert investigation of, data which indicate that the parent-therapist is sane or insane. It makes sense that this must have indeed been an important dimension of the patient's childhood—an important concern to him as a child—when we consider how afflicted has been the ego-functioning of at least one, and often both, of his two parents.

Similarly, I have found, and reported elsewhere, that a schizophrenic patient's expression of genuinely confused and delusional utterances may represent an unconscious effort to foster the creative imagination of the other person—the therapist, for example, the therapist perceived in the transference as being constricted, unimaginative, uncreative. I have seen this motive become clear and conscious in various of my patients. But in the instance of a hebephrenic woman it did not become clear to me until she physically loosened my too-tight shirt collar, which brought home to me the realization, in retrospect, of how many were the ways in which she had been trying, so to speak, to loosen my collar—trying to promote my living a freer and less obsessionally constricted life. I might add, parenthetically to any considerations about transference, that she has helped me greatly on this score. The schizophrenic patient's need to cure the therapist may dovetail in a useful way with the therapist's determination to become free from characterological obsessiveness.

Quite analogous is the schizophrenic patient's effort—a largely unconscious effort until it emerges from repression during the course of therapy—to relieve, by his crazy utterances and behaviour, depression in the other person. Depression is an important dimension in any schizophrenic patient; only after much therapy is he strong enough to feel it as his own, and until such time as he can, he has to project it upon the therapist (and other persons), and thus feels impelled to relieve it by schizophrenic symptoms which the other person may find infuriating, puzzling, or perhaps delightfully diverting, but in any case a way out of depression. Another way of viewing this phenomenon is to see that depression was prominent in the patient's parent(s) in his childhood, and in some instances oppressively permeated the whole family's life together; in the transference this becomes carried over to the therapist, who is often viewed as being on the verge of suicide. The suicidal feelings which are present, whether actively or latently, in every person (except those individuals who are too deeply schizophrenic for such feelings to be accessible to them) become mobilized in the therapist, making for one of the genuinely great difficulties in doing successful therapy with these patients. Seen in the overall context of the hospital, some of those patients who are most severely 'stuck' in their ego-development, year after year, are the hospital's well-known colourful characters, living legends, whose crazy antics, past and present, have served the function of relieving depression in the collective patients-and-personnel about them in the hospital community.

I personally have never felt more powerfully impelled towards suicide than I was during some months when a previously hebephrenic woman was working through her feelings towards me as being the personification, in the transference, of her long-depressed father. She had made clear to me that, at one time or another, each of her three other family members had been withdrawn, weeping, and 'yelling around about suicide'; but this had evidently been most severe in the father. He, a person much older than his wife, had fondly (though also enviously) told his daughter that she had 'all the vermilionishness of life', as she had once put it during the hebephrenic, highly neologistic earlier period of our work together. One of the ways in which she complemented him was by functioning as his own lost youth. She was both young, as he no longer was, and the girl he had never been and could never be. It was in part out of poignant experiences with her that I wrote a paper entitled, 'Schizophrenia and the Inevitability of Death' (1961*b*). The working-through of this aspect of her transference-symbiosis with me took years to accomplish.

For years she habitually went about looking like a little girl dressed up in vivid but miscellaneous and out-of-style clothing, often reminiscent of the 'flapper era' chronicled in, for example, the cartoons by John Held, Jr., in the *College Humor* magazine of the 1920s and '30s. I was often annoyed by her attire, and embarrassed by it as an advertisement of the therapeutic capabilities of the man, namely me, who had been her therapist for an embarrassingly long series of years; she often went to unstinting and at times highly creative effort to constitute such an advertisement of herself. All this had, of course, a transference root derived from her experience in 'advertising', by her schizophrenic symptoms, her parents who were painfully conscious of matters of social position. Her older brother once confided to me his concern lest the patient, who had shown no little murderousness during her life both at home and in the sanatorium, might be released from the hospital prematurely and might murder somebody. This was a reasonable concern; but I was startled when the brother went on to explain that he would not wish such a thing to happen, for the reason that it would 'embarrass the family'. I was both determined that my vulnerability to personal embarrassment should not lead me into trying to dictate what the patient should wear, and recurrently touched, moreover, by the little-girl delight which she evidently found in her own attire, so that I could not bear to hurt her feelings by going beyond comparatively gentle suggestions that, yes, the attire is pretty but the orange doesn't go very well with the purple; or, yes, the hat is pretty but the dress looks a bit out of style, say thirty years or so.

Then one day, a few weeks after we had found that we had each chanced to see and like the movie, 'The Sweet Bird of Youth', she came into the hour wearing, among other miscellaneous adornments (such as a black, scalloped slip and dramatic, blue-lensed eyeglasses) a taffeta skirt covered with giant splashes of colour, a skirt such as would be unlikely to be found anywhere but in a child's dream. She asked me eagerly, gesturing towards her skirt, 'Don't you think this looks like the sweet bird of youth?' It was this development which brought home to me the realization that, whereas all along I had felt that *I* was being tender to *her* in not bluntly opposing her wearing of such attire, she evidently was wearing it out of, in part, a tender concern for *me*—a concern to provide me, as a father in the transference, with Youth. I replied something like this, 'Alice, as a little boy I used to wear an aviator's helmet that buttoned down under the chin, like this—. As I say, I liked it, and I might for example come in here wearing it some day. I might want you to admire it—and possibly you would; but I think you might have *some* feeling that my aviator's helmet, buttoned down under my chin, would be a *bit* out of place'. She took this well, and I believe it was not so much the expressing of a gentle correction as, rather, the conveying to her that I could accept the loss of my own youth which helped her eventually to get over this particular symptom.

(IV)

The fourth variety of transference psychosis is manifested at a phase in therapy in which *the deeply and chronically confused patient, who in childhood had been accustomed to a parent's doing his thinking for him, is ambivalently (a) trying to perpetuate a symbiotic relationship wherein the therapist to a high degree does the patient's thinking for him, and (b) expressing, by what the therapist feels to be sadistic and castrative nullifying or undoing of the therapist's efforts to be helpful, a determination to be a separately thinking, and otherwise separately functioning, individual.* During my years of work at Chestnut Lodge, I have successively seen the basically transference nature of schizophrenic confusion; the intense though largely unconscious sadism which is being expressed in this confusion, by the subjectively helpless patient whom the dedicated therapist is trying to rescue from the confusion; and, lastly, the striving towards individuation which is at the core of those aspects of the patient's functioning which have seemed, heretofore, primarily intended sadistically to torture, and in one fashion or another to castrate, the therapist.

One chronically confused hebephrenic woman, who for years in her therapy evidenced much idiotic behaviour and on repeated psychological examinations was found to have a subnormal I.Q., had been trained by her father throughout her upbringing how to think. As a natural extension of this, he had coached her as to what to say in various social situations, and had taught her to memorize various witticisms which amused him and which she found essentially meaningless. She became schizophrenic during her teens, at a point where it had become evident that this idolized-father symbiotic partner of hers had, in actuality, feet of clay. She then oriented her life, for several years, around a delusional omnipotent figure, a kind of composite of powerful persons, real and imagined, from past and present life, and addressed hundreds of pleas for rescue, from the hospital, to, for example,

My Father, Zirey Edward Butcher
Head of the Marshall Airfields
All over the Place
    or
My Old Man . . .
Head the Boss of Radio City
Head of General Motors
The World's Fair
Head of Standard Oil
Head of the Conferences . . .
    or, in at least one instance,
. . . Head of Those Things.

A tiny sample of the vast extent to which her functional imbecility came from emotional, transference sources became evident in an hour when she was describing—against, as usual, massive confusion—her struggle to hold a job as a secretary, years ago, during an interim between two of her long successions of hospitalization. She managed to bring out her conviction that the customary salutation in a business letter, 'Dear Sir', is indicative of both promiscuity (as regards the 'Dear') and of boot-licking (as regards the 'Sir'). I had long ago found much evidence to indicate that her possessive father had forbidden her participation in either 'promiscuity' or 'bootlicking' to such an extent that it had been impossible for her to develop more than the rudiments of any friendships with other young people. It had long ago become clear that she had been given to feel that she must have no other gods before him— before him, who, she had quite literally believed up until her schizophrenic break, was omniscient.

In the transference relationship with me she would recount, with hebe-phrenic laughter, meaningless fragments of jokes that 'were going around New York' years before—always meaning, so I came to know, idiosyncratic jokes which she had heard from, specifically, her father. Always my failure to laugh in response to these unfunny 'jokes' was taken by her as confirmation that I was, like the mother upon whom she and her father had habitually heaped scorn, devoid of a sense of humour and therefore incapable of functioning upon the high plane occupied by that symbiotic twosome. For fully three years I was, in the transference, predominantly this scorned mother.

But then she began reacting to me as being, more and more clearly, the know-it-all father, and her confusion gradually took form as representing on the one hand a desperate effort to get me to clarify the awesome confusion with which she was genuinely afflicted, and on the other hand a mocking, sadistic, eroding kind of nullification of my efforts to be helpful to her in this very regard.

More than anything, I was patient; with seemingly endless patience and solicitude I tried to help this pitiably confused girl, and only later on did I realize that she had construed my overt calmness, gentleness, and patience as being evidence of the same maddeningly aloof, know-it-all quality she had come to hate—as therapy had by now established—in her father. It was characteristic of her to deny the fact of her own confusion; she had, no doubt, too little ego-strength to be able to face this awesomely helpless aspect of herself.

A turning-point came near the end of an hour filled with the usual inundatingly confused verbalizations from her. I had recurrently commented, 'That was puzzling, wasn't it?', or 'It's confusing to you, isn't it?'. Each time she had flatly denied that she was confused—had denied it in a way which I found progressively exasperating, since I felt very much confused most of the time myself, and since her tone, as well as her verbal content, was clearly one of confusion and puzzlement.

Finally, near the end of the hour, when for the *n*th time she had flatly disclaimed being confused, I burst out sarcastically and very exasperatedly, 'Well, if it's clear to *you*, congratulations, Louise! It sure as hell isn't clear to *me; I've* been confused by about 80 per cent of what you've been saying this hour. But if it's all clear to you, *congratulations*! You know, it's one thing to be confused and to *know* you're confused, and it's another thing to be confused and not even know you're confused. At least if you *realize* you're confused, that's a *beginning*!' Previously, I had been concerned to protect her from the realization of how very confusing I had long been finding her desperate efforts to convey her thoughts to me.

Significantly, it was in the very next day's session that she told me, more clearly than ever before, how exasperating it had been to her during her upbringing that her father would never admit that he was wrong about something, would never admit that there was something he didn't know. It was at this point that I realized in retrospect that one determinant of her years-long confusion had been an effort, apparently largely unconscious, on her part to thwart, and prove fallible, me as the know-it-all father in the transference.

Subsequently she was much more accepting of my efforts to help her in the resolution of her severe and chronic thought-disorder.

Another hebephrenic woman, who had likewise participated, until the onset of her schizophrenic psychosis, in an overtly idolizing but covertly competitive symbiotic relationship with her father, for several years placed me under extreme pressure—by reason of her manifest helplessness, despair, terror, and often mutely abandoned and unloved demeanour—to get me to do her thinking for her, as her father had evidently done in bygone years. Incessantly I was kept under pressure to guess aloud at the meanings which were supposedly nascent in her fragmentary, ambiguous, and half-inaudible speech, or in her oftentimes odd non-verbal communications. Despite the fact that she would almost invariably react with an undermining sneer when I did manage, by dint of flights of intuition, to guess correctly, I kept trying with dogged devotion—and, as became increasingly evident, I was trying overmuch to, as she phrased it, 'put words in my mouth'.

It was such infringement on her striving to think for herself, and to become free from the transference-symbiosis, that brought forth her most sadistic responses to me. In an earlier paper (1959a) I have conceptualized such responses as an effort to drive the other person crazy. She eventually came to make this sadistic motive quite explicit, in such statements as—near the end of an hour in which she had made clear, on the one hand, how much she suffered from genuine fragmentation of all her perceptual functions—'I hate doctors! That's why I make things mush!'

This was the same woman who had said, earlier in our work when I was trying, as usual, to rescue her from her despair-filled fragmentation, 'There's a weird doctor around here that doesn't make sense to me. He's metal— he's—everything', while looking uneasily about.

Rosenfeld (1954) states that

In the acute schizophrenic state the patient tends to put his self so completely into objects that there is very little of the self left outside the object. This interferes with most ego-functions, including speaking and understanding words . . .

And Bion (1956) presents some extremely stimulating concepts, to the effect that one of the essential features of schizophrenic personality is a hatred of reality, which is extended to all aspects of the psyche that make for awareness of it, such that his own perceptual ego-functions, as well as his attempted collaborativeness with the analyst, is subjected to hostile splitting-mechanisms.

It seems to me that the concepts of both Rosenfeld and Bion do not take into adequate account a factor inherent in the early family life of the patient, wherein the invasiveness of the symbiotic parent(s) was such as to prevent the child from meeting a genuine reality either outside himself or within himself as an individual. We need to see that it is not reality as such which the patient hates, but rather the only 'reality' which he has so far known, a symbiosis-derived pseudo-reality, a reality derived, in Brodey's (1959, 1961) terms, from the mother's (or, I would add, the father's) 'inner workings'. It is this 'reality', this facet of the pathogenic symbiosis, which the patient is health-ily—though seemingly so sadistically and castratively and destructively—determined to shed, in order to emerge and be born as an individual.

A chronically paranoid woman, whose mother, in the words of an uncle who gave us an admission history, had 'loved to dominate' this child and had given the girl, from her own isolated, eccentric, ambulatory schizophrenic social position, unequivocal but remarkably contradictory edicts as to how to think and behave in various situations, came to reveal, in the course of our several years of work together, various of these psychodynamics with unusual clarity.

Like one of the foregoing hebephrenic women, this patient became able to acknowledge the fact of her own confusion, defended against for years by vociferously uttered delusional certainties, only after I had come to experi-ence, and openly reveal, a deep confusion in myself in reaction to her force-fully- and tenaciously-expressed delusions, which I came eventually to feel as seriously eroding all the underpinnings of my sense of identity, all the things about myself of which I had felt most sure: namely, that I am a man, that I am a psychiatrist, that I am engaged in fundamentally decent rather than malev-olent work, and so on and so on. She now became able to say, simply and seriously, 'I don't know anything', and to evidence a steadily diminishing resistance to my therapeutic efforts.

I knew that the death of her mother had been one of the circumstances, if not the centrally significant circumstance, attending the onset of her paranoid schizophrenia, several years ago. A time came in our work when, in a spirit of unusually positive transference, although as usual she was delusional and confused, she was struggling unusually hard to try to understand and convey to me what she was experiencing during the course of the session. At one point she explained to me, 'You see, my mother was my mind', and this was said in such a tone as poignantly to convey the implication, 'and when I lost her, I lost my mind.' It was painfully clear during the hour to what an awesome extent she had indeed lost her mind, as measured by the incredible depth of her confusion, quite unreproducible here.

As far as her transference to me during this same session was concerned, I felt that all her productions, taken together, amounted to a vigorous effort to induce me to provide her with guidance, direction. She did make quite explicit her struggle at present to, as she put it, 'build a world', and was clearly trying to persuade me to work with her in figuring this out, or hopefully to show her how to do it. Part of the time she was working with pencil and paper, drawing a diagram of a very tall H, a turtle, an ark, a saucer, and one or two other items. Included in the notes I made subsequent to this session was the comment,

> What makes this so terribly difficult is that her competitiveness, her castrativeness, which is so much out of her awareness, is so strong as largely to nullify such efforts as I do make to respond to her indubitably sincere collaborativeness.

But it gradually became very clear to me, and confirmed by her, that the 'getting well' I sought to help her achieve was to her synonymous with getting castrated. This concept she acted out in various ways, in schizophrenic symptomatology which sometimes made one's flesh creep, as when—to mention but one among many diverse incidents—she stripped all the leaves off some luxuriant plants which she had been carefully nurturing in her room. She began to reveal more and more clearly that, in performing these various crazy acts, she was obediently following the directions which she heard coming from 'that woman in my head', who was evidently an introject, no matter how distorted by the patient's own anxiety and hostility, of the crazy mother of her childhood.

In one of the more amusing of our sessions, she suddenly reported to me, 'That woman in my head just said, ''Don't have anything to do with that frump out there''.' She confirmed my amused assumption that 'that frump' referred to me. At another point in the hour, she protested vigorously, when I had suggested, as had long been my custom 'Let's see what comes to your mind next', 'You keep asking me what's in my *mind—she's* in my mind; but she has nothing to do with *me!*' She went on to make it evident that she herself felt utterly ignored and unrelated-to by me, whenever I endeavoured, with those words, to encourage her to express herself. Usually we think of the person's mind as the locus and very core of his self; but she showed me that this was by no means true for her. It was evident, in retrospect, that when, all along, I had been endeavouring to help her explore and elaborate what was in her mind, she had been reacting as though my effort had been to stamp out finally her upward-struggling autonomy, to castrate finally her individuality, so to speak, by rendering permanent and total the sway which the introjected symbiotic mother already held over her ego-functioning.

Before leaving this discussion of the forms in which transference-psychosis is manifested, it should be noted that just as all these various forms may be shown by any one patient, at one time or another in the course of his psychotherapy, so is it impossible to demarcate clearly between transference-psychosis in general, on the one hand, and transference-neurosis on the other hand.

Freud (1911b) made the comment that

> We have long observed that every neurosis has as its result, and probably therefore as its purpose, a forcing of the patient out of real life, an alienating of him from reality . . . Neurotics turn away from reality because they find it unbearable—either the whole or parts of it. The most extreme type of this turning away from reality is shown by certain cases of hallucinatory psychosis which seek to deny the particular event that occasioned the outbreak of their insanity. But in fact every neurotic does the same with some fragment of reality . . .

Bion, in his paper in 1957 concerning the differentiation, in any one schizophrenic patient, between what he calls the psychotic personality and the non-psychotic personality, concludes the presentation of his theoretical formulations with,

> . . . Further, I consider that this holds true for the severe neurotic, in whom I believe there is a psychotic personality concealed by neurosis as the neurotic personality is screened by psychosis in the psychotic, that has to be laid bare and dealt with.

And in a paper in 1959, in which I described a phase of symbiotic relatedness in the transference-relationship between the schizophrenic patient and his therapist, as being at the core of the resolution of the schizophrenia, I included the general statement that

> . . . My experience indicates, further, that such a [symbiotic] relatedness constitutes a necessary phase in psychoanalysis or psychotherapy with either neurotic or psychotic patients, respectively . . . (Searles, 1959b).

THE 'TECHNICAL MANAGEMENT' OF TRANSFERENCE PSYCHOSIS

Bion conveys in his 1955 paper entitled 'Language and the Schizophrenic' a warning of the patient's tendency to project his own sanity upon the analyst, and of the massive regression which follows if this is condoned by the analyst. He states:

> . . . I have no doubt whatever that the analyst should always insist, by the way in which he conducts the case, that he is addressing himself to a sane person and is entitled to expect some sane reception . . .

And Rosenfeld, in his paper (1952b) concerning his analysis of an acute catatonic patient, writes,

> . . . My own approach was analytic, in so far as a great deal of what I was able to understand of the patient's words and behaviour was interpreted to him, and whenever possible, and that was frequently, the analytical material was related to the transference situation . . .

In principle, such an approach seems unassailably valid, and we recall some of the examples of the apparently dramatically beneficial results which followed from verbal interpretations of transference psychosis, as reported by Rosenfeld and others.

But in practice I, at least, seldom find it suitable to make verbal transference interpretations to the patient who—in contrast with the borderline-schizophrenic individual, for example—is still deep in chronic schizophrenia. Typically, such a patient is too unable to employ, or even hear, verbal communications to be able to make use of verbalized transference interpretations. Moreover, it is my experience that he actively needs a degree of symbiotic relatedness in the transference, which would be interfered with were the analyst to try, recurrently, to establish with him the validity of verbalized transference interpretations. I do not feel that the recognition of the patient's need for a relatively prolonged period—lasting, say, for several months—of predominantly non-verbal, symbiotic relatedness with the therapist is tantamount to one's fostering the patient's projection, upon one, of his own sanity. And I wonder whether such frequent, verbalized transference interpretations as Rosenfeld employs, as indicated in his reports of his work, are not suggestive of his own unconscious resistance to the development of the predominantly silent 'therapeutic symbiosis' phase which, in my experience, the patient so deeply needs in the course of the transference-evolution. I presume that what is needed is for the therapist to be so attuned to the patient's needs as to be able to maintain a dynamic balance between, on the one hand, some considerable degree of participating in symbiotic relatedness with him and, on the other hand, helping him at appropriate times to see the transference-meanings in what is transpiring, or has been transpiring, between the two participants.

In a session with a paranoid schizophrenic woman, after I had just endeavoured to call her attention, verbally, to something that had been going on between us, she looked greatly disconcerted, and told me, 'When you say things like that, I feel as though I had been riding with you in an airplane, and that I had just been dropped down into the bottom of the ocean.' Later on in the therapy, at a time when she had been trying for many months to make a body for herself out of all sorts of materials, she protested to me on one occasion, 'The minute I start to say something, you say something about, "Does this remind you of your mother, or does this remind you of your father, or somebody else?"—so naturally I don't feel that *I* exist!' I felt that she was making a valid and important point here, although by any ordinary standards I had not been overdoing such comments. I felt that she was clarifying a central determinant in her years-long lack of a sense of personal identity, which extended into her experiencing her body as not actually her own.

A hebephrenic man met, for a number of years, nearly every one of my comparatively infrequent verbalized questions with an antagonistic retort, 'I don't know you,' or 'I'm a stranger,' or 'I just got here.' It eventually dawned upon me, and was subsequently confirmed, that he heard each of these questions as conveying the covert, rejecting message which he himself spoke. That is, it became evident that to him the very fact that I would ask him a question—concerning either what he was experiencing at the moment, or some past event—was taken by him as a denial on my part that I knew him, was close to him, and had a great backlog of shared experience with him.

It was true that, as much as two years before I realized this, he had once replied to one of my questions with the disappointed and disgusted comment, 'There's no friendly intuition here!', in such a way as to make me realize that, if the degree of friendly intuition existed between us that he was hungering for, no words would be necessary. But one reason why I was so slow to make this later discovery is that this hebephrenic man would habitually tell not only me, but various other persons about him when they made overtures, 'I'm a stranger', and so on; hence I missed the personal significance of it in our relationship. This is all another way of pointing up the patient's need for a predominantly silent, basically symbiotic relatedness with the therapist.

I might mention that in a later predominantly wordless 'therapeutic symbiosis' phase of my work with the previously-mentioned paranoid schizophrenic woman, we were sitting in her room during one of the sessions, in a comfortable, fond silence, and she was peacefully knitting. I started to say something, and she interrupted me with, 'What's the matter—aren't you satisfied with what you're getting on your radar?' I started to protest, 'Yes, but—', whereupon she said, in the way a fond mother would firmly but gently admonish a little child, 'Then be *quiet.*'

I did not then attempt a transference interpretation, nor do I feel, in retrospect, that one was in order. Many times, earlier in our work, she had shown great pressure of speech, and had protested against my comparatively silent participation with the statement that she couldn't stand 'the intimacy of silence'. This I regard as an instance of the so frequent situations, with these very deeply ill patients, when it is essential for the therapist to be able not only to endure, but also to enjoy, a wide variety of transference-positions in relation to the patient, before the patient can become able, acknowledgedly and explicitly, to accept him as a *therapist* to such a degree as to be able to attend to verbalized transference-interpretations from him. To try to do this prematurely, before the therapeutic-symbiosis phase has been allowed to develop and has come towards the end of its usefulness to the patient, is tantamount to the therapist's using the concept of transference as a kind of shield to protect himself from the necessary degree of psychological intimacy with the patient, in a way quite analogous to the patient's own unconscious use of his delusional transference as a kind of shield to protect himself from experiencing the full reality of the therapist as a person in the present.

There is widespread agreement that it is inherent in therapy that the therapist functions as an auxiliary ego to the patient in the patient's struggle with inner conflicts, until such time as the patient, by identification with the therapist's strength, becomes able to make this greater strength part of his own ego. To the extent that the schizophrenic patient does not possess an observing ego of sufficient strength to permit the therapist usefully to make transference-interpretations, to that degree the therapist must be able to endure— and, eventually, to enjoy—various part-object transference-roles, until such time as the patient, *via* increasing ego-integration, becomes able to see the delusional-transference nature of this view of the therapist. Another way of saying this is that the patient develops ego-strength, in the face of his own id-impulses and pathogenic superego-retaliations, *via* identification with the therapist who can endure, and integrate into his own larger self, the kind of subjectively non-human part-object relatedness which the patient fosters in, and needs from, him.

Several writers have made clear that interpretations of transference psychosis must extend beyond the merely verbal level. Bion (1955), for example, comments:

> . . . for a considerable proportion of analytic time the only evidence on which an interpretation can be based is that which is afforded by the counter-transference.

He evidently uses the term 'counter-transference' to refer to the analyst's feeling-reactions to the patient's transference. He illustrates the role of the analyst's feelings in this regard by a description (quoted earlier here) of a successful transference interpretation derived, initially, only from Bion's own awareness of a fear in himself that the patient was contemplating a murderous attack upon him, without there having been at that moment any discernible outward change in the patient's demeanour.

Little, in one of her papers concerning patients in whom she finds a delusional transference to exist, emphasizes, concerning these patients, 'the supreme importance for them of body happenings', and says, albeit in somewhat tantalizingly vague phraseology,

> . . . the body events may become the interpretations. Verbalization then becomes the second stage in a two-stage process, both stages being necessary for real insight to be attained, but the second only effective as a result of the first, i.e. of the body happening.
> . . . Discharge, and consequent differentiation [out of the delusional basic unity], comes through some body event—a movement, a scream, salivation, etc.—by means of which some kind of bodily contact with the analyst occurs. Through repetitions of such events the patient comes gradually to recognize the difference between his body, his sensations, and his emotions, while those of the analyst are discovered as separate from his. The event has concerned two people, and the patient discovers himself as a person who has moved, screamed, etc., in relation to another person, whose separate existence, experience, movements, and responses can also be recognized. The delusion breaks up, recovery begins, and relationship becomes a possibility.
> The importance of these body happenings lies in the fact that in those areas where the delusion is operative the patient is to all intents and purposes literally an infant, his ego a body ego. For him, in these areas, only concrete, actual, and bodily things have meaning and can carry conviction . . . (Little, 1960).

The following comments by Little show how important she considers it to be, to the patient, that he be as it were free to feel at one with the analyst—in line with my own views; but she evidently feels less sure than I do that the analyst inevitably participates in this in reality, and that this mutuality of what I call the therapeutic symbiosis is indeed essential to a successful therapeutic outcome. That is, where I would say that the patient's 'delusion' of basic unity with the analyst needs to become a mutually shared reality between the two participants, she comments, variously, that

[Concerning one particular woman] . . . Her recovery has been based on this delusion of total identity with me, which has had to be gradually broken down, as far as factual reality is concerned, while the psychic reality of it has had to be preserved with the greatest care . . .

. . . the delusion [of unity with the analyst], although accepted as true for the patient, is not shared by the analyst (unless, unfortunately, he has something of a counter-transference psychosis).

. . . The underlying principle [of relevant analytic technique] . . . is that of acceptance by the analyst of the truth *for the analysand* of his delusion of absolute identity between them, his entering into it, and demonstrating both its psychic truth and its objective untruth.

. . . If the analyst is sufficiently one with his patient psychically, he experiences him, at times, as himself, or himself, at times, as the patient. But because of his unity with himself he also experiences what he says or does to be himself . . . (Little, 1960).

Boyer has reported upon his use of a modified analytic technique, in his office practice with schizophrenic patients, which apparently conforms more nearly to classical psycho-analysis than does any other reported approach by anyone treating such patients. Even he, while not making mention of any use of physical contact between himself and the patient in the course of his interpretations of delusional transference, does highlight the crucial significance of physical phenomena in these patients:

It is to be remembered that with inadequate differentiation of ego and id, tensions are often fixated to physical phenomena . . . In a previous report (Boyer, 1957) I have recorded a fragment of the history of a schizophrenic whose analysis was given tremendous impetus through repetitive direction of his attention to physical tension and movements . . .

. . . preverbal communications are of signal importance with many, if not all, regressed patients. The analyst's understanding of them and communication of their meanings enables patients not only to break through resistances and to help them to learn about realities, but to restore body-ego deficiencies and to separate self from nonself. In addition, their interpretation helps analysands to progress in ego growth to where they can accurately communicate in *words*. It is not unusual . . . that the words being *said* may have little importance as messages in themselves, but constitute the contributions of a decathected part of the self, while the meaningful cathexis is invested in the posture and movements of the moment (Boyer, 1961).

In general, while my own approach is far from being as abstemious as Boyer's appears to be, I cannot wholeheartedly accept Little's enthusiastic endorsement of physical contact; I have seen a number of clear-cut instances in which my declining to provide physical contact has been as helpful, in promoting the resolution of delusional transference, as has been my touching of the patient on other occasions. In a recent paper (Searles, 1963a), concerning the role of neutral therapist-responses in the therapy of the schizophrenic patient, I have emphasized that if one is to help him to become subjectively alive, one must be unafraid of functioning as the transference-representation of the subjectively unalive parts of the patient's self, or as the very early-perceived attributes of the mother, before she had emerged as a whole and alive and human being in the perception of the infant. Prior to such a development the mother, and comparably the therapist in the transference situation, is so very important to the patient—as one chronically paranoid patient phrased it, a Coke machine for the automatic gratification of his needs—that, from his view, the mother or the therapist must not have a separate aliveness. A therapist who is neurotically afraid of physical contact with people, including schizophrenic patients, to that degree complicates the recovery process in the patient; but so does the therapist who recurrently needs to reassure himself of his own living humanness, his own capacity for feeling, by a dramatically 'curative' employment of physical contact with the patient. In the latter instance, it is only ostensibly the trembling and frightened patient who is being helped by the therapist's reassuring touch; covertly the patient is thereby reassuring the therapist of the latter's own capacity for life and lovingness.

Milner (1952), in her beautiful account of her therapy of an 11-year-old boy who had found outer reality mechanized and soulless by reason of its unacceptingness of his own spontaneous creation, a difficulty she found traceable to a premature loss of belief in a self-created outer reality, describes how she helped him to achieve a healthy reality-relatedness through her acceptance of his treating her as being part of himself—as being his own malleable, pliable, 'lovely stuff', his 'chemicals', which he had created. Winnicott (1945, 1948), in the same vein has conjectured that the healthy mother helps her baby, in the nursing situation for example, towards an acceptance of external reality through helping him to experience this reality not as something alien to himself but as something self-created. I have described the patient-therapist relatedness during the 'therapeutic symbiosis' phase of therapy as being of essentially this same nature. We see here that what might be called a form of 'delusional transference'—the patient's reacting to the therapist as being an inanimate, or at least not separately alive, product of the patient himself—is really, in its nucleus, the primeval form of healthy, creative relatedness to external reality, and that this development could not occur if the therapist were unable to become comfortable with this 'inanimate' role in the transference.

A 32-year-old woman patient who had by now progressed far towards recovery from her chronic schizophrenia produced, in a number of sessions over the course of a month, material which illustrated memorably, for me, the point that a person can come to relinquish the oceanic ego-state, and to experience outer reality as such—can bear the loss involved in this develop- ment—only by finding an essential sameness between self and outer reality; her experience is, I think, closely comparable with that of Milner's boy- patient.

In the first of the sessions I wish to mention, she was talking about her recently-acquired room-mate, a woman whom I by now knew to personify, in many respects, my patient's own sicker—more paranoid, more self-ab- sorbed—former self, as she had been earlier in her treatment. She spoke with much feeling, including a particularly memorable, childlike naïveté. She told of having been for a walk with another woman patient and of how in the course of their walk they had come upon a little feather lying on the ground, which my patient, Edith, picked up. It so happened, she mentioned to me in her narrative, that her room-mate, an artist, had hung up a work of art she had done, a montage which had on it, among other things, a feather.

When Edith subsequently came into their room, her room-mate, Mrs Sim- mons, was in there and saw Edith coming in, wearing the little feather on her blouse. Mrs Simmons immediately said, 'Did you take my feather?', ac- cusingly. Edith explained to me that this was typical of Mrs Simmons—that is, it was characteristic of her to think of everything in terms of herself. Edith described how, in essence, she then had patiently but firmly pointed out to Mrs Simmons that no, this was not the latter woman's feather—that Mrs Simmons' feather was there on the montage, and that this was a different one which she, Edith, had just picked up out on the hospital grounds.

From here on in her account to me, Edith's tone took on a kind of childlike naïveté and hesitancy; but she went on determinedly, though finding it hard to express her thoughts in words. 'When I first came here, I was a little that way,' she said, and this made me smile a bit inwardly, because it was such an understatement. 'Then,' she went on, 'I sort of woke up, and said, ''There are so many people here—could be somebody else—we all have almost the same''.' She explained that it had been her seeing, in a department store window, dresses which were the same as one she was then wearing, and the same, likewise, as she had seen on various other women at that time during her trips into the community, that was the context in which she had awakened to this realization.

She then added that, in contrast to Mrs Simmons (who had been here in the sanatorium for only two months, in contrast to the several years of Edith's own residence here), when she, Edith, first came here, 'I didn't have anyone to tell me they had a feather'. This was said in a tone of painful deprivation, and I felt pained on hearing it, although this did not seem to be said with any aim of reproaching me for not having made clear to her that I, too, have a feather.

In a session near the end of that same month, she told me, 'Dr Searles, you know I've told you that I very seldom dream. But I had a dream the night before last. You remember the purse I have with flowers on the side of it? I dreamed that I rushed around so much that I lost the flowers from my purse, and I saw another woman pick them up and put them on *her* purse, and I said, [tone of strong protest] "*She's* taking *my* flowers!"'

She then went on, with much interest, to contrast the feeling she had had in the dream—describing it now in the following way: a sharp intake of the breath, with 'I lost my flowers!'—to the feeling she had had a few weeks previously when, while downtown shopping, she had seen a woman with a purse almost like her own, except that the other woman's purse had flowers on the top, whereas Edith's purse had flowers on the side. Edith described her feeling on that earlier, real-life occasion with a tone of pleasure, 'She has almost the same as mine!' In saying how different from this had been the feeling in the dream, she said, 'I guess I do feel that something has been taken away from me.'

It did not become established in that hour what the 'something' might be, and I was left with this as an unanswered question in my own mind. In the earlier years of our work, she had very often indeed expressed her conviction that she had been robbed; she had been unable for years to express a feeling of *loss* as such, but instead had felt deliberately robbed, of this or that person or thing, by maliciously inclined other persons including myself.

Then, in a session a very few days later, she described how the previous evening she had been in the nursing office, typing up the minutes of the recent ward-meeting, and Mrs Simmons had felt convinced, erroneously, that the paper Edith was using was from Mrs Simmons' art-tablet. Edith showed her that this was not the case—showed her that the tablet she was using was her own, with some of her own drawings in it, and went on, emphatically but not unkindly, 'Mrs Simmons, you have an illness, and I want you to get over it right this minute! You think everything is yours. I know, because I've been through it myself; I used to think that everything was—well, that everything concerned me, and was mine, and (here Edith's voice, in her telling me, became filled with a sense of loss) was gone.'

I felt that this material revealed how the paranoid person, involved as she had been, years earlier in her treatment, in a state of not-yet-completed ego-differentiation from the outside world, feels robbed of *everything*, and that this process of individuation can go on to completion, and the outside world be found acceptable and no longer made up of one's own stolen former contents, only upon one's finding an essential sameness between self and outer world—symbolized by the feathers, the flowered purses, and the identical women's dresses. By the same token, the patient can become individuated *vis-à-vis* the therapist only after she has come to find that the therapist possesses in reality essentially the same qualities which she has come to know in herself—that her various transferences to him, her various projections upon him, are not devoid of nuclei of interpersonal reality.

We begin to discover that this whole realm of various kinds of delusional transference, or transference-psychosis, can be seen by the therapist to be, and needs to be responded to by him as being, an effort on the part of the patient to build up whole-project interpersonal relationships and a whole-object ego-identity. All these can be seen as part-object phenomena through which the patient successively builds up, bit by bit, through processes of both projection and introjection, a psychological feeling-image of both himself and the mother-therapist as whole persons. One borderline patient experienced this process most explicitly in displaced terms in his relationship with his wife, clearly a mother-figure to him. In the course of his being absorbed successively with various parts of his wife—her genitals, her breasts, her nose, and so on—each part being the object of his fascinated attention when he was with her, over a period of months he built up to the realization that she was a whole person, and that he, no doubt partly through identification with these various part-attributes of her, was also a whole person.

The extent to which the therapist feels a genuine sense of deep participation in the patient's 'delusional transference' relatedness to him during the phase of therapeutic symbiosis—wherein the patient is reacting to him as being the personification of the Good Mother—is difficult to convey in words; it is essential that the therapist come to know that such a degree of feeling-participation is not evidence of 'counter-transference psychosis', but rather is the essence of what the patient needs from him at this crucial phase of the treatment. A hebephrenic woman who had evidenced intense antagonism towards me for several years eventually came to see me as the personification of the loving potentialities of her mother, and when, one day, as I was leaving her room at the end of a therapeutic session, she said fondly, 'Goodbye, Mother,' I simply replied, with like fondness, 'Good-bye, Betty.' This exchange had no quality of ungenuine role-playing about it; but on the other hand I felt that neither was any pathological misidentification involved. She could as well have said, 'Goodbye, Harold', without any shift in the emotional genuineness of this brief exchange. I felt it then, and have subsequently regarded it, as a landmark in terms of my deeply accepting the 'transference role' of mother to her, and in terms of her acceptance of me in that capacity.

A paranoid woman, who had reached the therapeutic-symbiosis phase of the transference after several years of comparably intense negative transference, suddenly asked in the midst of a highly productive session, 'You mean I own you?' I was not aware that I had been making any comments which could be so translated; but I had seen on a number of recent occasions how, in the midst of fond exchanges about whatever subject, she would suddenly ask, 'Are you proposing to me?', or 'Are you making love to me?' This time, when she asked, 'You mean I own you?', I replied, 'Well, I'm very much attached to you—if you call that owning me, then you own me.' I had never acknowledged so candidly how much a part of her I had come to feel, and it is noteworthy that this woman, who several years earlier in our work had shown an intensely paranoid reaction against feelings of fond intimacy, showed no such anxiety now. In the course of the next several months she came to express feelings of glowing adoration of me, viewed as an inexpressibly beautiful mother whose body was, the patient felt, interchangeable with her own; and now for the first time I began to get from her a picture of her mother not as multiple, suddenly changeable, and predominantly malevolent figures, but rather as having been, on at least some occasions during the girl's upbringing, a single, whole, healthy, and fond mother to her.

It has been my recurrent experience that one of the necessary developments in a long-delusional patient's eventual relinquishment of his delusions is for these gradually to become productions which the therapist sees no longer as essentially ominous and the subject for either serious therapeutic investigation, or argumentation, or any other form of opposition; rather, the therapist comes to react to these as being essentially playful, unmalignant, creatively imaginative, and he comes to respond to them with playfully imaginative comments of his own. Nothing helps more finally to detoxicate a patient's previously self-isolating delusional state than to find in his therapist a capacity to engage with him in a delightfully crazy playfulness—a kind of relatedness of which the schizophrenic patient had never had a chance to have his fill during his childhood. Typically, such early-childhood playfulness was subjected to massive repression, because of various intra-familial circumstances which I shall not try to elaborate upon here.

One of the ingredients of schizophrenia—in my experience, one of the regular ingredients—is a basically healthy and normal small-child playfulness which, for various reasons referable to the early environment, was early subjected to repression and has long been acted out in manifold ways, often highly destructive ways, by the patient, who is quite unaware of the extent to which he has come to play, in a destructively irresponsible spirit, with the irreplaceable and therefore-to-be-cherished-and-preserved relationships and situations in his life. In essence, the therapist has to become able to adapt to the patient's fiddling while Rome burns; at first the therapist endures this, later he comes to be quite comfortable in this setting despite its tragically wasteful aspects, and still later comes to enjoy the music and to share in producing it. At this juncture the patient, having gained the realization that he is not at heart a malevolent being for wanting to play, becomes interested at long last in putting out the fire, clearing away the rubble, restoring what can be restored, and building anew.

For the therapist thus to succeed, in the long run, in enlisting the patient's active co-operation in the therapy, he must be able to cope along the way with feelings of guilty irresponsibility on his own part. For example, not long ago I felt considerable guilt at discovering that I actually had come to regard with aesthetic appreciation the abundant delusions of a paranoid woman with whom I had long been working. I found myself drinking in, as it were, with appreciation and admiration, productions which my professional conscience told me I should continue, as I had for years, to struggle manfully to investigate with her, or somehow to counter. But as the sessions went on, my enjoyment became less and less tinged with guilt, and it was in this context that the patient came, for the first time, to speak with healthy pride of her own lifelong imaginativeness. I no longer reacted to this imaginativeness as being in any sense an enemy; I could now enjoy it, and participate in it with my own verbalized imaginatively 'crazy'—childishly playful—associations. For a number of years, earlier in her treatment, during what I term the ambivalently symbiotic phase of the therapy, when she had shown a high degree of anxiety and hostility of at times near-murderous proportions, I had surely done much of what Bion, in the following illuminating passages, describes his patient as having 'felt'—supposedly a transference-phenomenon without any basis in reality—that Bion had been doing:

. . . Throughout the analysis the patient resorted to projective identification with a persistence suggesting it was a mechanism of which he had never been able sufficiently to avail himself; the analysis afforded him an opportunity for the exercise of a mechanism of which he had been cheated. . . . There were sessions which led me to suppose that the patient felt there was some object that denied him the use of projective identification. In the illustrations I have given, . . . there are elements which indicate that the patient felt that parts of his personality that he wished to repose in me were refused entry by me . . .

Associations . . . showed an increasing intensity of emotions in the patient. This originated in what he felt was my refusal to accept parts of his personality. Consequently he strove to force them into me with increased desperation and violence. His behaviour, isolated from the context of the analysis, might have appeared to be an expression of primary aggression. The more violent his phantasies of projective identification, the more frightened he became of me. There were sessions in which such behaviour expressed unprovoked aggression, but I quote this series because it shows the patient in a different light, his violence a reaction to what he felt was my hostile defensiveness . . . (Bion, 1959).

It is particularly in the realm of playfulness that I have seen clearly before me the technical choice, whether to make a verbalized transference interpretation, or to accept, as it were, the transference-role which the patient is needing me to occupy. Repeatedly I have found that transference interpretations prove to be jarring and stultifying and essentially antitherapeutic until such time as the patient's experience of shared playfulness with me has become so customary that we can easily regain it, and the more clearly investigative 'work' aspects of what we are doing have become accepted as part of a basically enjoyable enterprise.

DELUSIONAL IDENTIFICATION

In this final section of the paper I shall attempt to illustrate the point that, just as the schizophrenic patient's symptomatology comes in the course of treatment to be revealed as consisting of manifestations of psychotic transference, so does this very symptomatology, or at any rate large increments of it, come to reveal an even deeper meaning as evidences of what might be called 'delusional identification'. That is, the patient's crazy behaviour needs to be seen as possessing, along with the psychotic transference root, a root in the form of an expressed identification with the therapist—an identification which, no matter how psychotically distorted, possesses a kernel of reality in terms of the therapist's real personality-functioning. It is essential for us to see this identificational determinant of the patient's illness, for only insofar as we can acknowledge and confirm these nuclei of reality in his identifications with us (no matter how reluctant we may be to discover, or scrutinize with unprecedented directness, the pertinent aspects of our own personality), can we foster his reality-testing ability and his confidence in that ability.

By way of contrast, Rosenfeld, in his in many respects excellent paper of 1952 entitled, 'Notes on the Psycho-Analysis of the Superego Conflict of an Acute Schizophrenic Patient', to my mind discounts the very real evidences of this particular mother's murderous possessiveness towards her son, the patient, and by the same token Rosenfeld seems unaware of the possibility that he himself was capable of murderous feeling in response to the patient's transference to him as a mother. We see no hint of Rosenfeld's awareness of such a possibility in his treatment of such data as the following:

. . . Once he said: "How can I get out of the tomb?" I felt here that he implied that in projecting his self, his depression, into me, he felt enclosed by me and so I became a tomb from which he wanted my help to be released . . . (Rosenfeld, 1952a).

In a footnote in the same paper, he expresses a point of view which certainly contains a valuable reminder of the essential importance of the intrapsychic realm in the patient—the realm which I have stressed in a recent paper ((1963b) concerning the family therapy of schizophrenia. But this passage is also a sample of his tendency to underestimate the etiological significance of early family-environmental factors, as well as the extent to which the schizophrenic patient in therapy is responding to real personality ingredients which the therapist is feeding, inevitably and constantly, into the patient-therapist relationship:

In some papers on schizophrenia particularly by American writers like Pious and Fromm-Reichmann the mother's hostile and "schizophrenogenic" attitude has been stressed. . . . In our analytic approach we know that it is futile and even harmful to the progress of an analysis to accept uncritically the patient's attempts to blame the external environment for his illness. We generally find that there exists a great deal of distortion of external factors through projection and we have to help the patient to understand his phantasies and reactions to external situations until he becomes able to differentiate between his phantasies and external reality (Rosenfeld, 1952a).

In another paper (1952b), Rosenfeld writes

. . . In my opinion the schizophrenic has never completely outgrown the earliest phase of development to which this object-relation [i.e., the patient's relating to the object by projective identification] belongs, and in the acute schizophrenic state he regresses to this early level . . .

I consider it essential for us to realize that no one ever does completely outgrow this (or, for that matter, any other) phase of development. When we realize this, we shall no longer overlook the extent to which we too share in the patient's projective-identification mode of relatedness—or, in my terms, we shall be able to see and accept the fact of our own participation in the symbiotic mode of relatedness between the patient and ourself.

Bion never acknowledges the possibility of his making, or having made, a real contribution to his patient's psychotic transference; typical is the passage, in his 'Attacks on Linking' paper (1959), concerning

> . . . *what he felt was* my refusal to accept parts of his personality . . . [italics mine].

It is in line with this viewpoint that he says, concerning the origin of the patient's pathological attitude towards linking,

> . . . On the one hand there is the patient's *inborn disposition to excessive destructiveness, hatred, and envy*: on the other the environment which, at its worst, denies to the patient the use of the mechanisms of splitting and projective identification . . . (Bion, 1959, italics mine).

When we see the extent to which the environment contributes to the patient's difficulty—when, in particular, we discover the extent to which he is reacting, in his psychotic transference to us, to real and intense sadism, murderous feeling, and so on in ourselves—we find little need, I think, to conjecture that as a newborn baby he possessed some inordinately great, inborn disposition to hostility. Whereas Bion (1959) refers to the patient's '*belief that* the analyst strives . . . to drive him insane [italics mine]', I have found much evidence, not only in my own work but from various colleagues' reports of theirs, that such a striving is indeed at work in the therapist, among various other intensely conflictual feelings towards the patient, during the so difficult ambivalently symbiotic phase of the therapy. It seems to me that relatively abundant transference interpretations might be used by the therapist in an unconscious effort not only to protect himself against symbiotic relatedness with the patient, but also to deny the extent to which his own sadism, so much at odds with his genuinely therapeutic intent, is playing a part in shaping and maintaining the patient's psychotic transference—to deny specifically the extent to which, at the deeper, symbiotic level, he is cruelly and destructively denying the patient access into himself.

In a paper in 1958, I described a number of instances of patients' acting out as being partially traceable to my own previously unconscious urges in the same directions, and mentioned the previous reports concerning this kind of phenomenon by Schroff (1957) and Barchilon (1958). Then in a later paper (1961a), concerning schizophrenic communication, I noted:

Particularly hard for the therapist to grasp are those instances in which the patient is manifesting an introject traceable to something in the therapist, some aspect of the therapist of which the latter is himself only poorly aware, and the recognition of which, as a part of himself, he finds distinctly unwelcome. I have found, time and again, that some bit of particularly annoying and intractable behaviour on the part of a patient rests, in the final analysis, on this basis; and only when I can acknowledge this, to myself, as being indeed an aspect of my personality, does it cease to be a prominently troublesome aspect of the patient's behaviour . . .

It is only more recently that I have become better aware of the *identificational* significance of these events: when, for example, the therapist is able to become aware of the relevant aspect of his personality to which the patient's acting-out behaviour has been a kind of caricatured reaction, he is thereby accepting the patient's struggle to identify with him. In an earlier paper I did note that the schizophrenic patient tends to identify first with those aspects of the therapist's personality which are least acceptable to the latter.

I have already given several instances of a variety of transference psychosis in which the patient endeavours ambivalently to get the therapist to do the patient's thinking for the latter—in line with a family background of a 'know-it-all' parent's doing the thinking during the patient's upbringing. Typically, such a parent has to maintain such a 'know-it-all' demeanour as a defence against inner confusion. I have described the beneficial result of my coming, eventually, to acknowledge freely my own confusion in response to such patients' extremely and often sadistically confusing verbalizations; and I believe that here again we can see in retrospect that the patient's confusion has had, among other determinants, a transference root in the form of a delusional identification with the very real confusion in the parent-therapist. The therapist's becoming able to be aware of and to acknowledge his own confusion helps to resolve the delusional, crazy quality of the patient's confusion. Particularly does it help to resolve the mocking, caricaturing, sadistic, or otherwise destructive aspects of the patient's efforts to identify with the therapist.

In one hour with a hebephrenic man, who was generally either utterly ignoring me or openly furious at me, and of whose yearning to identify with me I was quite unaware, I once put out my cigarette inside the top of his plastic wastebasket, after having first noted that it was empty. During the following session I was startled when, during one of the customary long silences, the wastebasket caught my eye: there was a black ring around the inside of the top of it where this heavily-smoking man, who had never done so before, had been using the wastebasket as an ash tray as he had seen me do. The potentially destructive nature of his identification startled me, for I felt no assurance that he took care, as I had, to make sure that the wastebasket was not full of paper.

Incidentally, I did not attempt a transference-interpretation at this point, for from long experience I knew that it would be like talking into the wind; but the incident had a long-run usefulness in helping me to be more alert to his need and his efforts to identify with this therapist of whom he ostensibly wanted no part whatever.

In my monograph concerning the nonhuman environment I presented, as an instance of the schizophrenic patient's inability to distinguish clear boundaries between his self and his nonhuman environment, the following incident from my work with a hebephrenic woman:

. . . [She] shockingly conveyed to me the statement that the whole left side of her head "is gone . . . caved in", speaking as if in reference to an inanimate object; one sensed her own horror and despair about this . . . (1960, p. 148).

In the years that have passed in my work with this woman since the above-noted incident occurred, two additional significances of this same symptom have come to light. About five years later, at a time when she had long since become—both subjectively, so far as one could determine, and objectively, as measured by my and other persons' responses to her—fully human, I made the following note:

The work with Pauline continues to show [as had been true, by that time, for many months], most prominently, her making clear her ambivalent efforts to achieve, and to avoid, a symbiotic relatedness with me as a representative of her father . . . [For example] about three weeks ago when I came up on the fourth floor to see another patient there, and stepped into Pauline's room for just a moment while the other patient was getting ready, Pauline once again made some reference to the left side of her head's being gone, or some similar terrible organic defect which I cannot precisely remember at the moment. This was almost exactly the kind of thing which she had expressed not very long after her admission here, and I found now that I reacted to it privately with a completely different connotation: I saw it as a very formidable effort to draw me into a kind of solicitude and a kind of taking over her life for her in a symbiotic fashion. Actually I did feel solicitude for her, but saw it, much more this time than I initially did, as a transference manifestation.

My different reaction this second time was probably due more to the change which had occurred in her—in terms of increased 'humanization'—than to an increase in insightfulness on my part over the intervening five years. At that earlier time such communications had emerged from such a 'nonhuman' over-all demeanour, and in such a vocal tone of horror and other-worldly despair and eeriness, as to make the listener (whether me or other personnel members) draw back in shock, and be quite blinded to any potential interpersonal-transference significance.

Slightly more than three years later still in our work, she was sitting nearby and looking at my face with a kind of private amusement, as I was saying something—I can't recall what. She asked, 'Is it all going to fall off?—Is it that bad?', rubbing her forehead and the top of her head as she spoke in such a way as to convey the idea that they—these areas of her body—were all crumbling. Her tone in asking this was a semi-serious one, and to this extent conveyed a genuine delusional experience; but her tone was also a semi-amused one. I replied, 'You do feel that I'm awfully *serious*, eh?'. She said, with warm and open amusement and without any tinge of delusional anxiety, 'Yes.' I had been aware for many years that among the personal eccentricities which survived the ravages of my personal analysis are a chronically worried look and a tendency to take everything too seriously; but I had not been aware that some of this patient's delusional behaviour was a reaction, in part, to this aspect of my personality. Each of her parents possessed this quality in abun-dance, which no doubt was relevant here; but I felt it better simply to ac-knowledge this real aspect of myself. To have made some transference inter-pretation at that juncture would, I think, have placed needless distance be-tween her and me, and would have vitiated my corroborating her own reality appraisal of the here-and-now situation.

The sequence which I have described, as occurring over the years of my work with this woman, is but one among many analogous ones which emerged as she became progressively human and progressively able to distinguish between literal and metaphorical meanings. As another brief instance, whereas there were occasions relatively early in our work when she seemingly perceived me as being inanimate—once, for example, looking at me in a kind of uncanny astonishment as I smoked a cigarette, and exclaiming to herself, 'What makes it smoke?'—several years later this bizarre perception of me devolved into a querying of me, clearly at this time as a transference representative of her compulsive father, as to whether I considered the way I lived to be really living. Her seeing me as being, in this figurative way, 'dead', contained, despite the element of transference distortion and exaggeration, a sufficiently realistic view of some of the aspects of my own compulsively work-oriented life for me to acknowledge the validity of the view of me which she was expressing.

At the end of one of the sessions during this same later period in our work, when I was about to go on a week's vacation, I commented, 'Well, I'll see you a week from Monday.' She replied in an ironic tone, as I was then starting out the door of her room, '*Try* again.' My first thought was that she meant by this that in her opinion our efforts during the session had been futile—as she had been indicating in many ways, both verbal and non-verbal, for years. But then another possibility occurred to me, and I asked, 'Do I sound defeated when I say that?', which she corroborated in a tone of delighted warmth and closeness. I had long known that she had viewed her father as being a disappointing quitter; but she had finally got the message across to me as to how defeated I, as I now realized in retrospect, often appeared and indeed felt, though I characteristically tend to repress such feelings. I believe it correct to think that the tremendous despair which this woman had shown during the first several years of our work, and which she acted out in myriad hebephrenically-fragmented forms of personality functioning, consisted in large part in a delusional identification with the despairing aspects of her father, her mother and, as the treatment relationship developed, myself.

A few months ago, a paranoid schizophrenic woman said to me, in reply to a verbalized interpretation I had just suggested to her, 'When you talk to me like that, I feel that I'm going to be led to the edge of the world and the people are going to decide whether I'll have to jump off or not'. I had known her to be living for years in a chaotically and terrifyingly delusional world, and when she said this I was momentarily awed, once again, by this glimpse into the vastly terrifying world in which she lived. But then this other viewpoint, concerning the possibility that I had unwittingly contributed to such a degree of delusional experience on her part, occurred to me, and I asked simply, 'Do you mean that I sound so portentous?', and she replied, even more simply, 'Yes'. Even more recent developments in our work have suggested that her having been living for so long in a terrifying psychotic world has been due, in part, to her delusional identification with what she has now come to call her 'fraidy-cat' therapist, who tends somewhat—as did her mother to a very great degree—to hide his own fearfulness behind the demeanour of the strong, calm parent-therapist.

In summary, it is my experience that even the most other-worldly, even the most 'crazy', manifestations of schizophrenia come to reveal meaningfulness and reality-relatedness not only as transference reactions to the therapist, but, even beyond this, as delusional identifications with real aspects of the therapist's own personality. When we come to see such meanings in the schizophrenic individual's behaviour, we come more and more to realize not only that he is now in the human fold but that, if only there had been someone all along wise and perceptive enough to know, and brave enough to acknowledge, he has never really been out of it.

REFERENCES

Abraham, K. (1908). 'The Psychosexual Differences between Hysteria and Dementia Praecox.' *Selected Papers*. (London: Hogarth, 1927.)

Barchilon, J. (1958). 'On Countertransference "Cures".' *J. Amer. Psychoanal. Assoc.*, **6**.

Bion, W. R. (1955). 'Language and the Schizophrenic.' *New Directions in Psychoanalysis*, ed. M. Klein, P. Heimann, and R. Money-Kyrle. (New York: Basic Books).

——— (1956). 'Development of Schizophrenic Thought.' *Int. J. Psycho-Anal.*, **37**.

——— (1957). 'Differentiation of the Psychotic from the Non-Psychotic Personalities.' *Int. J. Psycho-Anal.*, **38**.

——— (1959). 'Attacks on Linking.' *Int. J. Psycho-Anal.*, **40**.

Boyer, L. B. (1957). 'Uses of Delinquent Behavior by a Borderline Schizophrenic.' *Arch. Crim. Psychodyn.*, **2**.

——— (1961). 'Provisional Evaluation of Psycho-Analysis with Few Parameters Employed in the Treatment of Schizophrenia.' *Int. J. Psycho-Anal.*, **42**.

Brodey, W. M. (1959). 'Some Family Operations and Schizophrenia: A Study of Five Hospitalized Families each with a Schizophrenic Member.' *A.M.A. Arch. Gen. Psychiatry*, **1**.

——— (1961). 'The Family as the Unit of Study and Treatment-Workshop, 1959: 3. Image, Object and Narcissistic Relationships.' *Amer. J. Orthopsychiatry*, **31**.

Deutsch, H. (1942). 'Some Forms of Emotional Disturbance and their Relationship to Schizophrenia.' *Psychoanal. Quart.*, **11**.

Freud, S. (1911a). 'Psycho-Analytic Notes on an Autobiographical Account of a Case of Paranoia.' *S.E.*, **12**.

——— (1911b). 'Formulations on the Two Principles of Mental Functioning.' *S.E.*, **12**.

——— (1914). 'On Narcissism: an Introduction.' *S.E.*, **14**.

——— (1915). 'The Unconscious.' *S.E.*, **14**.

Glover, E. (1955). *The Technique of Psycho-Analysis*. (London: Baillière; New York: Int. Univ. Press.)

Hill, L. B. (1955). *Psychotherapeutic Intervention in Schizophrenia*. (Chicago: Univ. of Chicago Press.)

Katan, M. (1954). 'The Importance of the Non-Psychotic Part of the Personality in Schizophrenia.' *Int. J. Psycho-Anal.*, **35**.

Klein, M. (1946). 'Notes on Some Schizoid Mechanisms.' *Int. J. Psycho-Anal.*, **27**.

———, P. Heimann and R. E. Money-Kyrle, eds. (1955). *New Directions in Psycho-Analysis*. (New York: Basic Books.)

Little, M. (1958). 'On Delusional Transference (Transference Psychosis).' *Int. J. Psycho-Anal.*, **39**.

——— (1960). 'On Basic Unity.' *Int. J. Psycho-Anal.*, **41**.

Mahler, M. S. (1952). 'On Child Psychosis and Schizophrenia: Autistic and Symbiotic Infantile Psychoses.' *Psychoanal. Study Child*, **7**.

Milner, M. (1952). 'Aspects of Symbolism in Comprehension of the Not-Self.' *Int. J. Psycho-Anal.*, **33**.

Reich, A. (1953). 'Narcissistic Object Choice in Women.' *J. Amer. Psychoanal. Assoc.*, **1**.

Rosenfeld, H. (1952*a*). 'Notes on the Psycho-Analysis of the Superego Conflict of an Acute Schizophrenic Patient.' *Int. J. Psycho-Anal.*, **33**.

────── (1952*b*). 'Transference-Phenomena and Transference-Analysis in an Acute Catatonic Schizophrenic Patient.' *Int. J. Psycho-Anal.*, **33**.

────── (1954). 'Considerations Regarding the Psycho-Analytic Approach to Acute and Chronic Schizophrenia.' *Int. J. Psycho-Anal.*, **35**.

Schroff, J. (1957). 'Acting Out in a Patient with a Character Neurosis.' Unpublished paper submitted to the Education Committee of the Washington Psychoanalytic Institute.

Searles, H. F. (1958). 'The Schizophrenic's Vulnerability to the Therapist's Unconscious Processes.' *J. Nerv. Ment. Dis.*, **127**.

────── (1959*a*). 'The Effort to Drive the Other Person Crazy—An Element in the Aetiology and Psychotherapy of Schizophrenia.' *Brit. J. Med. Psychol.*, **32**.

────── (1959*b*). 'Integration and Differentiation in Schizophrenia.' *J. Nerv. Ment. Dis.*, **129**.

────── (1960). *The Nonhuman Environment in Normal Development and in Schizophrenia.* (New York: Int. Univ. Press.)

────── (1961*a*). 'Schizophrenic Communication.' *Psychoanal. and Psychoanal. Rev.*, **48**.

────── (1961*b*). 'Schizophrenia and the Inevitability of Death.' *Psychiatric Quart.*, **35**.

────── (1963*a*). 'The Place of Neutral Therapist-Responses in Psychotherapy with the Schizophrenic Patient.' *Int. J. Psycho-Anal.*, **44**.

────── (1963*b*). 'Some Aspects of the Family Therapy of Schizophrenia.' *Family Treatment of Schizophrenia*, ed. I. Boszormenyi-Nagy and J. L. Framo. (New York: Harper & Row.)

Szasz, T. S. (1957). *Pain and Pleasure—A Study of Bodily Feelings.* (New York: Basic Books.)

Winnicott, D. W. (1945). 'Primitive Emotional Development.' *Int. J. Psycho-Anal.*, **26**.

────── (1948). 'Paediatrics and Psychiatry.' *Brit. J. Med. Psychol.*, **21**.

10. Introjection, Reprojection, and Hallucination in the Interaction Between Schizophrenic Patient and Therapist

Norman Cameron

Freud has pointed out that psychotic persons are sometimes able to communicate their experiences with aspects of internal reality that are ordinarily inaccessible to normal and neurotic persons (4). This paper presents material from the intensive, psycho-analytically oriented therapy of a patient, over a period of three and a half years, which describes such experiences with exceptional clarity. These include the regressive reprojection of primitive superego functions in the form of an hallucinated mother image, the hallucination of the therapist under conditions of stress, and the subsequent introjection of a therapist image, followed by its apparent assimilation into a new ego-superego integration. After briefly describing the patient, I shall present clinical evidence of the incorporation and use of therapist attitudes, similar to that reported by Hoedemaker (6), but with examples also from dreams, one of them somnambulistic. I shall then go on to a lengthier account of the vicissitudes of the internal objects and of the introjected therapist image, and in an ensuing section attempt to discuss their significance.[1]

THE PATIENT

The patient, Grace L., a native of Cincinnati, when referred to me, was a 25-year-old single graduate student in the humanities at a coeducational college. She was living what seemed outwardly an effectual life, qualifying each year for a scholarship, and carrying a part-time job as well. She sought intensive therapy on the advice of her college psychiatrist, who had seen her once a week for three months, and now felt that she needed more time than he could spare. In her initial interview with me she complained of feeling tired and discouraged, of being in continual conflict over marriage and a career, of feeling shy and inadequate in relation to others, and of sleepwalking. She seemed vivacious, direct, anxious, and mildly perplexed. Apart from the sleepwalking and mild perplexity there was nothing to suggest the severity of what lay behind the complaints.

As therapy proceeded a graver clinical picture soon emerged. In spite of her outward effectual show, the patient was continually assailed internally by critical and accusing voices; she had serious difficulties in distinguishing between external and internal reality, and between herself and others; and she sometimes could not decide if she had been awake or asleep during what another person would have unhesitatingly called a dream. She called many of her experiences 'strange', 'weird', 'fantastic' and 'grotesque'—which they were—and she sometimes said that she herself could not understand what she was saying.

At the same time this intelligent and verbally gifted young woman was able to give spontaneous descriptions of her regressive and often archaic experiences with fidelity, undistorted by psychological sophistication. Her only contact with psychological science had been a one-semester college course which she said was 'mostly about eye-movements and colour vision', and had bored her. It is striking that throughout therapy she kept at her daily work successfully, first as a graduate student and then in a responsible teaching and supervising job. As time went on it became obvious that, as Freud has formulated it (2), the patient was 'in revolt' against primitive superego attacks from which she attempted with therapeutic help to liberate herself.

INCORPORATION AND USE OF THERAPIST ATTITUDES

It was my consistent experience with this sensitive, traumatized, resentful but superficially compliant person that she throve on firmness and bluntness in her therapist. Firmness gave her inner stability and bluntness gave her trust. The four clinical episodes which I have chosen to illustrate the incorporation and use of therapist attitudes all show this. Two of them also include unmistakable expressions of introjected material in manifest dreams. One is in the form of an hallucinated command, which ties up with her use of hallucination to be described in a later section. Here are the episodes.

Episode 1

In this episode the change in attitude was consciously experienced and immediate. Early in therapy, at the end of an hour filled with archaic material, the patient asked for a change in the time of the next hour, which I refused. She protested that she had something important to do in college at the assigned time. I told her that she would have to choose which was more important to her. She left, saying petulantly that, all right, she would come.

Next time she began the hour by saying that the preceding session had been a milestone. 'The whole hour seemed to be leading up to the end of the hour. When you stood firm that was a milestone, too. I've never really chosen before. Growing up is discovering what is most important. When I said to change it around, it would have been like slapping you in the face,' if the change had been allowed. This experience was followed by marked reduction in her flippancy toward her own behaviour, and an attitude of increased confidence in and respect for the seriousness of therapy. These changed attitudes, with the usual ups and downs, remained permanent.

Episode 2

Here the patient did not consciously recognize the source of her change in attitude; but the relationship is no less clear. Near the beginning of one hour Grace became infuriated with me over a blunt comment. She carried on an angry tirade, called me names and listing grievances against me. I told her there might be some truth in what she said, but that my comment still stood. Towards the end of the hour her anger subsided. Four days later this usually timid patient, who had never been able to endure serious criticism, reported that an angry teacher had made a public attack upon her supervisory methods. 'She was so excited about it! And I was trying to find out what there was in what she wanted to say. I was encouraging her to be difficult instead of just smoothing things over.' For some reason, she said, she was not afraid of 'disappearing' this time, as she had always done previously under similar circumstances.

The use Grace made of my incorporated strength is obvious. If I could take her tongue-lashing without becoming defensive or give ground, she could stand fast in the face of another's attack. If I did not wither and disintegrate under her assault—a fear she sometimes consciously experienced and directly expressed—she need not fear disintegration herself from a verbal barrage. If I could concede that there might be some truth contained in her angry talk, she could dare to take a detached attitude under comparable circumstances, and try to 'find out what there was' in what the excited woman wanted to say. The general process of testing limits went on continually; but this change also grew into an enduring ego attitude.

Episode 3

Here an introjected command is used by the patient four months afterward in a manifest dream. The command was originally given by the therapist under the following circumstances. During one therapeutic hour the patient became increasingly apathetic and incoherent, finally lapsing into almost inaudible mumbling and then silence. I said, 'Sit up!', and getting no response said it again louder. She sat up looking dazed, and said, 'I feel funny, queasy'. She soon regained contact and lay down of her own accord, saying, 'I'll feel better lying down'. The hour proceeded uneventfully.

Here is the dream four months later. 'I was bleeding myself for a good cause that I didn't know what it was. I was holding a bottle up and filling it with blood. I was getting weaker and weaker (she felt she was dying) and somebody said, "Sit up!" I sat up in bed (actually) feeling weak and woozy. There was nobody around, and somebody said, "Lie down again! If you sit up the blood will *really* run out!" So I lay down and I wanted to put all that blood back again. The dream just stopped.'

To rescue herself in a dream of gradual death, we see the patient using the same command that I had once used to bring her out of a catatonic-like state. It will be noticed that even the sense of her own statements made in the same long past therapeutic hour ('I feel funny, queasy' and 'I'll feel better lying down now') are also rendered, though less literally, in her manifest dream context.

Episode 4

The last episode illustrates the incorporation and use of therapist anger, which appears first as effective resistance to parental aggression, and later as a temper tantrum in a manifest dream. The background was the family's unflagging opposition to therapy, expressed in an endless succession of attempts at interference. There were, for example, repeated protestations to Grace that she was 'too normal' to spend all this time on herself 'in introspection'. Then a letter came containing the pious hope that she would not 'land up in a mental institution' because of therapy. An attempt was made to get 'confidential' information directly from me without the patient's knowledge. Finally, Grace received a special delivery letter warning her to get out of my hands at once.

The situation by this time had reached a point where the patient was becoming dangerously disturbed, caught between a desperate need for help and her extreme fear of the family, of their telephone conversations, their letters, and their hallucinated voices. She said, 'I feel I'm walking on the edge of a precipice and I'll fall in any minute now; this (therapy) is my last hope'. She spoke openly of suicide.

The day after the special delivery letter came it was decided to intervene vigorously. In the next hour, when the patient again expressed despair over the family's aggressive opposition, I said angrily that this was deliberate interference and I would not stand for it. I said that I refused to go on unless we were free from this constant interruption, and she could decide whether she wanted to go on or not. The day before she had remarked that, if I said so, she would not go home to Cincinnati this summer at all, probably hoping for my intervention then. I told her now, still angrily, that I would consider her going home an interruption of therapy, and for all I cared she could tell her family this.

Grace said next day that I had frightened her by my anger. Otherwise she made no direct reference to the hour. Three days later, however, she wrote a letter home, on her own initiative and without telling me beforehand, that disposed of both the question of continuing in therapy and of going home—at least for several months. I do not know what she wrote; but her whole attitude became firm and decisive, and her anxiety decreased dramatically. The immediate effect of her incorporating my open aggression was a spontaneous, decisive, and aggressive handling of a situation in which she had previously been helpless. The night after she sent the letter home she had the following dream, in which my angry outburst appears as her own, and at the same time a scarcely veiled oedipal situation is depicted.

'I was at the (student) health service and you were my doctor. There was a woman with blond hair. She was cold and aloof. She said it was the end of the year and she wondered if I'd mind changing doctors. I had a temper tantrum. I stamped my feet, jumped up and down, yelled and ran around the room. There was a catalogue and I tore it to shreds. I was damn mad. I know what it means—instead of taking everything I'm mad as hops!' Later in the hour the patient made the classic negation (3), 'It was not my mother', and added for good measure, 'It had nothing to do with my father'.

Here normal overt anger was used as a deliberate technical intervention to turn the tide of an internal battle that threatened to disintegrate the patient and drive her to suicide. The anger the therapist expressed was genuine anger; only the timing of its overt release was deliberate. Had the anger been mere simulation, this intuitively sensitive patient would only have been driven to further desperation, by finding deception where she needed trust. It will become clear in what follows that the patient was vividly aware of significant changes taking place in her internal economy.

VICISSITUDES OF INTERNAL OBJECTS AND INTROJECTION OF THE THERAPIST

In this section I shall give a clinical description of the vicissitudes of internal objects and of the introjected therapist image, and in an ensuing section attempt to discuss their significance. In my description I shall observe the following topical sequence:

(i) The operation of a concrete personified internal mother image, which functioned as a primitive superego, and of another internal critic which the patient called the *No-girl*.

(ii) The clear emergence of the hallucinated mother's voice, disowned and projected by the patient as part of a regressive attempt at ego-reorganization.

(iii) The appearance of my hallucinated voice in a moment of crisis, some months after a number of my attitudes in therapy had been incorporated; its use as a replacement for the mother's voice; and the subsequent fading away of the mother's hallucinated voice.

(iv) Return of the mother's voice during a period of deprivation (sudden hospitalization of the therapist), and its final disappearance.

(v) Introjection of the therapist image and use of this introject to further the process of forming new partial identifications.

(vi) The brief appearance of a male *Nay-sayer* during a period when all voices had been absent for some time.

(vii) The final return of critical female voices immediately following a severe experience of unexpected maternal rejection.

(i) The Mother and the No-girl

In most of the first hundred hours of therapy the patient included some form of complaint that her mother was continually interfering with her life. The complaints sounded like memories of petty nagging in childhood—mainly about being neat, clean, and tidy, showing good manners at the table, not leaving clothes lying about, etc.—plus current urgings to pay more attention to her appearance and to plan for marrying. In view of the fact that some of these urgings were actually included in current letters, and during visits home, I did not realize at first that this continual interference came also from an internal nagging presence, sometimes a voice, sometimes a more indefinite but still personified influence. Early in therapy the patient expressed irritation over all this, but no real anger. Her anger was openly expressed from the start towards a less clearly personified presence which the patient called an 'internal critic'.

In the nineteenth hour Grace for the first time spoke frankly of hearing a voice. This was the voice of the 'internal critic'. It did nothing but criticize her, so she named it the *No-girl*. Its function seemed to be restricted to the patient's current behaviour when she was with other people, and never in relation to being neat, clean, and tidy, having good table manners, not leaving clothes about, etc. It said such things as, 'Oh yes you did! You were noisy and tried to be the centre of attention. You were silly and unladylike. Cut it out— you can do it. Control yourself!' The patient said bitterly, 'If I'd been quiet as a mouse, I *swear* I don't know what she'd have said; but it would've been wrong!' The *No-girl's* criticism, she said, 'leads to a complete paralysis of the emotions. I go on acting as if nothing's happened, but I do everything wrong then, and I don't have any fun any more.'

The patient tried various ways of handling the *No-girl* which she described in therapy. 'I'm trying to disown her, to dissociate myself from her. She's so mean and hateful all the time. Sometimes at a party I'd like to push her over into a corner and cover her up and have a good time. But you could get divided, and then what would I be!' She began a kind of reality testing. She would string along a series of incidents in which she had actually done diametrically opposite things in social situations. But even so, the *No-girl* called every one of them wrong. The outcome of these reality-testing attempts seemed to the patient to make her situation hopeless. Actually they helped to rid her of this internal tyrant which, along with the personified mother image, had ruled her most of her life.

Next Grace began asking the opinions of people actually present about this or that social behaviour, during a card game or a coffee break, or during a dinner party. She always asked about something related to what the *No-girl* was attacking her for at the time, although she made it appear to her friends as if it were merely a question of what behaviour would be correct under such and such circumstances. She discovered by this means that, while usually the attacks were unjust, sometimes the *No-girl* turned out to be 'sounding a perfectly normal warning'. As the patient carried on this form of reality testing the *No-girl* gradually faded, while more realistic self-criticism began to take over. The situation became complicated, however, by the emergence of the mother's hallucinated voice, seeming now to come from the outside.

(ii) The Mother's Voice Outside

In the 150th hour Grace said that her mother had been giving her 'the third degree all the time by word of mouth' for several weeks.[2] This hallucination was obviously a new and startling experience for her. Since she had been hearing voices internally for fifteen years or more, it seemed to be the clear projection of the voice, coming apparently from without, that now impressed her. The serious attempt she made to understand this new phenomenon rings true.

'I hear the sound of her actual voice; it isn't just thinking to myself. It's outside me like over there in the corner. I think her part of me is being externalized. It's still there but it's becoming more obvious that it *is* her, and not me. I'm becoming more independent from her. Instead of rules and regulations'—i.e., instead of having a more abstract, impersonal superego—'she's kept on being part of me. I followed it as my conscience; and now it's more obvious that it *is* mother's voice and not *my* voice. I think what will happen is her voice will become more audible and disappear. I thought it would be the opposite. But it's becoming altogether audible, as if she's standing there and separate from me. It's as if mother were right in the room all the time, watching everything I did.' We shall return to the hypothesis contained in this statement of hers when we come to the discussion.

The patient made two other interesting observations about the voice. One was that the energy of her 'conscience machine' comes from her mother. The occasion was a shift in the maternal image hallucinated. Grace was living temporarily with an elderly woman; and she hallucinated this woman's face and voice telling her to tidy up. She said, 'Now it's Mrs X's voice, but I think the energy comes from my mother. This is the energy because my mother has said these things. I've no reason to think Mrs X cares. *This conscience machine goes on grinding it out; but the energy of this machine comes from my mother.*'

The second observation she made was that she had much less trouble distinguishing between herself and her mother's voice when they were in conflict than when they were in agreement. She said, 'I have a hard time distinguishing when I agree with her. If I disagree I can say, ''Shut up! I don't care!'' But when I agree I can't tell if I'm being obedient to her voice or to myself.' This experience seems to equate the hallucinated voice with a primitive superego function. Freud, in discussing the normal mature relation of ego and superego, wrote that 'as a rule we can distinguish them only when a state of tension, a conflict between them, has arisen' (5). Again a psychotic experience throws a relatively obscure early relationship into contemporary bold relief.

(iii) The Therapist's Voice Hallucinated

My voice was first hallucinated early in the second year when another direct attempt was made to get the patient home against her wishes, five months after the family interference had been stopped. This time a letter from her mother, enclosing a sizable check, told Grace of a big family reunion. It also revealed that the mother had found out about a teachers' meeting in Cincinnati at the same time, which the patient would ordinarily have attended. Grace was furious. She was in financial distress and she would have liked very much to be a part of the family reunion. But because she recognized the coercion in her mother's manoeuvring, she stuck by an earlier decision and did not go. She had to take an interurban bus trip before she could come to me for her next hour, so she put the case before me in imagination, arguing it logically, point by point. Suddenly she heard my voice saying out loud, 'I know you're really angry with your mother. Why don't you *say* so!' Now she began arguing with me out loud; but I insisted on repeating exactly the same thing, no matter what she said. Finally she gave up and began laughing. Here is her account.

'I wasn't angry with you for saying that; I knew you had to. I was bent on telling you I don't *have* to be angry. It's gone beyond that. I suppose I couldn't have been *so* secure or I wouldn't have minded that your voice kept coming back. I understand the goal is the independent personality arranging a way of establishing limits of yourself. You have to show people they can't invade your limits like that' (i.e. as her mother had just tried to do). 'When you've *made* boundaries you don't need to get angry. I know where I stand. I'm right and they're wrong. I guess that's one more step from indifference to compassion. Why did I keep hearing your voice? It was a new point of reference. It felt *good* to argue with you; and you got into such a ridiculous position, like a broken record.'

From this point on, my voice gained in importance while the mother's faded. There was some confusion at first. For example, once when I made a critical comment Grace asked me if I had actually said it, because it sounded like her mother's voice. Usually, she said, she differentiated on the basis of my tone of voice, manner, and actions—in which she included my general demeanour just before and after she lay down. By way of illustration she mimicked her mother's voice, and then mine, saying the same words. She was obviously engaged in another form of reality testing. A week after my voice appeared on the bus, she spoke of having got rid of her mothers; and a month later she remarked that she had not heard it for a long time. It did come back, but only once in its original form.

(iv) Return and Final Disappearance of the Mother's Voice

Unfortunately, three months after my voice appeared I was suddenly hospitalized with an acutely herniated intervertebral disc. Surgery was finally required, and I was kept from my office for nearly four months. During this period the patient held together well, but critical voices reappeared. She said upon my return, 'I count on you to be an ally against my critical self. She ran wild while you were away, criticizing me all the time and making me do things, pushing me. I guess she's a sort of amalgam of my mother and my sister. She used to be my mother. I don't think she really is any more.'

A month later Grace began hearing the voice of young Mrs Y, with whom she was temporarily living, just as she had heard Mrs X a year earlier. When alone, the patient could hear Mrs Y talking about her to other women, expressing surprise at her ineptness and ignorance in housekeeping matters. Also, Grace said, 'I have little conversations with her. I don't know that she has any existence. *She's a sort of a form of my mother*, because I know mother better than her. It's really my mother saying inane things that Mrs Y says or I imagine, but so obviously not true that I say "Too bad! I don't care!" Mother doesn't know the real me!' Soon after this the whole family returned to the attacks in hallucinated form when she bought a car she needed. Their harangue lasted ten days—'a whole chorus of voices'—and then for five months she made no allusion to family voices, although some form of internal critic was still active.

Just before the patient left for the Christmas holidays, and when she was very fatigued, her mother's voice reappeared clearly for a day, reproaching her for lying in bed late, but also saying, with unwonted sympathy, that she was working too hard. Next, back in Cincinnati, she experienced unprecedented good relationships with her mother. The mother even recounted intimately shared things from Grace's early childhood, which made the patient feel happy, such as having let her feel the baby kicking when the mother was pregnant. At the same time there was the old complaint that whenever Grace tried to talk about her current life, interests, and hopes, she met only silence from her mother or an abrupt change of topic.

The patient said on her return that this 'creature' who criticized her must represent her mother; but the mother's voice as such never came back. Within two weeks she said her hate for her mother had all gone; and she began expressing affection instead. There was a corresponding change in the tone of the mother's letters. Throughout the ensuing year Grace developed more and more realistic attitudes, recognizing her mother's many positive contributions to her personality structure, as well as the fact that her mother's failings seemed more the result of defect than of conscious malice. Outspoken expressions of pride in her mother as a woman emerged, along with increasing attention to her own femininity. Evidently, with the vanishing of the dangerous mother image, it became possible for the patient to intensify her identification with the external manifestations of the good mother in her actual mother's behaviour and appearance.

(v) Introjection of the Therapist

Running parallel with the return and final disappearance of the mother's voice there was evidence from time to time that my hallucinated voice was also active in the patient's internal economy. Occasionally Grace reported something it had said. She was having arguments with it, like the ones she had had with Mrs X and Mrs Y, but more or less in keeping with my actual attitudes. Once when something she quoted me as having said turned out to be her own thought, she said impatiently, 'It's the same thing'. During my four months' absence my voice did oppose the critics; but without reinforcement from my actual presence it could not prevail against them. 'I couldn't find you at the centre of my affection', she said, 'I couldn't have that in me or with me. You were a strong ally against this person; you went away and she got the best of me.'

During the next seven months there were occasional comments like, 'I keep hearing you'; but Grace did not volunteer any content, or indicate whether my voice was experienced as inside or outside. It seemed therapeutically contraindicated for me to enquire. However, on the day before the final appearance of the mother's voice (i.e., just before the patient went home for

Christmas), she made her first unmistakable statement of having introjected the therapist, which merits quotation in detail.

'I resent you. *It's because you're inside me that I resent you. I've taken you inside. It's the internal you that makes me mad.* Everything I do I have to tell you. Whether it's good or bad I have to come and tell you. I wanted to just have that evening and feel as I wanted to about it. But you had to pass judgement on it. I can remember when it happened. I was closing the garage door and you were suddenly there. Not your voice—I don't have hallucinations or anything like that. But you were there just the same; and we had an argument. You said, "You went ahead and did exactly the same thing you did before!" and I said, "I didn't! It was different!" I don't want to make this sound too neurotic; but I'm aware that you're involved, and it can't ever be simple any more. I don't mean you're always critical; but you were this time, and I didn't agree. Sometimes you say positive things, or seem to have a positive attitude—because it isn't your voice. Sometimes it is and sometimes it isn't—or I don't know if it is. This sounds all very strange; but that's the way it is. I'm sorry, that's the best I can describe it.'

A month later—and incidentally a week after saying that her hatred for her mother had gone—the patient reported arguing with me over her coming late and thus shortening her hour with me. Again introjection at a primitive level is obvious, as well as a clear recognition that my voice had now replaced her mother's.

'I've been arguing with you all morning before I came. You said, "You're late," I said, "I know I'm late. I got tied up and couldn't get here earlier." "Why didn't you *start* sooner?" "I *did* think I'd started early enough, but that damn car got stuck." "Why didn't you get up sooner?" "I was tired." "Why didn't you go to bed earlier?" "I shut up at this point. I just wasn't going to have you run my life. I've got something else besides you in my life. *You take the place of my mother—your voice. I don't know why I took your voice in.* You're not mad or nasty, just unpleasant, making me feel foolish and not letting me run my own life. I know you're not doing this at all. It must be the old *Witch*;[3] but not really. She doesn't say, "*Why didn't you get up earlier?*"' (inquiring voice). 'She says, "*Why didn't you get up earlier!*"' (nasty, attacking voice). 'It's distinctive. I hate her! That's why I make her into you.'

From this point on there was no further mention of my voice; and for a year—the fourth year of therapy—there was nothing said about female voices or the female 'internal critic'. A few times the patient said that what used to be her mother's voice was herself. Once she heard the male voice of her principal, 'a voice that was not quite a voice', reproaching her for not working harder. She remarked, 'It's really my voice talking to myself; but he gets into the form of it.' She spoke of experiencing 'a great pulling together, a feeling of wholeness, not just *trying* to be but *being*.' She added that she was not hearing voices any more and did not miss them.

(vi) The Male Nay-sayer

Four weeks later a male *Nay-sayer* put in a brief appearance. The patient spoke about him in three successive hours and never alluded to him afterwards. He first appeared suddenly as a disapproving voice during a Parent-Teachers' Association meeting when the patient's teaching methods were being criticized. Grace merely said that after a certain criticism the *Nay-sayer* was there for the rest of the evening.

The next night he appeared in a manifest dream, as her garage mechanic, who kept reproaching her for not taking better care of her car. 'This time', she related, 'I didn't say, "Yes, I've done all these things. I'm very sorry". I just said, "Haven't you heard about a God that forgives?" I said it out loud; I was sitting up in bed. But he knew things about me and kept piling them up, throwing past sins in my face. I said, "Haven't you heard about a God that takes care of people who sin because they don't know any better?" In the dream I said they would be forgiven—the things I've done without knowing, which plague me. You don't have to resurrect them all up in order to be forgiven for them.'

'The *Nay-sayer*,' she said, 'is definitely a man. It's a man accusing, or the masculine part of myself or integrated—no, I'm not making myself clear. He has a function that can't be denied, a part in the whole person. It's a man for me, a lot of rational and masculine characteristics, always fierce and sharp and aggravating. Men aren't always those things. It must be the picture of a man I had. My father wasn't like that at all. It's all tangled up. I don't want to be a man; so he can just be outside of me. I've discovered that a man can also be compassionate and still be a man.'

The next therapeutic hour followed a weekend, during which the patient had been pondering over the problem of why the *Nay-sayer* was a man. She said nothing new excepting a comment that she might have thought her mother was a man, when she was a child, since she had never been afraid of her father. She then spoke for the first time for years about her childhood fear of 'that terrible siren in the night' when the fire-engines went by. The *Naysayer* was never mentioned again. His probable dynamic significance will be discussed later.

(vii) Maternal Rejection and the Return of Critical Female Voices

After a year's absence the critical, attacking female voices came back suddenly, immediately after a severe, unexpected experience of maternal rebuff. The patient went home for the Christmas holidays. She fully expected a warm welcome because her Thanksgiving visit home had been successful, and there had been an affectionate exchange of letters for several months. The moment she got home, however, she noticed that her mother seemed 'miles and miles away, just like that first Christmas', i.e., three years earlier.

The climax of frustration came one evening when she made a direct appeal to her mother to listen to her plans and hopes for the future. Her mother paid no attention to her; she just went on reading a magazine. Even the father, a peaceable man, remonstrated with the mother over her ignoring Grace, but without result. So the patient talked about her plans and hopes to her father; but she felt sure her mother was listening behind the magazine. There were other unhappy incidents, and the patient finally left home feeling rejected, humiliated, angry, and, as she expressed it, 'emptied out.'

Back in her own apartment, the patient got a cool reception from her landlady. She jumped to the conclusion that this was because she had left the place in a mess. The next day she could 'hear two women's voices being catty' about her housekeeping; and later on the internal critic which she called the *Witch* came back, keeping up a running fire of nasty, critical, disparaging comment. This whole incident was obviously a setback, and a sign that some of the advances made during therapy were still unstable.

There were also encouraging signs. For one thing, the patient recognized the unreality of the two women's voices before coming to her first postholiday hour; and for another, the internal mother and the mother's voice did not return as such. It will be recalled that the internal mother, unmistakably personified, was prominent throughout the first year and a half of therapy; and it had probably been active for many years before. The *Witch* was always a much less personified entity than the internal mother, and less personified even than the *No-girl*. I assumed, therefore, that by no means all the ground gained had been lost. The fact remains, however, that this primitive level of self-control and self-criticism persisted; the critical, attacking female voice did not again disappear.

The setback necessitated a review of the patient's decision, made three months earlier, to leave therapy the following spring and take a position she greatly wanted in Seattle, where she also had good friends. During the ensuing month there were no signs of progressive ego disorganization and, excepting for the return of the *Witch*, the archaic material that came up was no different from what had been intermittently present during the preceding year of maximal improvement. Moreover, much of the good relationship with mother and the home was apparently restored through a reasonably affectionate correspondence. It was decided that the wisest thing would be not to attempt any interference with the patient's plans, in which she had frankly included the recognition that she might need further therapeutic help where she was going. Therapy was accordingly terminated by mutual agreement on the date originally set.

TERMINAL PSYCHOLOGICAL EXAMINATION[4]

Two weeks prior to termination a thorough psychological examination was carried out, and interpreted by the same psychologist who had tested the patient three and a half years earlier. Since his report represents an independent evaluation of important trends discussed in this paper, I shall give a summary of it as nearly as possible in the original wording.

To begin with, a persistence of archaic modes of thinking and of previously disturbed content was found. The patient was 'still likely to show moodiness and overalertness, to be concerned with filling up empty spaces, to feel enclosed and compressed, threatened with being robbed, out in the cold, dead', and to feel a grown-up in an infantile way. Some of her optimism was obviously forced.

In general, however, the test results indicated substantial improvement in orientation, more effective functioning, and better inner feeling. Energies available to the ego, free from conflict, appeared increased in quantity. The patient showed greater tolerance or awareness of regressive tendencies and a more realistic recognition of her limits. She seemed freer to recognize and acknowledge her subjective sense of confusion, and to speak of how things changed in appearance as she looked at them.

In the tests the patient seemed more freely egocentric, rebellious, assertive, and aggressive. There was less paranoid fearfulness and more neurotic or even normal fearfulness. She was better able to experience guilt, and not just hostile persecution from outside; and she was better able to tolerate direct sexual representations in fantasy, and to contemplate tender heterosexual relationships. The prospect of object loss or renunciation was less threatening to her; and she could contemplate it as something that could be used for better adaptation in the future. Separation could be tolerated, and so could non-compliance.

A relatively greater socialization was found than in much of the previous content. There was less lack of adequate communication in the Thematic Apperception Test (TAT), more real interaction between the person and the group, and less mutual destruction in conflict. There was more recognition of yielding and dependent feelings, more emphasis on being feminine and seeing femininity as involving grace, and less need to depict the female figure consistently as a saint and stronger than the man.

It was possible for the patient sometimes to see even the mother-figures in the TAT as benevolent. In several places, where the mother dies the daughter can feel compassion even though she hates the mother; and she can recognize that she has not been an adequate daughter. In one story the mother-figure was a hostile schemer in the tests three and a half years ago. Now she is represented as someone who appears in the identification figure's thoughts once in a while; and although these thoughts keep recurring, they do not affect her because she knows it is just a thought, and the mother is not really with her.

DISCUSSION

Internal Critics from the Past

Early in therapy, as we have seen, the patient distinguished two internal critics, both female, one of whom she identified definitely as her mother, and the other much less definitely as the *No-girl*. The two seemed to be performing different though overlapping functions. The mother's criticisms were confined to chiding and nagging Grace for petty failings characteristic of normal childhood, and urging her to make herself attractive so that she could marry. To the therapist they sounded complaining, trivial, and relatively naïve.

The *No-girl*, by contrast, sounded sophisticated and seemed to be operating more on terms of equality with the patient. Its special function seemed to be that of berating and ridiculing current social behaviour, particularly where Grace's personal integrity, self-respect, and interpersonal competence were involved. This internal critic was often conspicuously present in the midst of social activities; and it also gave Grace rather cruel, straight-from-the-shoulder talks when she got home from a date, a party, an informal get-together or a teachers' meeting.

There was a person who had actually performed such functions during most of her life, who seemed to have these characteristics, and had always exerted a domineering and primitive influence, which Grace experienced as more sadistic than her mother's but less dangerous. This person was an older sister. In real life Grace had been able to fight back and argue when her sister attacked, just as she now did with the *No-girl*. She said of her childhood, however, 'I took on her pattern as much as I could, but it's much more in keeping with her nature than mine.' In the case of the sister as also in the case of the actual mother, there was plenty of evidence—in the form of letters, long-distance calls and events during Cincinnati visits—that the attitudes and methods ascribed to the *No-girl* had substantial foundations in external reality.

It is impossible to say how much of the patient's initial complaining about maternal interference and nagging was experienced at the time as recall, how much as vague internal voice, how much as influence, and how much as hallucination. The same is true of the *No-girl*, whose identity remained always somewhat obscure in spite of its probable origin in sister identifications.[5] The patient seemed to experience many gradations between feeling criticized by something vaguely ego-alien within her and hearing voices say things which she could more or less repeat. The unclarity of this whole picture, and its variability even within a single hour, suggest that the patient's level of effective ego organization fluctuated within wide limits, a suggestion supported by frequent shifts between archaic and mature ego functioning in other areas, not reported in this paper.

Therapeutic Regression and the Mother's Reprojected Voice

What did emerge clearly was the frank hallucination of the mother's voice, now experienced as coming from the outside. The patient was startled, but in no way frightened by this new phenomenon. On the contrary, she at once assumed that it was a necessary step towards getting rid of her mother's internal persecuting voice. It is remarkable that a psychologically naïve person should arrive at such a conclusion, when one considers that hallucinations were not recognized as signs of restitution and attempts at recovery until the present century (1,2). Nor was Grace altogether disappointed. For with the help of another hallucinated voice she did get rid of her mother's voice completely, internal as well as external.

Two other assumptions may be added to the one the patient made. One is that the slow growth during therapy of a new sense of trust made it possible for the patient to dare regress to a point where the mother appeared as an hallucinated separate existence outside herself. Grace could not have done this without feeling confident that she would be protected. It is this confidence that explains her being undaunted by the sudden apparition of a concrete presence which had previously seemed extremely dangerous. She had already given voice by this time to a multitude of archaic fears that she might be swallowed up and destroyed, expressed in direct and not merely in symbolic form.

We can also assume that the patient's ability to separate off the mother image, reproject it, and then dare to face it, was the product of a long process of normally aggressive interaction between therapist and patient. After many months of continual testing, at first in the therapeutic situation and later outside it as well, Grace discovered that contrary to her lifelong conscious expectation she destroyed no one by her aggressivity, and was not herself destroyed. On the contrary, as she dared more and more, she experienced a growing sense of her own identity which she frequently expressed. I assume that her internal relationship with the bad mother image underwent parallel transformations until, as soon as the patient could risk regressing sufficiently, the image erupted as something separate from her evolving self-representations.

The Hallucinated Therapist Voice as Replacement Therapy

I assume further that when Grace hallucinated my voice she was taking another step towards recovery, and towards freeing herself ultimately from dependence upon me. But my voice went through a different course of transformation, and functioned differently in a new internal relationship. To begin with, the mother's voice had been internally present in one form or another for many years. Its presence grew out of the originally symbiotic mother-infant unity which, in this case, had never adequately differentiated into two distinct persons. There had never even evolved a workable distinction between the actual and the internalized mother. The patient's final step, in what has just been discussed, seemed to be a disowning projection of the mother image followed by its gradual disappearance from consciousness and the preconscious—presumably through some process of assimilation.

My voice, on the other hand, seems first to have appeared as a disowning projection—as something heard outside the self which could be argued with and laughed at. This first appearance coincided in time with the beginning disappearance of the external hallucinated mother's voice, which faded out and stayed away until my four months' absence. I call the process *replacement therapy* because my real voice, my hallucinated voice, and later my clearly introjected voice, became substitutes for the hallucinated mother image and ultimately replaced it. The therapist supplied this facility in a usable form, and the patient utilized it in accordance with her own internal needs.[6]

Why was the therapist hallucinated before being experienced as an introjected object? Innumerable attempts at partial identification had preceded this dramatic projection, many of them undoubtedly successful. On a number of occasions Grace had reported experiences of being unable to distinguish between herself and me. Evidently in moments of deep regression my image entered into a temporary symbiotic relationship with her, comparable to that which she experienced with the mother image. It seems to me that her hallucinating me on the outside was a restitutional achievement, a synthesis, in which she succeeded in putting me on a par with her already externalized hallucinated mother. The two could now confront each other, and be equated, in a form that lay within internal reality but seemed to her outside it. When my image was hallucinated, in a moment of urgent need, it could stand for the first time as an entity on the threshold of the patient's psychic system before entering it—to make use of Grace's imagery, like a trusted friend about to be invited in.

FURTHER STEPS IN REPLACEMENT THERAPY: INTROJECTION AND ASSIMILATION

The next step, introjection of my image as an internal object, did not occur in one dramatic moment. It probably took place over a period of many months of therapy, preceded and accompanied by the incorporation of my attitudes. I cannot say how long my voice operated as a disowning projection, from the outside, and exactly when it became entirely internal. The two phases seemed to overlap. What we do know is that fifteen months elapsed between the day when the patient first hallucinated my voice and the day when she spoke definitely of having taken me inside.

The occurrence of introjection here is not merely inferred. The patient herself described the 'taking in' with naïve directness. My image had originally appeared outside when she was in the act of defying her mother's power and needed my help. Now it was transformed into an internal reality which performed some of the superego functions previously performed by the now evicted mother. It discharged these duties differently, more in accord with my basic therapeutic attitudes and not in the spirit of the old internal voices. For example, whereas the maternal voice had consistently nagged, belittled, and attacked, mine only confronted or opposed Grace without disparagement; and whereas the internal mother pressed forward, encroached, and threatened, the internal therapist remained firm and available, but detached. It was again the patient herself who expressed these basic distinctions; and it was her continual reality testing, in relation both to therapeutic interaction and to the home, that made further discrimination learning possible for her.

What finally became of the male introject? It ultimately disappeared from consciousness and the preconscious, as had the personified internal mother. I assume that while serving as a kind of 'ego ally' and 'superego substitute'—the former in the sense of the patient's formulation, the latter in the sense used by Pious (8, 9), Wexler (11), and Hoedemaker (6)—it was gradually integrated into the more mature ego-superego organization, as a new set of values with more realistic goals, demands, and ideals.

There is special significance in the fact that the male Nay-sayer emerged in the midst of a year of freedom from voices, and then quickly disappeared. It indicates that something was going on all this time beneath the surface, some process of ego-superego reintegration. Judging by what Grace actually said, a new and impressive kind of identification was crystallizing which included strong masculine components, something she was already calling the masculine part of herself with a function she could not deny.

This was a new kind of identification for Grace, because her childhood home had always been dominated by a dangerous, unpredictable mother who made the father appear weak and ineffectual. She could have taken strength from her mother and compassion from her father; but to her the strength seemed too destructive and the compassion seemed defenceless. The therapist as she experienced him apparently bridged the gap—first through a process of archaic introjection, and subsequently through processes of partial identification, derived both from the introject and from the therapist still present in the therapeutic interaction.

It was obvious from her introjection and use of therapist attitudes early in therapy that this patient was capable of making relatively stable, new partial identifications. We know that these new partial identifications preceded in time the more primitive and drastic introjection of the therapist. We can assume that after this wholesale introjection process occurred, the now continuously present male introject could be used to help form partial identifications which both supplemented and balanced new partial identifications with the toned-down mother image—the ones which made it possible for Grace to accept her own femininity and take pride in it.

These last assumptions are related to Loewald's thesis (7) that an early identification with the father stands against the threatening possibility 'of sinking back into the structureless unity from which the ego emerged'. There was abundant clinical material in this case that expressed clearly and consciously the conflict over need for a structureless union with the mother and a terrifying dread of it. Grace often felt at conscious levels that she was actually only an extension of mother, and sometimes that her mother was an extension of herself.

The handicaps of operating in adulthood at such archaic levels are all too obvious. There is perhaps also an advantage. It may still be possible for a patient, who is operating at archaic levels part of the time, to use the equivalents of early partial identifications in ways that a more maturely developed psychic system could not. It may even still be possible—and this case suggests it—to introject massively with archaic completeness in adulthood, and then be able to assimilate the new introject as an infant might, so that it disappears as such, but some of its properties do not.

The Witch

The internal critic that returned toward the end of therapy, following the maternal rebuff, resembled the one that had appeared two years earlier, after the therapist had disappeared suddenly into the hospital. Grace called it *Witch, Creature*, or *She* during both periods. Like the *No-girl*, it seemed to represent a more mature level of functioning than did the original internal mother. The patient expressed much uncertainty about the nature and identity of the *Witch*. Once she called it an amalgam of her mother and her sister. At times she felt that it represented her mother in some way. At times she called it a part of herself or another form of herself, at other times not herself at all but other people, and again herself in the form of someone else. Some of what the voice said she recognized spontaneously as things I once had said. Often the voice sounded like normal imagining, and many of its accusations were felt as bits of painless truth.

As the date fixed for interrupting therapy approached, Grace drew the unexpected conclusion that she really needed this internal critic, with all its harshness and bluntness, both for self-control and for protection against the world. The *Witch* had evidently also changed character and acquired useful potentialities. It seemed now to be an intermediate product of the therapeutic interaction, and of environmental pressures, which might function as a substitute for the internal mother, the *No-girl* and the therapist, until something better integrated and more stable could be worked out. This would probably be achieved most successfully with further therapeutic help.[7]

SUMMARY

(i) Clinical material has been presented which describes clearly certain regressive experiences not ordinarily accessible to normal and neurotic persons. Transformations in the identity and function of 'internal critics' during therapy are documented, including a sudden disowning reprojection of the mother's voice and, later, hallucination of the therapist's voice in a moment of critical need.

(ii) The patient spontaneously interpreted the clear hallucination of her mother's voice as a step towards differentiation and recovery; and it is assumed that hallucination of the therapist's voice had a similar significance.

(iii) The subsequent introjection of the therapist is reported by the patient with naïve directness. This event is soon followed by a fading out of the mother's voice; and the patient experiences the new introject as taking over some of its functions.

(iv) It is assumed that the new introject was gradually assimilated into the maturing ego-superego reorganization, that its internal presence supplemented the continued therapeutic interaction in forming new partial identifications, and that these balanced new feminine identifications were evident in the clinical material.

(v) The brief emergence of a new male critic, during a year-long period of apparent freedom from internal and external voices, seems to justify the assumption that a slow process of assimilation was going on beneath the surface during this 'silent' period. The male critic, which the patient somewhat reluctantly identified as a part of herself, expressed maturing attitudes of open aggression tempered by compassion.

(vi) Finally, a previous internal female critic reappeared and persisted, following an experience of severe maternal rejection in external reality. The old internal persecuting mother did not reappear, new partial identifications with the actual mother and the therapist were not lost, and, just before terminating therapy, the patient said that she would need this critic as a source of self-control and self-protection.

NOTES

1. The writer wishes to acknowledge the many valuable suggestions and interpretations made by Dr William L. Pious during therapy in this case, and by both Dr Pious and Dr Hans W. Loewald during preparation of the paper.
2. The several weeks included the period leading up to her putting a stop to family interference, described above as Episode 4.
3. The *Witch* was one name used by the patient to refer to her internal critic that seemed to have replace the *No-girl* and the mother.
4. The material in this section is abstracted from the report of Dr Roy Schafer.
5. Pious (10) has pointed out the additional possibility that the *No-girl* may act as a restitution from a sense of aloneness, and on another level may represent the patient, identifying with the mother in expressing hatred of herself.
6. Although 'voices' are emphasized in this account, as they were by the patient, there was abundant evidence that much more was being experienced than a bodiless auditory hallucination.
7. Two years later this patient was able to fall in love for the first time in her life and to marry.

REFERENCES

(1) Freud, S. (1911, English trans. 1925). 'Psycho-analytic Notes upon an Autobiographical Account of a Case of Paranoia (Dementia Paranoides).' *S.E.* **12**.
(2) ——— (1914, English trans. 1957). 'On Narcissism: an Introduction.' *S.E.* **14**.
(3) ——— (1925, English trans. 1950). 'Negation.' *C.P.*, **5**.
(4) ——— *New Introductory Lectures on Psychoanalysis*. (New York: Norton, 1933.)
(5) ——— (1926, English trans. 1936). *The Problem of Anxiety*. (New York: Norton).
(6) Hoedemaker, E. D. (1955). 'The Therapeutic Process in the Treatment of Schizophrenia.' *J. Amer. Psychoanal. Assn.*, **3**, 89–109.
(7) Loewald, H. W. (1951). 'Ego and Reality.' *Int. J. Psycho-Anal.*, **32**, 10–18.
(8) Pious, W. L. (1949). 'The Pathogenic Process in Schizophrenia.' *Bull. Menninger Clinic*, **13**, 152–159.
(9) ——— (1950). 'Obsessive-compulsive Symptoms in an Incipient Schizophrenic.' *Psychoanal. Quart.*, **19**, 327–351.
(10) ——— Personal communication.
(11) Wexler, M. 'The Structural Problem in Schizophrenia: the Role of the Internal Object.' *Psychotherapy with Schizophrenics*, ed. E. B. Brody and F. C. Redlich (New York: Int. Univ. Press, 1952.)

11. Phases of Patient-Therapist Interaction in the Psychotherapy of Chronic Schizophrenia

Harold F. Searles

At the end of three years of doing intensive psychotherapy with chronically schizophrenic patients, I found myself occupied, for a comparatively brief period, with the question of whether I should go ahead and devote myself, for an indefinite number of further years—perhaps for the whole remainder of my professional career—primarily, to this line of endeavour. I decided in favour of doing this, out of a feeling of having found myself in the course of my personal analysis, in the course of these early years in the crucible of the intensive psychotherapy of schizophrenia, and in the course of my developing marital-family life. The question of whether I am a human being, possessed of the feeling-capacities which activate human beings, had been affirmatively put to rest, and I felt able now to approach this psychotherapy in a new and workmanlike spirit, sure that my basic potential for this work was there in me, and curious to see what truly professional *techniques*, quite beyond the countertransference-ridden flounderings of the neophyte, one could develop in grappling with this remarkably complex job that clearly needed doing.

The nine years which have passed since then, while confirming for me the validity of that shift in my feeling-orientation, have none the less forcibly brought home to me the realization that the 'technique' of psychotherapy with schizophrenia is best spelled out in terms of an evolutionary sequence of specific, and very deep, feeling-involvements in which the therapist as well as the patient becomes caught up, over the course of what has emerged, for me, as—in necessarily broad and schematic terms—the 'normal' and predictable over-all course of psychotherapy with the chronically schizophrenic person. This paper, then, will attempt both to highlight the crucial role of feelings in the therapeutic relationship, and to delineate what I have found to be this 'normal' over-all pattern of the psychotherapeutic course which that relationship follows over the years of the patient's treatment.

The therapist's feeling-involvement in this therapeutic work is, for various reasons, a deep one, and personal analysis does not spare him from such involvement, but rather makes his feelings more available to him for the deep involvement which is so necessary.

First, the very length of time required for this therapy tends to foster a deep involvement on his part, such that the hours he has spent with the patient over the course of, say, six or eight or ten years, become deeply a part of all that the years have brought for him—the joys and sorrows, the triumphs and bereavements.

Secondly, the various forms of intense transference on the part of the schizophrenic individual tends forcibly to evoke complementary feeling-responses, comparably intense, in the therapist. Mabel Blake Cohen (1952) has made the extremely valuable observation, for psychoanalysis in general, that:

. . . it seems that the patient applies great pressure to the analyst in a variety of non-verbal ways to behave like the significant adults in the patient's earlier life. It is not merely a matter of the patient's seeing the analyst as like his father, but of his actually manipulating the relationship in such a way as to elicit the same kind of behaviour from the analyst . . .

It is not too much to say that, in response to the schizophrenic patient's transference, the therapist not only *behaves like* the significant adults in the patient's childhood, but experiences most intimately, within himself, activated by the patient's transference, the very kind of intense and deeply conflictual feelings which were at work, however repressed, in those adults in the past, as well as experiencing, through the mechanisms of projection and introjection in the relationship between himself and the patient, the comparably intense and conflictual emotions which formed the seed-bed of psychosis in the child himself, years ago.

A third reason for the necessarily deep feeling-involvement on the part of the therapist is inherent in the nature of early ego-formation, the healthy reworking of which is so central to the therapy of schizophrenia. Spitz (1959), in his monograph concerning the early development of the ego, repeatedly emphasizes that emotion plays a leading role in the formation of what he describes as the 'organizers of the psyche' (which he defines as 'emergent, dominant centres of integration') during the first eighteen months of life. He says, for example, that:

. . . the road which leads to this integration of isolated functions is built by the infant's object relations, by experiences of an affective nature. Accordingly, the indicator of the organizer of the psyche will be of an affective nature; it is an affective behaviour which clearly precedes development in all other sectors of the personality by several months.

This brings us back to my other main topic, namely the phases comprising the over-all course of psychotherapy with the chronically schizophrenic person. Within recent years I have become growingly convinced that it is possible to delineate such phases amongst the complex, individualistic, and dynamic events of clinical work. One can take heart, in this difficult effort at conceptualization, from Freud's delineation of the successive phases of libidinal development in healthy maturation, from Erikson's (1956) portrayal of the process of identity formation as a gradual unfolding of the personality through phase-specific psycho-social crises, and from Hartmann's (1956) statement, concerning the process of evolution of the reality principle in healthy development, that:

> The impact of all stages of child development—the typical conflicts, the sequence of danger situations, and the ways they are dealt with—can be traced in this process.

The successive phases which in my experience best characterize the psychotherapy of chronic schizophrenia, with each of which the remainder of this paper will deal in turn, are (A) the 'out-of-contact' phase, (B) the phase of ambivalent symbiosis, (C) the phase of preambivalent symbiosis, (D) the phase of resolution of the symbiosis, and (E) the late phase—that of establishment, and elaboration, of the newly won individuation through selective new identifications and repudiation of outmoded identifications.

The first three of these phases retrace, in reverse, the phases by which the schizophrenic illness was originally formed. To my way of thinking, the aetiological roots of schizophrenia are formed when the mother-infant symbiosis fails to resolve into individuation of mother and infant—or, still more harmfully, fails even to become at all firmly established—because of deep ambivalence on the part of the mother which hinders the integration-and-differentiation of the infant's and young child's ego. The child fails then to proceed through the normal developmental phases of symbiosis and subsequent individuation; instead, the core of his personality remains unformed, and ego-fragmentation and dedifferentiation become powerful, though deeply primitive, unconscious defences against the awareness of ambivalence in the object and in himself. Even in normal development, one becomes a separate person only by becoming able to face, and accept ownership of, one's ambivalent feelings of love and hate toward the other person. For the child who eventually goes on to schizophrenia, the ambivalance with which he had to cope in his relationship with his mother was too great, and his ego-formation too greatly impeded, for him to be able to integrate his conflictual feeling-states into an individual identity.

My theoretical concepts have been fostered by Mahler's (1952) paper on autistic and symbiotic infantile psychoses and by Balint's (1953, 1955) writings concerning phenomena of early ego-formation which he encountered in the psychoanalysis of neurotic patients. In 1958, I ventured to express my conviction that a symbiotic relatedness between patient and therapist constitutes a necessary phase in the transference-evolution of successful therapy with either psychotic or neurotic patients, although it is particularly prominent and important in the former group (1958c). I have noticed with great interest, therefore, that Mahler & Furer (1960) emphasize that:

> Our first therapeutic endeavour in both types of infantile psychosis [i.e. both autistic infantile psychosis and symbiotic infantile psychosis] is to engage the child in a 'corrective symbiotic experience'. . . .

Loewald (1960a), too, reports that what I call a symbiotic relatedness occurs in the schizophrenic patient's transference to the therapist: in his way of phrasing it,

> . . . If ego and objects are not clearly differentiated, if ego boundaries and object boundaries are not clearly established, the character of transference also is different, in as much as ego and objects are still largely merged. . . .

It is now time to embark upon a description of the successive phases of therapy with the chronically schizophrenic adult patient.

(A) THE 'OUT-OF-CONTACT' PHASE

I do not term this the 'autistic phase', for the reason that the world 'autistic' has come to have a certain connotation, in psychodynamic theory, which I regard as invalid and therefore do not advocate. Specifically, the term 'autistic', as generally used, conjures up Freud's (1911) psychodynamic formulation of schizophrenia as involving withdrawal of libido from the outer world and its subsequent investment in the self—as involving, in other words, a regression to narcissism. My own view is that there occurs instead, in schizophrenia, a regressive dedifferentiation toward an early level of ego-development which has its prototype in the experience of the young infant for whom inner and outer worlds have not yet become clearly distinguishable as such (see chapter 5). This is in line with the formulations of Werner (1940), and Loewald (1960a) follows the same reasoning in his previously mentioned paper.

To the degree that the patient is schizophrenic, this phase predominates during the early months, and in many instances the early years, of his therapy. Characteristic of this phase is the circumstance that his feelings are unavailable to himself and are not conveyed in his interpersonal relationships; hence the therapist experiences comparatively little in the way of feeling responses to the patient's behaviour, except for a sense of strangeness, of alienness, in reaction to the bizarre symptomatology into which the patient's feeling-potentialities have long ago become condensed—the hallucinations, the delusional and neologistic utterances, the stereotyped and manneristic non-verbal behaviour, and so on. It is seldom that the therapist feels that the patient even perceives him, sufficiently undistortedly so that the therapist can sense that he is a person in the here-and-now is being seen, or heard, or otherwise perceived, by the patient who much more often shows, instead, every evidence of being lost in a world of chaotically disturbed and distorted perceptions. Patient and therapist, so long as this phase endures, clearly have not yet entered into a deep feeling-relatedness with one another.

The feeling-orientation in the therapist which best serves a constructive approach to the patient and his bizarre symptomatology, and best facilitates the traversing and resolution of this phase of the therapy, is a calm, neutral, investigative orientation. By contrast, the inexperienced therapist is apt to approach the patient in a spirit of urgent need to relieve the suffering of this deeply and tragically ill person. One is helped to relinquish such an attitude, which to the extent that it predominates, renders constructive therapy impossible, by realizing a number of things about the patient. First, as Szalita-Pemow (1952) helped me to see, the patient's individuality, his sense of personal identity, resides largely in his psychotic symptoms; thus the therapist is reacted to as threatening to rob him of his individuality, by 'curing' him of his illness. He has no conception of psychological health in our experience of this term; for him, 'getting well' is tantamount to a restoration of the state—the anxiety-ridden, unendurably boring, or what-not, state—which he experienced just before he originally became overwhelmed by the psychosis. Basically, 'getting well' is, for him, tantamount to loss of his individuality through return to symbiotic relatedness, toward which he is constantly being impelled by the inner drive which never ceases to pull him back toward the world of people. Also, for him, 'facing reality' is a very different thing from the therapist's being able to face the reality of *his* life; the reality of the patient's own life, which must eventually be confronted if he is ever to become well, is a reality overfull of tragedy and loss.

We need to realize, in the same vein, that the patient is not solely a broken, inert, victim of the hostility of persons in his past life. His hebephrenic apathy or his catatonic immobility, for example, represent for one thing an intensely active striving toward unconscious, regressive goals, as Greenson (1949, 1953) has helped to highlight in his papers on boredom and apathy in neurotic patients. The patient is, in other words, no inert vehicle which needs to be energized by the therapist; rather, an abundance of energy is locked up in him, pressing ceaselessly to be freed, and a hoveringly 'helpful' orientation on the part of the therapist would only get in the way. We must realize that the patient has made, and is continually making, a contribution to his own illness, however unwittingly and however obscure the nature of this contribution may long remain.

It is particularly when the therapist sees the dimensions of the patient's hostility, of his sadism, that he realizes that, on balance, the sufferer is doing what, on the over-all, he *wants* to do at the moment. When this understanding comes home to the therapist, he does not need to struggle to maintain some artificially neutral-screen façade, but comes to *feel* on the over-all neutral toward the patient whom he sees to be both loving and hateful, and whom, he increasingly realizes, he himself is capable of both loving and hating.

The therapist's hand can be strengthened, in effecting this change, by his identifying with his predecessors who have reported in the literature their achievement of such an attitude toward their work. Winnicott (1949), for example, points out how inevitably is hatred a component of the therapist's, as well as the normal mother's, feelings toward, respectively, the patient or the child. Knight (1940) describes his having found that, in the psychotherapy of paranoid patients, the use of such time-honoured techniques as reassurance, reeducation, and tactfulness in dealing with the patient's homosexual wishes only causes him to become increasingly paranoid because, Knight saw, the patient has real hatred and this is what the anxiety is mainly about. Heimann (1955) finds it best not to try to convince the paranoid patient of one's good will, or to avoid coming to terms with his delusional material, and clearly sees the sadism involved in her patient's suffering. Hayward & Taylor (1956) find that 'when a patient is suffering, the decision as to whether to give comfort or to attack is often very difficult', and Hayward's recovered schizophrenic patient tells him, in retrospect, 'You should never have stood by and let me torture you by crucifying myself and making you watch my suffering. You should have forced me to come down or at least thrown rocks at me', and reminds him that 'people need practice in hating without guilt or fear, just as much as loving'.

The therapist, operating from this basic feeling-orientation, can meet usefully a wide variety of typical problem-situations; I can mention only a few. In response to the patient's manifestation of delusional thinking, he will be aware that, for the patient, the delusions represent years of arduous and subjectively constructive thought, and are therefore most deeply cherished. He will not forget that obscured in them is an indeed indispensable nucleus of reality-perception. He will not become caught up in either disagreeing or agreeing with the delusional view, but will try to help the patient explore the feelings which this delusional world-view causes him to feel—the dismay, the shock, the despair, and fear, and so on. Not only here, but in general, free from any absorbingly urgent need of his own to 'cure' the patient, he will remain attentive to what the *patient* is experiencing. He will couch his remarks in terms of the patient's own presumed point of view, and when the patient is able to express a feeling—whether of fear or loneliness or anger or what-not—the therapist will usually content himself with simply acknowledging the feeling and encouraging its further elaboration, rather than rushing verbosely to somehow relieve the patient of it. Likewise, when a patient is having vigorously to disavow any feeling about a clearly affect-laden matter, the therapist will remain in tune with the patient's own feeling experience, by remarking, 'I gather you don't find yourself having any particular feeling about this',—or, better, will make no mention of feelings—rather than trying to overcome the unconscious denial by asserting; 'But surely this *must* make you very angry (or hurt, or what-not)'. Similarly, in responding to the expressions of an archaic, harsh superego in the patient, rather than setting himself up as the spokesman, the personification, of the repressed id-impulses, he will realize that it is in the superego that the patient's conscious self—his personal identity—mainly resides; thus he will seldom urge the patient to recognize sexual or aggressive feelings within, and will more often acknowledge how strong a sense of protest or outrage the patient feels upon perceiving these in others.

To the extent that the therapist is free from a compulsion to rescue the suffering patient, he can remain sufficiently extricated from that suffering to be able to note significant sequences in the appearance of such symptoms as hallucinations, verbalized delusions, and so forth, and thus be in a position to be genuinely helpful. Even when on an auto ride with a patient, or grappling with the latter's physical assault, the therapist may on occasion be able to allow himself sufficient detachment to help the patient to link up this immediate experience, clarifyingly, with forgotten situations from earlier life; such 'action interpretations' may be especially important to the patient whose memory, and whose capacity for abstract thinking, are severely impaired.

In working with the patient during weeks or months of silence on the latter's part, he will not, out of a compulsion to help the tragic victim of schizophrenia, rack his brain with diligent therapeutic efforts focused upon the patient, who is already afflicted with overwhelming intrapsychic pressures. Rather, the therapist will feel free to let his thoughts roam where they will, leaf through magazines, do some serious reading of current interest to him, and otherwise see to his own personal comfort and freedom from anxiety. This may at times involve periodic letting off of steam at the inarticulate patient; but such blasts do, in my experience, no harm to the patient and help one to become again, for a relatively long period, genuinely accepting of this difficult situation. Thus one places on the over-all a minimum of pressure upon the patient who is already paralyzed with pressure, and keeps oneself in a comparatively unanxious and receptive state which, better than anything else, helps eventually to relieve the patient's anxiety and unlock his tongue. Sooner or later, like a bright dawn pushing back a long night, the patient will put his rusty vocalization capacities to work in venting reproach, contempt, and fury upon the therapist for doing, as the former sees it, nothing to help him.

In general, while aware that the parents responded to the patient in certain ways—such as by condemnation, reproach, contempt, or what-not—which promoted illness in the child, the therapist will refuse to tie his own hands with any self-imposed injunction to make his own behaviour always an antidote for such early trauma, and never to engage in such responses himself. He knows that there will be times when such responses are the only realistic ones to make to a given piece of behaviour on the patient's part, and he rests assured that if the patient were never able to find *anything* of the latter's mother or father in the therapist, the transference-reliving, and eventual resolution, of the schizophrenic illness would be impossible. One could postulate with some confidence that a person whose intrafamilial relationships had been so warped as to lead to schizophrenia would quite simply be at a loss to know how to relate, would have insufficient tools from past experience for relating, to a hypothetically ideally loving-and-mature therapist.

The therapist learns to take fewer and fewer things for granted in this work, learns to question more and more of his long-held assumptions and discard many of them. He learns that one does not set a ceiling upon any human being's potential growth. He finds recurrent delight in the creative spontaneity with which the schizophrenic patient pierces the sober and constricting wrappings of our culture's conventions, and he discovers that humour is present in this work in rich abundance, leavening the genuine tragedy and helping to make it supportable. While developing a deep confidence in his intuitive ability, when working with the severely fragmented or dedifferentiated patient he will not jump too quickly to attempt communicational 'closure' (in the Gestalt sense), but will leave it in the patient's hands to do, no matter how slowly and painfully, the parts of the communicational work which only the latter can do. Meanwhile, he will not need to shield himself, through the maintenance of an urgently and actively 'helpful' or 'rescuing' attitude, from feeling at a deep level the impact of the fragmented and dedifferentiated world, with its attendant feelings, in which the patient exists. The unfolding of such feeling-experiences, which will be elaborated in my portrayal of the next phase of the therapy, the 'urgently helpful' therapist-attitude is unconsciously designed to avert, comparable to the defensive function, in the patient, of the latter's schizophrenic delusions.

I hope to have made it sufficiently clear that, in describing a basically neutral feeling-orientation toward the patient, I am not thereby recommending that the therapist should assume, and hold to, any rigid professional role of 'the psychiatrist'. My experience of this coincides with that indicated by a number of workers in this field. Robert A. Cohen (1947) reports, concerning his therapy of a paranoid schizophrenic woman, 'the patient's unfavourable reception of any remark which smacked of the usual psychiatric jargon', and learned to avoid becoming so interested in the *content* of her delusions as to lose track of their *feeling*-implications for the patient. Lidz & Lidz (1952) point out that: 'More paranoid patients, in particular, can participate in treatment but cannot be treated in the sense of having another person control or manage them'. Bullard (1960) offers to the paranoid individual 'not interpretations but, rather, hypotheses for the patient to consider as possibly shedding some light on the problems he is exploring'. The basic orientation I recommend is well described in Loewald's (1960a) remarks about psychoanalytic work,

. . . Through all the transference distortions the patient reveals rudiments at least of that core (of himself and 'objects') which has been distorted. It is this core, rudimentary and vague as it may be, to which the analyst has reference . . . and not some abstract concept of reality or normality, if he is to reach the patient. If the analyst keeps his central focus on this emerging core he avoids moulding the patient in the analyst's own image or imposing on the patient his own concept of what the patient should become. It requires an objectivity and neutrality the essence of which is love and respect for the individual and for individual development . . .

(B) THE PHASE OF AMBIVALENT SYMBIOSIS

To the extent that the therapist's basic orientation toward the patient is a neutrally investigative one, one free from a compulsive need to help and to love the patient, but one open, rather, to the sensing of hateful as well as loving feeling-tones in the therapeutic relationship, he comes progressively to detect the intense ambivalence which has been locked within the patient's psychotic symptomatology. He detects this, before the patient himself has become able to experience and verbally express such ambivalence, through the awareness of sudden fluctuations of his own feelings in reaction to the patient's verbal and non-verbal communications. He finds his feelings toward the patient switching unexpectedly from, for example, tenderness to contempt, or from fury to grief, or what-not. He finds himself experiencing, on occasion, feeling-states which are quite ineffable and foreign to his memory and which, despite whatever roots in his own preverbal childhood, can usefully be regarded as samples of the feeling-states at work in the patient himself, though more probably than not outside the latter's awareness as yet.

The prolonged silences, or obscurity of verbal communication, or both, which characterize the work with the chronic schizophrenic patient have served to foster a progressive weakening of ego-boundaries between patient and therapist. That is, in this situation of clouded communication, projection and introjection on the part of each participant is facilitated to an extent which is seldom if ever seen in an analyst's work with a neurotic patient, for in the latter instance the frequent and clear verbalizations, from each participant, tend to keep *relatively* clearly highlighted the ego-boundaries between the two participants. Thus there develops a generous reality-basis for the symbiotic transference which the schizophrenic patient tends powerfully, in any case, to form with his therapist. The therapist's own ego-boundaries are weakened not only in reaction to the prolonged silences and in reciprocity to the patient's transference, as indicated in the above-mentioned comment by Mabel Blake Cohen, but also for the reason that regression toward symbiotic relatedness tends to occur in the therapist himself as an unconscious defence against the intense and deeply ambivalent feelings—of helplessness, fury, loathing, tenderness, grief, and so on—evoked by his relationship with the schizophrenic patient, long prior to that relationship's having become strong enough, and well-defined enough, to permit his recognition of these feelings, and any full-scale expression of them, toward the patient.

As I have described in earlier papers (1958c, 1959a, b), the therapist at times will find himself in the extremely uncomfortable state of experiencing two quite different, and subjectively unrelated, feeling-attitudes toward the patient simultaneously. Particularly in instances in which one or another parent was psychotic, the patient tends to form such a subjectively ego-splitting kind of transference toward the parent-surrogate therapist. The relatedness between patient and therapist comes, sometimes for several months, to bear many of the earmarks of a mutual effort to drive one another crazy (1959a). I have described elsewhere (1958a) some of the manifestations of the patient's vulnerability, during this phase, to the disturbing impact of the therapist's unconscious processes.

More and more the therapist comes to feel enmeshed, as it were, in the patient's own ego-fragmentation and dedifferentiation. The therapy has a sticky feel about it; the therapist feels restrained from any decisive actions, incisive comments, or even clear-cut and unambivalent feelings toward the patient. His resentment, rage and hatred toward the latter are tormentingly guilt-provoking in nature; and his tender and loving feelings are hardly less burdensome and guilt-provoking. He feels that he does not truly love the patient, but has only an ugly lust which will not stand the light of day; and when he does feel that his love is more of a parent-to-child order, his love feels guiltily possessive. He is painfully aware of being like a jealous Pygmalion concerning this Galatea with whom is he at once blessed and afflicted: he looks to his colleagues for succour, but deeply resents any participation from a third person—psychiatric administrator, therapeutic supervisor, nurse, or whomever—as an intrusion into his own private domain. One other simple earmark of this phase of ambivalent symbiosis is the circumstance that the relationship with this patient has assumed an absorbing, unparalleled *importance* in the therapist's life, an importance which not only jars with such relationships with other staff members as impinge upon the situation, but which he experiences also as a competitive threat to his most personal and cherished non-professional relationships.

At its fullest intensity, this phase is experienced by the therapist as a threat to his whole psychological existence. He becomes deeply troubled lest this relationship is finally bringing to light a basically and ineradicably malignant orientation toward his fellow human beings. He feels equivalent to the illness which is afflicting the patient; he is unable to distinguish between that illness and himself. This is not sheer imagination on his part, for the patient is meanwhile persistently expressing, in manifold ways, a conviction that the therapist constitutes, indeed, the affliction which threatens to destroy him and with which he, the patient, is locked in a life-and-death struggle. In my theoretical view, the therapist is now experiencing the fullest intensity of the patient's transference to him as the Bad Mother.

The patient's own ego-boundaries may be so unclear that it may be impossible to know whether, when he speaks, he is uttering thoughts which are subjectively his 'own', or rather giving voice to what he assumes the therapist to be thinking but not expressing. The therapist will often find it similarly impossible to know whether a predominant feeling-tone of anger, or grief, or what-not is welling primarily from the patient or from within himself.

Murderous feelings arising within the therapist tend particularly, in contrast to more readily acceptable feelings, to become projected upon the patient, whose own oftentimes prominent assaultive tendencies offer a ready reality-basis for such projections. The therapist in these circumstances is prone, for various reasons some of which are quite obvious, to the development of intense murderous feelings. These result from the intense frustration of his therapeutic endeavours, the threat to his individuality arising from the symbiotic relatedness with the patient, and his residua of infantile omnipotence brought to bay during the mutual regression which this symbiosis involves, such that the therapeutic relatedness often takes the form of a raging struggle between two gods. There supervenes, thus, all the murderousness of the thwarted infant not only in the patient but in himself also.

Uncomfortable though it is for the therapist to feel afraid of the murderous patient, it is still harder for him to realize the full extent of his own murderousness toward the patient, and to see that the latter is unaware of feeling murderous and is experiencing, instead, intense fear of the therapist who is viewed as murderously insane. It is more acceptable to the therapist's super-ego to feel intimidated than intimidating, and the realization that the patient is deathly afraid of one tends, at least initially, to weaken one's own feeling of control over one's rage.

I have reported elsewhere (1958a) a dream which I had during the course of my work with a hebephrenic man whom I had been viewing, for some months, as being a dangerous, uncontrollable person. In the dream, during a desperate struggle between us he got his hands on a knife-like letter-opener. But then *he* took *me* into custody and at the end of the dream he was functioning as a kind of sheriff's deputy, marching me out to turn me over to the authorities. This dream was one of the developments which helped me to

268 PSYCHOTHERAPEUTIC ENCOUNTERS WITH PSYCHOSIS

become aware of massive, previously-repressed rage in myself which I had been projecting upon the patient. A colleague reported to me in a supervisory hour, two weeks ago, the uneasy feeling that he and the patient were presently in a state of ostensible calm which was really the calm, he sensed, of the eye of a hurricane; he felt that there was some as-yet-undefined fury in the patient which was looming somewhere. But in last week's supervisory session he reported various intimations of a previously unsuspected quantity of rage in himself, such that he said, 'I'm not sure now whether the hurricane is in her, or in me'.

More often than not the therapist is, unlike the colleague just mentioned, unaware that a state of symbiosis is developing, or has long been established, between the patient and himself. This state of affairs is easier to detect in one's colleagues than in oneself. When one becomes alert to the significance of this phase of the therapy with the schizophrenic person, one is struck by how frequently one hears therapists make, in supervisory sessions or in staff presentations, such comments as 'There's been a lot of anger this past week', without specifying in *whom*; or, likewise, 'There's a manicky mood around— there's a lot of giggling'; or, 'There is a very strong dependency there', without specifying *where*. The therapist may make repeated slips of the tongue concerning the sexual identity of the patient—a response not only to the deep-seated sexual confusion in the patient which has now come to light, but a function also of the therapist's lack of differentiation between his own sex and that of the patient. He may say, 'I started seeing her in [a cold, wet sheet] pack', in such an ambiguous tone as to make one wonder momentarily whether he means that she was in pack, or he was in pack, or both were in packs. On rare occasions one may hear: 'The first period when he was my therapist was—I mean, the first period when I was his therapist was. . . .' One becomes alert to such clues in one's own presentations also.

The dissolution of ego-boundaries between patient and therapist is only a major aspect of a more general dedifferentiation-and-disintegration of ego-functions which occurs in both participants (although to a much lesser, and therefore more subtle, degree in the therapist, of course, than in the patient) as the symbiotic relatedness develops. Thus the therapist, losing temporarily his ability fully to differentiate between fantasy and reality, may react to various of his sexual fantasies about the patient with as much guilt as though they represented consummation in behavioural reality, and may feel jealous of the hallucinatory figures with which the patient is immersed in a seemingly lively and intimate interaction, as though these hallucinatory figures were to be compared on a par with himself (Searles, 1961b). On occasion, too, during this phase, childhood scenes have welled up in my memory with an almost overpoweringly tangible reality. One feels from time to time, too, the impact of some previously unglimpsed fragment of the patient's past, conveyed to one now by him in ways that are largely non-verbal and hard to objectify.

Before this phase of ambivalent symbiosis can give place to the succeeding one in the therapeutic sequence, the relationship between patient and therapist must gradually grow, through the resolution of innumerable and increasingly severe tests of the kind mentioned above, sufficiently strong so that the therapist can endure the fullest intensity of the patient's hostility, focused directly upon him. In contrast to the warnings given by Sullivan (1956), Hill (1955), and many other writers, to the effect that such a development means that the therapy has foundered irretrievably, I have come to see this, both in my own work and in that of my colleagues, as an utterly essential therapeutic development. The patient can never become deeply a whole person unless he has this chance to, in Hoedemaker's (1955) way of describing it, identify with the therapist who survives the fullest intensity of this kind of attack to which the patient was exposed in childhood and from which he, the patient, had to flee into psychosis. And complementarily, I have found that it is an equally essential part of this phase that the therapist finds himself gradually coming, step by step, to express openly—even though not as often as he feels it within—the very fullest intensity of his own hatred, condemnation, and contempt toward the patient, expressing these in ways which are unconsciously patterned after those ways by which the parents expressed their destructively negative feelings toward the patient as a child; the therapist's responses are so moulded, in powerful degree, by the patient's transference, and it is thus that the patient is at last able to cope successfully with, symbolically, the parents' destructiveness, recapitulated in the therapist's side of the transference relatedness. The deep reassurance which therapist as well as patient derive from finding repeatedly that each can survive the other's, and his own, baring of hatred at its fullest means that the foundation for the next therapeutic phase, that of full—or, genetically speaking, preambivalent—symbiosis has now become established.

(C) THE PHASE OF FULL, OR PREAMBIVALENT, SYMBIOSIS

This phase, which is ushered in gradually and—as in the instances of the other phases I am describing—with unceasing fluctuations toward both earlier and later phases, most often makes its presence known in terms of the therapist's finding, to his surprise, that his largely silent hours with the patient are no longer a source predominantly of conflict and anguish to him, but rather a source mainly of pleasureful contentment, contentment which his superego at first reacts against as being reprehensible in view of the still formidable degree of illness in the patient after the passage of these many months of treatment. Or the therapist may discover, in the course of work with a largely verbal patient, that their verbal encounters have somewhere along the way lost their disturbing, anxiety-provoking and hurtful quality, and are now predominantly, though largely deniedly, cherished by both himself and the patient.

The therapist comes more and more unconflictedly to accept, now, both the feelings of a Good Mother who has a godlike importance to the little infant in the patient, as well as his own equally infantile-dependent feelings toward the patient as a similar Good Mother; the therapeutic relatedness, having progressed to the preambivalent mother-infant symbiosis, oscillates between the therapist's being now in the one position, now in the other, toward the patient.

I cannot overemphasize the extent to which it is the little child in each participant upon whom mutual trust must eventually be placed, for therapy to succeed; in the biblical phrase, '. . . and a little child shall lead them'.[1] Psychotherapy with the schizophrenic patient tends naturally to involve the therapist's feelings at the level of his own early childhood experiences. He powerfully responds to the patient as being an omnipotent mother, both because the latter's history of prolonged symbiotic relatedness with the mother has fostered strongly maternal qualities in the patient, and also because the present deeply undifferentiated state of the patient's ego gives the therapist the impression of unlimited potentialities for the therapist's own gratification.

One's love for the patient is now experienced as boundless and unthreatening, no longer a threat to, for example, one's relationship with one's wife and children, but rather a confirmation of one's ability to love whomever. The sexual components of the love are no longer experienced as predominant, but submerged in a kind of boundless, fundamentally maternal, *caring for* the patient. This love, experienced toward the patient who is a member of one's own sex, is no longer experienced, as it was previously, as being any threat to one's sexual identity. Such hateful feelings as do from time to time arise become progressively guilt-free and actively enjoyable, on the over-all much subordinate in power and frequency to loving feelings, and increasingly rapidly revealed as defensive against the intensely tender love which underlies them. One comes to see that, at this level of dedifferentiation, 'love' and 'hate' are one, and that any intense and overt relatedness is, in effect, love. One of my patients, during such a phase, expressed her realization that 'There's a very thin line between love and hate'.

The patient's formerly archaically harsh superego is seen progressively, now, as no longer a giant foreign body in the patient-therapist relatedness, but rather as the vehicle for the patient's expression of his most deeply denied, but by the same token, most intense and intimate, love for the therapist-mother. Comparably, the therapist finds that his own vestiges of infantile omnipotence, fanned to flame by the 'struggle-between-two-gods' nature of the ambivalent phase of symbiosis, give way to a realization, and deep acceptance, of his inability to 'cure' the patient through any exercise of rageful, godlike authority—his inability, that is, to bend the patient to his will by 'curing' him. There emerges in him then a feeling-orientation which, achieving what I have experienced as a 'gentle victory' over the domineering god-infant in oneself, is felt, for all its quiet gentleness, to be awesome in its power: a loving acceptance of the immediate relatedness with the patient, founded upon the knowledge that one's now full and unswerving dedication to his recovery, mingled with the patient's own increasingly liberated striving toward health, comprise together a current which is carrying the therapeutic process forward. Out of this whole-hearted commitment of feeling by both patient and therapist, we understand the accuracy of the comment made by Bak (1958), that to the degree that the adult person is truly mature, there is in him no realm of the superego, demarcated as such within the over-all functioning of the personality; and of Anna Freud's (1946) observation that ' . . . our picture of the super-ego always tends to become hazy when harmonious relations exist between it and the ego. We then say that the two coincide. . . .'

The therapist experiences not only the above-mentioned sense of whole-hearted commitment to the therapeutic relationship, at a depth which, he now realizes, despite all his previous expenditures of effort and feeling, he never felt before; he responds to the patient, during the therapeutic session, as being of boundless personal importance to him, and becomes progressively unafraid to acknowledge this on occasions when the patient needs such acknowledgment. It is not too much to say that the therapist feels the patient as necessary, even, to complete himself; temporarily and acknowledgedly, that is, he feels toward the patient that which the 'schizophrenigenic mother' was not strong enough either to acknowledge or to relinquish: the need for the patient to complete her own personality. For years we have been accustomed to totally damning this phenomenon as wholly destructive, and productive of schizophrenia; we need to realize that the core of any human being's self esteem is traceable to the healthy infant's experience that he is indeed needed to complete the psychological wholeness of the mothering person; it is there, I have come to believe, that the core of the *raison d'etre*, for each of us, is to be found.

By the same token, the therapist should not be ashamed to receive from the patient such help in personal integration as the patient is able to provide; in this regard I fully concur with Whitaker & Malone (1953). The healthy child's self esteem is strengthened by the experience that, just as his mother needed him to complete herself in his infancy, she now finds him deeply helpful in fostering her personal integration, her maturing. We should be able to have the courage to see, and acknowledge, these aspects of the symbiotic core of therapeutic interaction, when we see that, as long ago as 1923, Groddeck (1923) had the courage to describe how, in his treatment of one of his patients:

> . . . Her childlike attitude towards me—indeed, as I understood later, it was that of a child of three—compelled me to assume the mother's role. Certain slumbering mother-virtues were awakened in me by the patient, and these directed my procedure. . . . And now I was confronted by the strange fact that I was not treating the patient, but that the patient was treating me; or, to translate it into my own language, the It of this fellow-being tried so to transform my It, did in fact so transform it, that it came to be useful for its purpose. . . . Even to get this amount of insight was difficult, for you will understand that it absolutely reversed my position in regard to a patient. It was no longer important to give him instructions, to prescribe for him what I considered right, but to change in such a way that he could use me.

The therapist, at moments when he is in the position of the mother in the mother-infant symbiosis, may have vivid fantasies of giving suck to the patient as a happily nursing infant; Warkentin & Taylor (Whitaker, 1958) have described the physical accompaniments of such fantasies, and I, too, have experienced these in my work with a number of patients. It is equally important that the therapist become able to accept his nursing-infant fantasies toward the patient, whether female or male, for otherwise the patient cannot learn to deeply accept his own desires to nurture—the primeval basis for all givingness. I find it impressive, in this connexion, that Sechehaye (1951), Eissler (1951), Schwing (1954), Hayward & Taylor (1956), Whitaker & Malone (1953) and many other therapists are in agreement concerning 'the absolute necessity for a happy infantile experience with a good mother before the patient can begin to grow toward adult reality' (Hayward & Taylor, 1956), and it is of additional interest that the recovered schizophrenic patient reported by Hayward & Taylor, who gave a detailed account of her therapy as she saw it in retrospect, 'stressed that the happy nursing experience was the most important single part of her therapy'. I am trying here to describe something of how this particular phase of the therapy, this 'happy infantile experience with a good mother' phase, actually manifests itself, particularly in terms of the therapist's experiences during it.

A mutual spirit of childlike playfulness is another prominent characteristic of this phase. Because the ambivalent stage of the symbiotic transference-relatedness has been successfully traversed and the stratum of preambivalent lovingness attained, the lack of structure, the lack of rigidly defined boundaries between patient and therapist, or between such intrapsychic realms as those of remembered 'reality' and those of creative fantasy, or those of concrete imagery and those of metaphorical or allegorical or otherwise highly figurative imagery, is experienced no longer as a threatening kind of dedifferentiation, but rather as giving both participants the unfettered opportunity to playfully trade places with one another (and even, in one instance in my experience, to imaginatively trade various body-parts with one another), and to playfully gambol about all these various realms of psychological experience in a mix-up which is oftentimes thoroughly merry to both of them. One finds something which one had never thought possible: confusion itself, usually regarded in psychiatry as so tragically destructive to the patient and threatening to his therapist, can be actively pleasureful in an atmosphere where a sufficient degree of mutual trust has been reached so that, where hate for all practical purposes does not exist, confusion is no longer tantamount to vulnerability, and ego-structure need not be thrown up as a poorly erected bulwark against external threat, but can form at its own pace as, primarily, a growing organization for the expression of increasingly complex inner potentialities and, therefore, needs.

It is appropriate at this juncture to note the impact upon the over-all hospital environment of the foregoing phase in the psychotherapeutic relationship, namely the phase of ambivalent symbiosis, and of this phase of full or preambivalent symbiosis. In the former phase the patient-therapist relationship tends to foster incessant and severe splits among the group of patients-and-personnel on the ward, pervading, at times, the social structure of the whole hospital. By the same token, the deep ambivalence in the patient, as well as the not inconsiderable ambivalence roused responsively in the therapist in the course of the therapy, tend to make their relatedness the ready instrument for the expression of already existing, latent disagreements rife in the social environment surrounding them; thus, of the ambivalence which permeates this larger social environment, their therapeutic relationship is at once cause and victim. Such ambivalently symbiotic phenomena in the larger social structure of the hospital have been well described by Stanton & Schwartz (1954), Main (1957), Perry & Shea (1957) and others; I have reported my own experience with, and interpretations of, such phenomena (1959b).

Many a therapeutic relationship miscarries and the therapist and patient, unable to face and resolve the intense, mutual hatred which is evoked by the symbiotic phase of the psychotherapy, repress this hatred, project it on to various figures in the surrounding social matrix of the hospital, and become locked into a relatedness in which they both share the fantasy of being lovingly at one. But this is not the truly preambivalent phase of the transference-symbiosis which they are experiencing; rather it is, as those responsible for the long-run management of the hospital are painfully and irritatedly aware, predominantly a *folie-à-deux* between patient and therapist, in which symbiosis is functioning mainly as a defence against the recognition of mutual hatred. This development is so common that I have come reluctantly to conclude that there is no sure criterion by which one can know, for long periods of time, whether one is involved in a genuinely preambivalent symbiosis with the patient, or rather in the predominantly paranoid symbiosis which is a defence against hatred; there is no kind of litmus paper which will definitely tell us, and we must remain openminded to the ever-present possibility that, for example, a basically constructive, subjectively preambivalent symbiosis will be misused unconsciously from time to time, by both participants, to keep out of awareness increments of particularly intense hostility.

Even in those treatment-relationships where a healthy, preambivalent symbiosis is in full sway, it is not always easy for the social environment to take. The therapeutic relationship even here needs a kind of delicate handling, much as a pregnant woman needs special care from her environment even when the pregnancy is progressing well. For example, neither therapist nor patient is yet ready for any third person to come upon the scene as a consistently valued, and openly acknowledged, contributor to their mutual therapeutic work. Further, the subjectively irresponsible playfulness and contentment, so genuinely healing in itself and so central an ingredient of the preambivalent symbiosis, nonetheless strains the faith and patience of others on the hospital staff who have little or no opportunity to participate in the favourable developments I have been describing, and who are aware mainly of such conspicuous

factors as the patient's already-long hospitalization, his persisting manifestation of various chronic symptoms in his daily life on the ward, and perhaps,
the intimations from the family that this hospitalization cannot be underwrit-
ten indefinitely.

'They were going around on a merry-go-round—no, not on a merry-go-
round, because that implies movement', snorted a supervisor at a recent staff
conference, concerning the therapeutic relationship between a hebephrenic
woman and her therapist who were, from my view, in the midst of the phase
of preambivalent symbiosis at a time when, for extraneous reasons, the therapist had had to leave the Lodge to return to his distant home-country. 'Going
around on a merry-go-round' is a beautiful way of describing the kind of
therapeutic interaction in which it is so important for the patient and therapist
to become able freely to participate, but which is so difficult for the hospital
organization to permit. I myself, who 'know' these things as well as I know
anything about the therapy of schizophrenia, feel, when in the role of supervisor hearing from a therapist concerning his work during such a phase,
unenjoyably aware of being an 'outsider' to the so-intimate two-person relatedness I am hearing about at second hand, and must work against my
tendency to express envious resentment to the therapist through admonitions
and reproaches that he should buckle down to the business of psychotherapy
with the patient—the worst possible supervisory response at this phase of the
therapy. By contrast, the sheepish therapist obtains invaluable help from his
supervisor's realization that what is going on in therapy is the very essence of
what is good for the patient, confirming the therapist's own courage to go on
doing this in the face of the reproaches of his own all-too-conscientious
superego.

(D) THE PHASE OF RESOLUTION OF THE SYMBIOSIS

The complex individualistic needs of the two participants, and thus their
respective strivings for individuality, will not tolerate indefinitely the perpetuation of the therapeutic symbiosis. The basic function of this symbiosis
is, after all—despite the intense regressive gratification which it holds in
itself—a maturational one: it provides the patient, and to a not insignificant
degree the therapist also, with a basis for renewed, and healthier, development of individuality. Thus, after a period extending from, as best I have been
able to determine, a few months to one or two years, the dynamic equilibrium
of the therapeutic relatedness shifts increasingly toward resolution of the

symbiotic phase. The initiative for this shift may be manifested first by either patient or therapist, and it is my impression that the resolution process—that is to say, the process of both participants' coming to be subjectively, and to function as, individual persons, rather than partners in symbiosis—proceeds by turns, with now the one, and now the other, showing the greater push toward emancipation. I shall describe first the therapist's experiences when the initiative is in his hands, and then his experiences in reaction to the patient's showing such initiative.

One of the therapist's typical feelings, in the former instance, is a quiet, subjectively unaccountable, but deeply memorable sense of apartness from the patient, a feeling-realization that the patient is outside oneself—a realization that the patient is a person 'over there', a person afflicted with a schizophrenic illness which is, likewise, 'over there' in the patient. One facet of the therapist's realization is, then, that he—the therapist—is not the patient's illness. This shift in feeling-orientation is at times experienced, also, as a sensation of now being, at long last, 'out of love with' the patient—a feeling always, for me, tinged with some guilt in those instances in which the patient is still showing much need for persisting symbiosis with me beyond the time when I have now 'outgrown' it.

On other occasions, the therapist experiences a resolution of the symbiosis, or at least a step in this resolution-process, not in this quiet and subjectively inscrutable way, but rather with a sudden sense of *outrage*. The very word '*out*rage' is significant, and the feeling it designates is qualitatively different from annoyance, anger, or even rage. He feels outrage at this or that chronic regressive symptom in the patient, or outrage at the latter's whole regressive symptomatology, and always outrage at the unreasonableness of the demands which the patient has been making upon him, these many months or years. He sees the enormity of these demands which the patient has been placing, through his illness, upon him and other persons, and sees clearly the folly of acquiescing further to these regressive demands. He is suddenly and vigorously determined to give no more of his long-time dedication, now seen as misplaced dedication, to the gratification of these demands, which he formerly saw as infant-needs which it would be unthinkable to brush aside.

The therapist sees now, by the same token, the full interpersonal offensiveness of the patient's defence-mechanisms, whereas he possessed heretofore a high degree of tolerance for such offensiveness in his patient and maintained a devoted effort to see, and empathize with, the anxiety, the hurt, the loneliness, and so on, against which the patient has been unconsciously protecting himself through the use of these defence-mechanisms. In my work with, for example, one paranoid schizophrenic man who chronically manifested intense scorn and sarcasm in his dealings with other persons including myself, for nearly two years I had experienced increasing forebearance toward, and sympathy with him as I saw more and more clearly the feelings of hurt, disappointment, and so on which the scorn and sarcasm were serving to maintain under repression. But then, with the advent of the resolution-of-symbiosis phase, it forcibly dawned upon me how genuinely obnoxious, to me as well as to others, he was being with his scorn and sarcasm, the defensive function of these notwithstanding.

In other words, one now holds the patient highly responsible for his symptoms. One now leaves in his hands the choice as to whether he wants to spend the remainder of his life in a mental hospital, or whether he wants, instead, to become well. In every instance that I can recall from my own experience, I have found occasion to express this newly won attitude to the patient himself, emphasizing that it is all the same to me. These are no mere words, but the expression of a deep and genuine feeling-orientation. One cares not, now, how callous this may sound, nor even whether the patient will respond to it with suicide or incurable psychotic disintegration; and one feels and says this while casting one's own professional status, too, into the gamble, not to mention the potential feelings of lasting remorse to which one might be subject in case one's communication had such an irremediably destructive effect upon the patient. Thus, in effect, one braves the threat of destruction born to the patient and to oneself, in taking it into one's hands to declare one's individuality, come what may.

It may well be that individuation—the resolution of symbiosis—innately contains, even in the healthy maturation of the young child, this element of going ahead in the face of such a life-and-death threat. Incidentally, if this is true, we have here the primordial determinant of democracy's tenet that it is better to brave death than to live as any other than a politically free individual.

Part of this new attitude on the therapist's part is a readiness to let the patient 'stew in his own juice', in contrast to his having often found himself, previously, vicariously expressing the patient's feelings in the symbiosis which then obtained. Likewise, he feels a new freedom to express his own individual thoughts and feelings to the patient as an individual—or as, at any rate, one whose nascent individuality is increasingly in evidence—without being hampered by concerns as to whether he is being inconsistent toward the latter, or is treating the latter unfairly in comparison with his other patients—a not unimportant aspect of the work, when one has two or three patients on the same hospital ward.

The therapist feels a clear realization, with all this, of the fact that he himself is no longer indispensable to the patient; he realizes, that is, that he himself is not the only conceivable therapist who can help the patient complete the journey to health. He can look about him and see various colleagues who, he can readily imagine, would fill this capacity as well as, or possibly better than, he can fill it. He feels now a lively appreciation of, a genuine welcoming of, the invaluable contributions to the patient's recovery which have been made, are being made, and will continue to be made, by nursing personnel, relatives, various of the other patients on the ward, and so on. This is in marked contrast to the therapist's feeling earlier in the work, a grandiose feeling but, I think, a feeling quite essential to the development and maintenance of the therapeutic symbiosis, of being a God the Creator in the therapeutic situation, of being the only conceivable Pygmalion for this Galatea; that feeling was, after all, of a piece with the mother's sensing of her own god-like indispensability to her so-needful infant. The therapist's subsequent realization, now, that these others are helping in major ways to meet the patient's needs, comes predominantly as a deeply reassuring one; but it has, obviously, affective ingredients of deflation and loss.

One sees the loss-aspect of the therapist's experience more clearly at those junctures when the patient, rather than the therapist, is manifestly showing a determination to grow free of the symbiosis. One of my most frequent experiences as a supervisor is that of helping a therapist to explore his feelings of dissatisfaction and despair about a current therapeutic relatedness in which, he is consciously convinced, the schizophrenic patient is showing discouraging stasis, but in which the patient is actually evidencing, as shown by various subtle clues, all too many indications of a growing, though still somewhat submerged, determination to slough off the symbiosis in which the therapist has a far deeper feeling-investment that he cares to acknowledge to himself. The therapist paradoxically finds himself despairing, for example, just at the time when the patient has actually been opening up unprecedentedly deep areas for investigation—areas of fondness and dependency toward the therapist, areas of confusion or other disturbed subjective experience, and so on. One unconsciously employs, as therapist, the same defence-mechanisms against recognising the beginning resolution of the symbiotic phase as one employed, earlier, against the recognition that this phase of symbiosis was becoming more and more deeply established—namely the defence-mechanisms of denial and reaction-formation: the denial of how well the work is actually proceeding, denial of how much the patient means to oneself, denial of how deeply cherished are the gratifications which one is obtaining or has been obtaining, denial of how deep is the sense of loss which further change will bring; and reaction-formation feelings of impatience and dissatisfaction, as part of one's struggle to maintain under repression feelings of contentment, satisfaction, and accomplishment.

I think it correct to say that the therapist, no matter how mature or experienced, inevitably reacts somewhat against any move on the patient's part into a new area of feeling, a new area of psychotherapeutic investigation. This is partly for the reason, as I have mentioned elsewhere (1961a), that the patient's sense of identity is so deeply invested in the old way of experiencing things, the old and familiar way of relating to the therapist, that he, the patient, would experience a major threat to his sense of identity if the therapist were somehow able to welcome with unambivalently open arms this move into a new area of experiencing and interpersonal relating. But it is partly for the reason, too, that the therapist has a more or less deeply imbedded emotional investment in the familiar, more predominantly symbiotic mode of relatedness with the patient, and hence reacts against the threat of personal loss with which the patient's new growth as an individual confronts him.

I have had the experience of finding that a hebephrenic woman, with whom I had been involved for a number of years in an increasingly unambivalent and pleasurable symbiotic relatedness, had come to radiate, now—with disconcerting suddenness, so it felt to me—a self-containment which, by all logical standards, was a most welcome therapeutic development. Instead of her making unceasing efforts for me to be all persons to her and to satisfy her every need almost before it arose, she now spent the hours with me in saying little, but mainly in looking at me calmly, appraisingly, and objectively. She was not being actively rejecting to me, in either word or facial expression, as she had been on innumerable occasions much earlier in our work, particularly during the phase of ambivalent symbiosis. But I felt a distinctly unpleasurable sense of being apart from her; I could not help feeling rejected in the face of a development which I knew represented, for the first time, the establishment of a genuine sense of self on her part.

For the patient to become firmly established as, subjectively, an individual person, he must come to accept that, although he can contribute to the healing of other persons'—including his therapist's—psychological difficulties, he cannot cure them in any total sense, and therefore does not have to hold himself responsible for curing them. He can proceed, therefore, with the getting-well process, the process of becoming an increasingly healthy person, without *guilt* for being, and increasingly becoming, a separate individual. This is one of the dividends which the relinquishment of infantile omnipotence yields to the patient—a relinquishment which is part of the relinquishment of the mother-infant symbiosis in the transference.

From the therapist's view, he must come to accept that, although the patient has been of deeply personal help to him, the patient cannot totally 'cure' him—that he will have to struggle toward increasing maturity, increasing personal integration-and-differentiation in future courses of work with the patients who will succeed this one, and he may glimpse, now, the basic truth—if it be that, and I surmise that it is—that the ideal of 'complete maturity' is only one of the disguises worn by the persistent striving, within him, toward infantile omnipotence. Loewald (1960b) speaks of the valuable role, in superego formation in healthy development, of manageable increments of disillusionment. The successful resolution of the symbiotic phase of therapy with the schizophrenic patient requires, likewise, that each person be able to integrate his disillusionment about his own, and his partner's, powers, shrunken now from omnipotent to life-size proportions.

It has seemed to me, both in my own work and in the material reported by colleagues in supervision and elsewhere, that the patient has first to demonstrate to himself that the therapist is not omnipotent, but rather—at this moment, at least—totally helpless, before he can feel it permissible to go ahead and function, capably, as an individual. This seems in part a function of the vulnerability to guilt-about-being-a-separate-person to which the schizophrenic person—and, I believe, to a lesser extent the neurotic person also—is so prone. It is as though he has to exhaust every possibility of getting help from the therapist—about whatever issue is at hand—before he can himself allow his own constructive potentialities to come to the fore, and meet the issue at hand in his own functioning individuality. Thus it is no coincidence that the emergence of the patient's individuality tends to occur in a setting of the therapist's feeling more than usually helpless in the situation. One can think of it from the viewpoint, also, that no one, whether adult patient or healthy child, would give up a therapist (or, respectively, a parent) who is, as far as can be determined, omnipotent; human beings are, if nothing else, practical, and this would be simply impractical: it would make no sense to individuate oneself from such an omnipotent being.

It is worth noting, further, that if the therapeutic relationship is to traverse successfully the phase of resolution of the symbiosis, the therapist must be able to brave not only the threats of suicide or psychotic disintegration on the patient's part, and of the professional and personal destruction to himself which might be a correlate of such outcomes; he must brave also the threat, which seems at times to be of a comparable order of magnitude, that the patient will, after these arduous years have passed and the homestretch is in sight, change therapists. It is as though the patient, by presenting the therapist with this threat of separation and finding that the latter can face it squarely without resort to panicky efforts to re-establish their erstwhile mother-infant symbiosis, gains the reassurance that the therapist will allow him to become a person in his own right, and to regard the recovery from psychosis as predominantly the patient's own achievement, rather than as a feather in the therapist's cap.

An important step in individuation for one of my patients, with whom I had been working for seven years, occurred when I allowed her to use my telephone, during one of her sessions with me, to call the Director of Psychotherapy for an appointment to discuss her desire for a change of therapists. In retrospect I have seen this as a crucial experience for her, that I freely allowed her to do this although her changing therapists would have meant a great personal loss to me, and although I felt it quite possible that she might succeed in that endeavour.

Incidentally, my readiness to face this development was, I think, one factor which enabled her to explore soon afterward, in her sessions, her desires, repressed since childhood, for a different set of parents. This transference-development tends, I think, to occur comparatively late in treatment, when the therapist is likely to think the patient painfully ungrateful for wanting, in the transference, a different therapist. I have mentioned elsewhere (1961a) how apt the patient is to press for a change of therapists just at a time when he is threatened with the beginning recognition of how greatly he himself has changed, a recognition which tends to disrupt his still-tenuous sense of personal identity; in the context of this paper, the patient tends to flee from the recognition of his having undergone the great change of individuation— tends, in Erich Fromm's (1941) phraseology, to flee from the freedom of individuality, by seeking a symbiotic relationship with a new therapist.

The resolution-of-symbiosis phase is always complicated, often to a marked degree, by the resistances which various persons in the patient's life between therapeutic sessions, including the family members, various of the nursing personnel and, it may be, various of his fellow patients, pose to his becoming a separate person and depriving them, therefore, of such symbiotic gratifications as the therapist himself has come to know, and reluctantly to relinquish, in the transference-relationship. It is by now a truism that the family members, no matter how genuinely fond of the patient and devoted to him they are at a conscious level, are particularly likely to withdraw him from the hospital just at the point when his individuation is promising to become established; and the therapist is not the only member of the hospital personnel who inevitably acquires, over the years, a deep emotional investment in the patient's remaining ill and symbiotically oriented toward the more significant ones among his fellow human beings. But that aspect of the matter has been discussed already in the literature to a considerable extent, and any detailed examination of it would carry us beyond the intended focus of the therapeutic relationship itself with which I am primarily concerned here.

(E) THE LATE PHASE

This phase extends from the resolution of the therapeutic symbiosis up through the completion of the therapy. It is a long phase, for only with the resolution of the symbiotic mode of relatedness is the patient capable of genuine object-relatedness and able, therefore, to cope with the matters with which psychoanalysis of the neurotic individual ordinarily deals. Only now, that is, is he ready for psychoanalysis; thus this phase requires a number of years of continued work.

Now that his symbiotic mode of relatedness has been resolved, the patient becomes involved in a better differentiated, more selective, process of de-repression of identifications from the past, with acceptance into his own ego of those identifications which are predominantly useful to him, and relinquishment of those which have proved unuseful, or pathological. He shows a similar capacity for forming, or rejecting, part-identifications with figures in current life, including the therapist. This process is well described in some of Erikson's (1956) words about identity formation, where he says that this ' . . . arises from the selective repudiation and mutual assimilation of child-hood identifications, and their absorption in a new configuration . . . '.

The patient now evidences increasingly much, not only in therapeutic sessions but in his daily life, the demeanour of a healthy child or adolescent; he belatedly evidences, that is, those normal developmental phases which, be-cause of the severity and early onset of the schizophrenigenic personality-warp, he had barely known in his biological childhood and adolescence. From a childhood which earlier in therapy he had experienced as unrelievedly black, he now remembers, with powerful affects of love and grief, positive experiences with his parents and other figures in his childhood, and there is a consequent freeing-up of useful identifications with those persons' strengths. Thus the strength which helps him to become well derives not only from his positive identifications with the therapist and other figures from current life in the hospital; there is also, and most importantly, this ingredient of his making contact with the strengths in his own past.

To an extent far greater than in the neurotic, however, the patient is likely for at least several months to present himself—and no doubt genuinely to feel—as a naïve little child who doesn't know anything, and who therefore needs to be taught all over again, and correctly this time, how to live. The therapist, aware that so much of what the child learned from family members was indeed pathological and that a high degree of social isolation outside the family prevented his learning innumerable things about everyday life which were common currency among his age-mates, will be under extraordinary pressure to assume the function of a teacher or counsellor. I believe that the patient may benefit from, or at least not be greatly harmed by, the therapist's assuming on occasion such a function. But the therapist rapidly finds himself, here, on thin ice, in danger of losing touch with the only consistently solid function he has in the patient's life—that of psychotherapist. The words of Spitz (1959) concerning psychoanalysis are forcefully applicable here, and the therapist will do well to recall them:

> The essence of psychoanalytic treatment is that it does not direct, advise, educate. It liberates the personality and permits it to make its own adjustments. . . . No directive or educative measures in the commonly accepted sense of the terms are necessary. Indeed, they can only disturb the natural process, which is so highly individualistic as to make it impossible for the particular therapist to direct it in its minute details. Any direction required is provided actually by the transference situation. This insures a process of developmental unfolding free from the anxieties, perils, threats of the original situation.

The patient has been exposed in actuality, prior to the psychotherapy, to more of adult-life experience than he realizes as yet, and the naïve-child orientation is eventually seen in retrospect to have represented a powerful, though unconscious, striving to keep the therapist enshrined as an omniscient parent, while himself avoiding the fullness of his childhood disillusionment with the parent(s) and avoiding, thus, the responsibility for his own going on to adulthood. If the therapist persists in adhering to his psychotherapeutic function, the next unfolding of the transference consists, in my experience, in the patient's deeply disillusioned and scornful conviction that the therapist is in no measure qualified to be an omniscient general manager of the patient's life but is, quite the contrary, crazy. This is the development which Hill (1955) evidently had in mind in describing the schizophrenic patient's experience of the conclusion of therapy:

. . . one hears very little about gratitude from these patients. What happens is that, in the process of taking in the goodness [i.e. identifying with the good qualities of the doctor] and incorporating it actually into himself, the patient manages to make the sort of split that is comfortable to all of us. He is good, and the baldness is left with the doctor. Even the illness is left with the doctor. Sometimes it is quite striking that the patient comes to believe that the doctor is thoroughly psychotic, quite in the fashion in which he himself has been psychotic.

This is a very regular development in my work with patients, as I have reported previously (1959a); but, unlike Hill, I feel it essential for the patient's future welfare that the psychotherapy be pursued far beyond this point, until the craziness has been well resolved, rather than simply left in this projected form upon the therapist. It is subsequent to this that there is a differentiation, in the transference, of those intense affects—murderousness, envy, loneliness, fear, and above all deeply denied love (Searles, 1958b)— which lay behind the parents' craziness. The added ego-strength which the patient has acquired in the course of his psychotherapy enables him to experience derepressed feeling along these paths with a clarity of delineation, and depth of intensity, which he could not subjectively experience previously— no matter how intense were the affects which he acted out during the phase of ambivalent symbiosis. And the therapist is unprecedentedly free now to experience within himself, and on crucial occasions to express, the reciprocal feelings inherent in these transference-positions in which he finds himself, with a minimum of the conflict and guilt which had been so prevalent during the ambivalently symbiotic phase.

It is during this late phase of the therapy that the onset of the patient's psychosis becomes clarified; he is finally able to experience, and integrate, the emotions which at that much earlier date had had to be repressed, and defended against by the advent of psychosis. For example, I have had the experience, at once fulfilling and somehow awesome, of finding that a patient who had become schizophrenic at the age of fifteen and had spent nineteen years predominantly in mental hospitals, had now reached a point, after ten years of intensive psychotherapy with me, where the secondary elaborations of her hebephrenic illness had been sufficiently unravelled so that the material of her original delusions was now coming to the fore, but in a way progressively understandable to both of us.

As the patient makes emotional contact with the various previously repressed areas of his past experience, bit by bit, he eventually reaches the realization that, despite all the years of illness, as one patient expressed it with great relief, 'I'm still myself'. In other words, there is eventually established a sense of continuity of identity, combining the person he felt himself to be prior to the psychosis with the emotions and attitudes manifested in the psychosis, long unacceptable to the conscious ego, but now accepted as a part of it. It is on the basis of such a newly achieved ego strength and such a firmer sense of personal identity that he is now able to take his stand and assess the personalities of figures from present and past life. I remember how impressed I was with one schizophrenic woman, for example, when after three years of therapy she became able to express, in a single breath, her realistic disapproval of certain qualities in her mother, in her father, and in me. Earlier in our work she had possessed far too little of a sense of individuality to be able to objectify these three so-important figures, so clearly and simultaneously. She became, as do other patients in the late phase of the work, equally able to express admiration and fondness toward parents and therapist.

Because the therapy of these patients usually requires a considerable number of years, the therapist may find it particularly difficult to be receptive to the expression of some feelings which the patient can face only after several years of treatment. The therapist, keenly aware that, say, five or six or seven years of intensive psychotherapy have elapsed, may feel threatened and therefore impatient at the patient's finally becoming able to explore the depths of the latter's discouragement and despair, or—as I mentioned before—wish for a different parent in the transference, or regressive strivings. It is only through the therapist's being fully aware of the therapeutic progress represented by the patient's becoming conscious of these feelings, and able now to express them verbally rather than having to act them out as in the foregoing years of the treatment, that he is able to help the patient on toward completion of the therapeutic investigation, rather than toward a rerepression of these feelings for an indefinite time longer.

Similarly, because the therapist has seen the patient to be, earlier in the therapy, such a deeply fragmented person, he tends to retain a lingering impression of the latter's fragility, an impression which may interfere with his going along at the faster pace which the patient, a very different and far stronger person now, is capable of setting. But even this memory-image of the fragile patient, carried with the therapist, has a natural function in the course of the psychotherapy, for it is only very late in the work that the patient himself is able to realize how very ill, how very fragile, he indeed once was; until he becomes strong enough to integrate this realization into his self-image, the therapist has to be the bearer of this piece of the patient's identity. This process is analogous to the well-known phenomenon in which each major forward stride in the patient's therapeutic growth is accompanied, or presaged, by the therapist's suddenly seeing in the patient a new and healthier person (Searles, 1958c, 1959b); there, too, the impact of the development falls primarily, for a time, upon the therapist rather than the patient. The patient himself, because his sense of identity is still, during the earlier therapeutic phases to which I am referring at the moment, relatively tenuous, is easily overwhelmed—in one patient's words, 'Knocked out'—by the realization of the extent to which he is now changed, even though this change be, in our view, a most beneficial and welcome one.

Another characteristic of the late phase—and I am not attempting to describe, here, all such characteristics—is the circumstance that various of the patient's adult strivings may be found more deeply repressed than his infantile strivings. That is, it may well prove easier for the therapist to contemplate (Searles, 1957), and easier for the nursing personnel to recognize and at least partially gratify, various of the patient's infantile and small-child oral needs, than to help him to face squarely his powerful adult-desires, mobilized and given shape in the course of the psychotherapy but still painfully thwarted by reason of his long hospitalization—his desires to marry and procreate and bear adult responsibilities. Sometimes the patient's expression of such desires, particularly if he or she has been so long hospitalized that various of these must be accepted as losses or deprivations which can never be made up, is at least as poignant for the therapist to hear as were the earlier-expressed yearnings for infantile and childlike gratifications. He realizes to what an extent, for probably many months now, it is the more *mature* areas of the patient's personality which have been the more deeply repressed ones (Searles, 1961a), and that, in contrast to some of the views expressed by Freud (1915), the maturation-process is so deep-reaching that it leaves no changeless core of the personality, no eternally-infantile id, unchanged by it.

The evolution of the reality-relatedness between patient and therapist, over the course of the psychotherapy, is something which, so far as I know, has received little more than passing mention in the literature (Searles, 1961c). Hoedemaker (1955), in a paper concerning the therapeutic process in the treatment of schizophrenia, stresses the importance of the schizophrenic patient's forming healthy identifications with the therapist, and Loewald (1960a), in his paper concerning the therapeutic action of psychoanalysis in general, repeatedly emphasizes the importance of the real relationship between patient and analyst, but only in the following passage alludes to the evolution, the growth, of this relationship over the course of treatment:

> . . . Where repression is lifted and unconscious and preconscious are again in communication, infantile object and contemporary object may be united into one—a truly new object as both unconscious and preconscious are changed by their mutual communication. The object which helps to bring this about in therapy, the analyst, mediates this union. . . .

It has been my distinct impression that the patient's remembrance of new areas of his past—his manifestation of newly derepressed transference reactions to the therapist—occurs only hand in hand with the reaching of comparable areas of feeling in the evolving reality-relatedness between patient and therapist (1958b). For example, he does not come to experience fond memories of his mother until the reality-relatedness between himself and the therapist has reached the point where the feeling between them has become, in reality, predominantly positive. Loewald's words, quoted above, imply to me that an increment of transference-resolution slightly antedates, and makes possible, the forming of each successive increment in the evolving reality-relationship between patient and analyst. It has been my impression, by contrast, that the evolution of the reality-relatedness proceeds always a bit ahead of, and makes possible, the progressive evolution-and-resolution of the transference, although to be sure the latter, in so far as it frees psychological energy and makes it available for reality-relatedness, helps greatly to consolidate the ground just taken over by the advancing reality-relationship. Loewald (1960a) thinks of it that

> . . . The patient can dare to take the plunge into the regressive crisis of the transference neurosis which brings him face to face again with his childhood anxieties and conflicts, *if* he can hold on to the potentiality of a new object-relationship, represented by the analyst.

But it seems to me that this new object-relationship is more than a potentiality, to be realized with comparative suddenness, and *in toto*, toward the end of the treatment with the resolution of the transference. Rather it is, so it has seemed to me, constantly there, being built up bit by bit, just ahead of the likewise evolving transference-relationship. Pertinent here is Freud's (1922) having pointed out that projection—which is, after all, so major an aspect of transference—is directed not 'into the sky, so to speak, where there is nothing of the sort already', but rather on to a person who provides some reality-basis for the projection.

In the final months of the therapy, the therapist clearly sees the extent to which the patient's transferences to him as representing a succession of figures from the latter's earlier years, have all been in the service of the patient's unconsciously shying away, to a successively decreasing extent, from experiencing the full and complex reality of the immediate relatedness with the therapist in the present. The patient at last comes to realize that the relationship with a single other human being—in this instance, the therapist—is so rich as to comprise all these earlier relationships, so rich as to evoke all the myriad feelings which had been parcelled out and crystallized, heretofore, in the transferences which have now been resolved. This is a process most beautifully described by the Swiss novelist Hermann Hesse (1951) winner of the Nobel Prize in 1946, in his little novel, *Siddhartha*. The protagonist, in a lifelong quest for the ultimate answer to the enigma of man's role on earth, finally discovers in the face of his beloved friend all the myriad persons, things, and events which he has known, but incoherently before, during the vicissitudes of his many years of searching.

It is thus that the patient, schizophrenic or otherwise, becomes at one with himself, in the closing phase of psychotherapy. But although the realization may come to him as a sudden one, it is founded on a reality-relatedness which has been building up all along. Loewald (1960a) in his magnificent paper to which my brief references have done less than full justice, suggests, as I mentioned, something of the role which transference-resolution plays in the development of this reality-relatedness. I suggest that the evolution of the 'countertransference'—not countertransference in the classical sense of the therapist's transference to the patient, but rather in the sense of the therapist's emotional reactions to the patient's transference—forms an equally essential contribution to this reality-relatedness. This paper has been primarily an attempt to describe the evolution of what might be called—in this special sense—the therapist's typical 'countertransference' to the schizophrenic patient, over the course of successful psychotherapy.

CONCLUDING REMARKS

In my attempt to highlight the paramount place which emotions—emotions in the therapist as well as in the patient—hold in the psychotherapy of schizophrenia, I would not wish to leave the impression that the therapist should strive to be immersed continually in a kind of emotional blood-bath. On the contrary, as I described it at the outset, the emotionally charged transference-evolution which has been traced here can develop, and run a relatively unimpeded course, only if the therapist is sufficiently sure of his capacities for feeling so that his basic emotional orientation can be an investigative, rather than for example a compulsively 'loving', orientation. Moreover, each of these patients—and, I think, this is true to a lesser degree of the neurotic patient also—needs in the course of the therapy to project upon the therapist the subjectively unfeeling, nonhuman and even inanimate, aspects of himself, and thus to see his therapist, in the transference, as the representation of the parents who were, to the child's view, incapable of human feeling, as has been the patient himself in his own view (Searles, 1960; see also chapter 5). Only by thus re-externalizing his pathogenic introjects can the patient make contact with his own feeling-capacities and come to know, beyond any further doubt, that he is a human being. This aspect of the transference, this aspect of the healthy reworking of very early ego-differentiation, cannot be accomplished unless the therapist is able to be self-accepting while spending hour after hour without finding in himself any particular feeling whatever toward the patient. He must be sufficiently sure of his own humanness so that he can endure for long periods the role, in the patient's transference-experience, of an inanimate object, or of some other percept which has not yet become differentiated as a sentient human being.

In the course of writing this paper, the realization has dawned upon me that the therapist recurrently experiences guilt in reaction to the arousal of one or another kind of emotion in himself, during the course of his work with the schizophrenic patient, on the basis of a rekindling of the therapist's infantile-omnipotence. Such a temporary regression on the therapist's part, to the level of infantile-omnipotence, is his major unconscious defence against the realization, and deep and consistent acceptance, of the fact that not only the patient but he also is in the grip of a process, the therapeutic process, which is comparable in its strength to the maturational *process* in the child—which is, indeed, this same process in a particular context, the context of psychotherapy of the adult schizophrenic person. The more experienced and confident the therapist becomes in this work, the more deeply does he realize that this process is far too powerful for either the patient or himself to be able at all easily to deflect it, consciously and wilfully and singlehandedly, away from the confluent channel which it is tending—with irresistible power, if we can

290 PSYCHOTHERAPEUTIC ENCOUNTERS WITH PSYCHOSIS

give ourselves up to the current—to form for itself. When the therapist sees this, he realizes how illusory has been his subjective omnipotence, but also how groundless has been his subjective guilt.

NOTE

1. Isaiah xi. 6.

REFERENCES

Bak, R. C. (1958). The role of aggression in psychic conflict. Presented at the 7 November 1958 meeting of the Washington Psychoanalytic Society.

Balint, M. (1953). *Primary Love and Psycho-Analytic Technique*. New York: Liveright.

Balint, M. (1955). Friendly expanses—horrid empty spaces. *Int. J Psycho-Anal.* **36**, 225.

Bullard, D. M. (1960). Psychotherapy of paranoid patients. *A.M.A. Arch. Gen. Psychiatry,* **2**, 137.

Cohen, M. B. (1952). Countertransference and anxiety. *Psychiatry,* **15**, 231.

Cohen, R. A. (1947). The management of anxiety in a case of paranoid schizophrenia. *Psychiatry,* **10**, 143.

Eissler, K. R. (1951). Remarks on the psychoanalysis of schizophrenia. *Int. J. Psycho-Anal.* **32**, 139.

Erikson, E. H. (1956). The problem of ego identity. *J. Amer. Psa. Ass.* **4**, 56. Quote is from p. 68.

Freud, A. (1946). *The Ego and the Mechanisms of Defence*. New York: International Universities Press. Quote is from pp. 5–6.

Freud, S. (1911). Psycho-analytic notes upon an autobiographical account of a case of paranoia (Dementia Paranoides). In *Collected Papers,* **3**. London: Hogarth Press (1953).

Freud, S. (1915). Thoughts for the times on war and death. In *Collected Papers,* **4**. London: Hogarth Press (1953).

Freud, S. (1922). Certain neurotic mechanisms in jealousy, paranoia and homosexuality. In *Collected Papers,* **2**. London: Hogarth Press (1953).

Fromm, E. (1941). *Escape From Freedom*. New York and Toronto: Rinehart.

Greenson, R. (1949). The psychology of apathy. *Psychoanal. Quart.* **18**, 290.

Greenson, R. (1953). On boredom. *J. Amer. Psa. Ass.* **1**, 7.

Groddeck, G. (1923). *The Book of the It*. London: Vision Press (1950). Quote (also included in the paper by Hayward and Taylor listed below) is from pp. 262–3.

Hartmann, H. (1956). Notes on the reality principle. In *The Psychoanalytic Study of the Child,* **11**. New York: International Universities Press.

Hayward, M. L. & Taylor, J. E. (1956). A schizophrenic patient describes the action of intensive psychotherapy. *Psychiatric Quart.* **30**, 211.

Heimann, P. (1955). A combination of defence mechanisms in paranoid states. In *New Directions in Psycho-Analysis*. Ed. by M. Klein, P. Heimann and R. E. Money-Kyrle. New York: Basic Books.

Hesse, H. (1951). *Siddhartha*. New York: New Directions.

Hill, L. B. (1955). *Psychotherapeutic Intervention in Schizophrenia*. Chicago: The University of Chicago Press. Quote is from p. 206.

Hoedemaker, E. D. (1955). The therapeutic process in the treatment of schizophrenia. *J. Amer. Psa. Ass.* **3**, 89.

Knight, R. P. (1940). The relationship of latent homosexuality to the mechanism of paranoid delusions. *Bull. Menninger Clin.* **4**, 149.

Lidz, R. W. & Lidz, T. (1952). Ed. by E. B. Brody & F. C. Redlich. Therapeutic considerations arising from the intense symbiotic needs of schizophrenic patients. In *Psychotherapy with Schizophrenics.* New York: International Universities Press.

Loewald, H. W. (1960a). On the therapeutic action of psycho-analysis. *Int. J. Psycho-Anal.* **41**, 16.

Loewald, H. W. (1960b). Internalization, separation, mourning and the superego. Presented at the 10 December 1960 meeting of The American Psychoanalytic Association in New York City.

Mahler, M. S. (1952). On child psychosis and schizophrenia—autistic and symbiotic infantile psychoses. In *The Psychoanalytic Study of the Child,* 7. New York: International Universities Press.

Mahler, M. S. & Furer, M. (1960). Observations on research regarding the 'symbiotic syndrome' of infantile psychosis. *Psychoanal. Quart.* **29**, 317.

Main, T. F. (1957). The ailment. *Brit. J. Med. Psychol.* **30**, 129.

Perry, S. E. & Shea, G. N. (1957). Social controls and psychiatric theory in a ward setting. *Psychiatry,* **20**, 221.

Schwing, G. (1954). *A Way to the Soul of the Mentally Ill.* New York: International Universities Press.

Searles, H. F. (1957). Oedipal love in the countertransference. Presented at the 7 December 1957 meeting of The American Psychoanalytic Association in New York City. *Int. J. Psycho-Anal.* **40**, 180, 1959.

Searles, H. F. (1958a). The schizophrenic's vulnerability to the therapist's unconscious processes. *J. Nerv. Ment. Dis.* **127**, 247. (Also in German translation, under the title 'Die Empfänglichkeit des Schizophrenen für unbewusste Prozesse im Psychotherapeuten'. *Psyche,* **12**, 321, 1958.)

Searles, H. F. (1958b). Positive feelings in the relationship between the schizophrenic and his mother. *Int. J. Psycho-Anal.* **39**, 569. (Also in German translation, under the title, 'Positive Gefühle in der Beziehung zwischen dem Schizophrenen und seiner Mutter'. *Psyche,* **14**, 165, 1960.)

Searles, H. F. (1958c). Integration and differentiation in schizophrenia. Presented at the 6 December 1958 meeting of The American Psychoanalytic Association in New York City. *J. Nerv. Ment. Dis.* **129**, 542, 1959.

Searles, H. F. (1959a). The effort to drive the other person crazy—an element in the aetiology and psychotherapy of schizophrenia. *Brit. J. Med. Psychol.* **32**, 1.

Searles, H. F. (1959b). Integration and differentiation in schizophrenia: an over-all view. *Brit. J. Med. Psychol.* **32**, 261.

Searles, H. F. (1960). *The Nonhuman Environment in Normal Development and in Schizophrenia.* New York: International Universities Press.

Searles, H. F. (1961a). Anxiety concerning change, as seen in the psychotherapy of schizophrenic patients—with particular reference to the sense of personal identity. Presented at the 5 December 1959 meeting of The American Psychoanalytic Association in New York City. *Int. J. Psycho-Anal.* **42**, 74.

Searles, H. F. (1961b). Sexual processes in schizophrenia. Presented at the 10 December 1960 meeting of The American Psychoanalytic Association in New York City. *Psychiatry,* **24**, Supplement to No. 2, 87.

Searles, H. F. (1961c). The evolution of the mother transference in psychotherapy with the schizophrenic patient. In *Psychotherapy of the Psychoses*. Ed. by A. Burton. New York: Basic Books.

Sechehaye, M. A. (1951). *Symbolic Realization*. New York: International Universities Press.

Spitz, R. A. (1959). *A Genetic Field Theory of Ego Formation*. New York: International Universities Press. Quotes are from pp. 84 and 100.

Stanton, A. H. & Schwartz, M. S. (1954). *The Mental Hospital*. New York: Basic Books.

Sullivan, H. S. (1956). *Clinical Studies in Psychiatry*. New York: Norton. See p. 351.

Szalita-Pemow, A. (1952). Personal communication.

Werner, H. (1940). *Comparative Psychology of Mental Development*. New York: International Universities Press.

Whitaker, C. A., editor (1958). *Psychotherapy of Chronic Schizophrenic Patients*. Boston and Toronto: Little, Brown. See remarks by J. Warkentin and J. E. Taylor on pp. 79–84.

Whitaker, C. A. & Malone, T. P. (1953). *The Roots of Psychotherapy*. New York: Blakiston.

Winnicott, D. W. (1949). Hate in the countertransference. *Int. J. Psycho-Anal.* **30**, 69–74.

Index

Laing, R. D.
Lewin, B. D., xxvii–xxix, 136
Libido
    libidinal cathexis, xx
    libidinal theory, 11–12
Lidz, R. W., 264
Lidz, T., 35, 38, 46 *n*7, 264
Lipinski, J. F., xiv
Little, M., 179, 180, 183, 188–89, 190,
    216–17
Loewald, H. W., 17, 32, 259, 264–65, 280,
    287, 288
London, N. J., 1, 3

McGlashan, T. M., 143
Mahler, M. S., 29, 46 *n*10, 144, 191, 259
Main, T. F., 274
Malone, T. P., 272
Manic-depressive illness
    affective psychoses, 31
    elation in, xxvii–xxix
    Lewin's theory of oral triad, xxviii–xxix
    mania in, xxvii–xxix
    symptoms, xxvii–xxix
Masochism, in paranoia, 118–30
Mayer-Gross, W., 119
Melancholia, 76 *n*11
Milner, M., 218
Modell, A. H., 108
Mother-child relationship, 108–14, 225–26,
    238–39

Narcissism, 66, 69–70, 148–49, 155–57
    defenses and, 78–97
Niederland, W. G., xx–xxii
Novey, S., 9, 35, 45 *n*1
Noyes, A. P., 102
Nunberg, H., 120

Objects
    internal objects, 238–46
    Klein's theory, xxiv–xxv, 140 *n*3
    mental representations, 24–27, 28–30
    part objects, 184–85, 221
Orality, oral triad, xxviii

Paranoia
    homosexuality in, xviii–xx, xxii–xxiii,
        118–30

masochism in, 118–30
persecution by a group, 127–28
Parsons, T., 35
Patient-therapist interaction
    ambivalent symbiosis, 265–69
    conclusion of therapy, 282–88
    full symbiosis, 269–75
    out-of-contact phase, 259–65
    in psychotherapy of schizophrenia, 256–
        90
    resolution of symbiosis, 275–82
Perceval, John, xii, xxiii–xxiv
Perry, S. E., 274
Piaget, J., 25, 106
Pious, W. L., 15, 30, 44, 225
Pope, M. G., Jr., xiv
Pötzl, O., 76 *n*13
Primitive thinking, 16–17
Projection, xviii–xix, xxiii, 99–100
    body projection, 64–67
    "influencing machine" as, 72–73
Projective identification, 185–88
Psychotherapy of psychoses
    Freud's views, 148–51
    historical review, 147–74
    hospital environment and, 273–74
    introjection of therapist in, 243–45
    patient-therapist interaction in, 256–90
    reprojection in, 249–50
    therapist attitudes in, 234–38
    transference in, 180–84
    transference psychosis in, 177–231

Rado, S., 131
Rapaport, D., 17, 32, 33, 40, 103
Reality
    break with, 33–35
    disavowal of, 34–35
    disturbances of, 17–18
    integration, 32–36, 39–40
    testing, 32–36, 239–40
Regression
    developmental, 38–39, 41
    ego, 80–82
    Freud's classification of, 85
Reich, A., 195
Róheim, G., 120
Rosenblatt, B., 45 *n*1
Rosenfeld, H., 15, 44, 144, 157, 169, 170–

X